YU-GI-OH!: DUELIST VOL. 16
The SHONEN JUMP Manga Edition

STORY AND ART BY
KAZUKI TAKAHASHI

Translation & English Adaptation/Joe Yamazaki
Touch-up Art & Lettering/Eric Erbes
Design/Andrea Rice
Editor/Jason Thompson

Managing Editor/Frances E. Wall
Editorial Director/Elizabeth Kawasaki
Vice President & Editor in Chief/Yumi Hoashi
Sr. Director of Acquisitions/Rika Inouye
Sr. Vice President of Marketing/Liza Coppola
Exec. VP of Sales & Marketing/John Easum
Publisher/Hyoe Narita

In the original Japanese edition, YU-GI-OH!, YU-GI-OH!: DUELIST and
YU-GI-OH!: MILLENNIUM WORLD are known collectively as YU-GI-OH!.
The English YU-GI-OH!: DUELIST was originally volumes 8-31
of the Japanese YU-GI-OH!.

Printed in the U.S.A.

Published by VIZ Media, LLC
P.O. Box 77010
San Francisco, CA 94107

SHONEN JUMP Manga Edition
10 9 8 7 6 5 4 3 2 1
First printing, August 2006

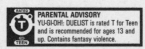

www.viz.com

PARENTAL ADVISORY
YU-GI-OH!: DUELIST is rated T for Teen
and is recommended for ages 13 and
up. Contains fantasy violence.

THE WORLD'S
MOST POPULAR MANGA

www.shonenjump.com

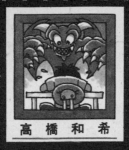

高橋和希

MANY OF THE FAN LETTERS I RECEIVE HAVE ORIGINAL
ILLUSTRATIONS OF CARDS AND MONSTERS ON THEM.
THEY ARE SO UNIQUE AND WELL DRAWN! (I COULDN'T
DRAW THAT WELL AT THEIR AGE!) WHEN I DESIGN A
MONSTER, I THINK OF THE CHARACTER WHO WILL BE
USING IT AND THE SHAPE OF THAT CHARACTER'S
"HEART." ROUND HEART...SPIKY HEART...KIND
HEART...UGLY HEART. THE MONSTERS ARE CREATED
FROM THIS FOUNDATION. IS THE MONSTER OF YOUR
HEART STRONG AND COOL?
        —KAZUKI TAKAHASHI, 2000

Artist/author Kazuki Takahashi first tried to break into
the manga business in 1982, but success eluded him
until **Yu-Gi-Oh!** debuted in the Japanese **Weekly
Shonen Jump** magazine in 1996. **Yu-Gi-Oh!**'s themes
of friendship and fighting, together with Takahashi's
weird and wonderful art, soon became enormously
successful, spawning a real-world card game, video
games, and two anime series. A lifelong gamer,
Takahashi enjoys Shogi (Japanese chess), Mahjong,
card games, and tabletop RPGs, among other games.

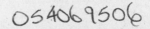

SHONEN JUMP MANGA

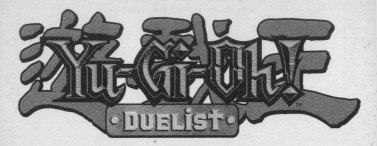

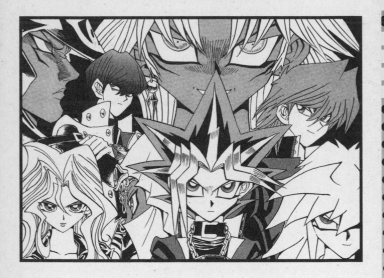

Vol. 16
THE BATTLE CITY FINALS
STORY AND ART BY
KAZUKI TAKAHASHI

THE STORY SO FAR...

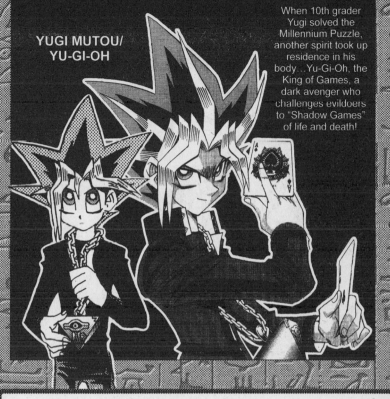

YUGI MUTOU/
YU-GI-OH

When 10th grader Yugi solved the Millennium Puzzle, another spirit took up residence in his body…Yu-Gi-Oh, the King of Games, a dark avenger who challenges evildoers to "Shadow Games" of life and death!

YUGI FACES DEADLY ENEMIES!

Using his gaming skills, Yugi fights ruthless adversaries like Maximillion Pegasus, multimillionaire creator of the collectible card game "Duel Monsters," and Ryo Bakura, whose friendly personality turns evil when he is possessed by the spirit of the Millennium Ring. But Yugi's greatest rival is Seto Kaiba, the world's second-greatest gamer—and the ruthless teenage president of Kaiba Corporation. At first, Kaiba and Yugi are bitter enemies, but after fighting against a common adversary—Pegasus—they come to respect one another. But for all his powers, there is one thing Yu-Gi-Oh cannot do: remember who he is and where he came from.

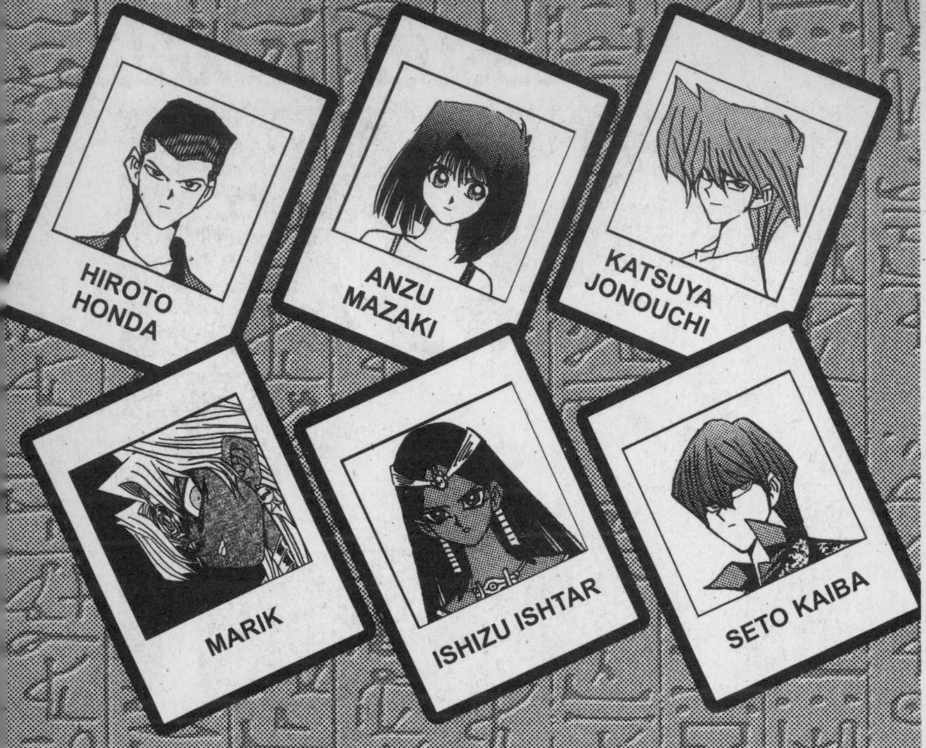
HIROTO HONDA
ANZU MAZAKI
KATSUYA JONOUCHI
MARIK
ISHIZU ISHTAR
SETO KAIBA

THE TABLET OF THE PHARAOH'S MEMORIES

Then one day, when an Egyptian museum exhibit comes to Japan, Yugi sees an ancient carving of himself as an Egyptian pharaoh! The curator of the exhibit, Ishizu Ishtar, explains that there are seven Millennium Items, which were made to fit into a stone tablet in a hidden shrine in Egypt. According to the legend, when the seven Items are brought together, the pharaoh will regain his memories of his past life.

THE EGYPTIAN GOD CARDS

But Ishizu has a message for Kaiba as well. Ishizu needs Kaiba's help to win back two of three Egyptian God Cards—the rarest cards on Earth—from the clutches of the "Rare Hunters," a criminal syndicate led by the evil Marik, Ishizu's brother. In order to draw out the thieves, Kaiba announces "Battle City," an enormous "Duel Monsters" tournament. As the tournament rages, Yugi, Kaiba and Marik struggle for possession of the three God Cards. But Marik has a trump card…the mind-altering power of the Millennium Rod! Brainwashing Yugi's friend (and fellow duelist) Jonouchi, Marik forces the two best friends to fight one another, handcuffed to a ticking time bomb. Can Honda and Kaiba rescue them before the loser feeds the fishes at the bottom of Domino Bay?

Yu-Gi-Oh! Duelist

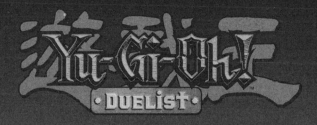

Vol. 16

CONTENTS

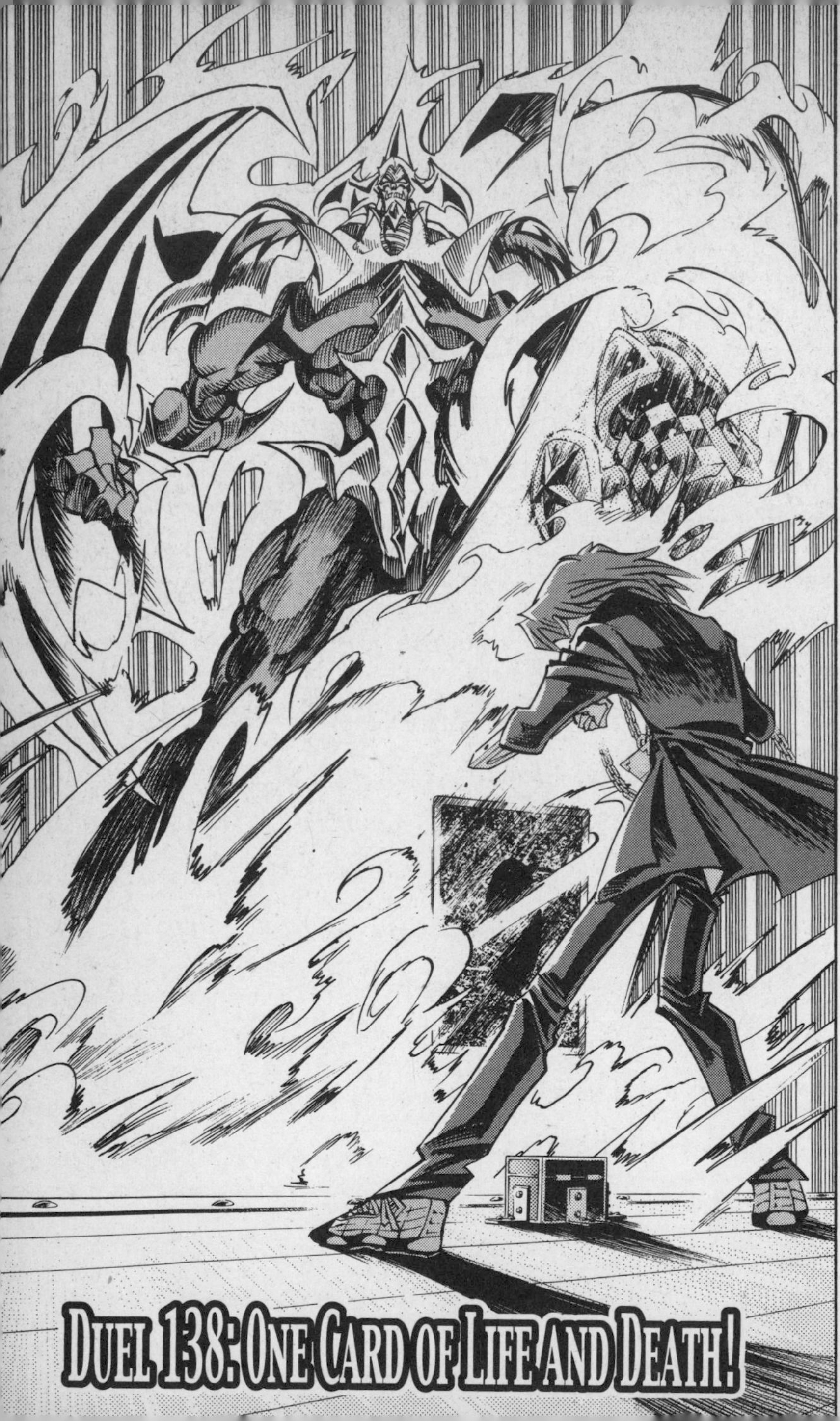

Duel 138: One Card of Life and Death!

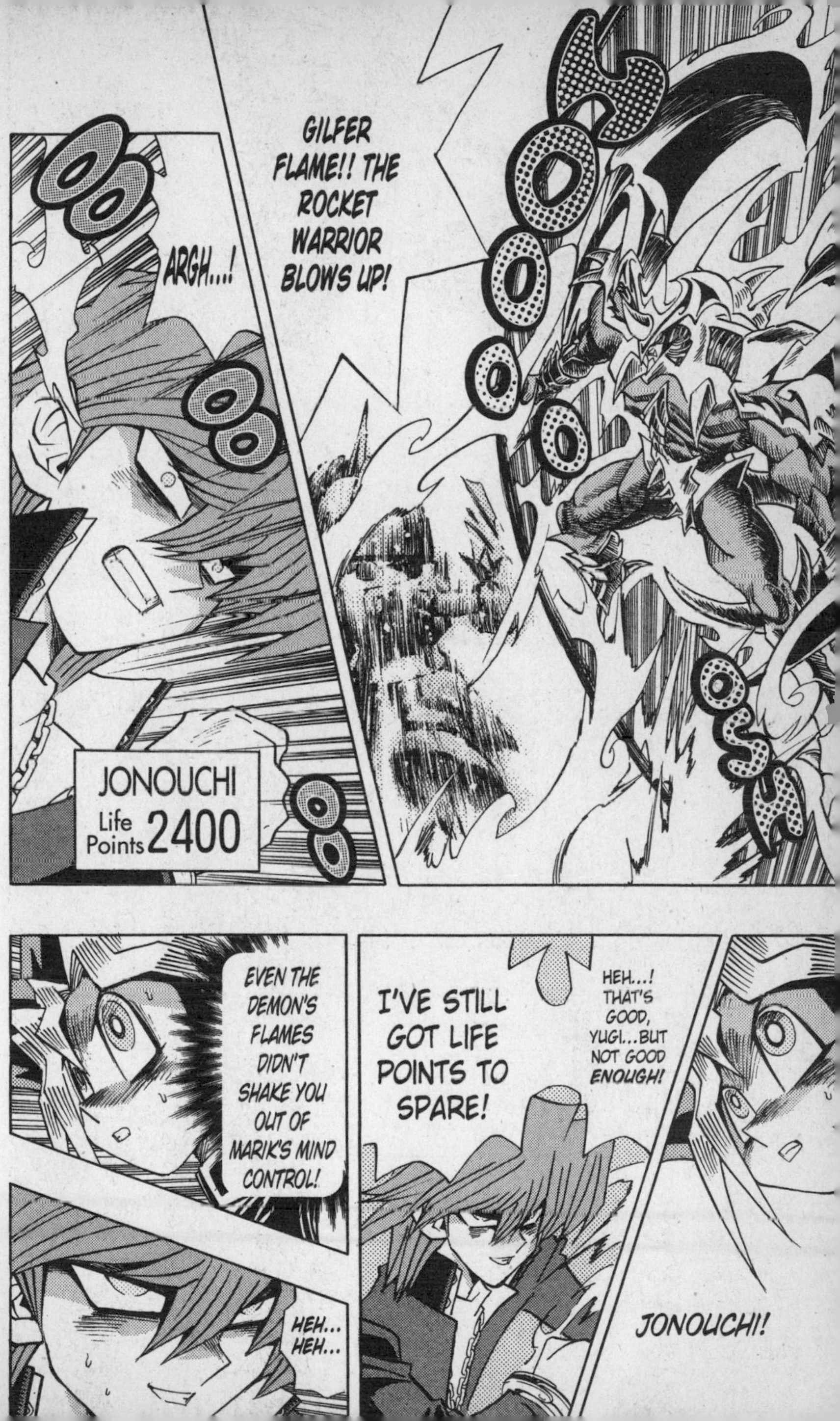
GILFER FLAME!! THE ROCKET WARRIOR BLOWS UP!
ARGH...!
JONOUCHI Life Points 2400
JONOUCHI!
HEH...! THAT'S GOOD, YUGI...BUT NOT GOOD ENOUGH!
I'VE STILL GOT LIFE POINTS TO SPARE!
EVEN THE DEMON'S FLAMES DIDN'T SHAKE YOU OUT OF MARIK'S MIND CONTROL!
HEH... HEH...

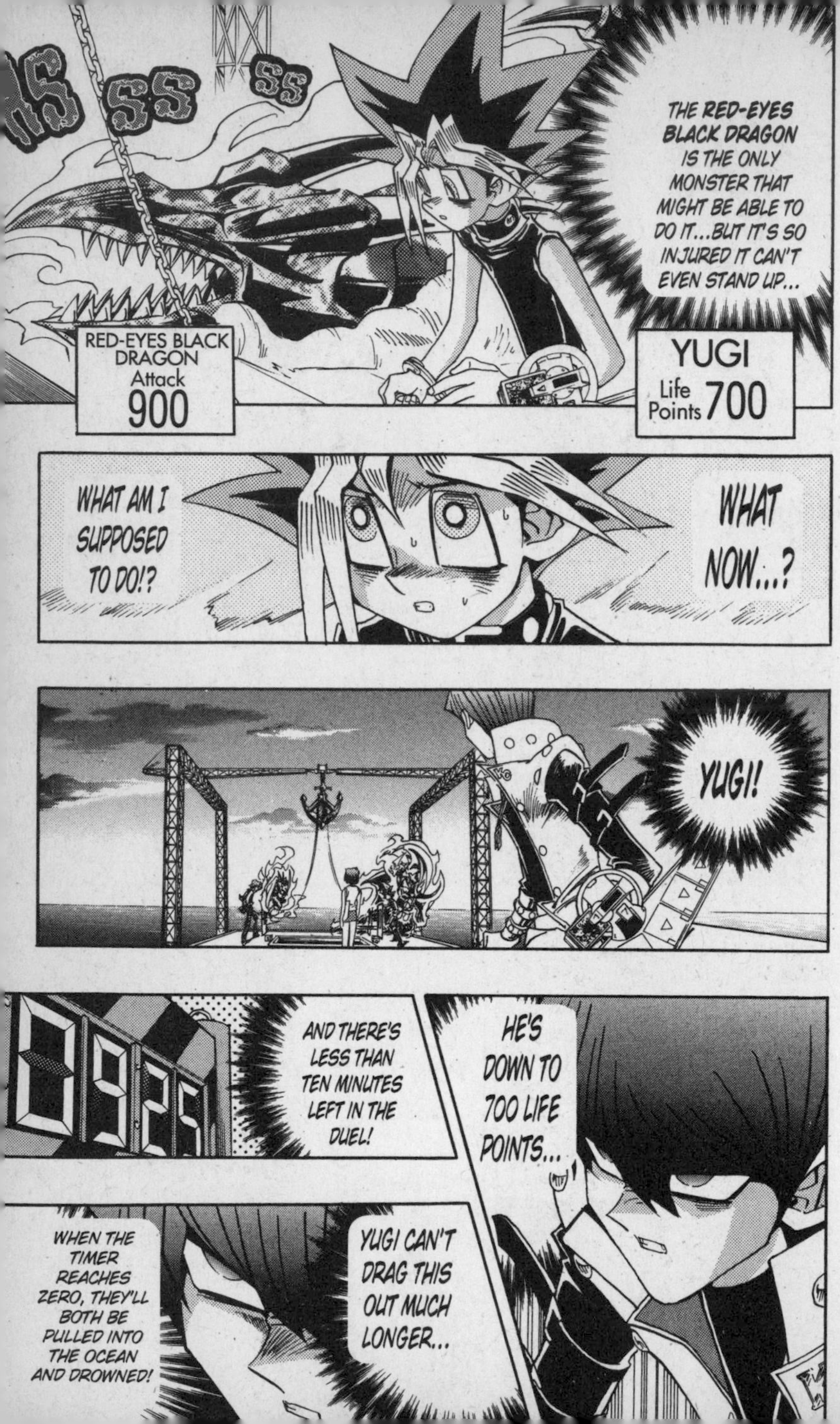
THE RED-EYES BLACK DRAGON IS THE ONLY MONSTER THAT MIGHT BE ABLE TO DO IT...BUT IT'S SO INJURED IT CAN'T EVEN STAND UP...
YUGI Life Points 700
SS
SS
RED-EYES BLACK DRAGON Attack 900
WHAT NOW...?
WHAT AM I SUPPOSED TO DO!?
YUGI!
HE'S DOWN TO 700 LIFE POINTS...
AND THERE'S LESS THAN TEN MINUTES LEFT IN THE DUEL!
YUGI CAN'T DRAG THIS OUT MUCH LONGER...
WHEN THE TIMER REACHES ZERO, THEY'LL BOTH BE PULLED INTO THE OCEAN AND DROWNED!

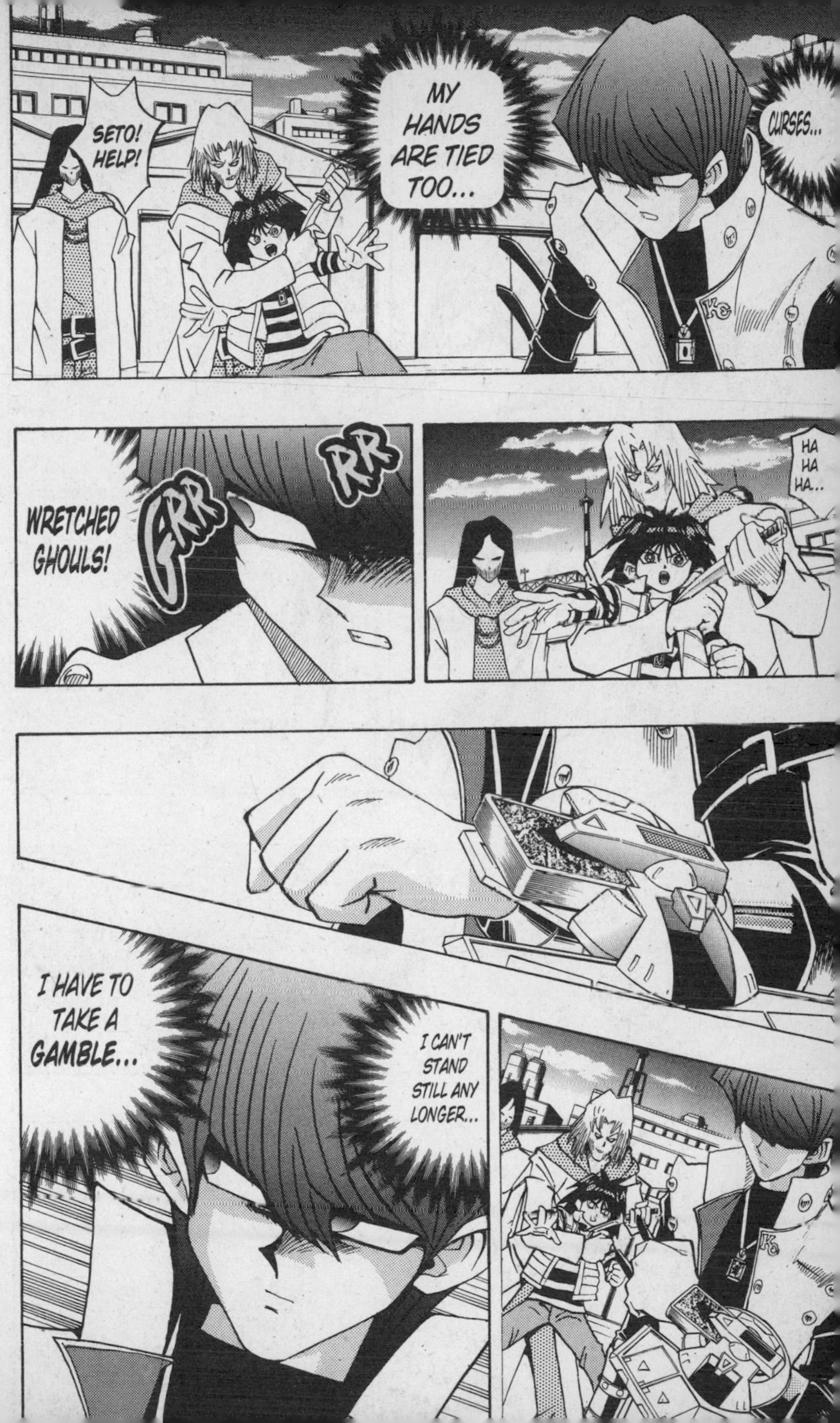
CURSES...
MY HANDS ARE TIED TOO...
SETO! HELP!
HA HA HA...
RR
GRR
WRETCHED GHOULS!
I CAN'T STAND STILL ANY LONGER...
I HAVE TO TAKE A GAMBLE...

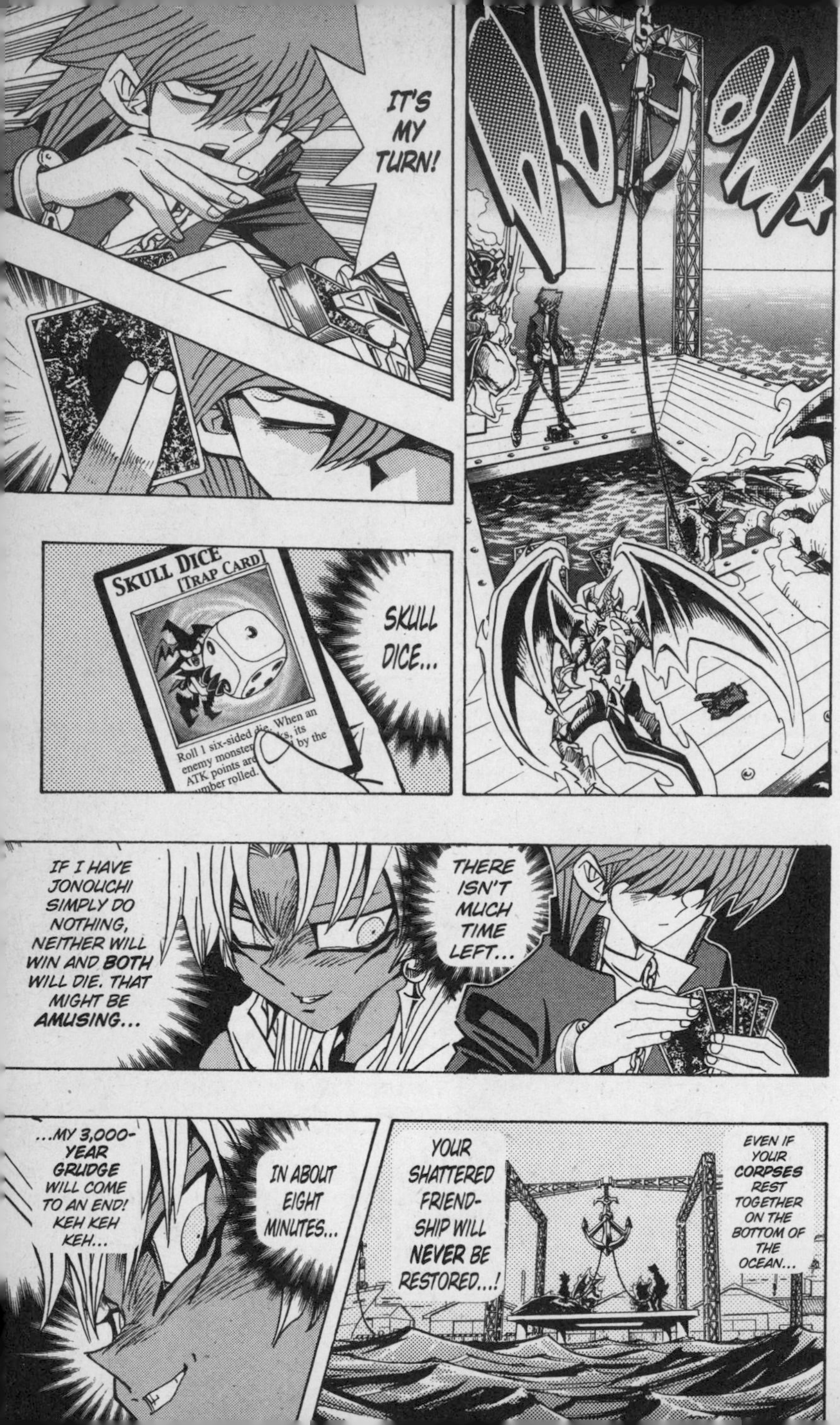
IT'S MY TURN!
SKULL DICE [TRAP CARD]
Roll 1 six-sided die. When an enemy monster
ks, its
ATK points are
by the
umber rolled.
SKULL DICE...
THERE ISN'T MUCH TIME LEFT...
IF I HAVE JONOUCHI SIMPLY DO NOTHING, NEITHER WILL WIN AND BOTH WILL DIE. THAT MIGHT BE AMUSING...
EVEN IF YOUR CORPSES REST TOGETHER ON THE BOTTOM OF THE OCEAN...
YOUR SHATTERED FRIEND-SHIP WILL NEVER BE RESTORED...!
IN ABOUT EIGHT MINUTES...
...MY 3,000-YEAR GRUDGE WILL COME TO AN END! KEH KEH KEH...

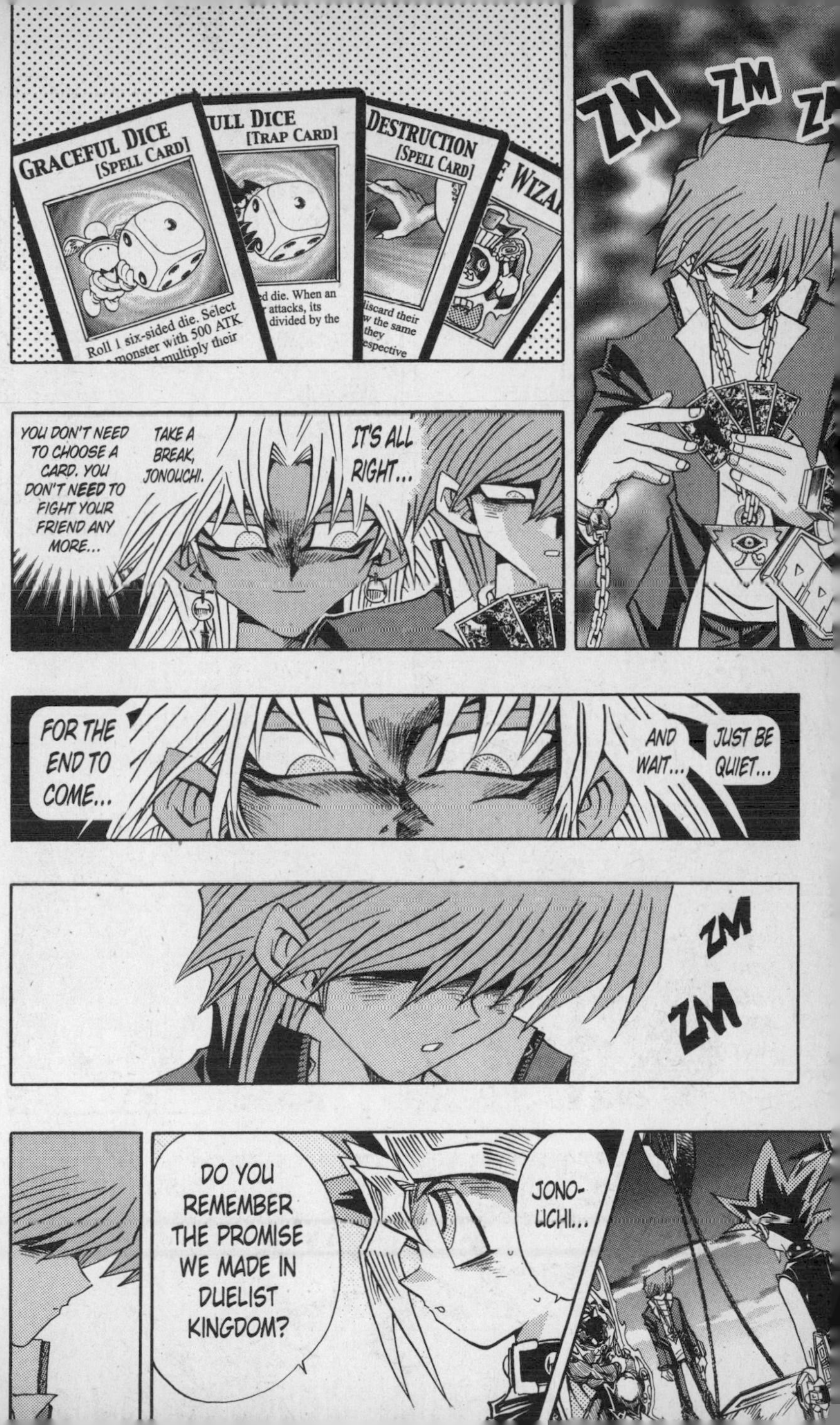

ZM ZM
GRACEFUL DICE
[SPELL CARD]
Roll 1 six-sided die. Select
monster with 500 ATK
multiply their
ULL DICE
[TRAP CARD]
d die. When an
attacks, its
divided by the
DESTRUCTION
[SPELL CARD]
iscard their
w the same
they
espective
E WIZA
IT'S ALL RIGHT...
TAKE A BREAK, JONOUCHI.
YOU DON'T NEED TO CHOOSE A CARD. YOU DON'T NEED TO FIGHT YOUR FRIEND ANY MORE...
JUST BE QUIET...
AND WAIT...
FOR THE END TO COME...
ZM
ZM
JONO-UCHI...
DO YOU REMEMBER THE PROMISE WE MADE IN DUELIST KINGDOM?

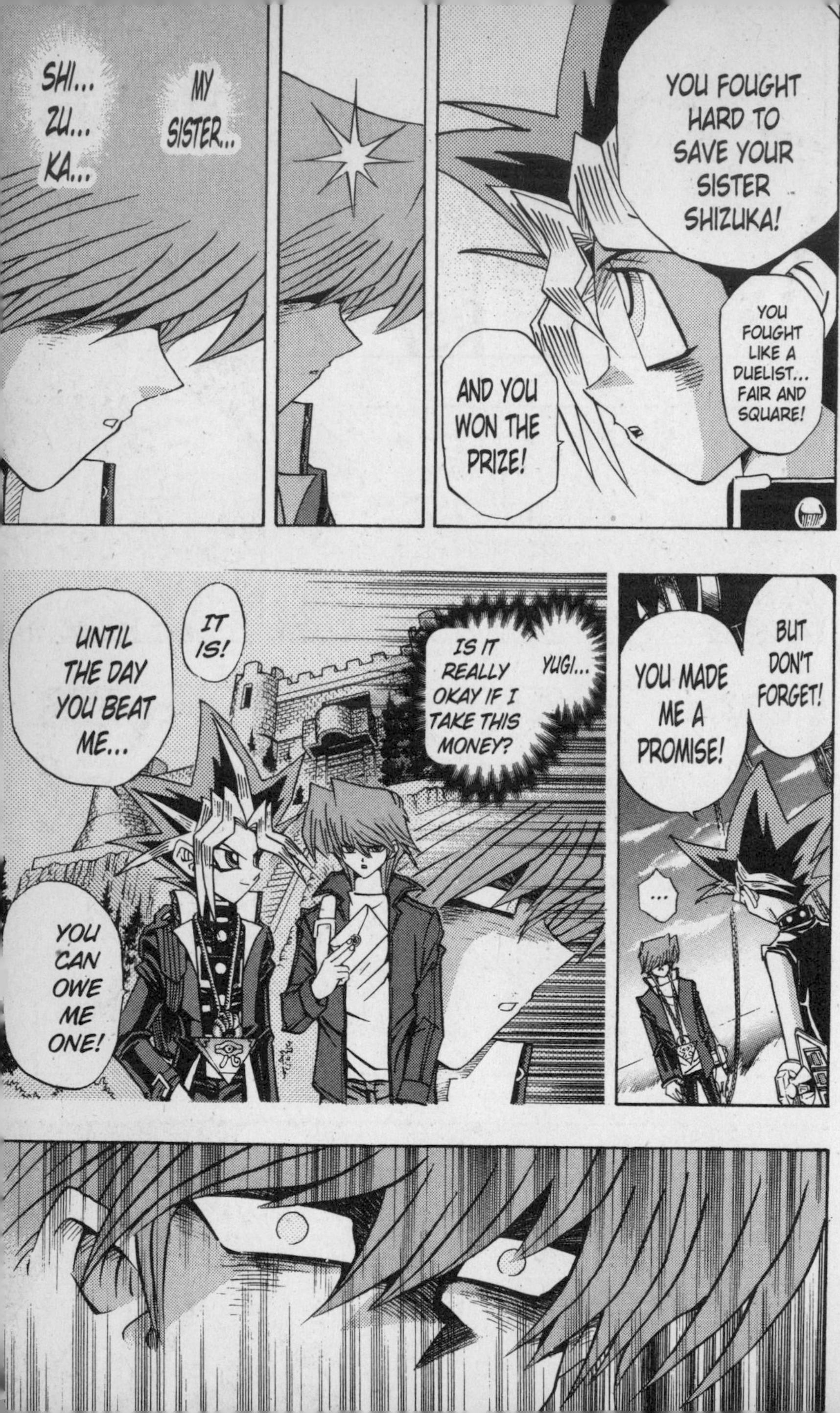
YOU FOUGHT HARD TO SAVE YOUR SISTER SHIZUKA!
YOU FOUGHT LIKE A DUELIST... FAIR AND SQUARE!
AND YOU WON THE PRIZE!
SHI... ZU... KA...
MY SISTER...
BUT DON'T FORGET!
YOU MADE ME A PROMISE!
...
YUGI...
IS IT REALLY OKAY IF I TAKE THIS MONEY?
IT IS!
UNTIL THE DAY YOU BEAT ME...
YOU CAN OWE ME ONE!

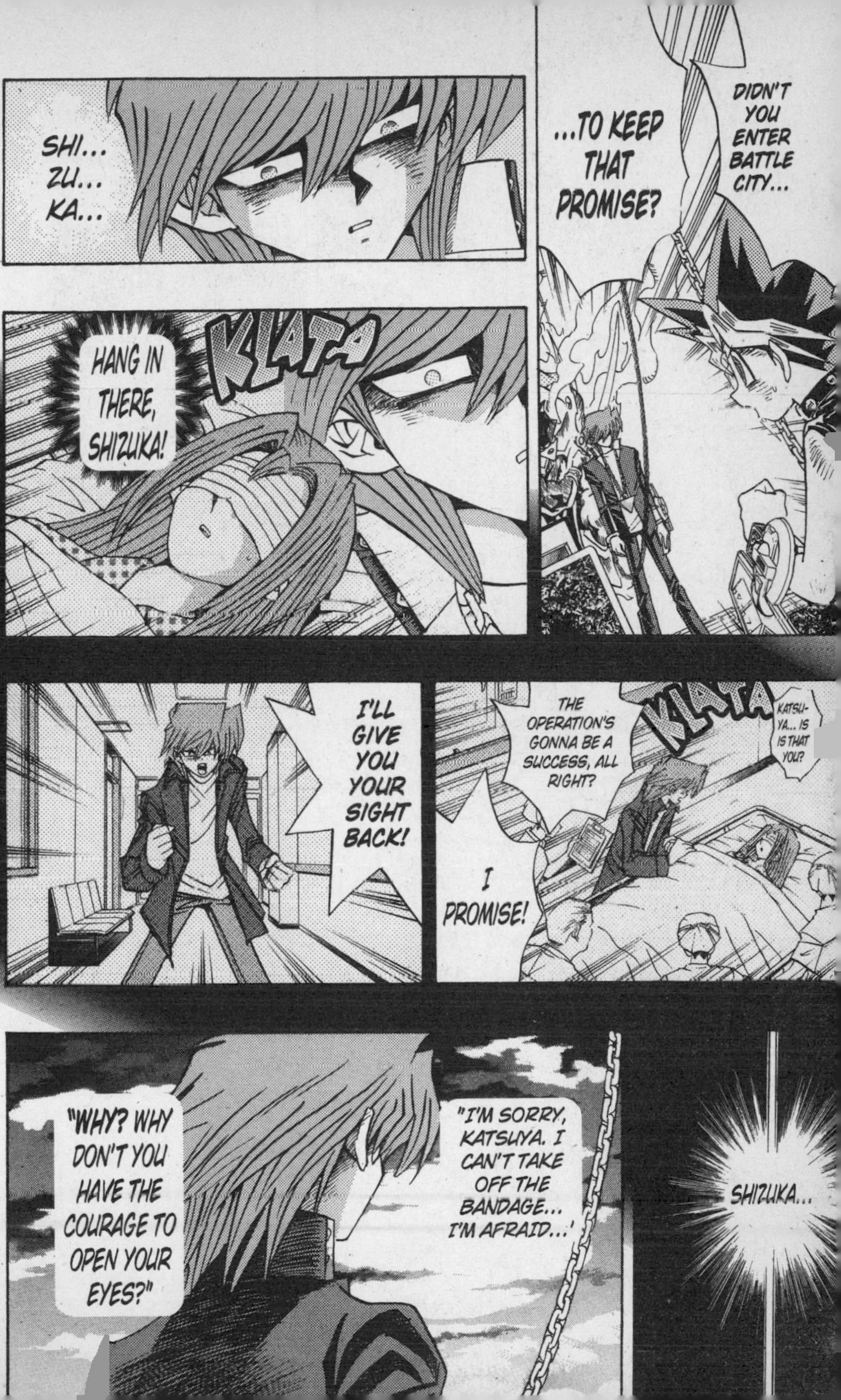
DIDN'T YOU ENTER BATTLE CITY...
...TO KEEP THAT PROMISE?
SHI... ZU... KA...
KLATA
HANG IN THERE, SHIZUKA!
KLATA
KATSUYA... IS IS THAT YOU?
THE OPERATION'S GONNA BE A SUCCESS, ALL RIGHT?
I PROMISE!
I'LL GIVE YOU YOUR SIGHT BACK!
SHIZUKA...
"I'M SORRY, KATSUYA. I CAN'T TAKE OFF THE BANDAGE... I'M AFRAID...'
"WHY? WHY DON'T YOU HAVE THE COURAGE TO OPEN YOUR EYES?"

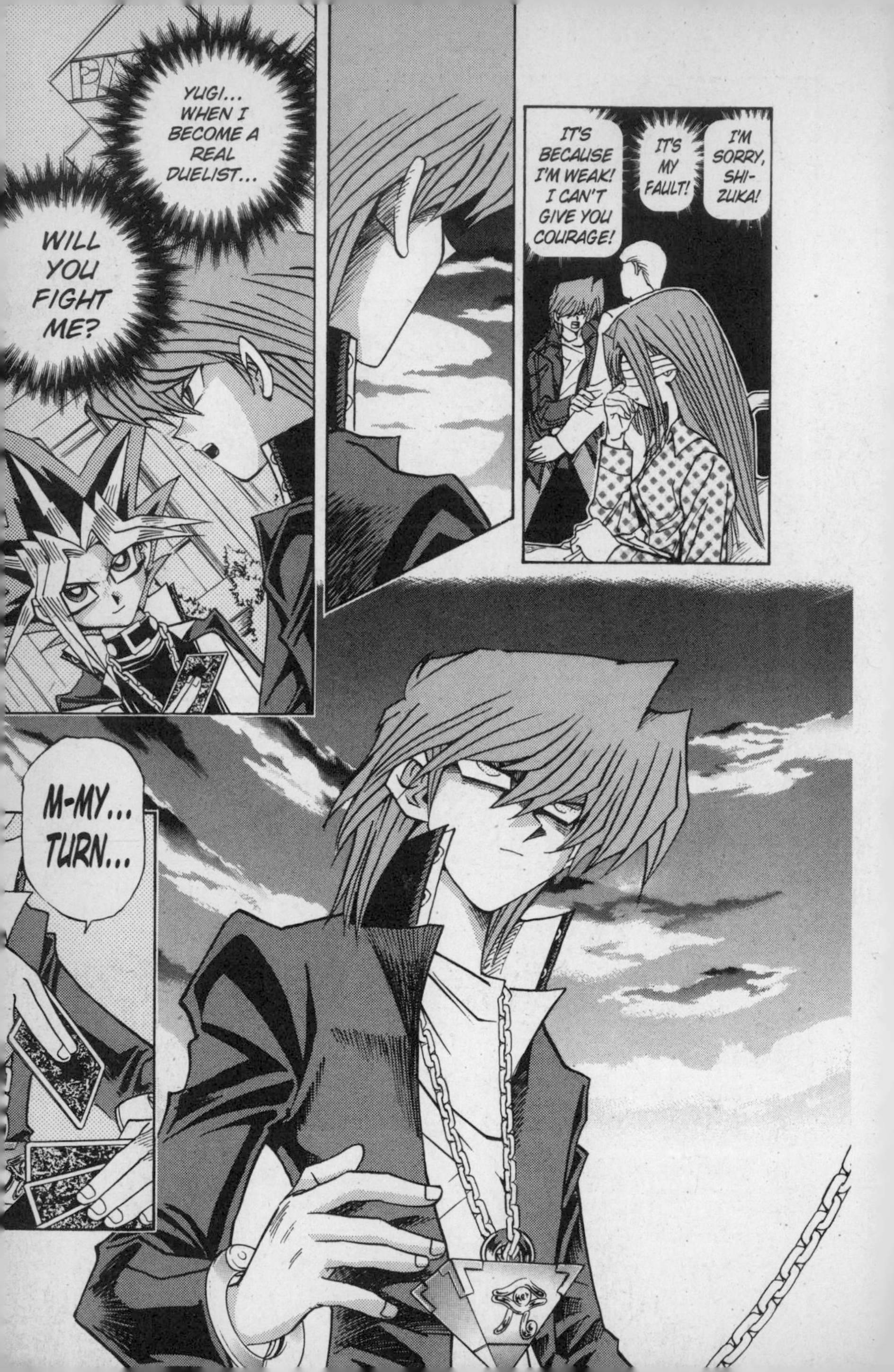
I'M SORRY, SHI-ZUKA!
IT'S MY FAULT!
IT'S BECAUSE I'M WEAK! I CAN'T GIVE YOU COURAGE!
YUGI... WHEN I BECOME A REAL DUELIST...
WILL YOU FIGHT ME?
M-MY... TURN...

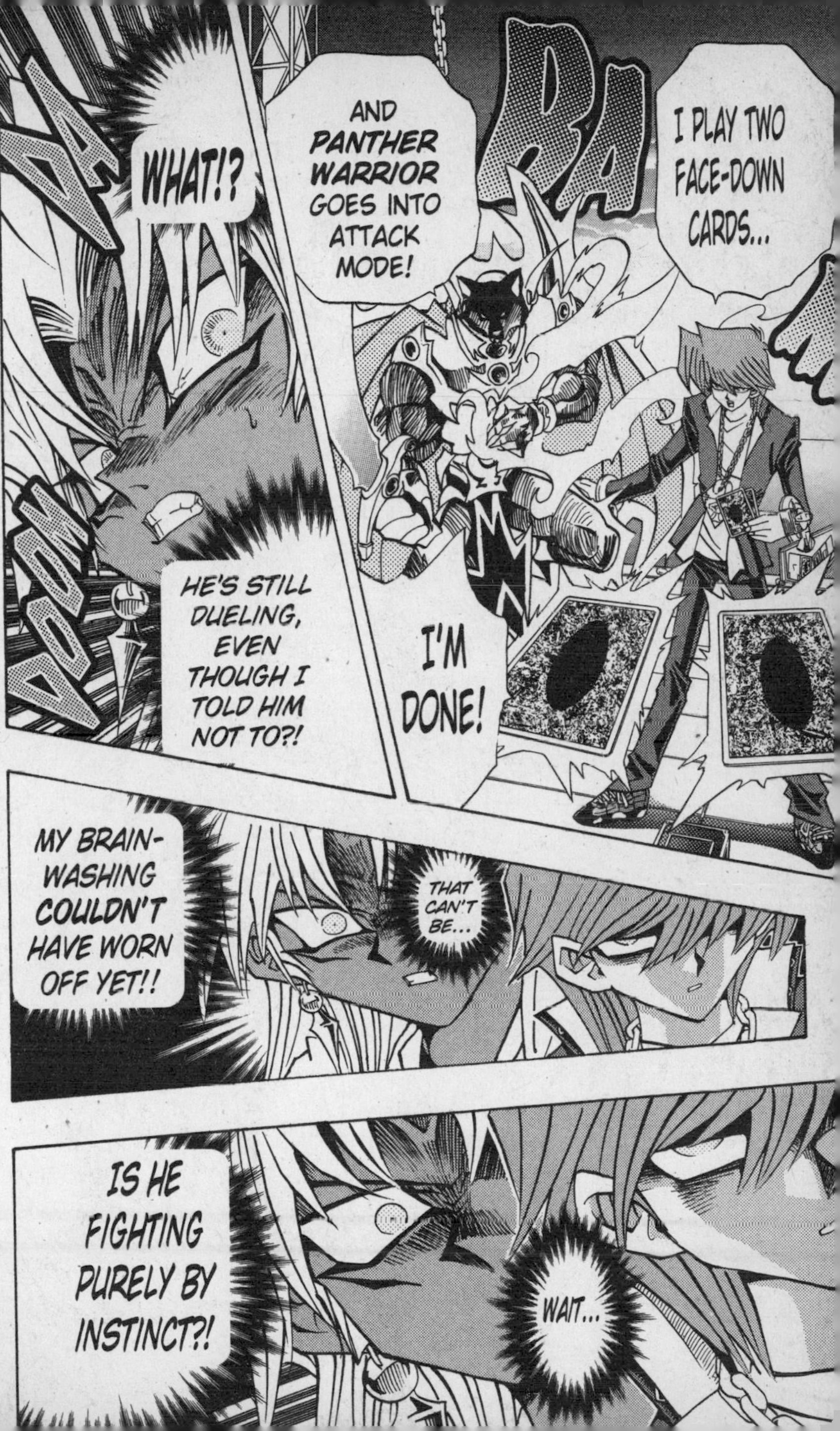
RA
I PLAY TWO FACE-DOWN CARDS...
AND PANTHER WARRIOR GOES INTO ATTACK MODE!
I'M DONE!
WHAT!?
HE'S STILL DUELING, EVEN THOUGH I TOLD HIM NOT TO?!
THAT CAN'T BE...
MY BRAIN-WASHING COULDN'T HAVE WORN OFF YET!!
WAIT...
IS HE FIGHTING PURELY BY INSTINCT?!

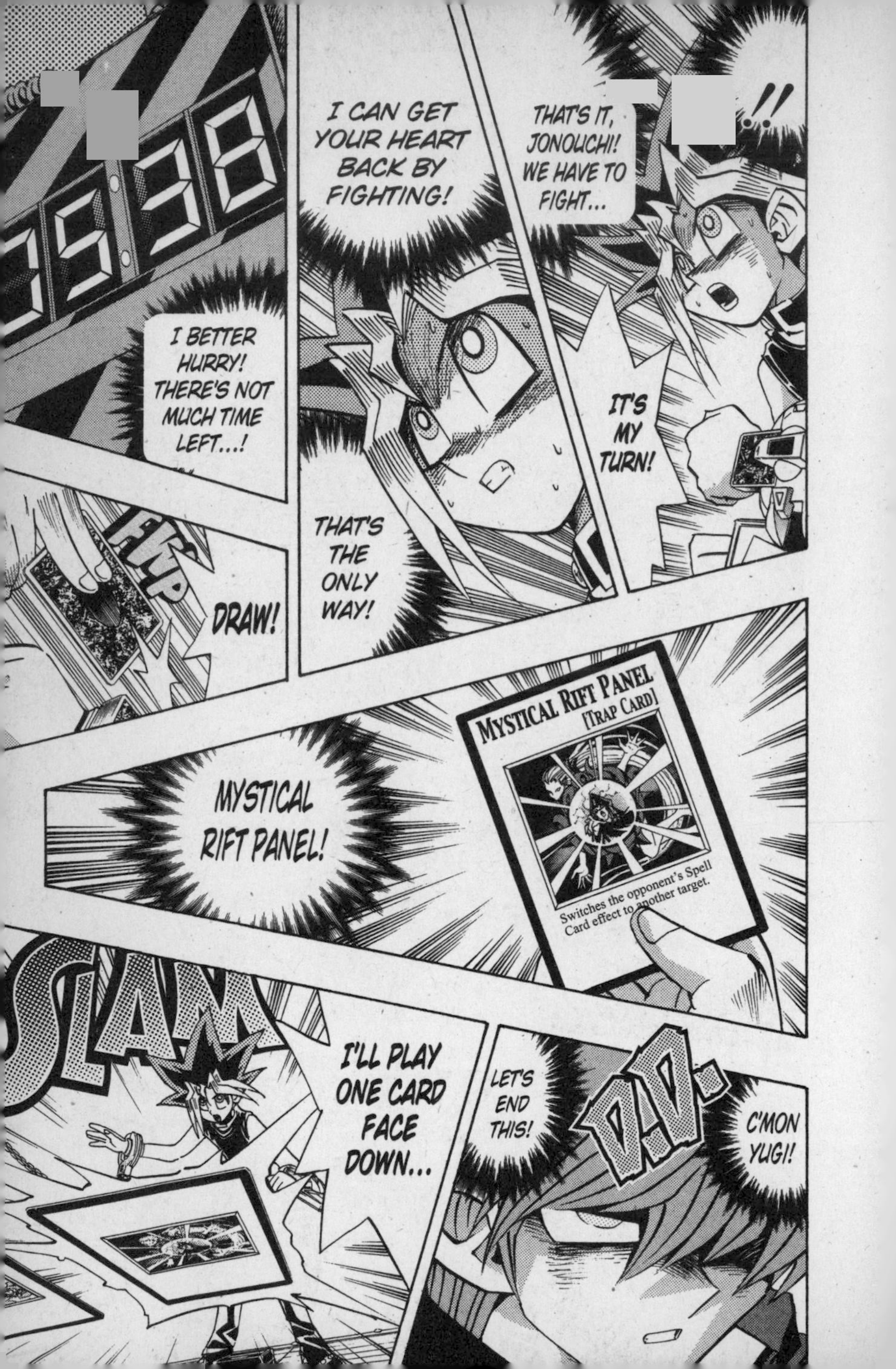

THAT'S IT, JONOUCHI! WE HAVE TO FIGHT...
IT'S MY TURN!
I CAN GET YOUR HEART BACK BY FIGHTING!
THAT'S THE ONLY WAY!
I BETTER HURRY! THERE'S NOT MUCH TIME LEFT...!
DRAW!
MYSTICAL RIFT PANEL!
MYSTICAL RIFT PANEL
[TRAP CARD]
Switches the opponent's Spell Card effect to another target.
C'MON YUGI!
LET'S END THIS!
I'LL PLAY ONE CARD FACE DOWN...
SLAM

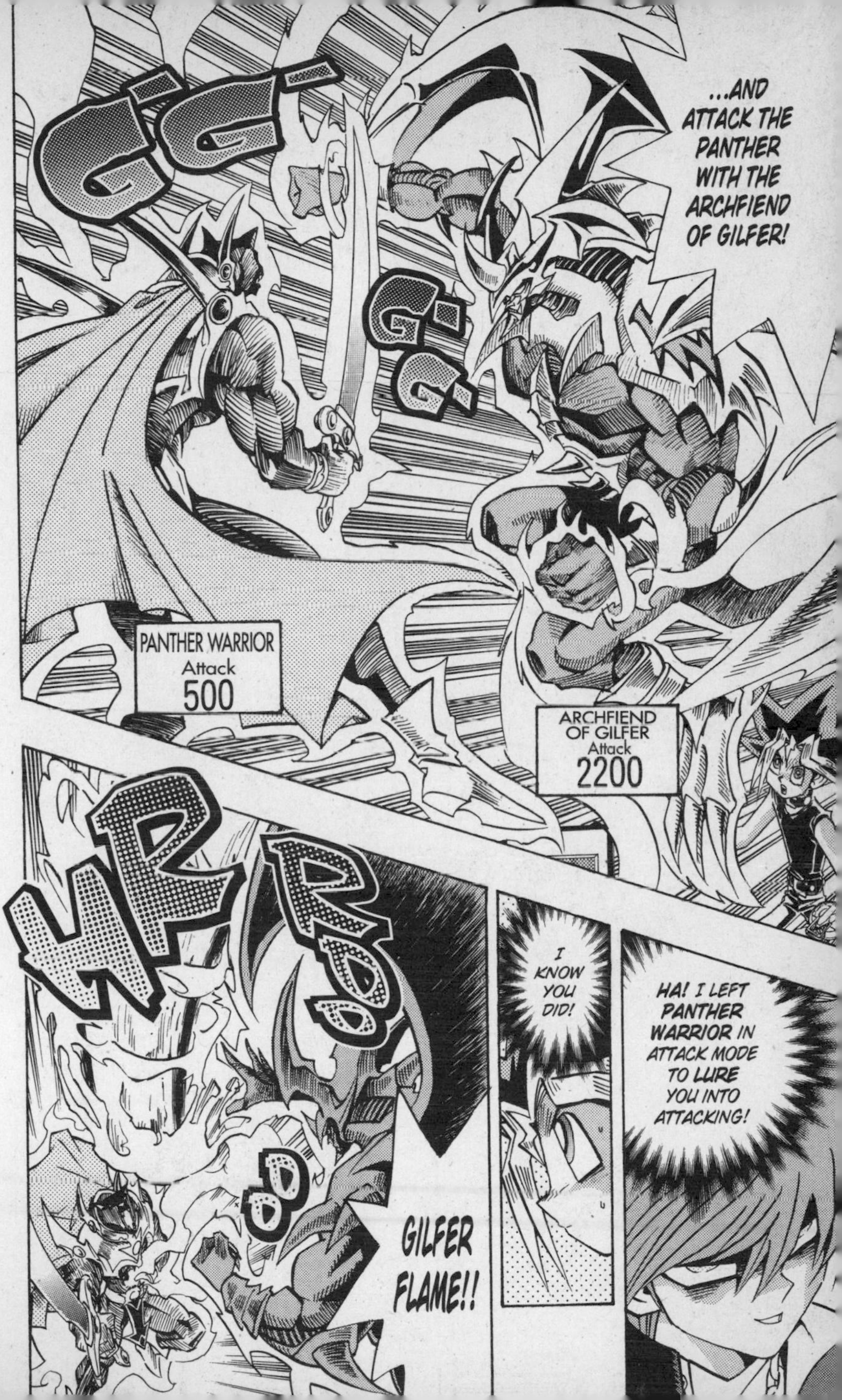
...AND ATTACK THE PANTHER WITH THE ARCHFIEND OF GILFER!
ARCHFIEND OF GILFER Attack 2200
PANTHER WARRIOR Attack 500
HA! I LEFT PANTHER WARRIOR IN ATTACK MODE TO LURE YOU INTO ATTACKING!
I KNOW YOU DID!
GILFER FLAME!!

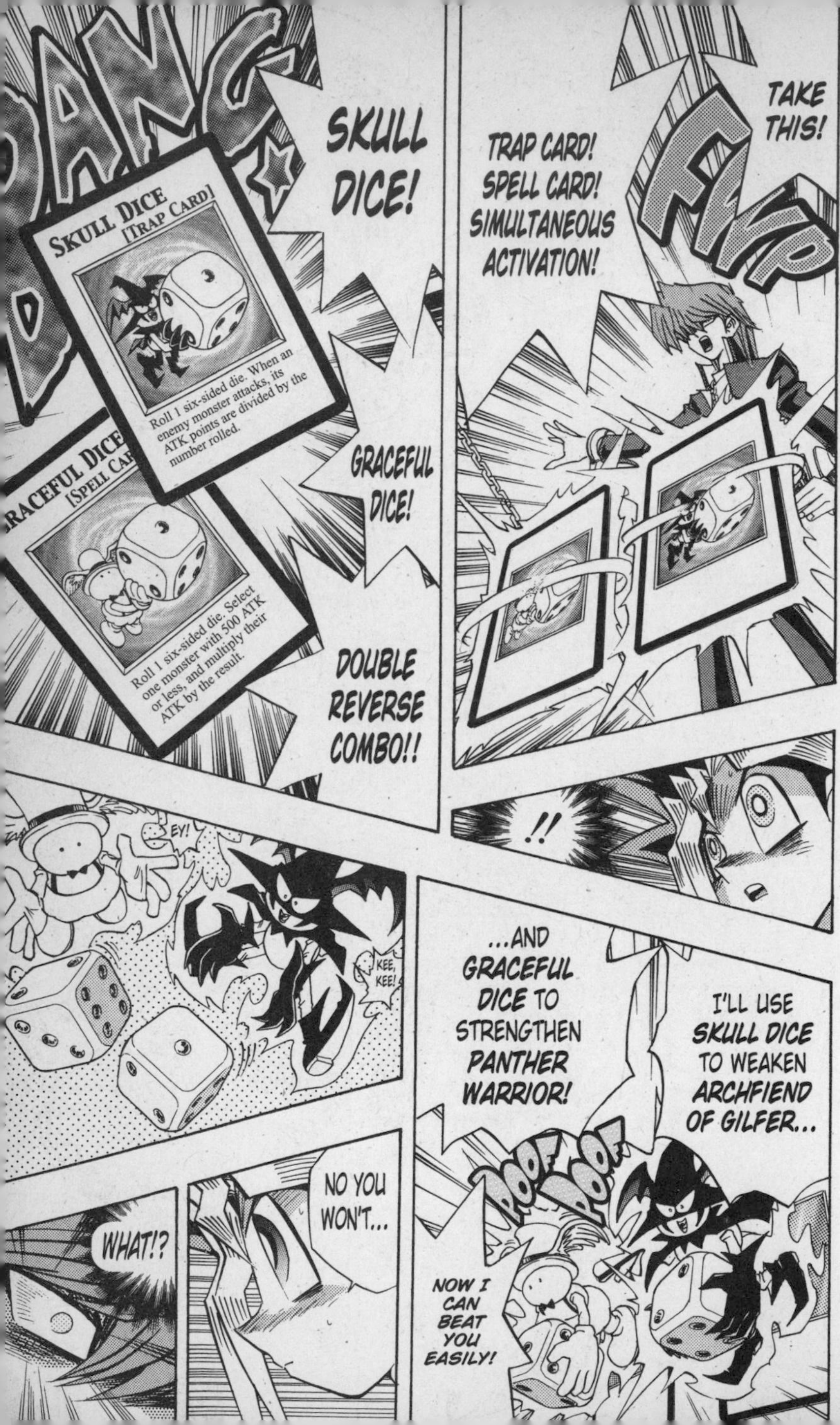

TAKE THIS!
FLIP
TRAP CARD! SPELL CARD! SIMULTANEOUS ACTIVATION!
BANG
SKULL DICE [TRAP CARD]
Roll 1 six-sided die. When an enemy monster attacks, its ATK points are divided by the number rolled.
GRACEFUL DICE [SPELL CARD]
Roll 1 six-sided die. Select one monster with 500 ATK or less, and multiply their ATK by the result.
SKULL DICE!
GRACEFUL DICE!
DOUBLE REVERSE COMBO!!
!!
EY!
KEE, KEE!
I'LL USE SKULL DICE TO WEAKEN ARCHFIEND OF GILFER...
...AND GRACEFUL DICE TO STRENGTHEN PANTHER WARRIOR!
POOF POOF
NOW I CAN BEAT YOU EASILY!
NO YOU WON'T...
WHAT!?

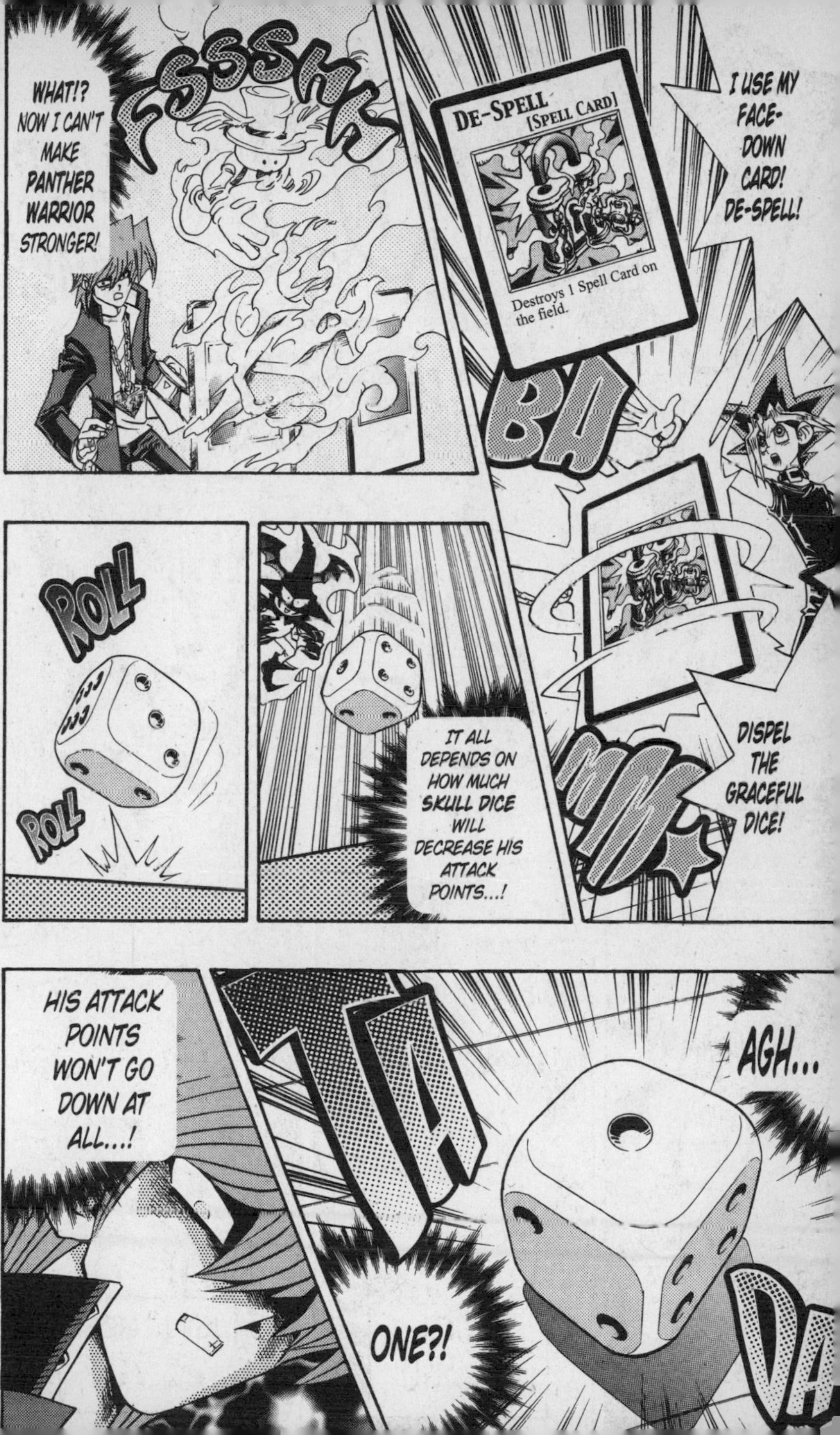
I USE MY FACE-DOWN CARD! DE-SPELL!
DE-SPELL
[SPELL CARD]
Destroys 1 Spell Card on the field.
BA
DISPEL THE GRACEFUL DICE!
FSSSH
WHAT!? NOW I CAN'T MAKE PANTHER WARRIOR STRONGER!
IT ALL DEPENDS ON HOW MUCH SKULL DICE WILL DECREASE HIS ATTACK POINTS...!
ROLL
ROLL
AGH...
ONE?!
HIS ATTACK POINTS WON'T GO DOWN AT ALL...!

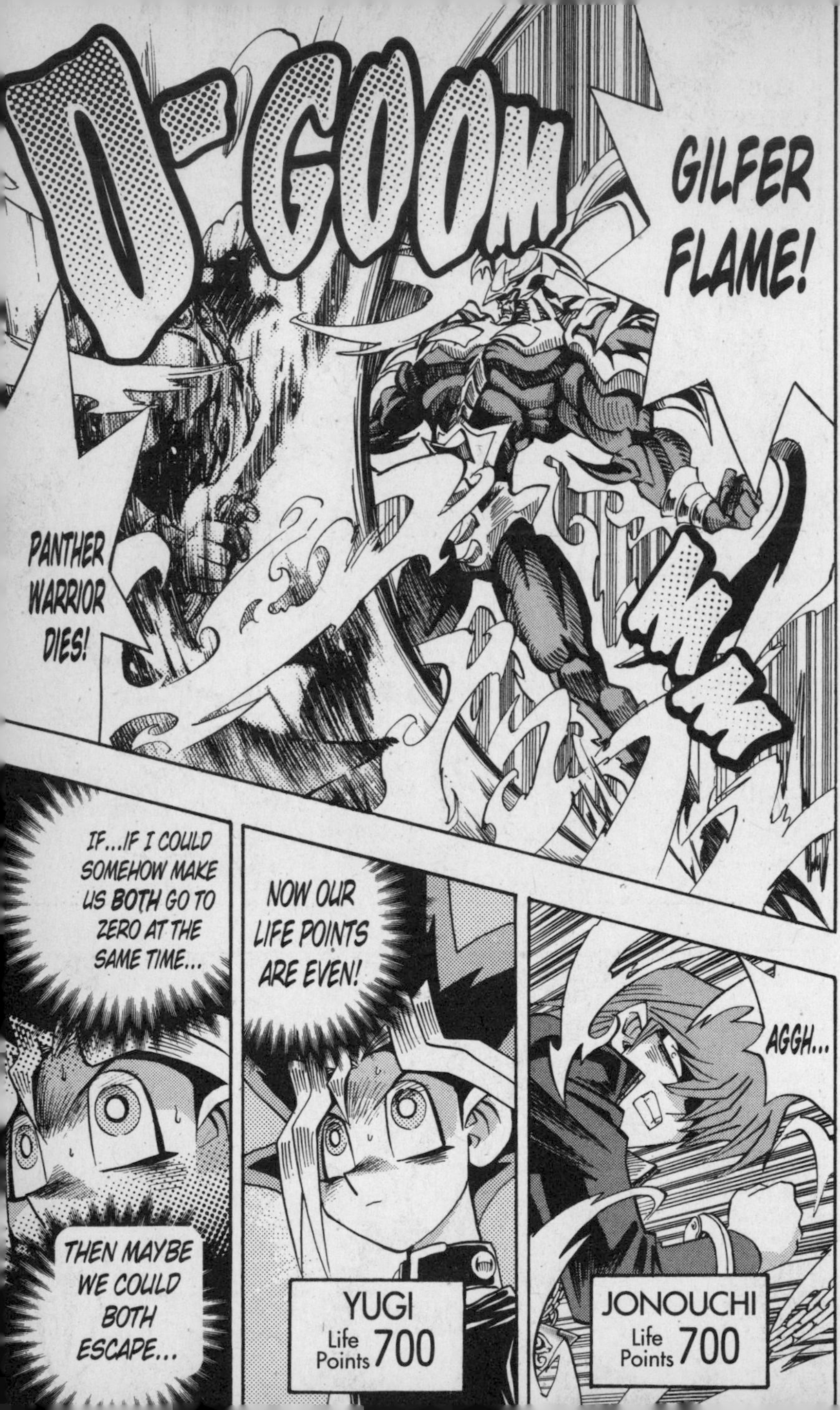
GILFER FLAME!
D-GOOM
PANTHER WARRIOR DIES!
AGGH...
JONOUCHI Life Points 700
NOW OUR LIFE POINTS ARE EVEN!
YUGI Life Points 700
IF...IF I COULD SOMEHOW MAKE US BOTH GO TO ZERO AT THE SAME TIME...
THEN MAYBE WE COULD BOTH ESCAPE...

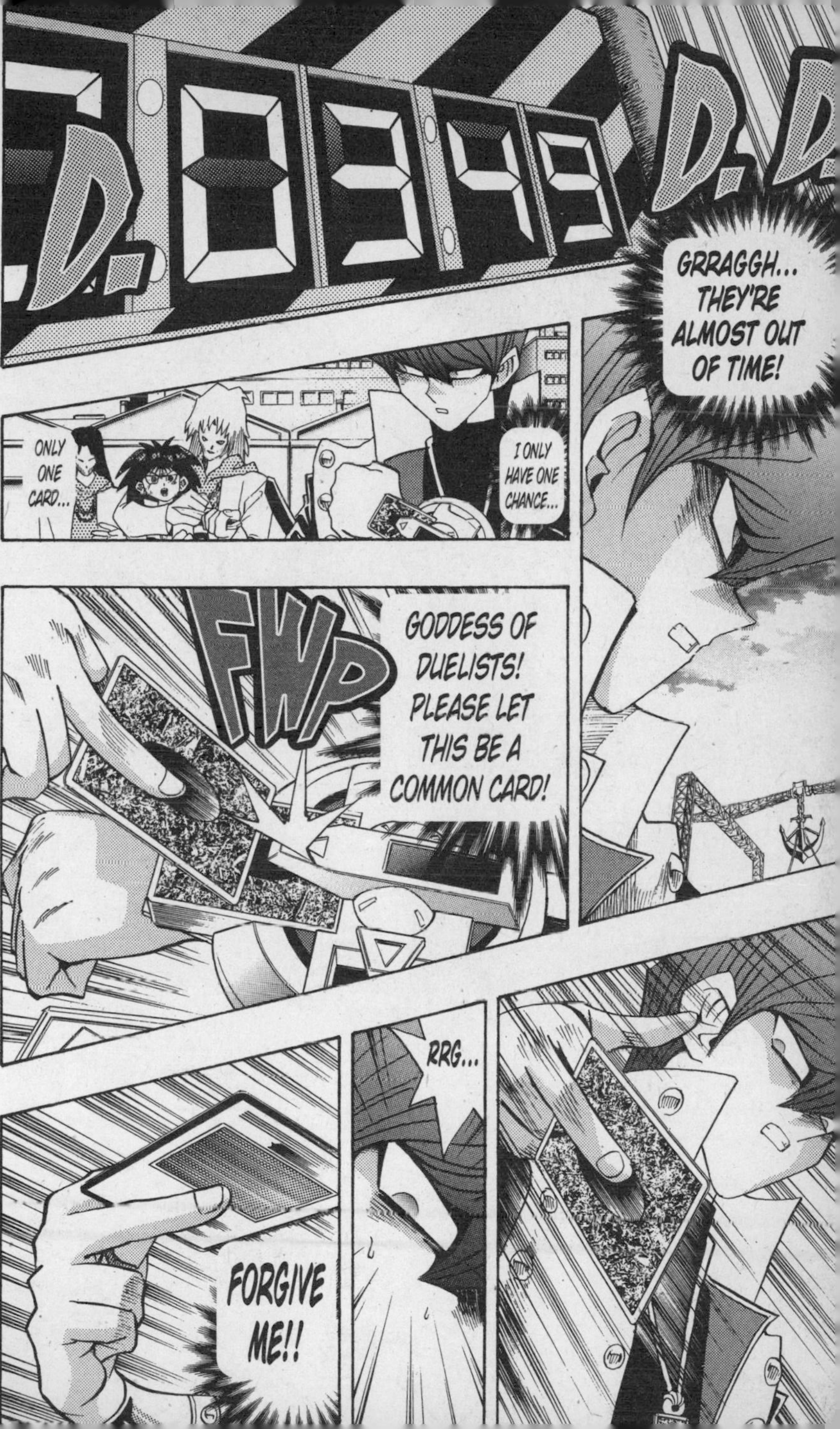
.D. 0349 D.D
GRRAGGH... THEY'RE ALMOST OUT OF TIME!
I ONLY HAVE ONE CHANCE...
ONLY ONE CARD...
FWP
GODDESS OF DUELISTS! PLEASE LET THIS BE A COMMON CARD!
RRG...
FORGIVE ME!!

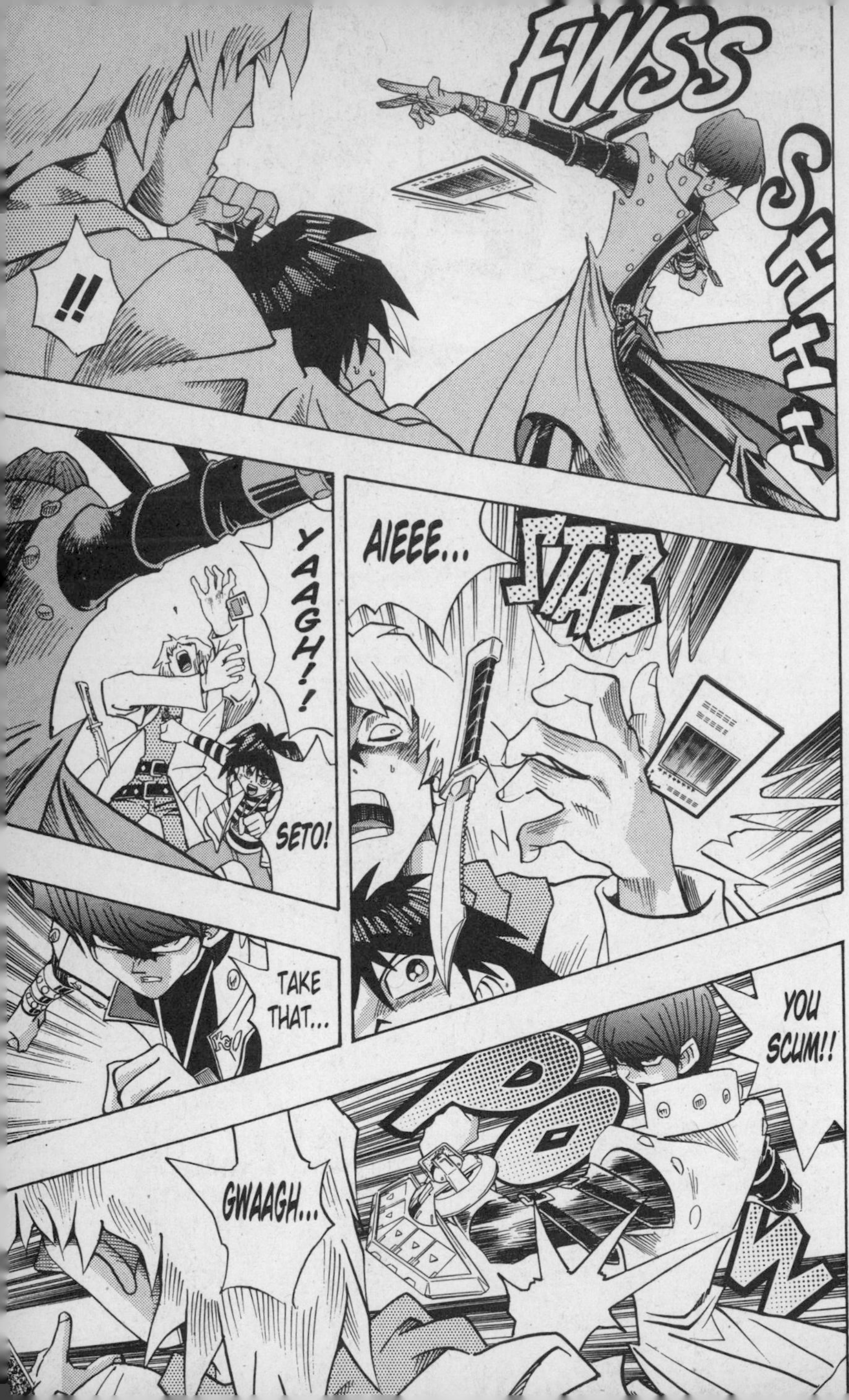
FWSS
SHHH
!!
STAB
AIEEE...
YAAAGH!!
SETO!
TAKE THAT...
YOU SCUM!!
POW
GWAAGH...

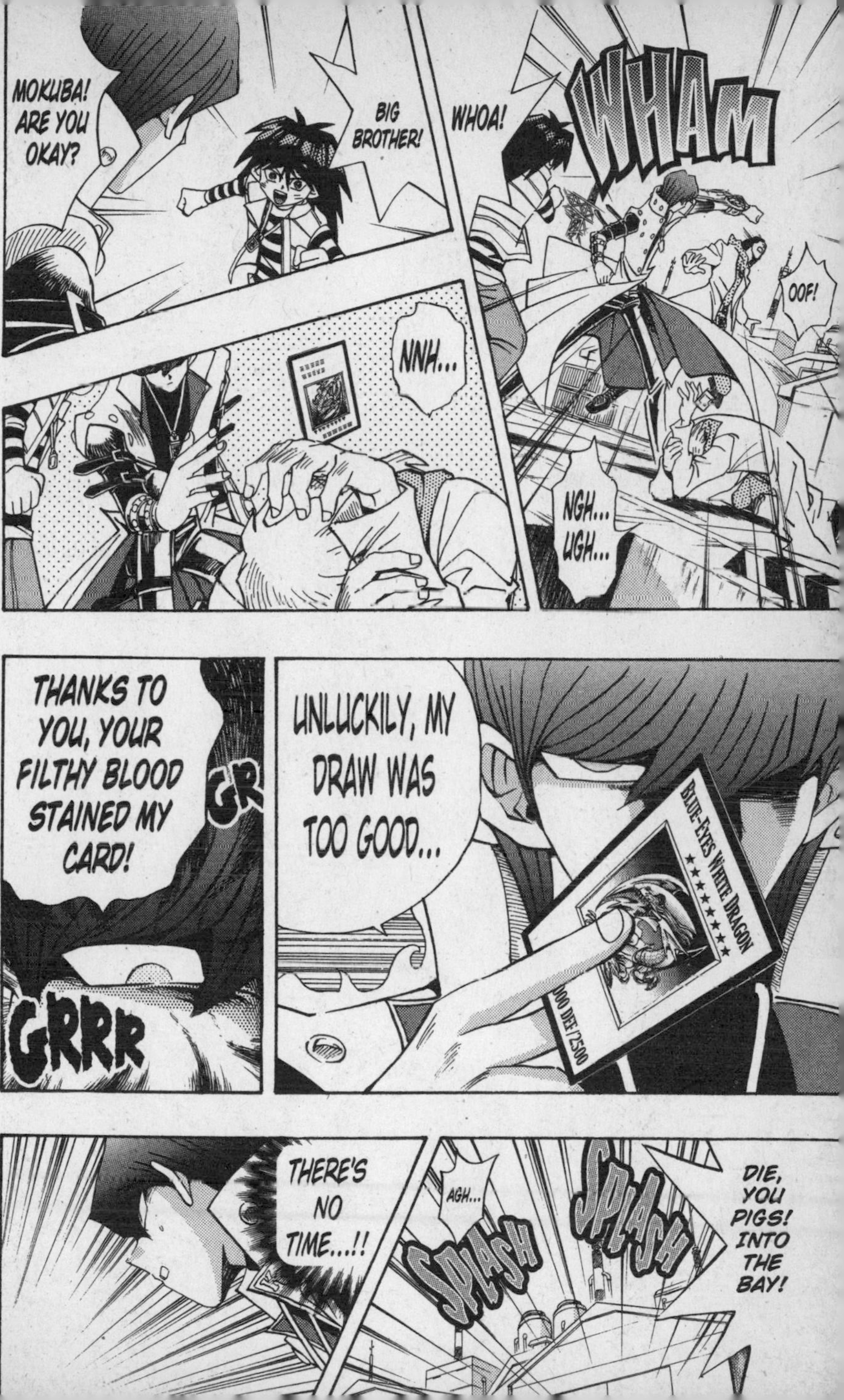
WHOA!
WHAM
OOF!
NGH... UGH...
BIG BROTHER!
MOKUBA! ARE YOU OKAY?
NNH...
UNLUCKILY, MY DRAW WAS TOO GOOD...
BLUE-EYES WHITE DRAGON
DEF/2500
THANKS TO YOU, YOUR FILTHY BLOOD STAINED MY CARD!
GR
GRRR
DIE, YOU PIGS! INTO THE BAY!
SPLASH
SPLASH
AGH...
THERE'S NO TIME...!!

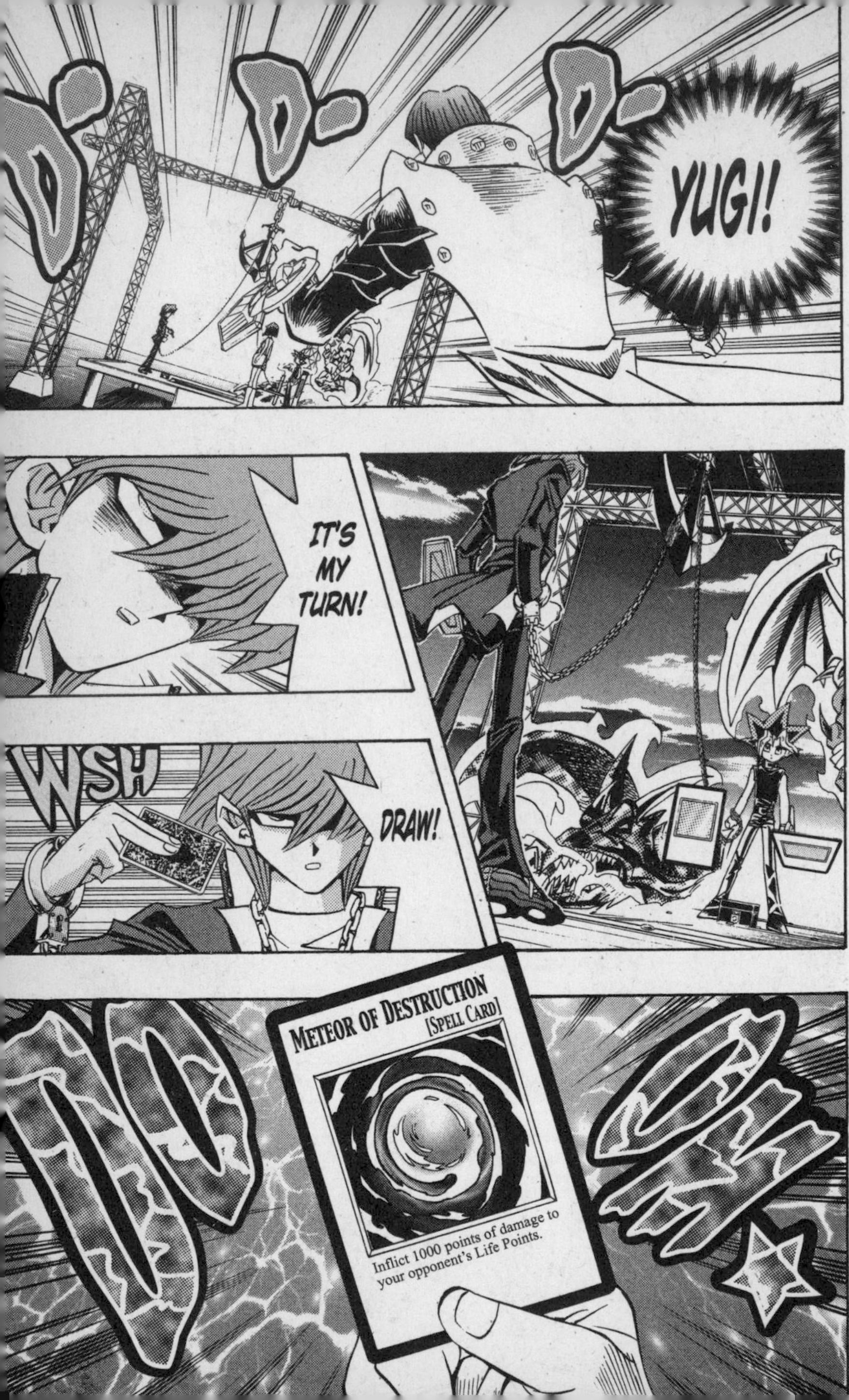
D-D-D-
YUGI!
IT'S MY TURN!
WSH
DRAW!
METEOR OF DESTRUCTION
[SPELL CARD]
Inflict 1000 points of damage to your opponent's Life Points.

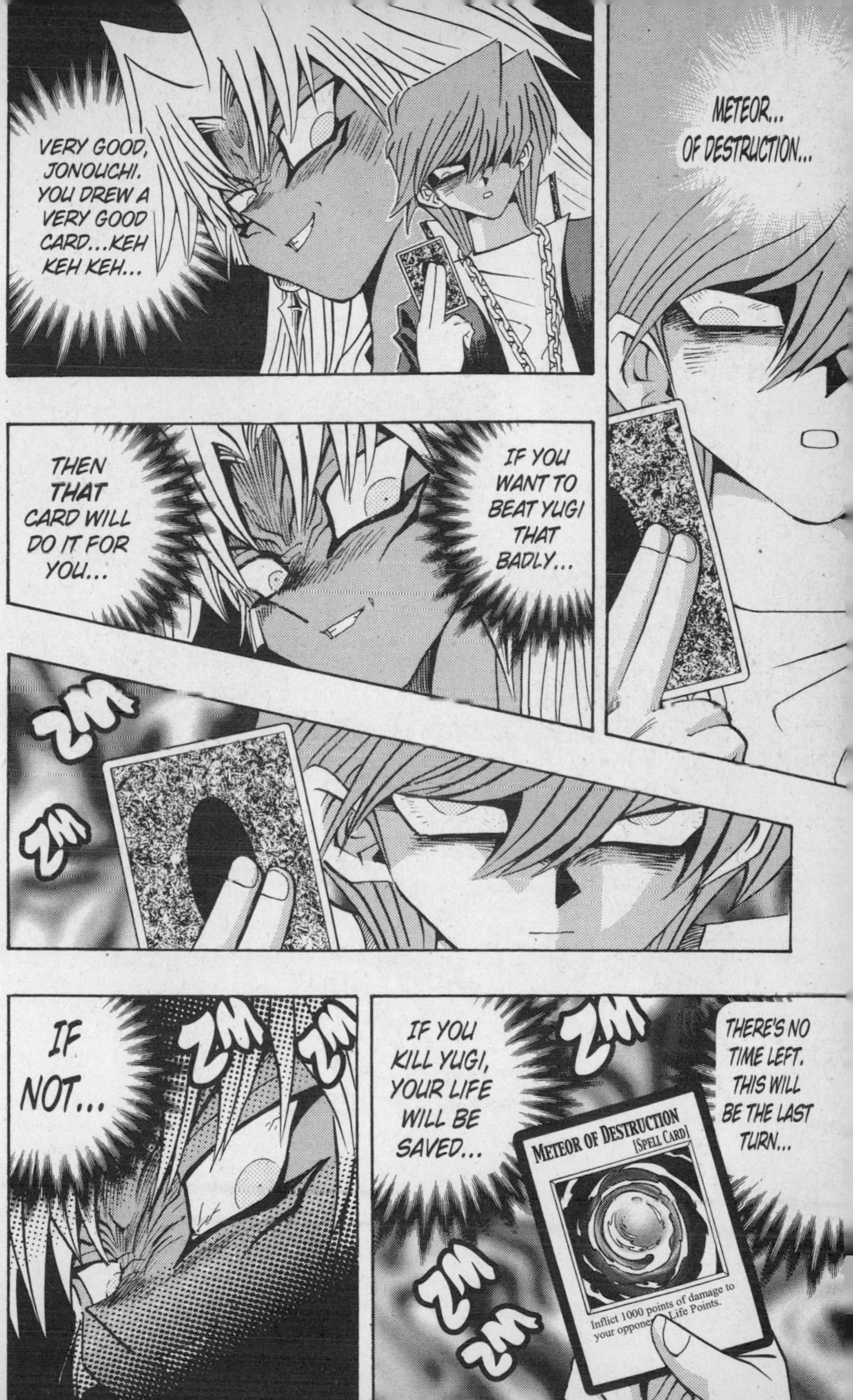
METEOR... OF DESTRUCTION...
VERY GOOD, JONOUCHI. YOU DREW A VERY GOOD CARD...KEH KEH KEH...
IF YOU WANT TO BEAT YUGI THAT BADLY...
THEN THAT CARD WILL DO IT FOR YOU...
ZM
ZM
THERE'S NO TIME LEFT. THIS WILL BE THE LAST TURN...
IF YOU KILL YUGI, YOUR LIFE WILL BE SAVED...
ZM
METEOR OF DESTRUCTION
[SPELL CARD]
Inflict 1000 points of damage to your oppone Life Points.
ZM
ZM
IF NOT...
ZM
ZM

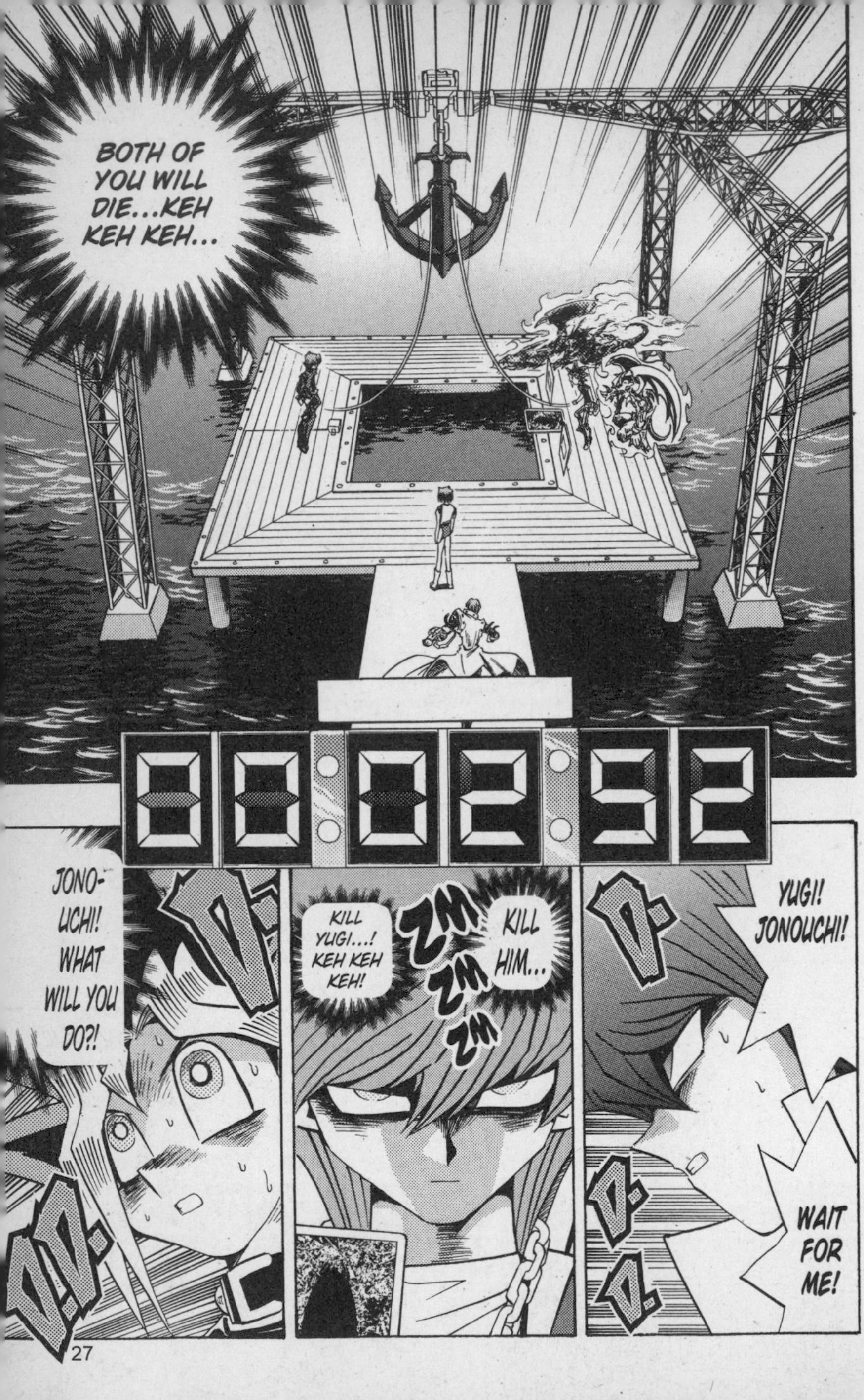
BOTH OF YOU WILL DIE...KEH KEH KEH...
YUGI! JONOUCHI!
WAIT FOR ME!
KILL HIM...
ZM ZM ZM ZM
KILL YUGI...! KEH KEH KEH!
JONO-UCHI! WHAT WILL YOU DO?!

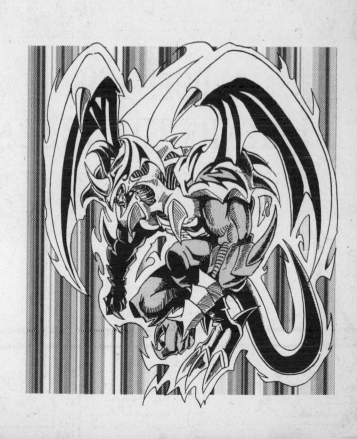

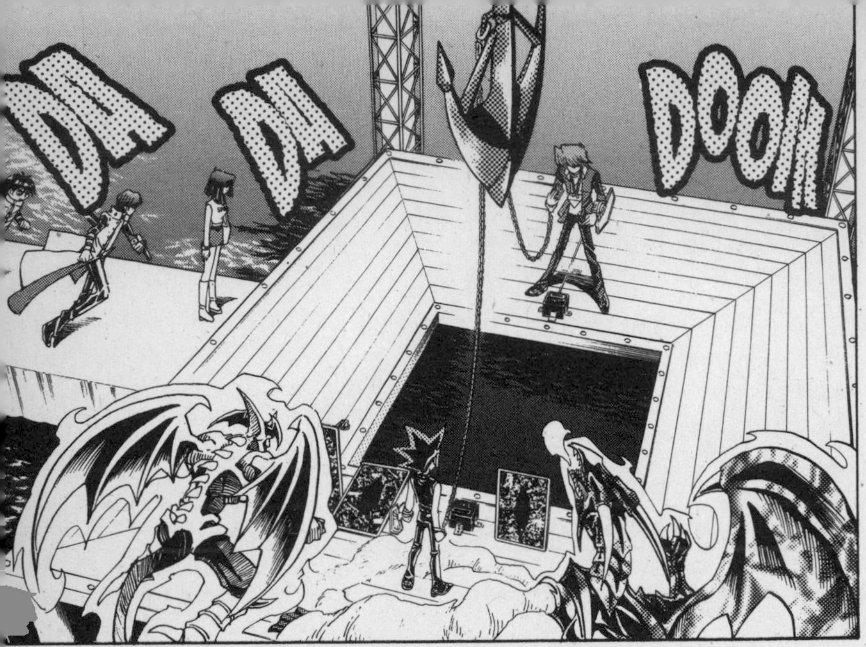
DA
DA
DOOM

Duel 139: Friends till the End

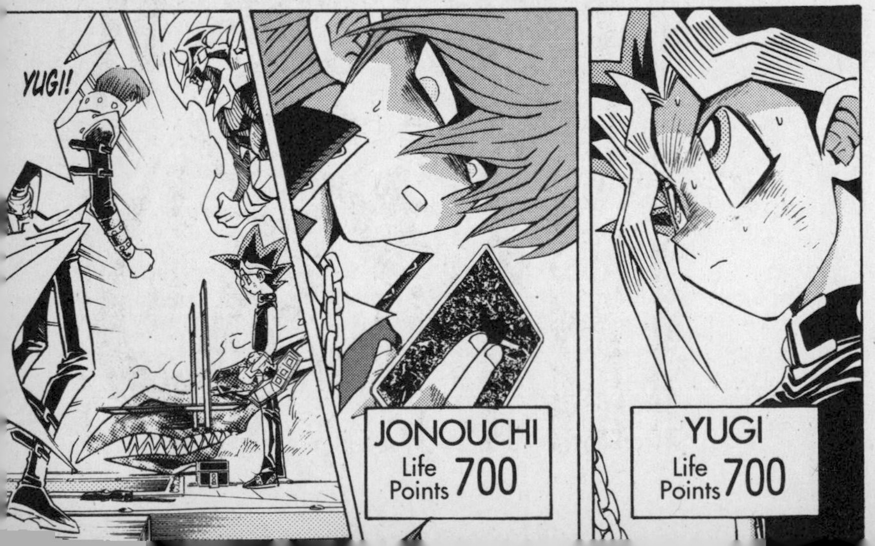
YUGI
Life Points 700
JONOUCHI
Life Points 700
YUGI!

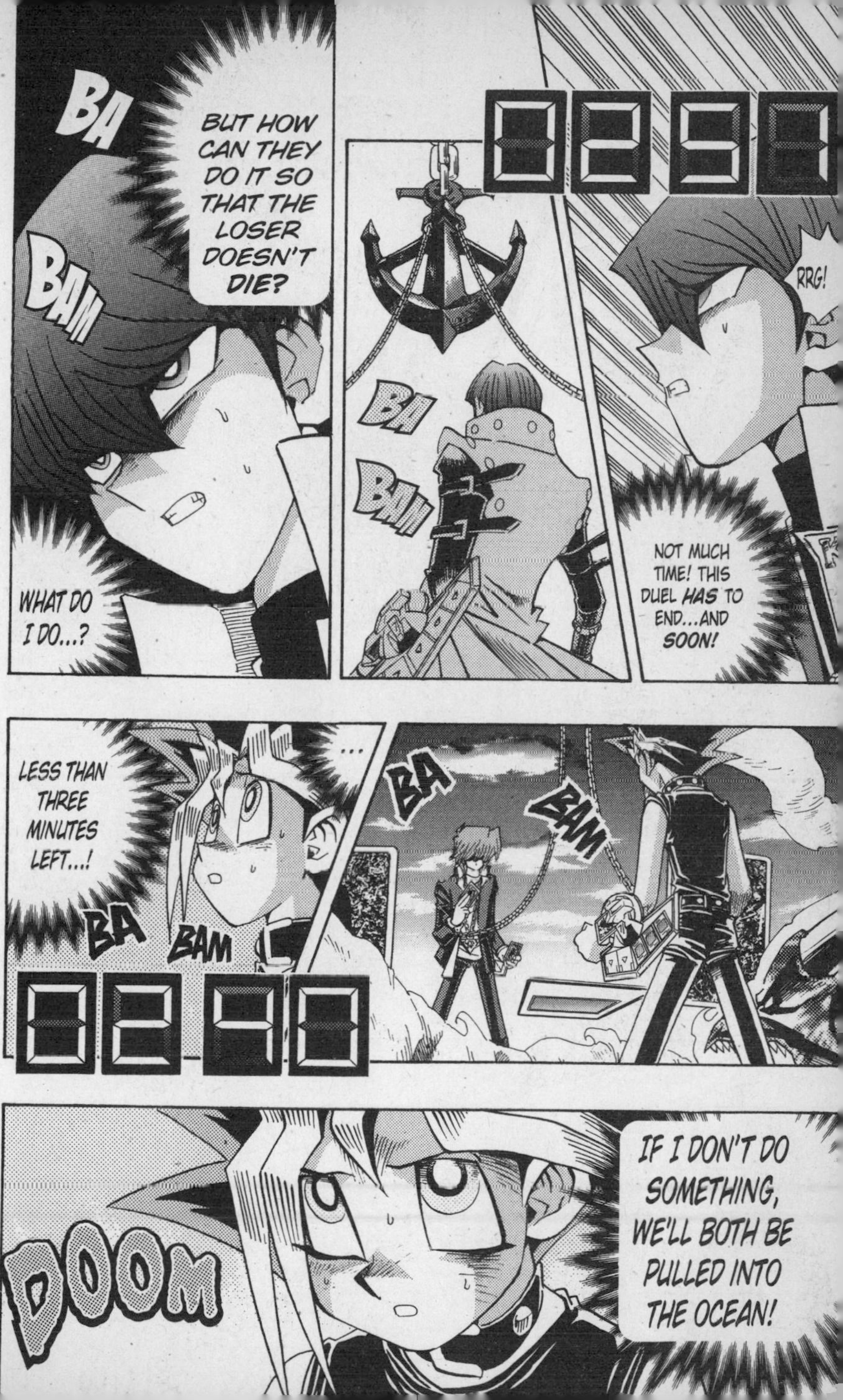
RRG!
NOT MUCH TIME! THIS DUEL HAS TO END...AND SOON!
BA
BAM
BA
BUT HOW CAN THEY DO IT SO THAT THE LOSER DOESN'T DIE?
BAM
WHAT DO I DO...?
BA
BAM
...
LESS THAN THREE MINUTES LEFT...!
BA
BAM
IF I DON'T DO SOMETHING, WE'LL BOTH BE PULLED INTO THE OCEAN!
DOOM

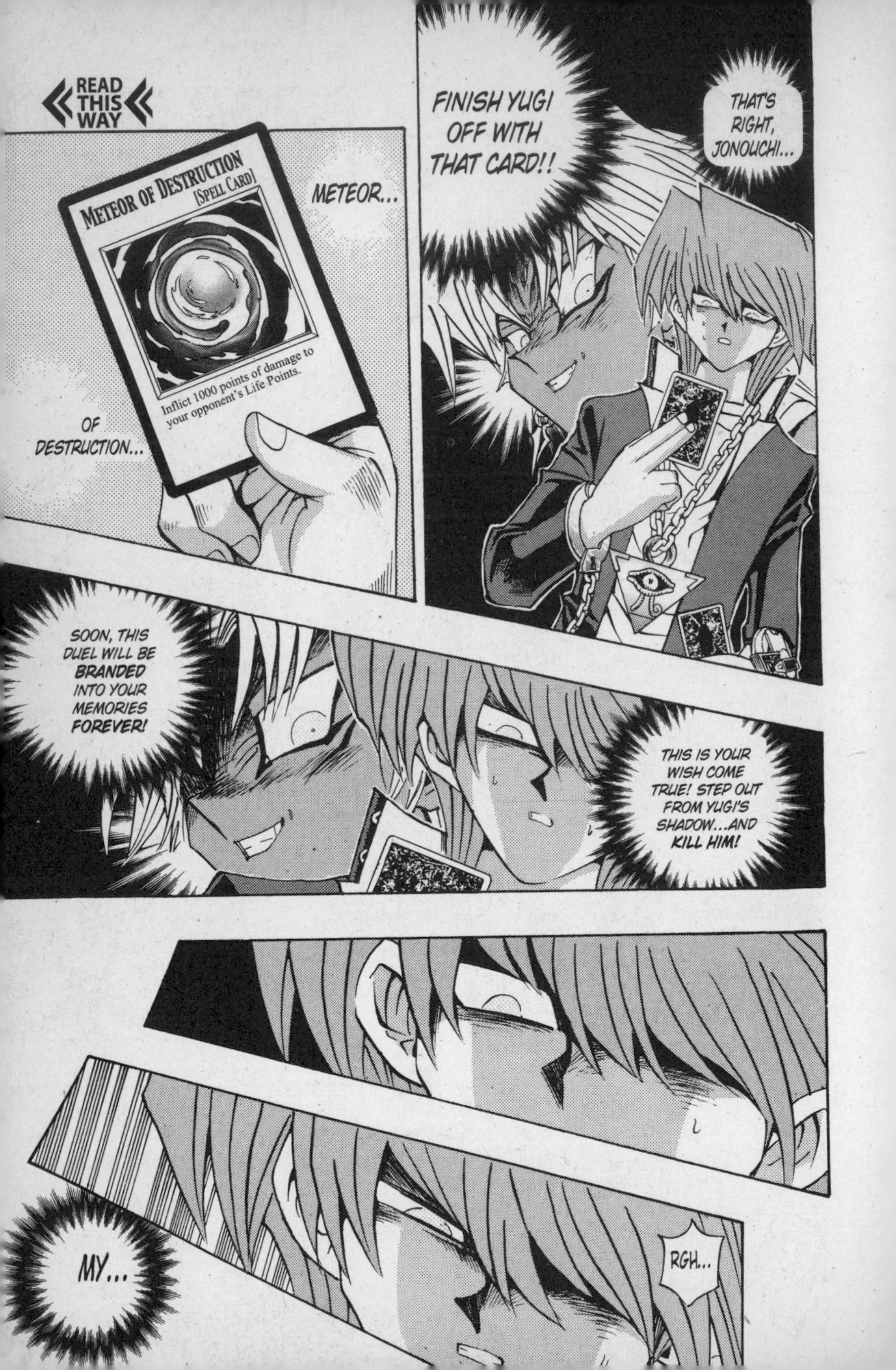
READ THIS WAY
THAT'S RIGHT, JONOUCHI...
FINISH YUGI OFF WITH THAT CARD!!
METEOR...
METEOR OF DESTRUCTION
[SPELL CARD]
Inflict 1000 points of damage to your opponent's Life Points.
OF DESTRUCTION...
SOON, THIS DUEL WILL BE BRANDED INTO YOUR MEMORIES FOREVER!
THIS IS YOUR WISH COME TRUE! STEP OUT FROM YUGI'S SHADOW...AND KILL HIM!
RGH...
MY...

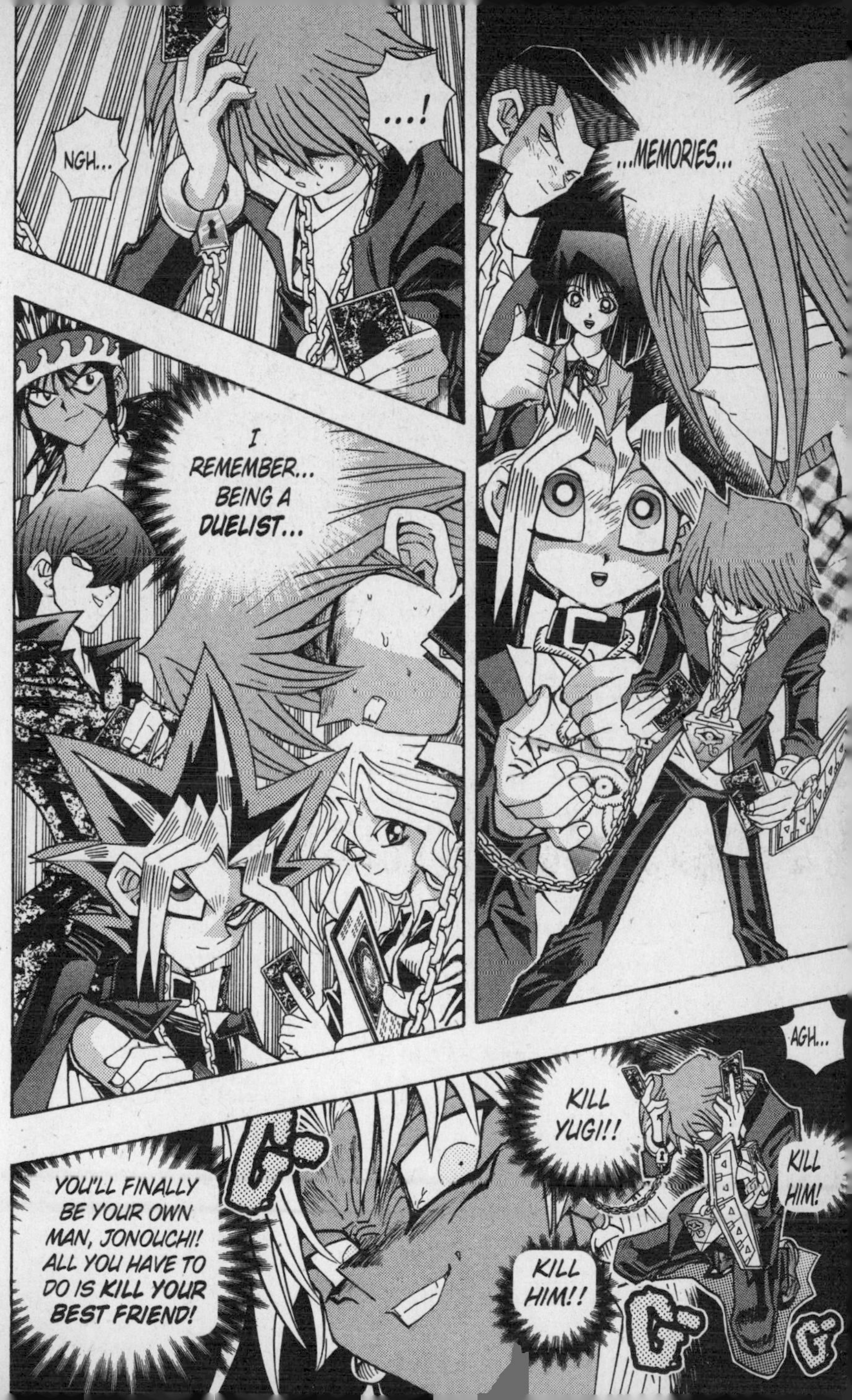
...MEMORIES...
...!
NGH...
I REMEMBER... BEING A DUELIST...
AGH...
KILL HIM!
KILL YUGI!!
G-
KILL HIM!!
YOU'LL FINALLY BE YOUR OWN MAN, JONOUCHI! ALL YOU HAVE TO DO IS KILL YOUR BEST FRIEND!
G-
G-

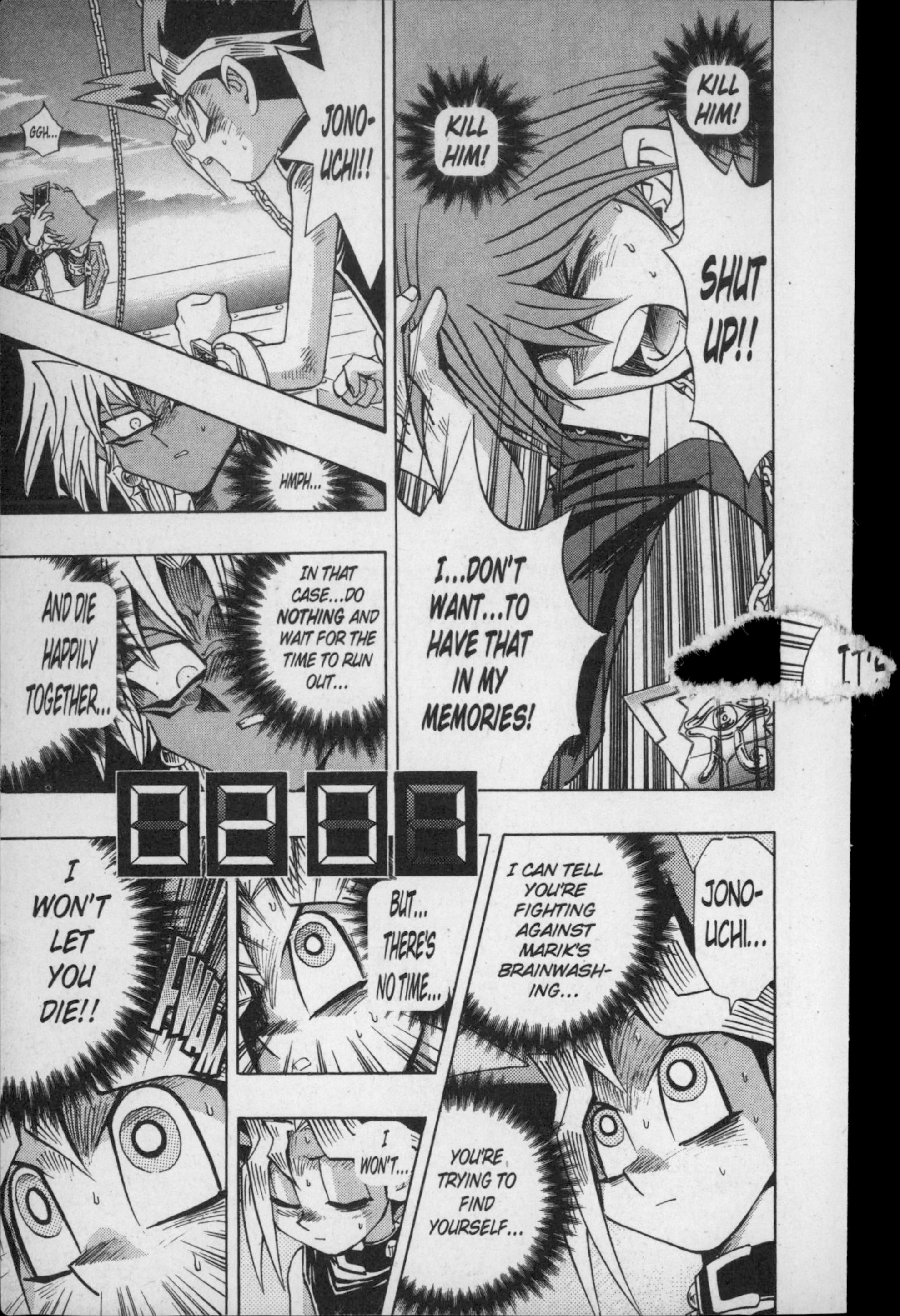
KILL HIM!
KILL HIM!
SHUT UP!!
JONO-UCHI!!
GGH...
HMPH...
I...DON'T WANT...TO HAVE THAT IN MY MEMORIES!
[redacted] IT'
IN THAT CASE...DO NOTHING AND WAIT FOR THE TIME TO RUN OUT...
AND DIE HAPPILY TOGETHER...
JONO-UCHI...
I CAN TELL YOU'RE FIGHTING AGAINST MARIK'S BRAINWASHING...
YOU'RE TRYING TO FIND YOURSELF...
BUT... THERE'S NO TIME...
I WON'T...
I WON'T LET YOU DIE!!

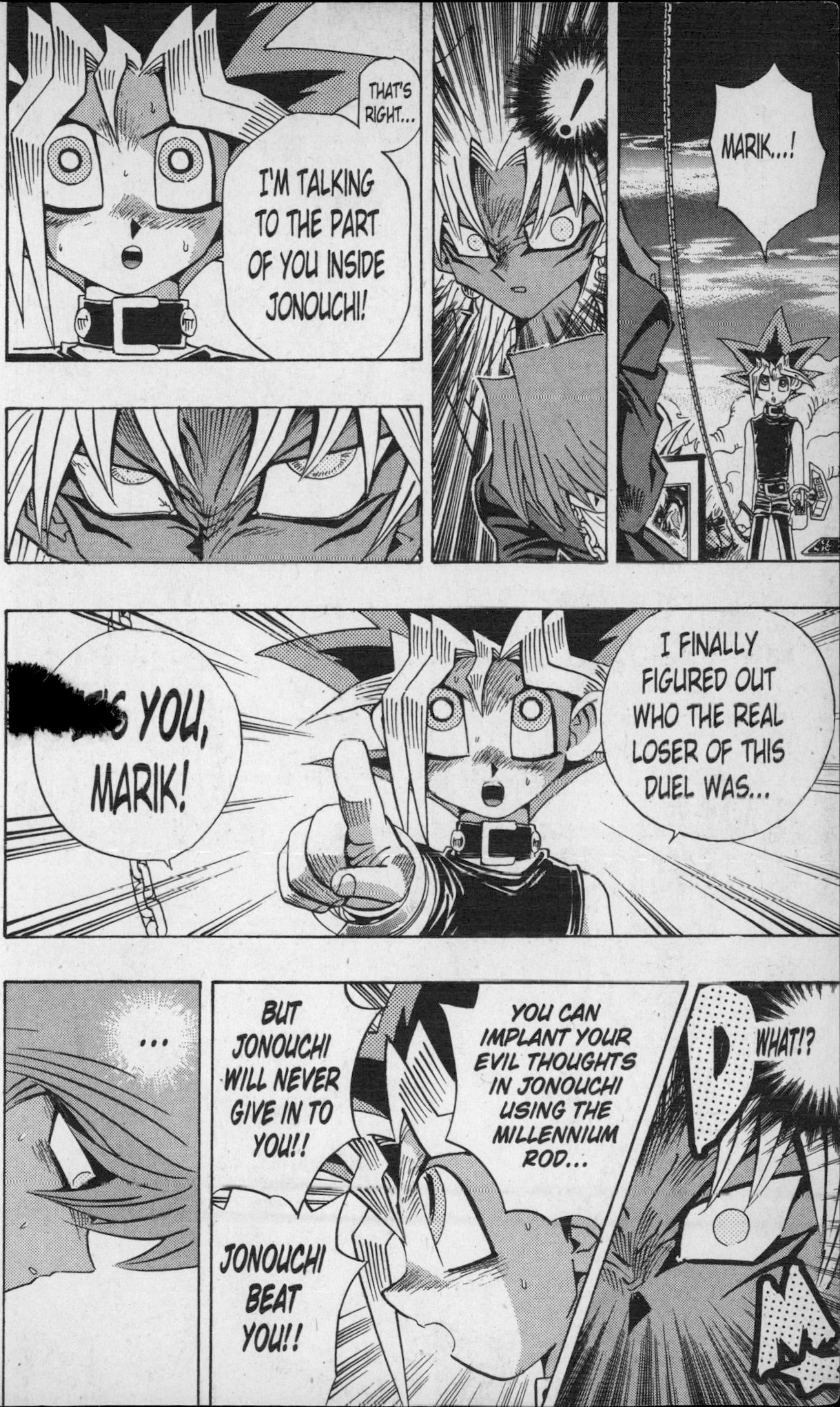
MARIK...!
!
THAT'S RIGHT...
I'M TALKING TO THE PART OF YOU INSIDE JONOUCHI!
I FINALLY FIGURED OUT WHO THE REAL LOSER OF THIS DUEL WAS...
S YOU, MARIK!
WHAT!?
YOU CAN IMPLANT YOUR EVIL THOUGHTS IN JONOUCHI USING THE MILLENNIUM ROD...
BUT JONOUCHI WILL NEVER GIVE IN TO YOU!!
JONOUCHI BEAT YOU!!
...

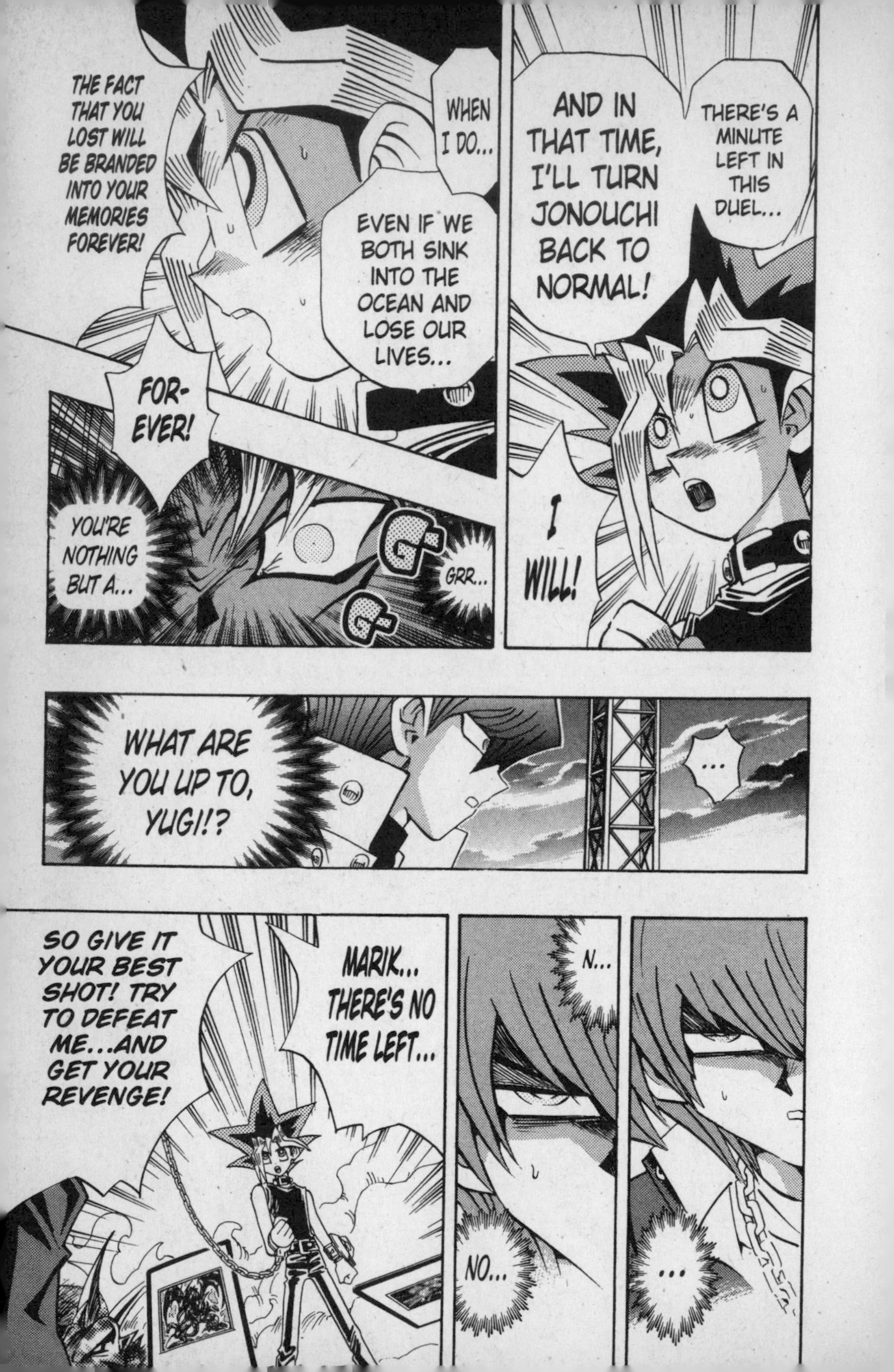
THERE'S A MINUTE LEFT IN THIS DUEL...
AND IN THAT TIME, I'LL TURN JONOUCHI BACK TO NORMAL!
I WILL!
WHEN I DO...
EVEN IF WE BOTH SINK INTO THE OCEAN AND LOSE OUR LIVES...
THE FACT THAT YOU LOST WILL BE BRANDED INTO YOUR MEMORIES FOREVER!
FOR-EVER!
YOU'RE NOTHING BUT A...
GRR...
...
WHAT ARE YOU UP TO, YUGI!?
...
N...
NO...
MARIK... THERE'S NO TIME LEFT...
SO GIVE IT YOUR BEST SHOT! TRY TO DEFEAT ME...AND GET YOUR REVENGE!

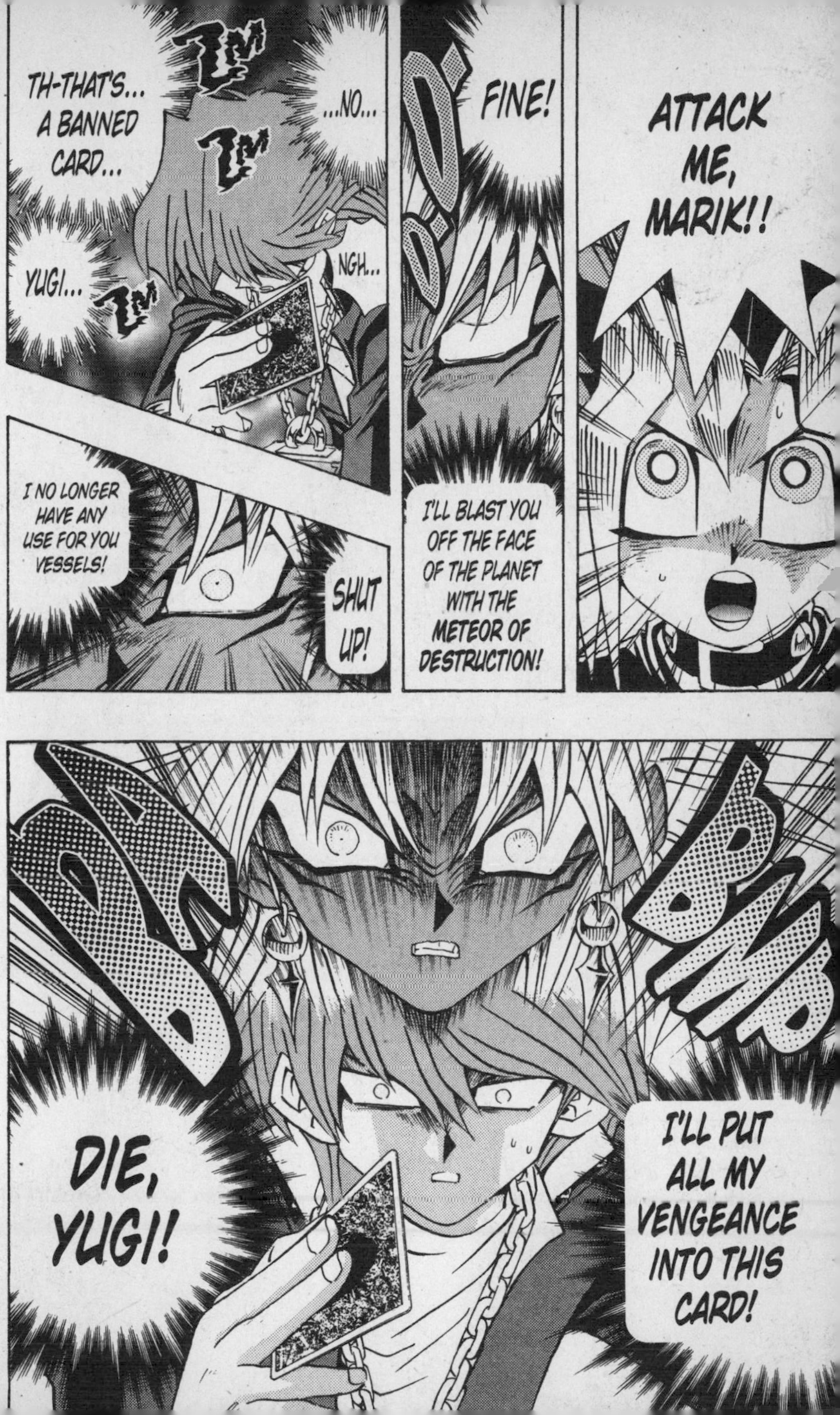
ATTACK ME, MARIK!!
FINE!
I'LL BLAST YOU OFF THE FACE OF THE PLANET WITH THE METEOR OF DESTRUCTION!
...NO...
TH-THAT'S... A BANNED CARD...
NGH...
YUGI...
SHUT UP!
I NO LONGER HAVE ANY USE FOR YOU VESSELS!
I'LL PUT ALL MY VENGEANCE INTO THIS CARD!
DIE, YUGI!

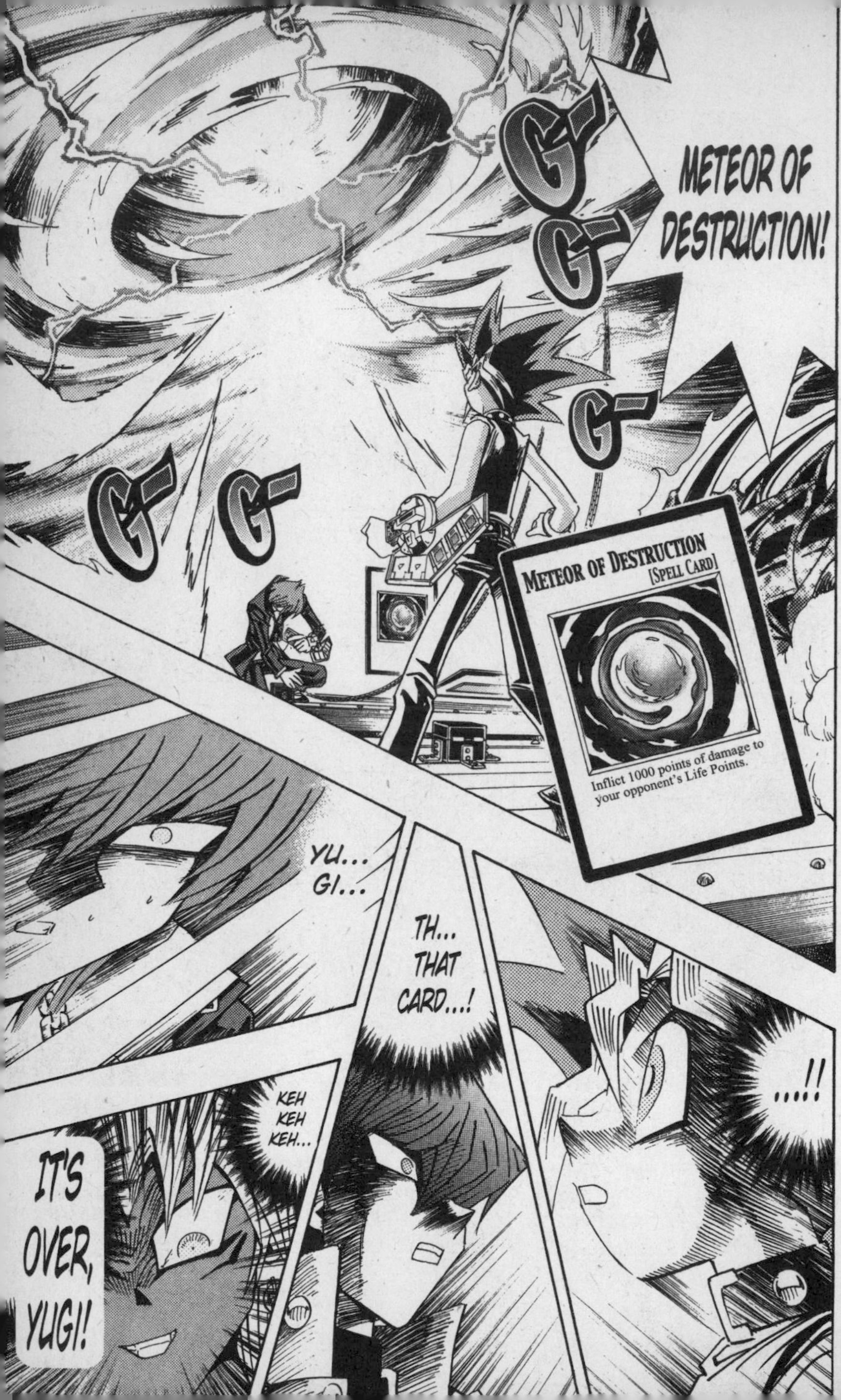
METEOR OF DESTRUCTION!
G- G- G-
G- G-
METEOR OF DESTRUCTION
[SPELL CARD]
Inflict 1000 points of damage to your opponent's Life Points.
YU... GI...
...!!
TH... THAT CARD...!
KEH KEH KEH...
IT'S OVER, YUGI!

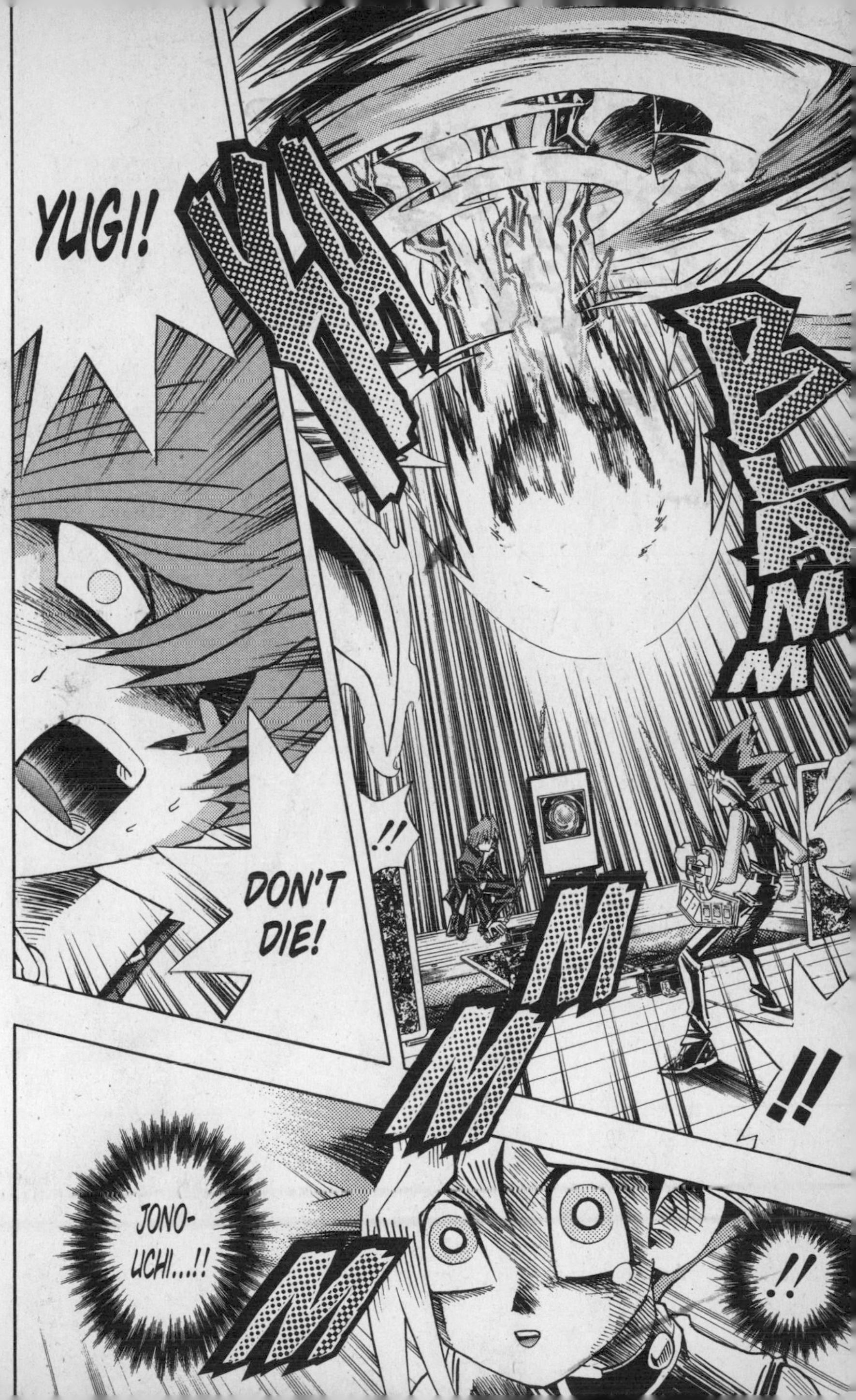

!!
!!
YUGI!
DON'T DIE!
!!
JONO-UCHI...!!

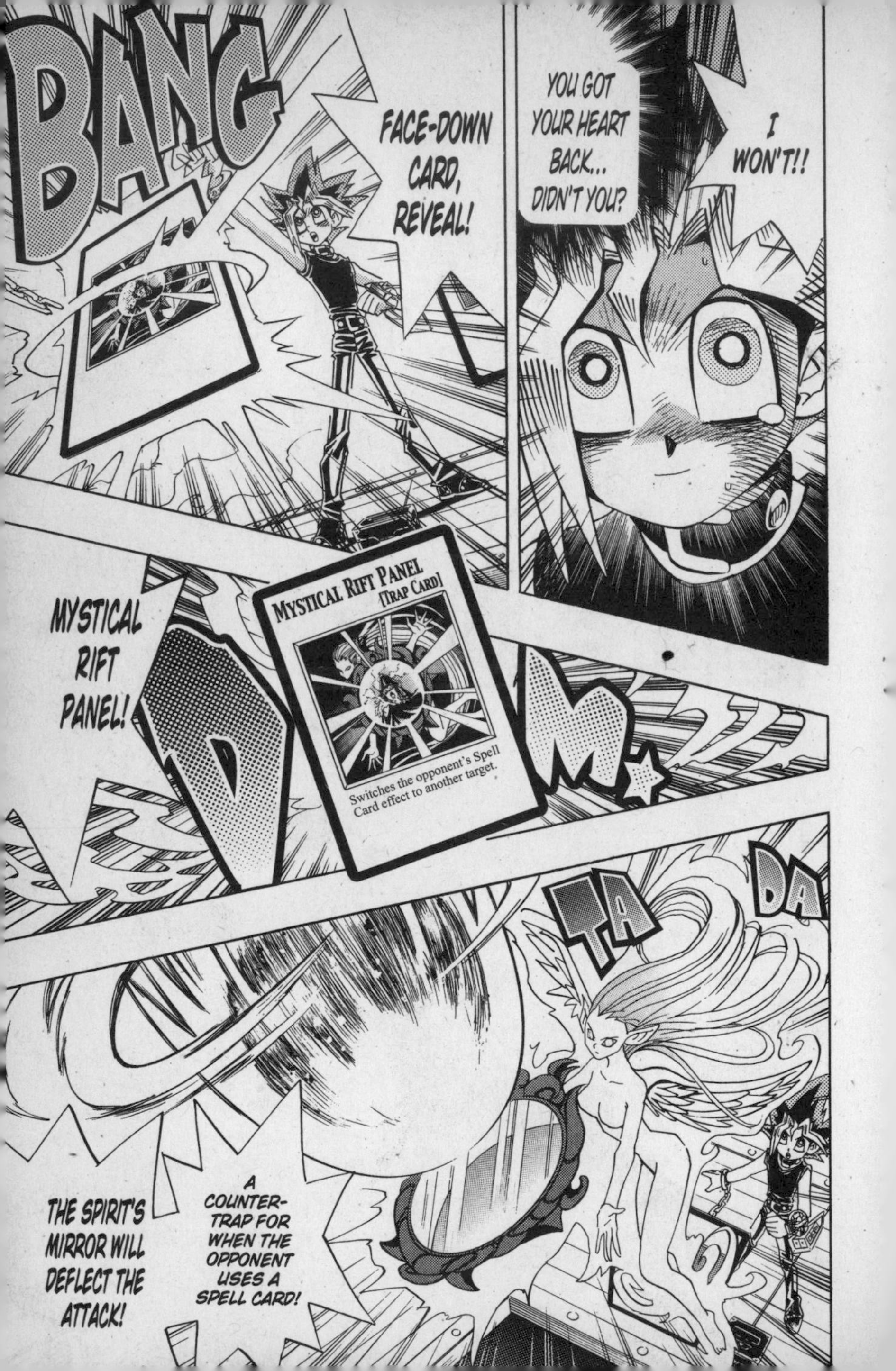
I WON'T!!
YOU GOT YOUR HEART BACK... DIDN'T YOU?
FACE-DOWN CARD, REVEAL!
BANG
DOM★
MYSTICAL RIFT PANEL
[TRAP CARD]
Switches the opponent's Spell Card effect to another target.
MYSTICAL RIFT PANEL!
TA DA
A COUNTER-TRAP FOR WHEN THE OPPONENT USES A SPELL CARD!
THE SPIRIT'S MIRROR WILL DEFLECT THE ATTACK!

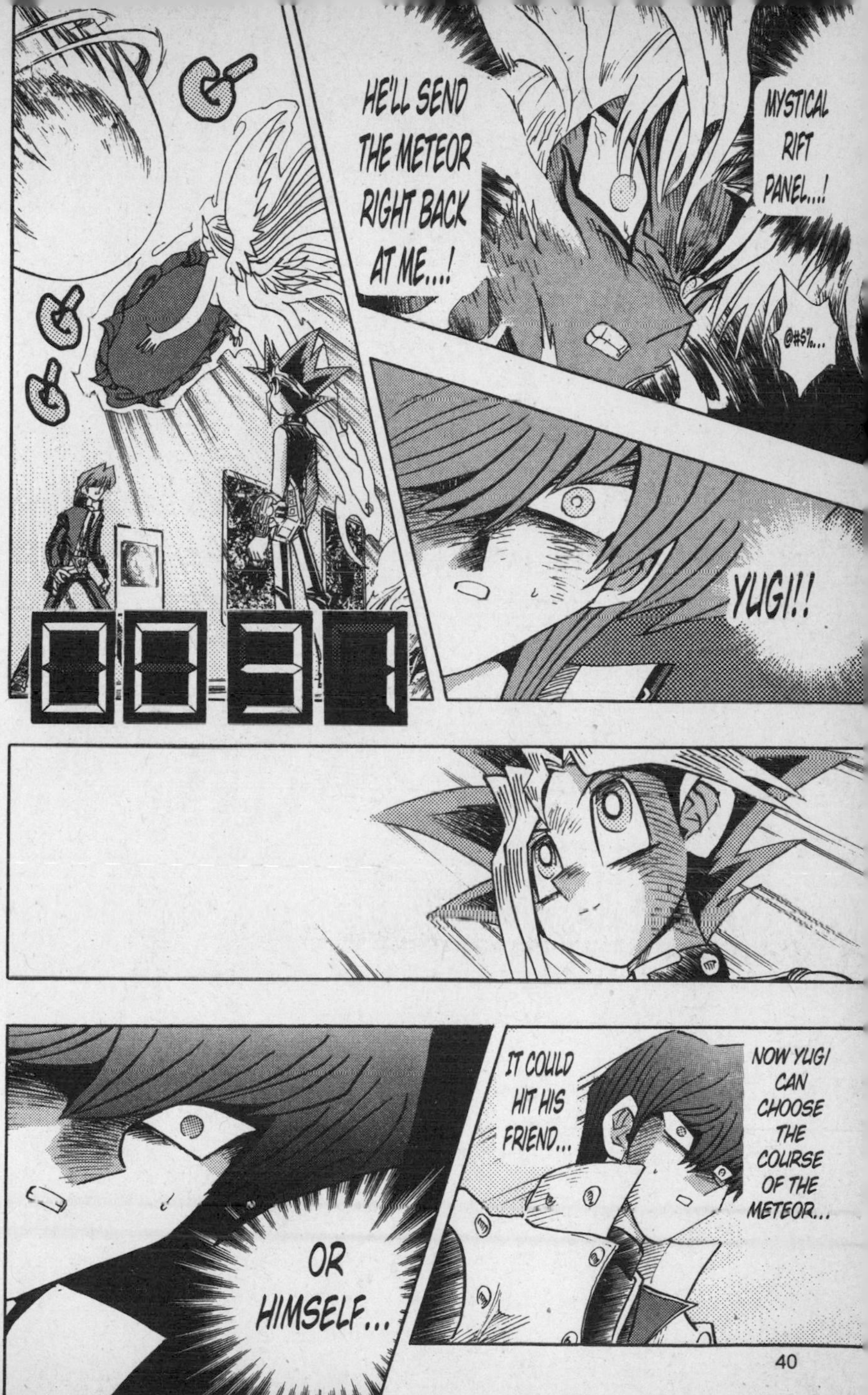

MYSTICAL RIFT PANEL...!
HE'LL SEND THE METEOR RIGHT BACK AT ME...!
@#%...
YUGI!!
00371
NOW YUGI CAN CHOOSE THE COURSE OF THE METEOR...
IT COULD HIT HIS FRIEND...
OR HIMSELF...

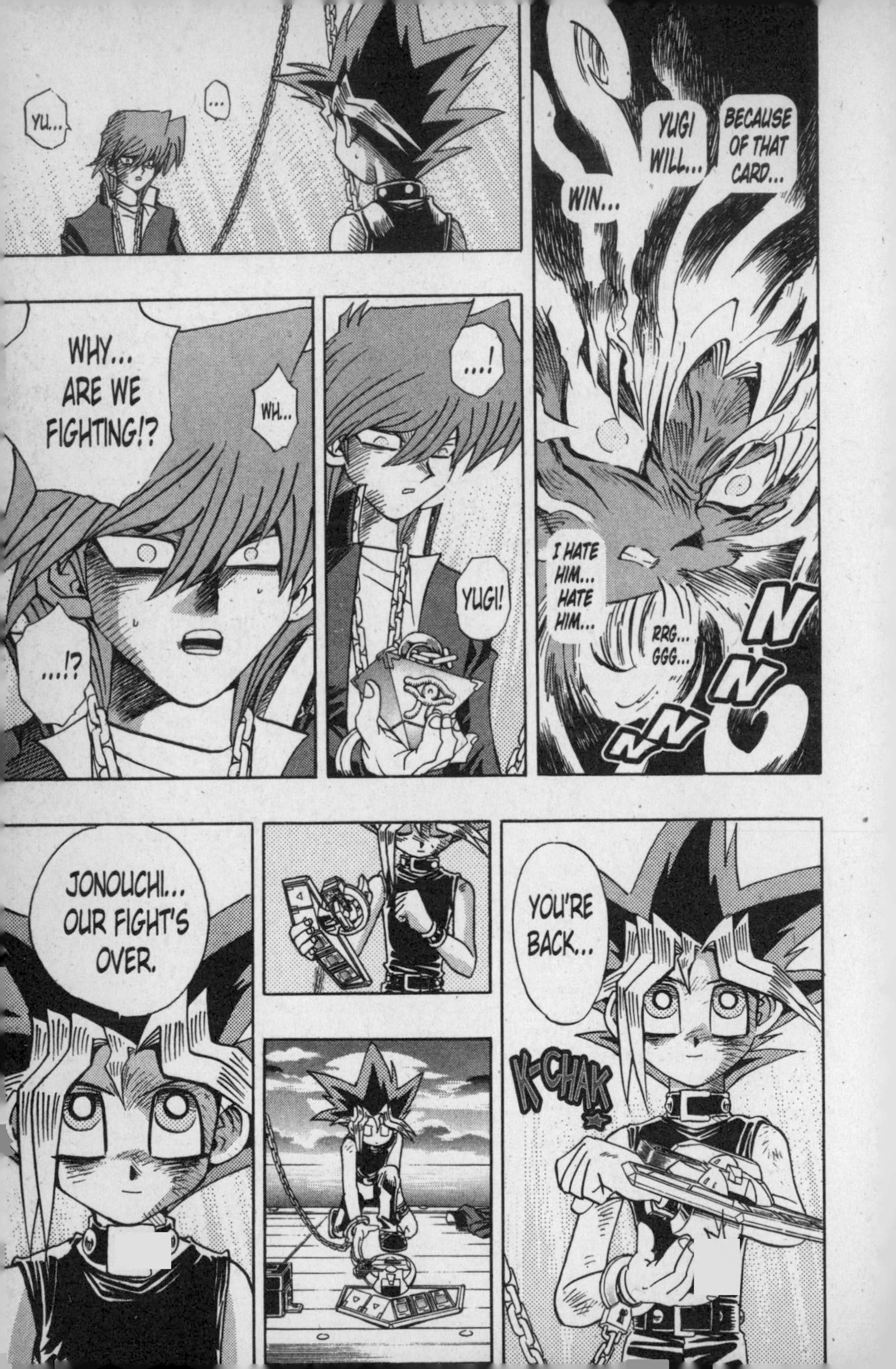
BECAUSE OF THAT CARD...
YUGI WILL...
WIN...
I HATE HIM... HATE HIM...
RRG... GGG...
NNNN
...
YU...
...!
YUGI!
WH...
WHY... ARE WE FIGHTING!?
...!?
YOU'RE BACK...
K-CHAK
JONOUCHI... OUR FIGHT'S OVER.

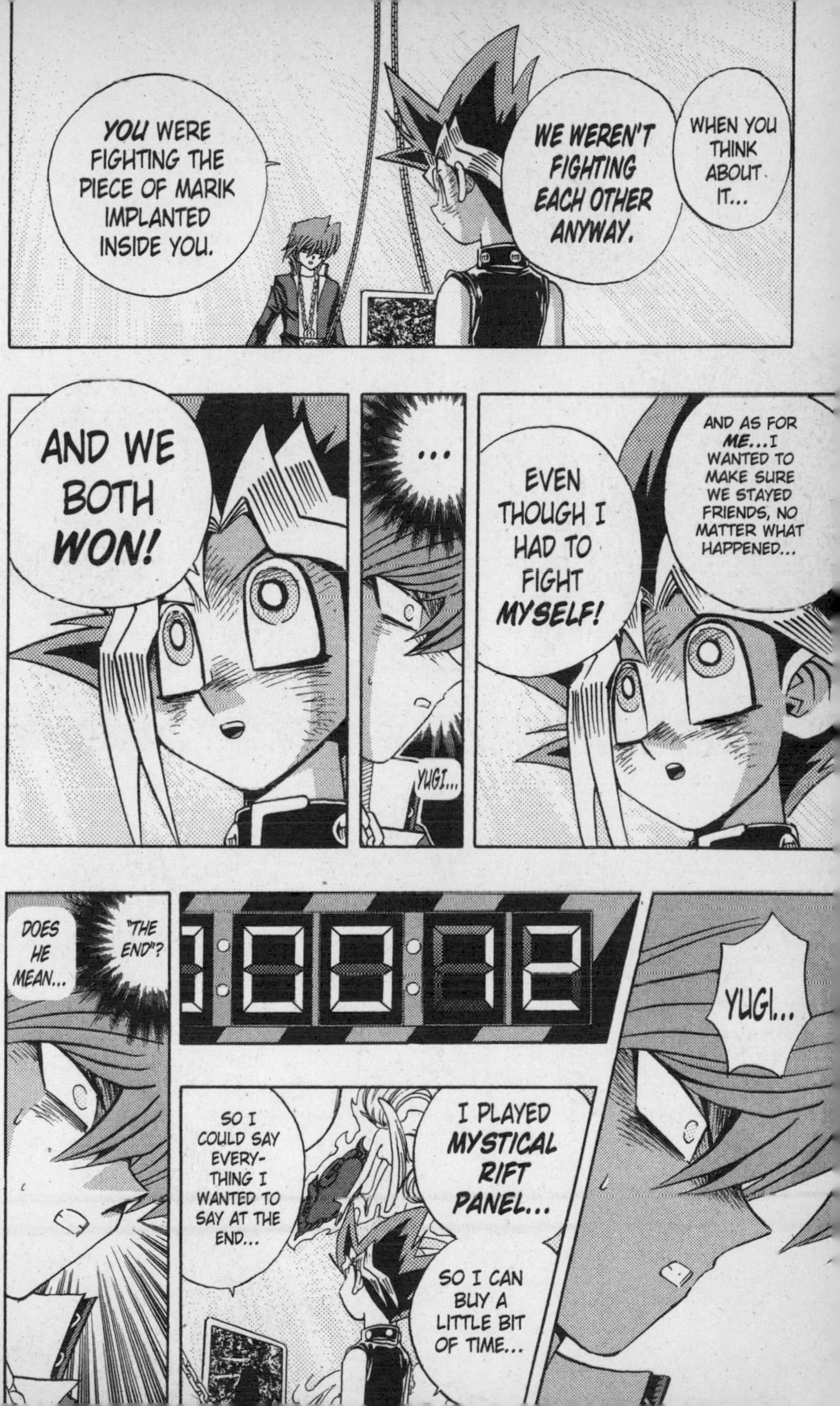
WHEN YOU THINK ABOUT IT...
WE WEREN'T FIGHTING EACH OTHER ANYWAY.
YOU WERE FIGHTING THE PIECE OF MARIK IMPLANTED INSIDE YOU.
AND AS FOR ME...I WANTED TO MAKE SURE WE STAYED FRIENDS, NO MATTER WHAT HAPPENED...
EVEN THOUGH I HAD TO FIGHT MYSELF!
...
YUGI...
AND WE BOTH WON!
YUGI...
I PLAYED MYSTICAL RIFT PANEL...
SO I CAN BUY A LITTLE BIT OF TIME...
SO I COULD SAY EVERYTHING I WANTED TO SAY AT THE END...
"THE END"?
DOES HE MEAN...

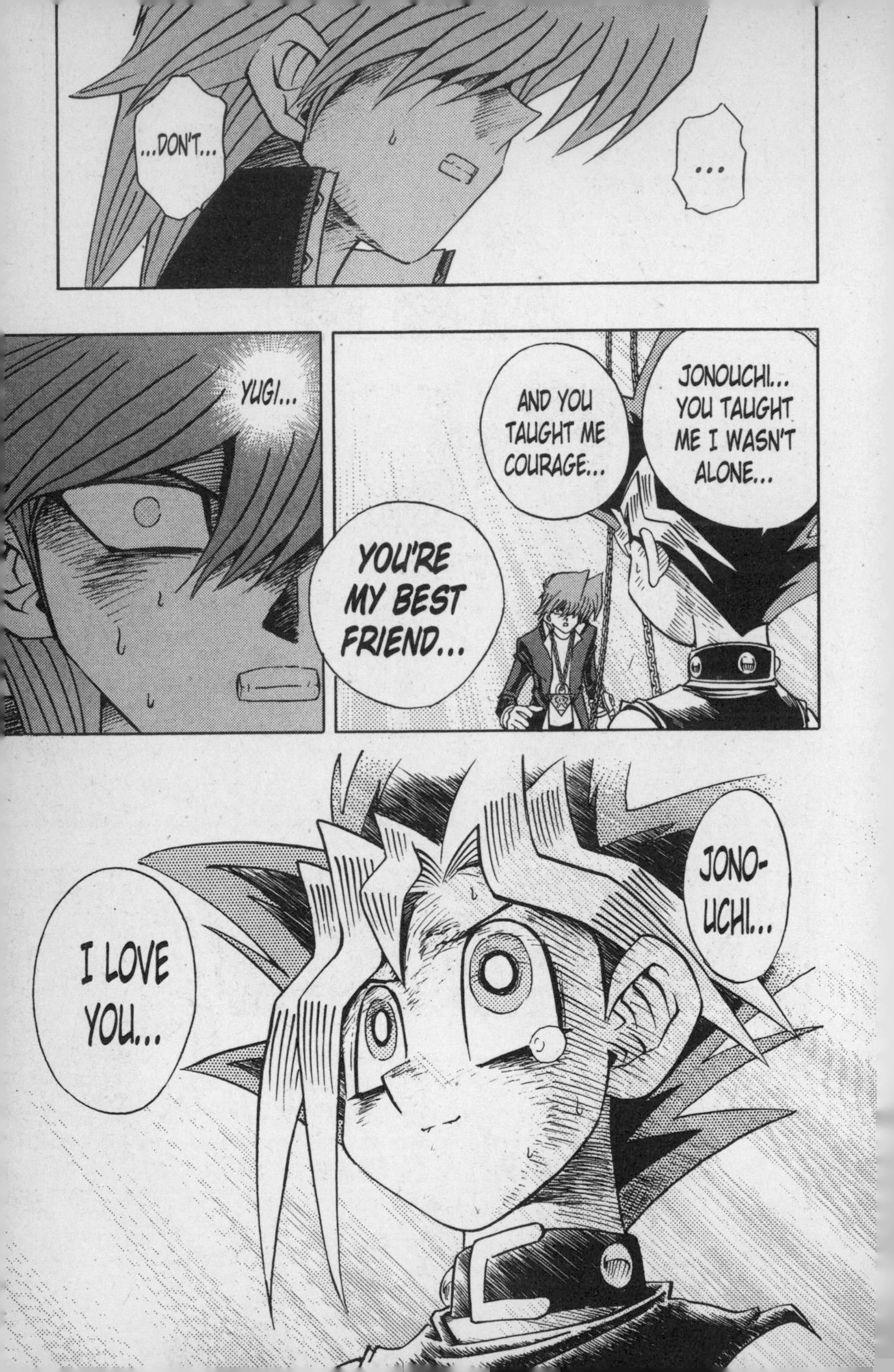
...
...DON'T...
JONOUCHI... YOU TAUGHT ME I WASN'T ALONE...
AND YOU TAUGHT ME COURAGE...
YOU'RE MY BEST FRIEND...
YUGI...
JONO-UCHI...
I LOVE YOU...

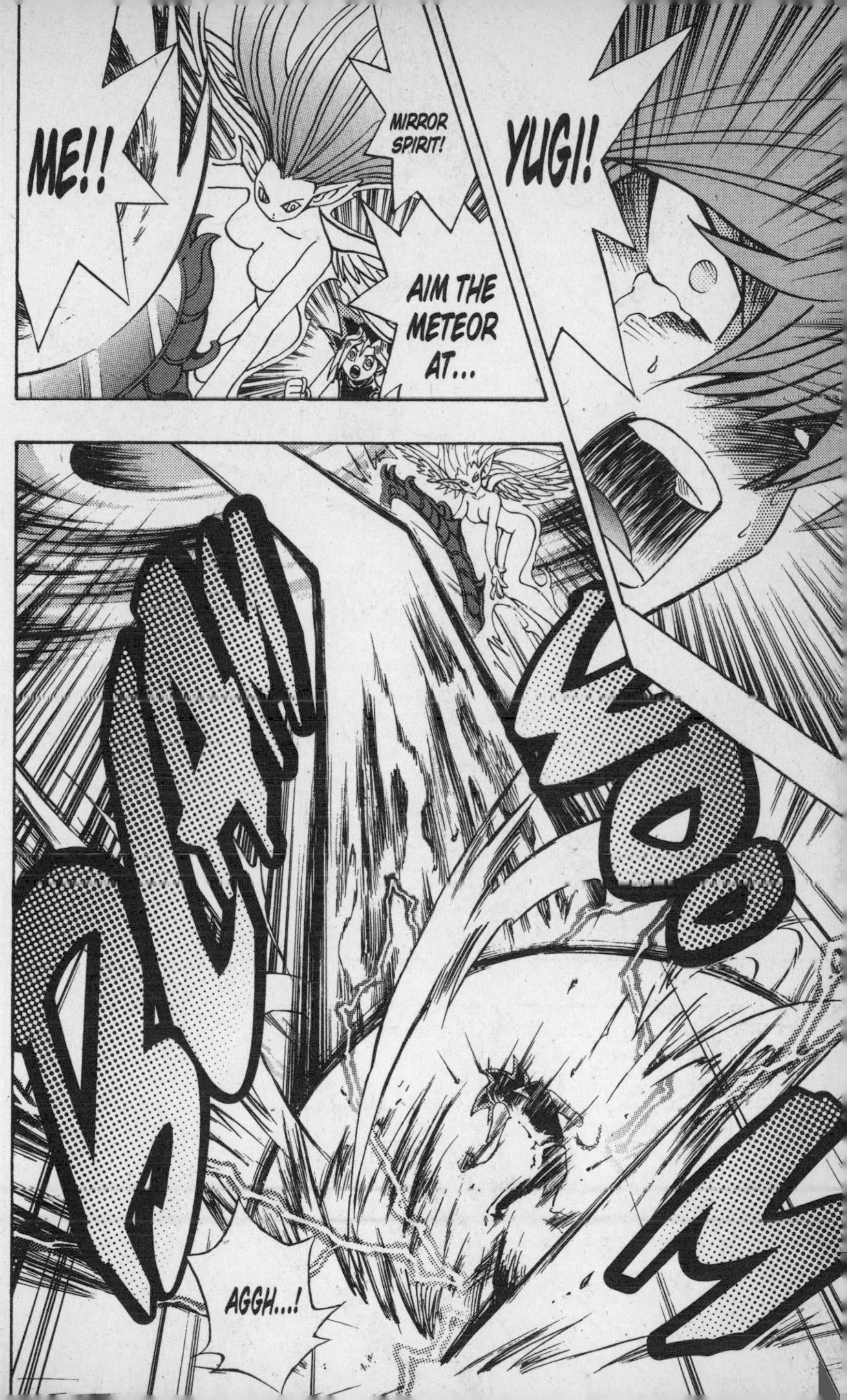
YUGI!
MIRROR SPIRIT!
AIM THE METEOR AT...
ME!!
AGGH...!

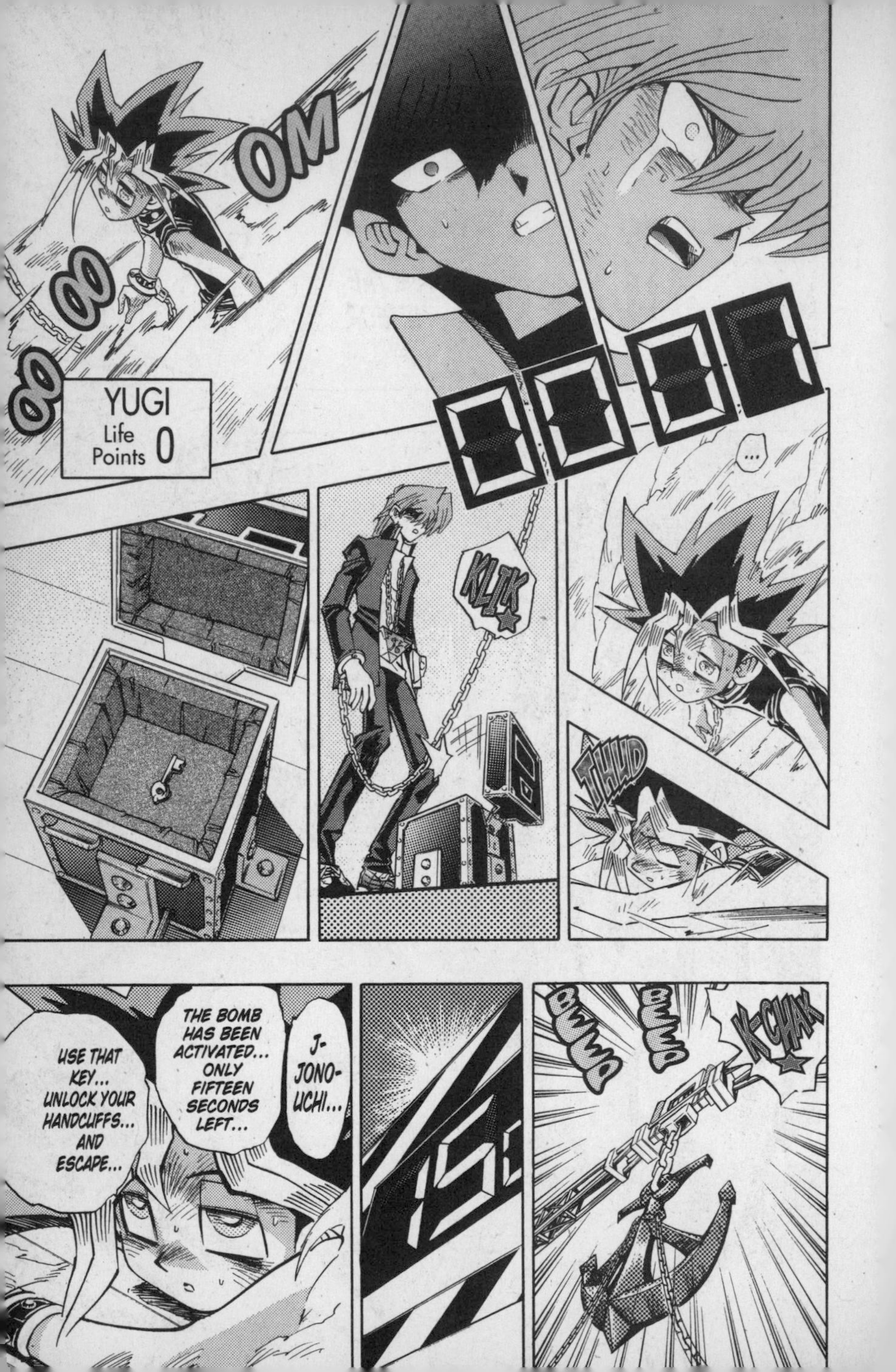

OM
YUGI
Life Points 0
...
THUD
KLIK
K-CHAK
J-JONOUCHI...
THE BOMB HAS BEEN ACTIVATED... ONLY FIFTEEN SECONDS LEFT...
USE THAT KEY... UNLOCK YOUR HANDCUFFS... AND ESCAPE...

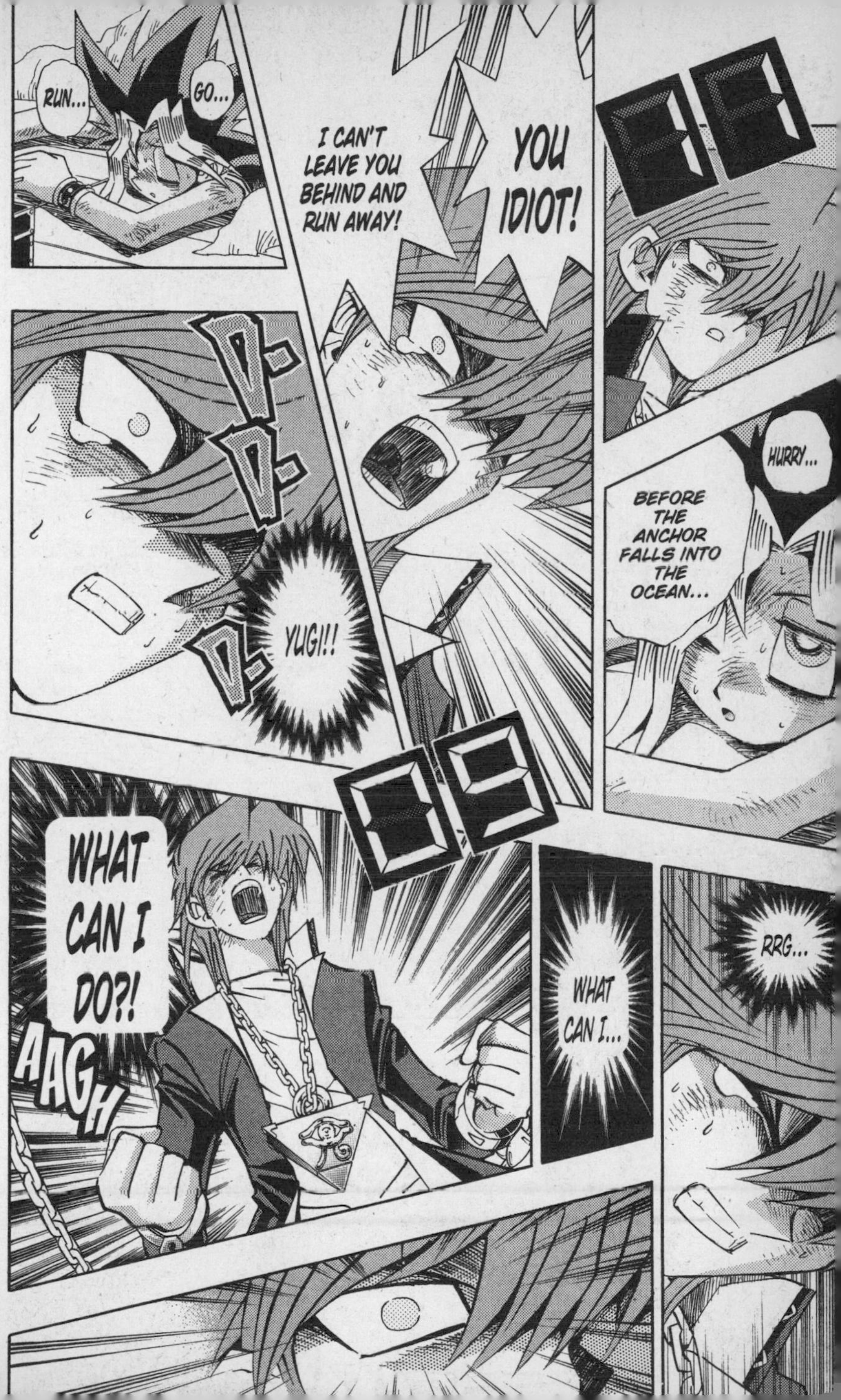

HURRY...
BEFORE THE ANCHOR FALLS INTO THE OCEAN...
YOU IDIOT!
I CAN'T LEAVE YOU BEHIND AND RUN AWAY!
GO...
RUN...
YUGI!!
RRG...
WHAT CAN I...
WHAT CAN I DO?!
AAGH

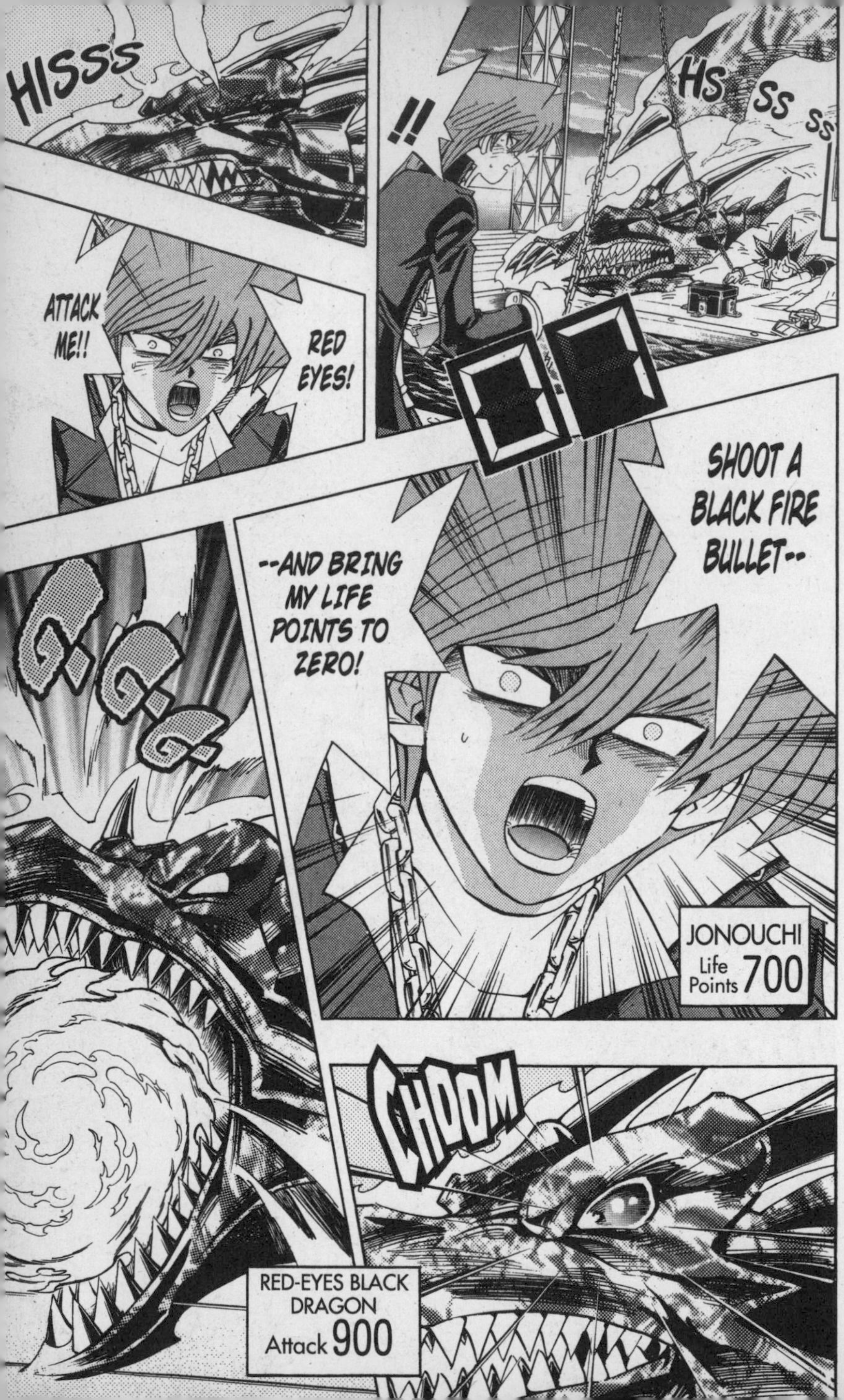
!!
HS SS SS
HISSS
RED EYES!
ATTACK ME!!
SHOOT A BLACK FIRE BULLET--
--AND BRING MY LIFE POINTS TO ZERO!
JONOUCHI Life Points 700
G.. G.. G..
CHOOM
RED-EYES BLACK DRAGON Attack 900

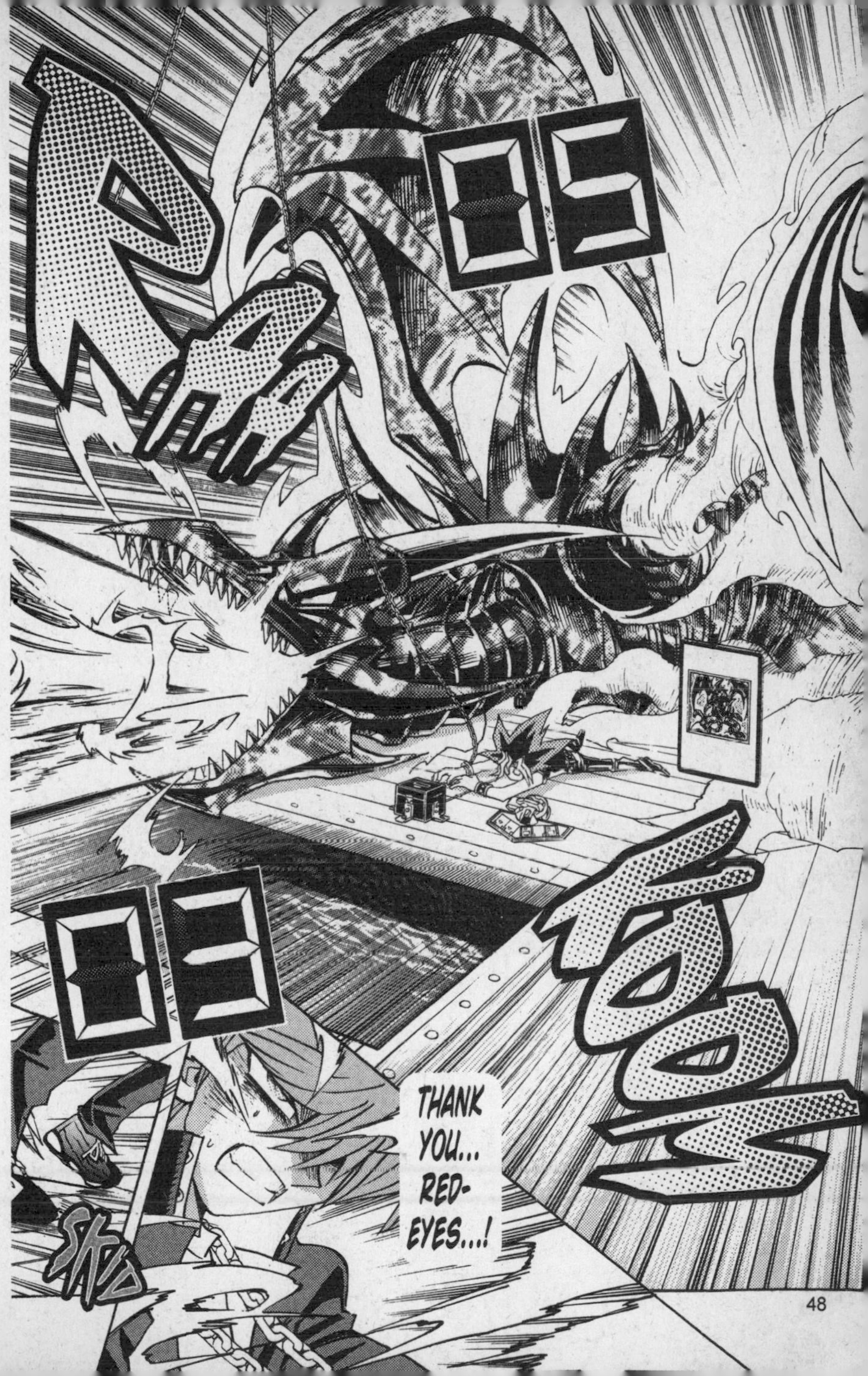
THANK YOU... RED-EYES...!
SKID

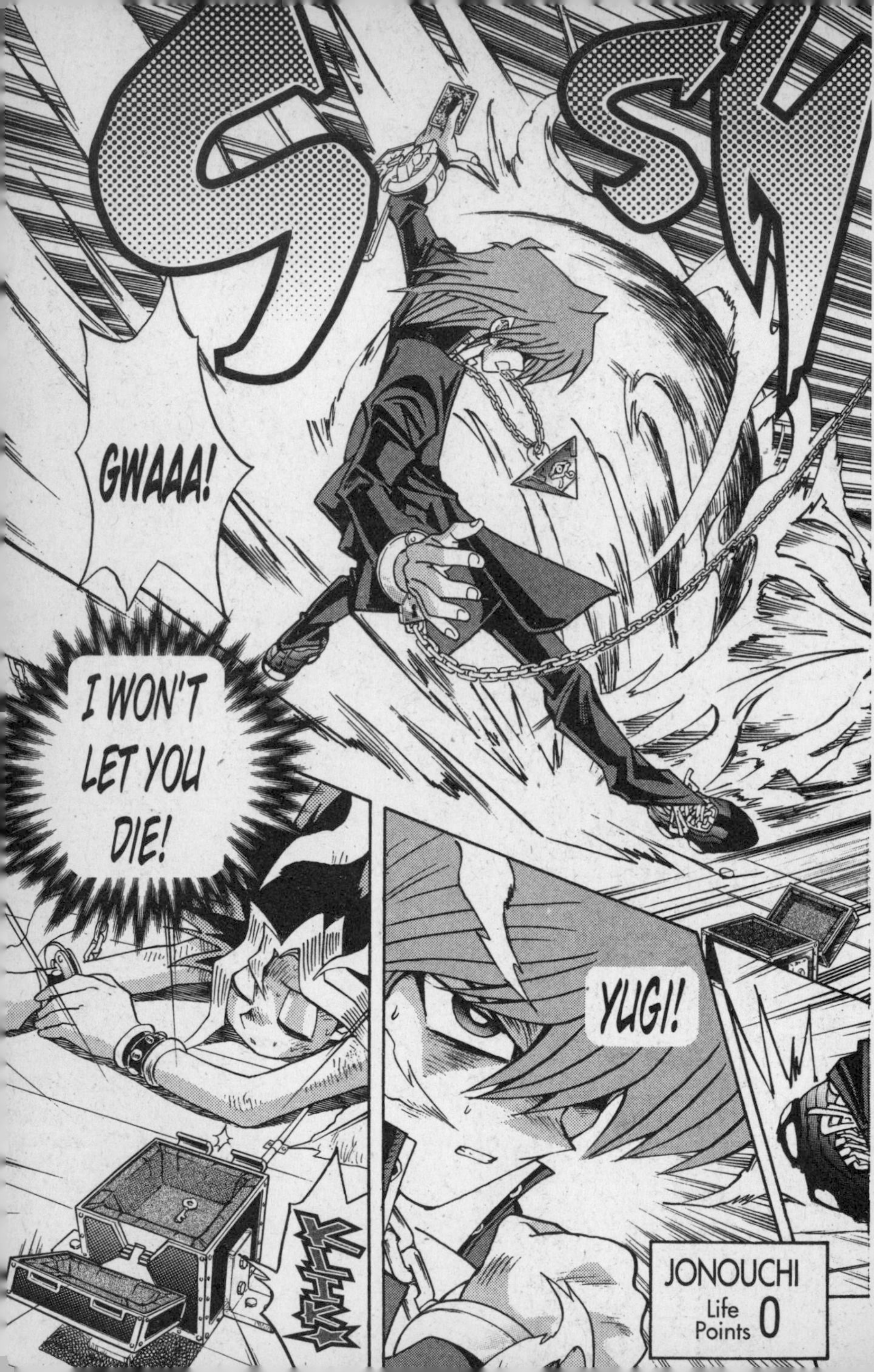
GWAAA!
I WON'T LET YOU DIE!
YUGI!
JONOUCHI Life Points 0

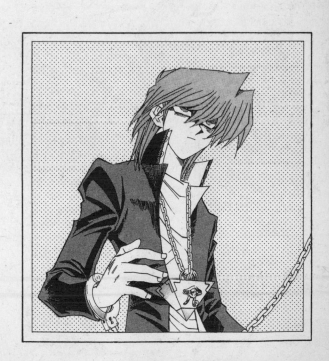

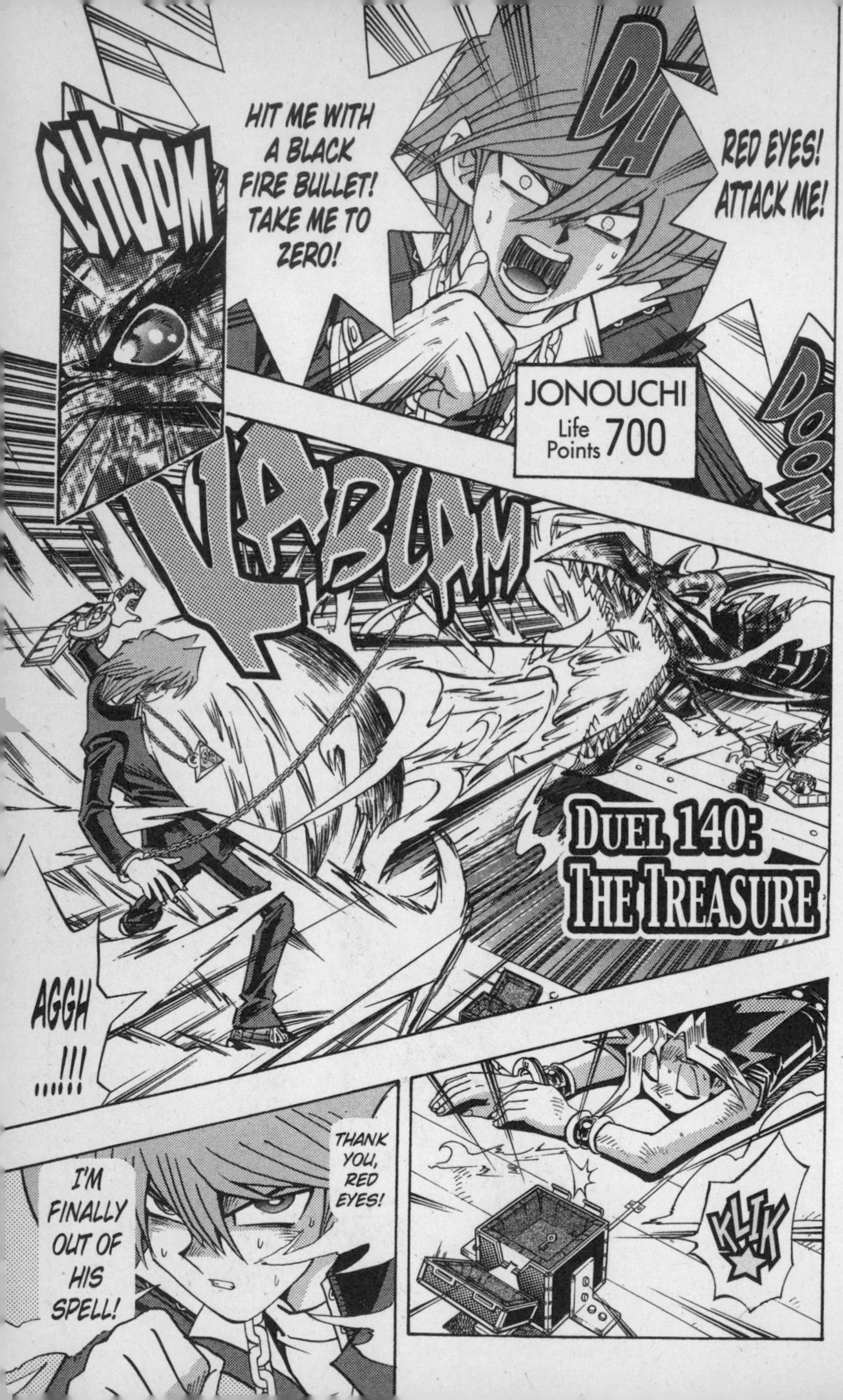
DA
RED EYES! ATTACK ME!
HIT ME WITH A BLACK FIRE BULLET! TAKE ME TO ZERO!
JONOUCHI Life Points 700
DOOOM
CHOOM
VABLAM
DUEL 140: THE TREASURE
AGGH ...!!!
KLIK
THANK YOU, RED EYES!
I'M FINALLY OUT OF HIS SPELL!

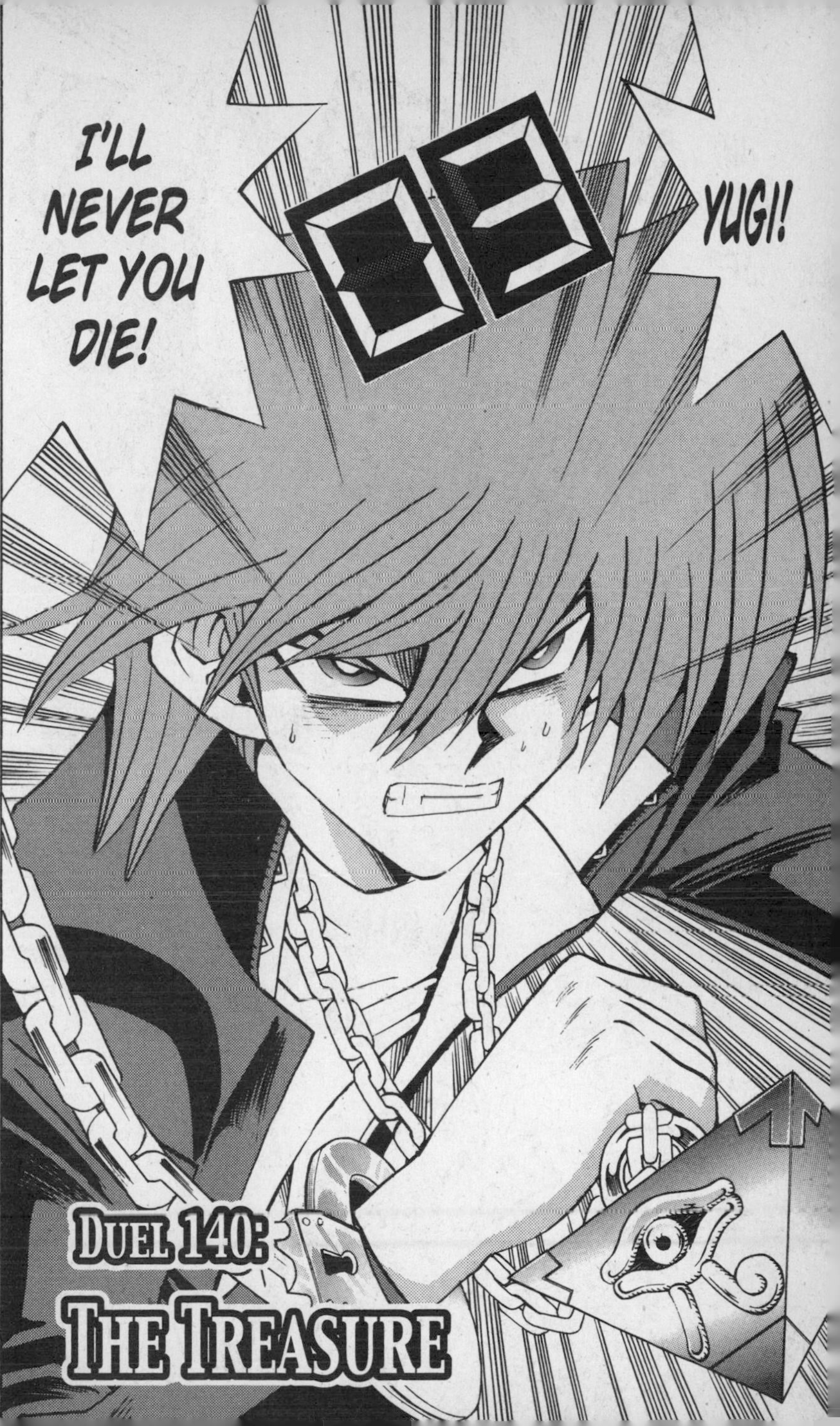
YUGI!
I'LL NEVER LET YOU DIE!
DUEL 140:
THE TREASURE

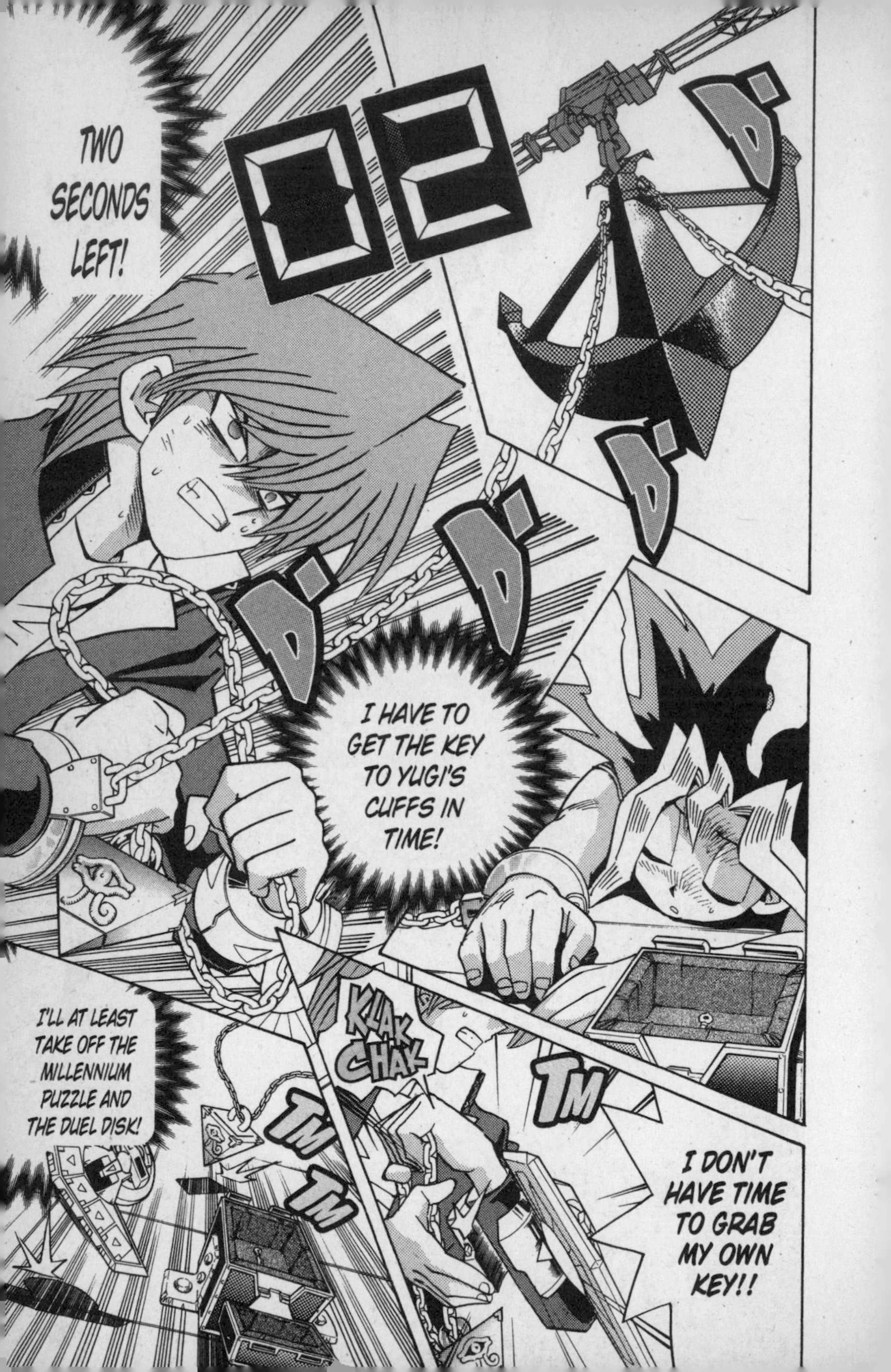
02
TWO SECONDS LEFT!
I HAVE TO GET THE KEY TO YUGI'S CUFFS IN TIME!
KLAK CHAK
TM
I DON'T HAVE TIME TO GRAB MY OWN KEY!!
TM
TM
I'LL AT LEAST TAKE OFF THE MILLENNIUM PUZZLE AND THE DUEL DISK!

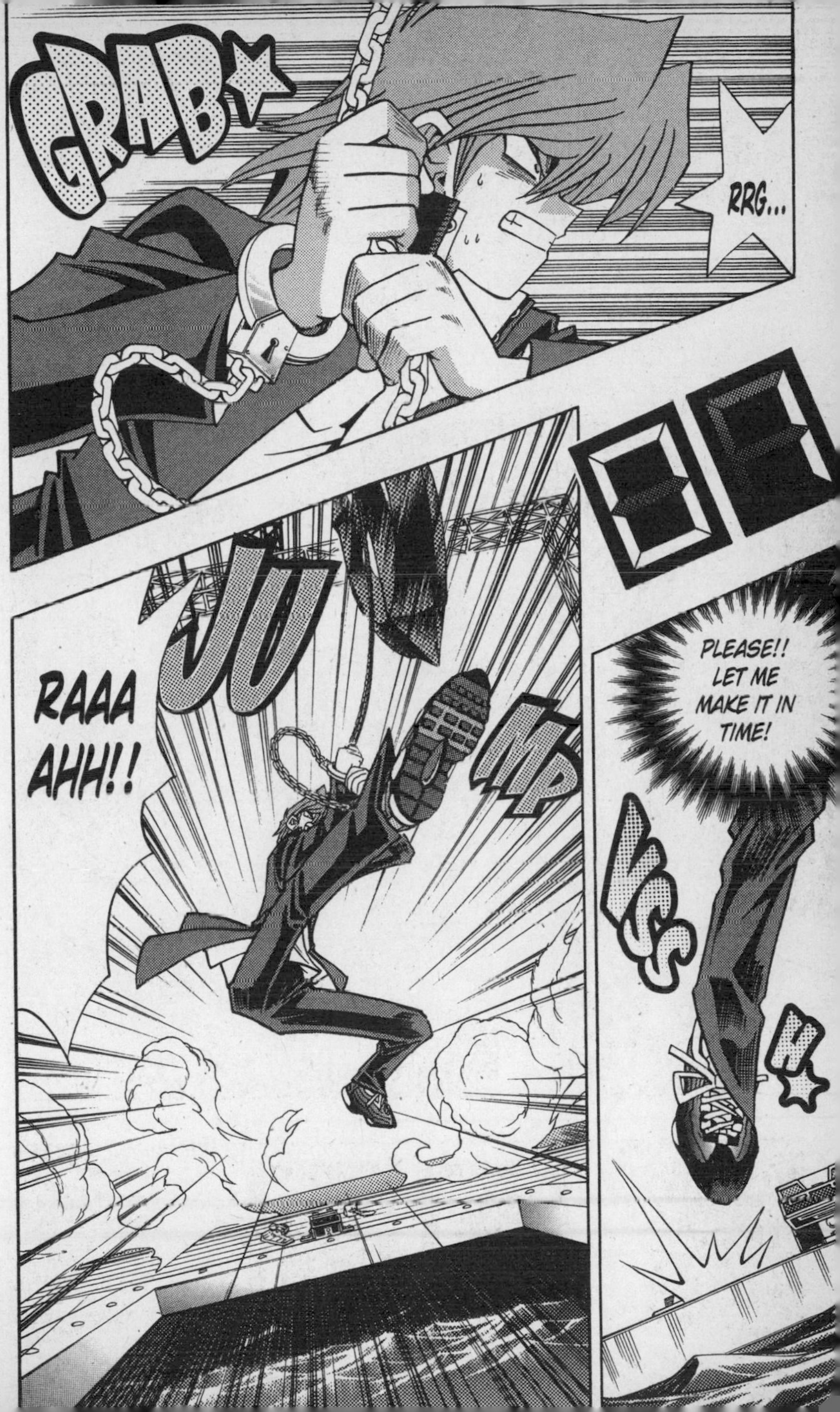
GRAB
RRG...
PLEASE!! LET ME MAKE IT IN TIME!
JUMP
RAAA AHH!!

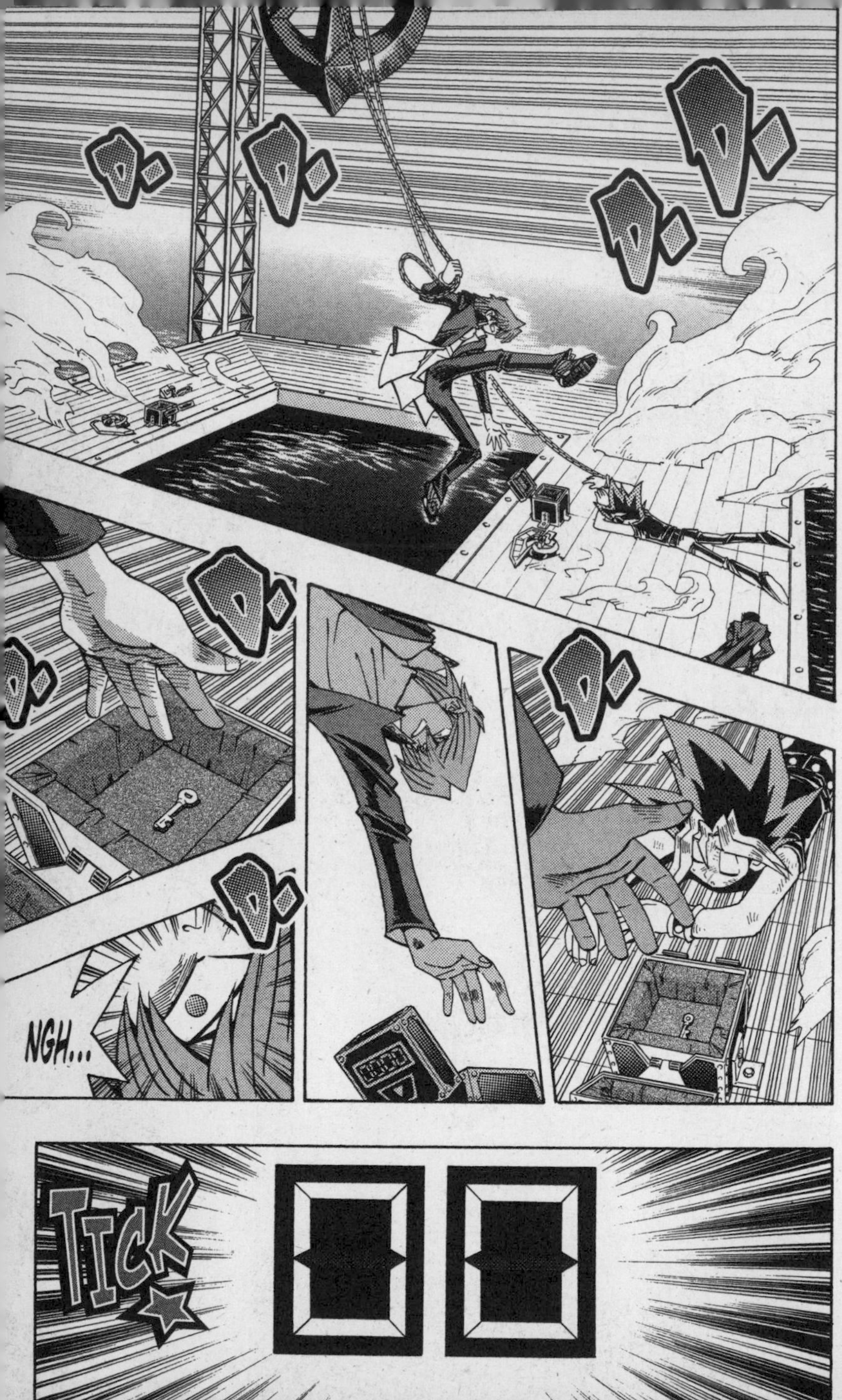
D.
D.
D.
D.
D.
D.
D.
D.
NGH...
TICK
00

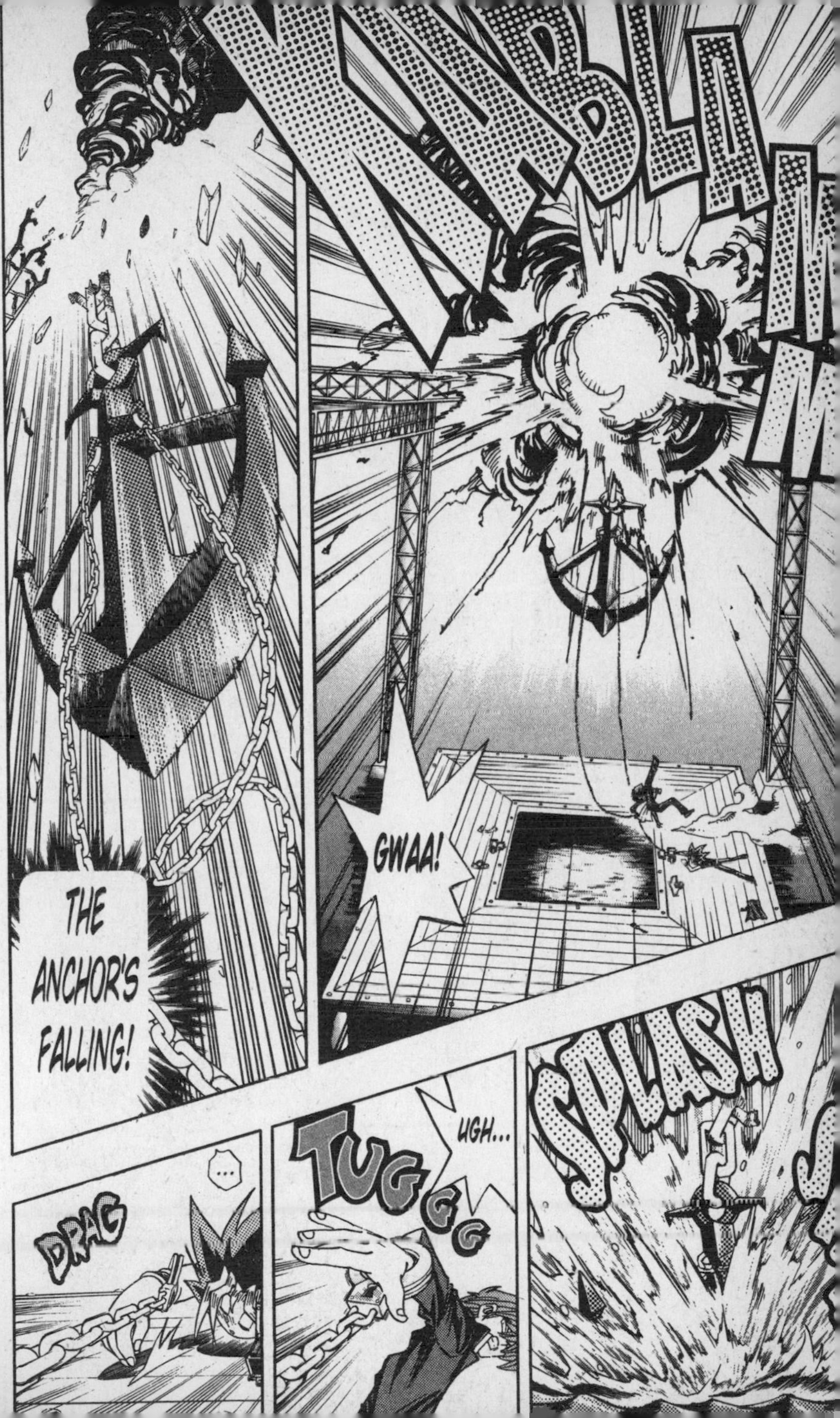

BLAM
GWAA!
THE ANCHOR'S FALLING!
SPLASH
UGH...
TUGGG
...
DRAG

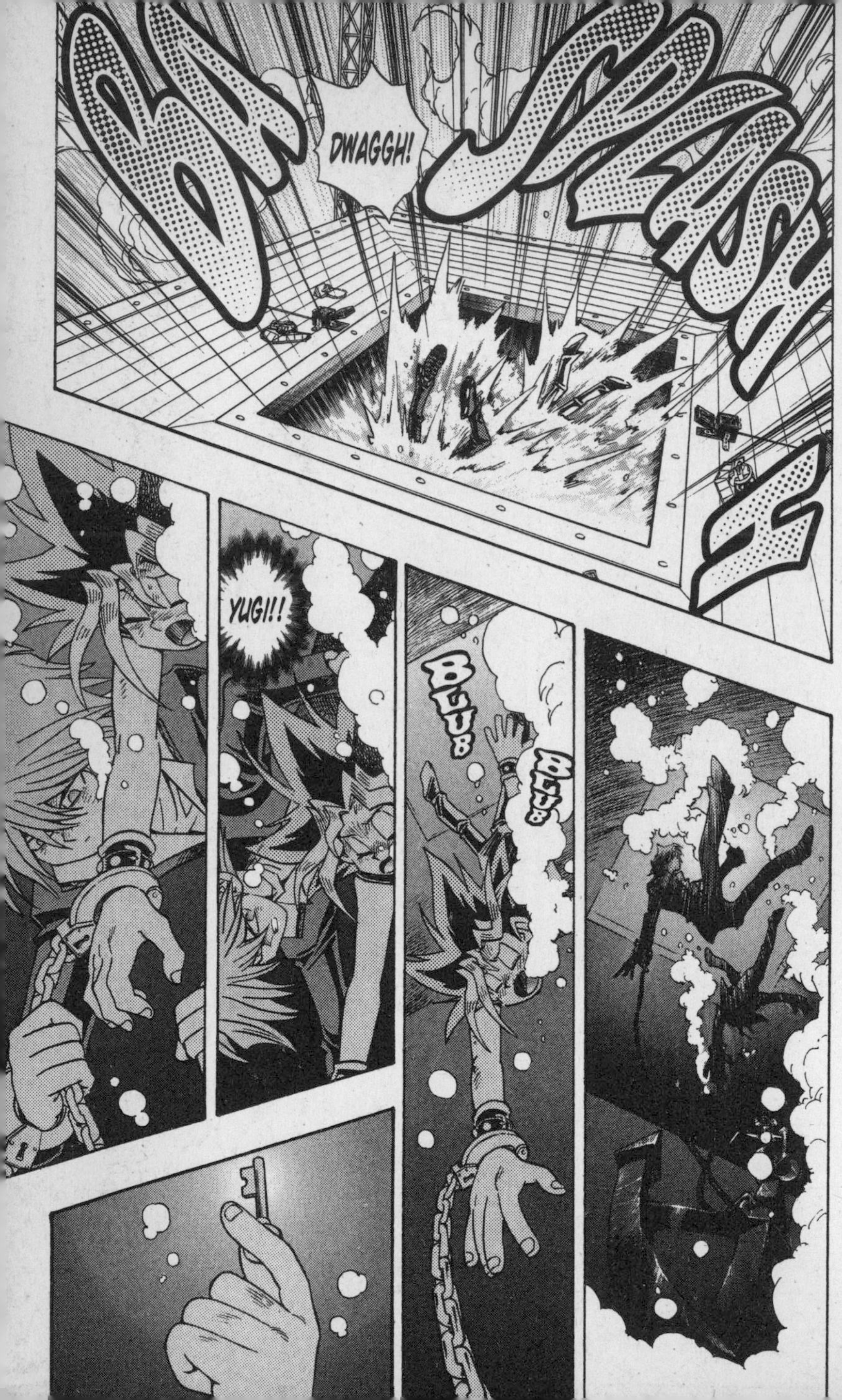
SPLASH!
DWAGGH!
BLUB
BLUB
YUGI!!

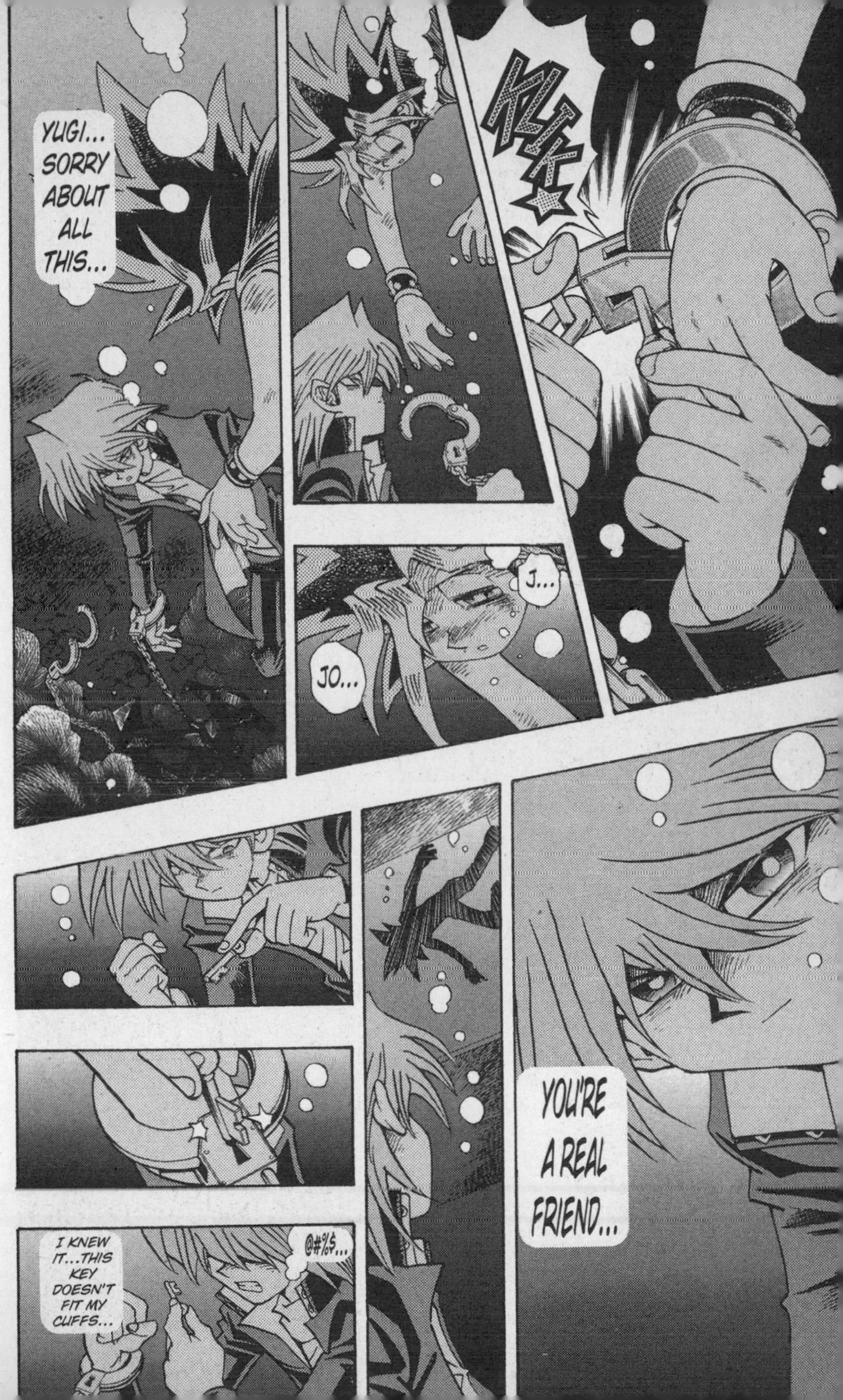
KLIK
J...
JO...
YUGI... SORRY ABOUT ALL THIS...
YOU'RE A REAL FRIEND...
@#%$...
I KNEW IT...THIS KEY DOESN'T FIT MY CUFFS...

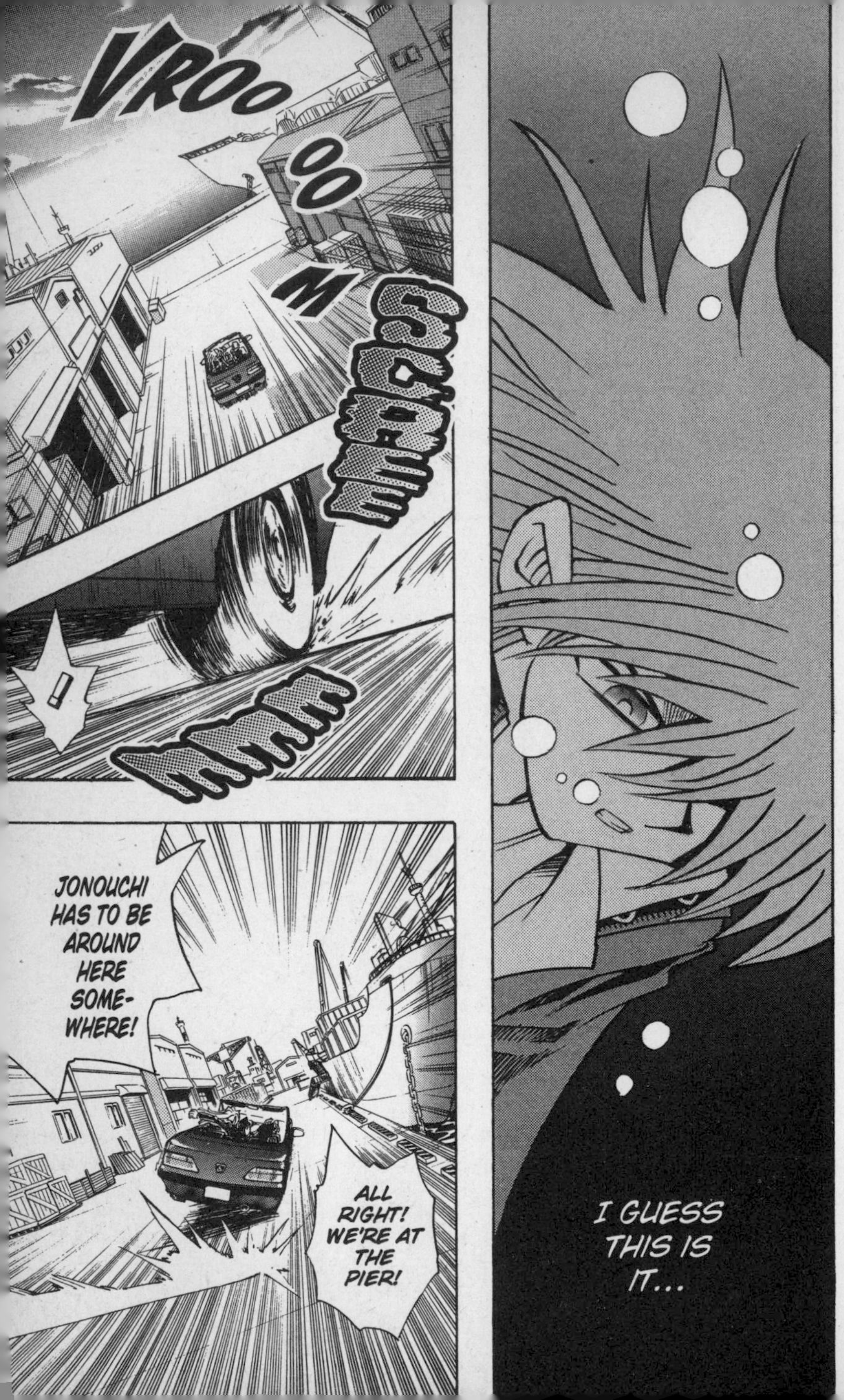
I GUESS THIS IS IT...
VROOOOM
SCREEE
!
JONOUCHI HAS TO BE AROUND HERE SOME-WHERE!
ALL RIGHT! WE'RE AT THE PIER!

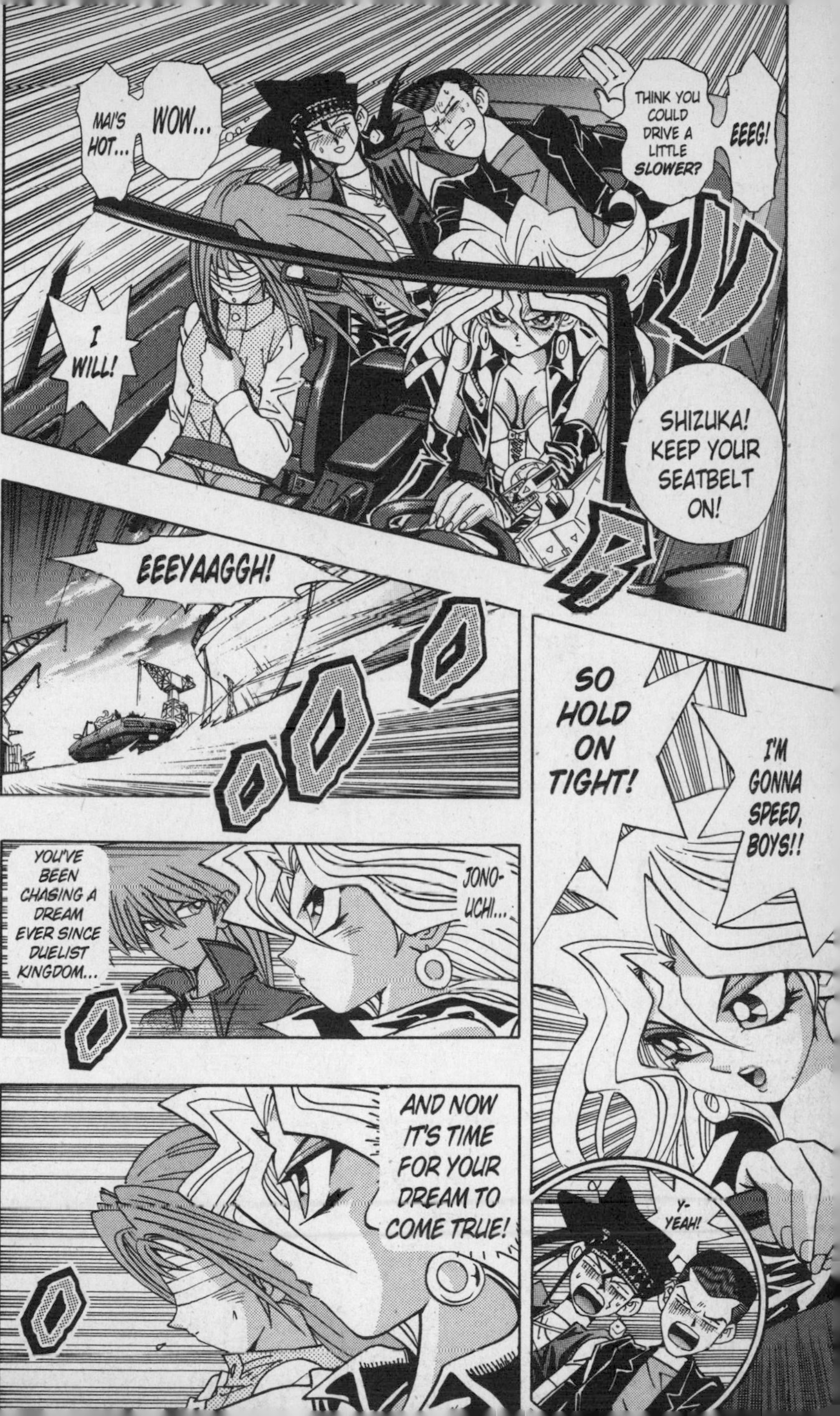
EEEG!
THINK YOU COULD DRIVE A LITTLE SLOWER?
WOW...
MAI'S HOT...
SHIZUKA! KEEP YOUR SEATBELT ON!
I WILL!
I'M GONNA SPEED, BOYS!!
SO HOLD ON TIGHT!
Y-YEAH!
EEEYAAGGH!
JONO-UCHI...
YOU'VE BEEN CHASING A DREAM EVER SINCE DUELIST KINGDOM...
AND NOW IT'S TIME FOR YOUR DREAM TO COME TRUE!

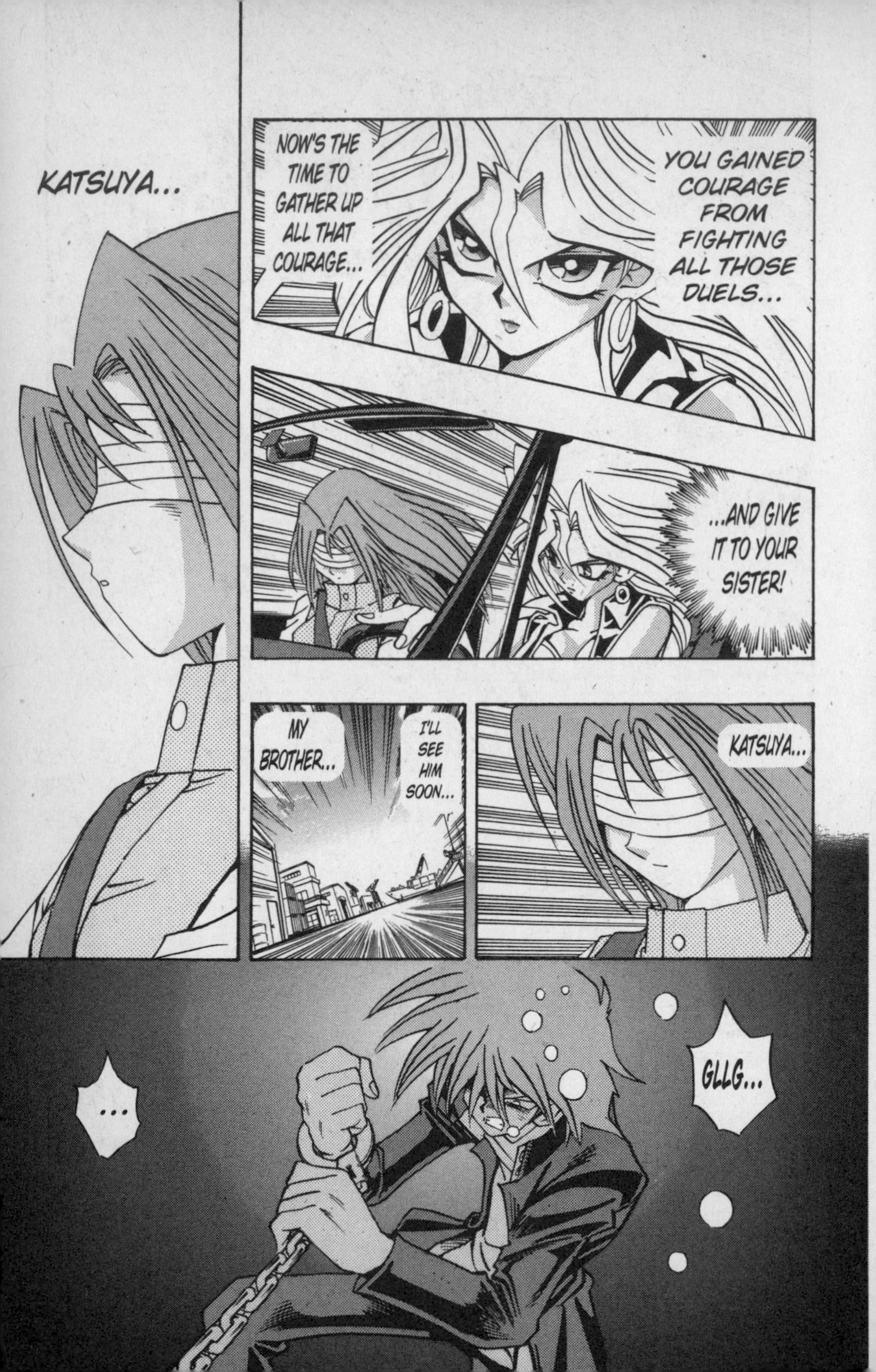
YOU GAINED COURAGE FROM FIGHTING ALL THOSE DUELS...
NOW'S THE TIME TO GATHER UP ALL THAT COURAGE...
...AND GIVE IT TO YOUR SISTER!
KATSUYA...
I'LL SEE HIM SOON...
MY BROTHER...
KATSUYA...
GLLG...
...

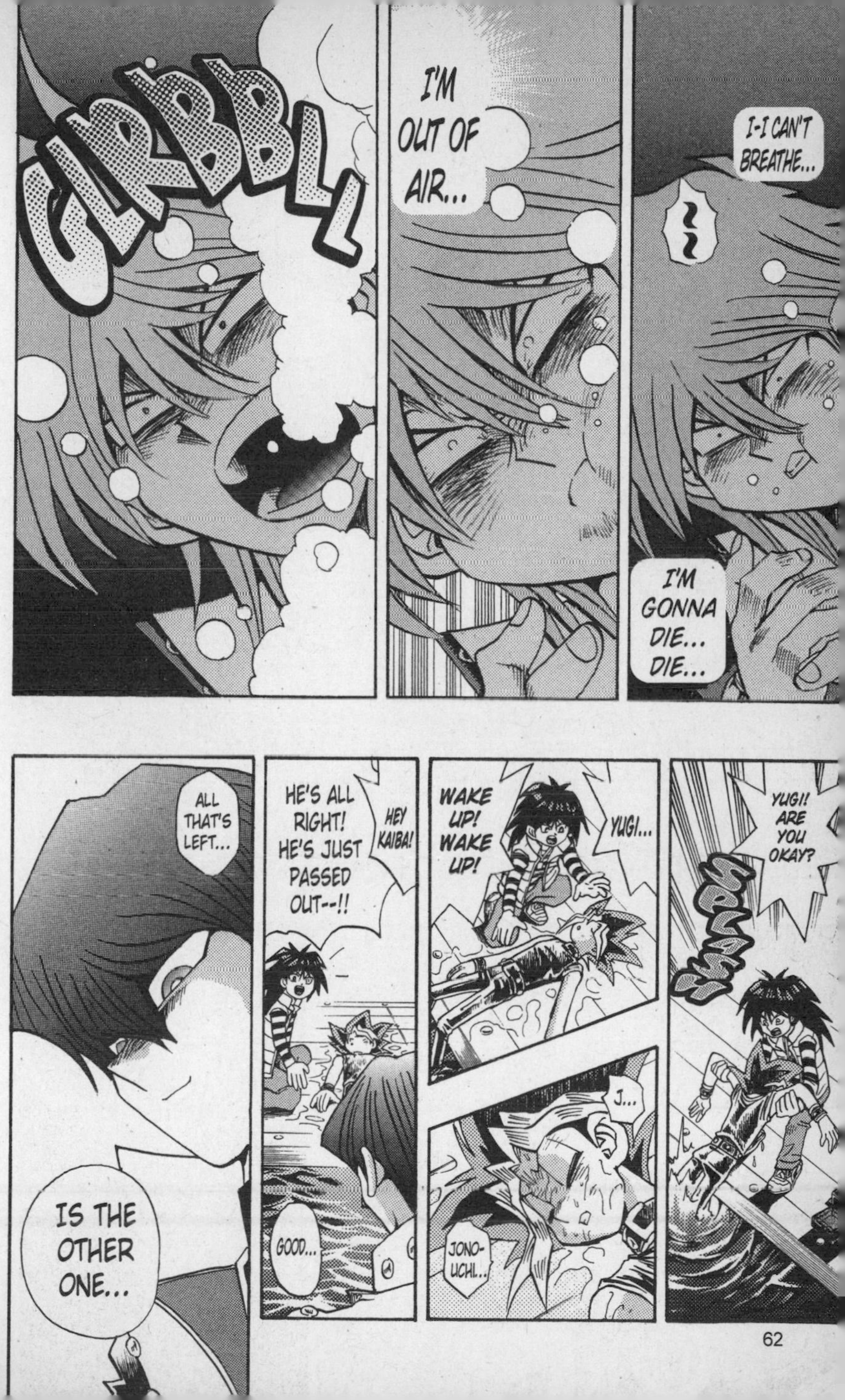
I-I CAN'T BREATHE...
I'M GONNA DIE... DIE...
I'M OUT OF AIR...
GLRBBLL
YUGI! ARE YOU OKAY?
SPLASH
YUGI...
WAKE UP! WAKE UP!
J...
JONO-UCHI...
HEY KAIBA!
HE'S ALL RIGHT! HE'S JUST PASSED OUT--!!
GOOD...
ALL THAT'S LEFT...
IS THE OTHER ONE...

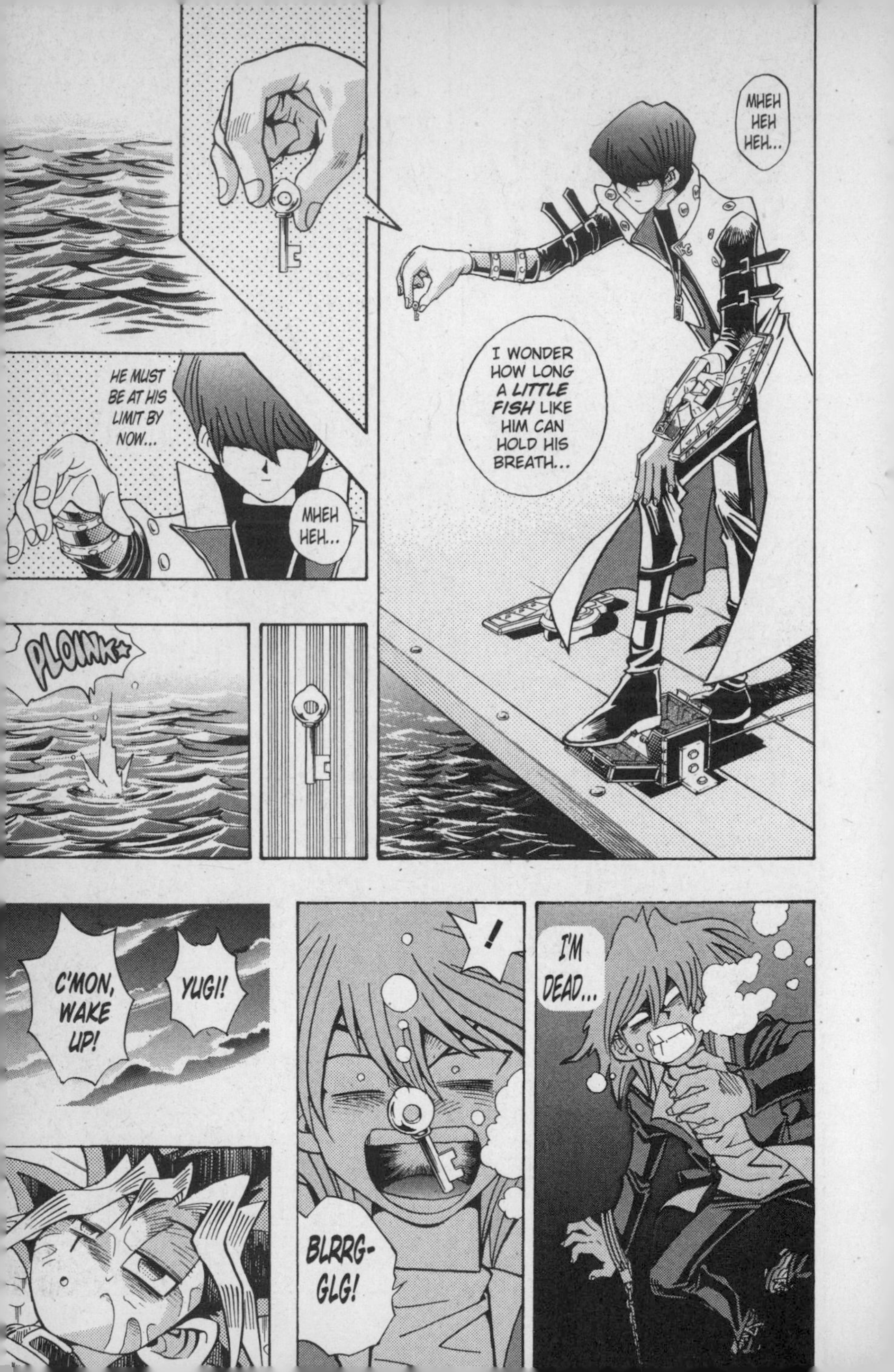
MHEH HEH HEH...
I WONDER HOW LONG A *LITTLE FISH* LIKE HIM CAN HOLD HIS BREATH...
HE MUST BE AT HIS LIMIT BY NOW...
MHEH HEH...
PLOINK
I'M DEAD...
!
BLRRG-GLG!
YUGI!
C'MON, WAKE UP!

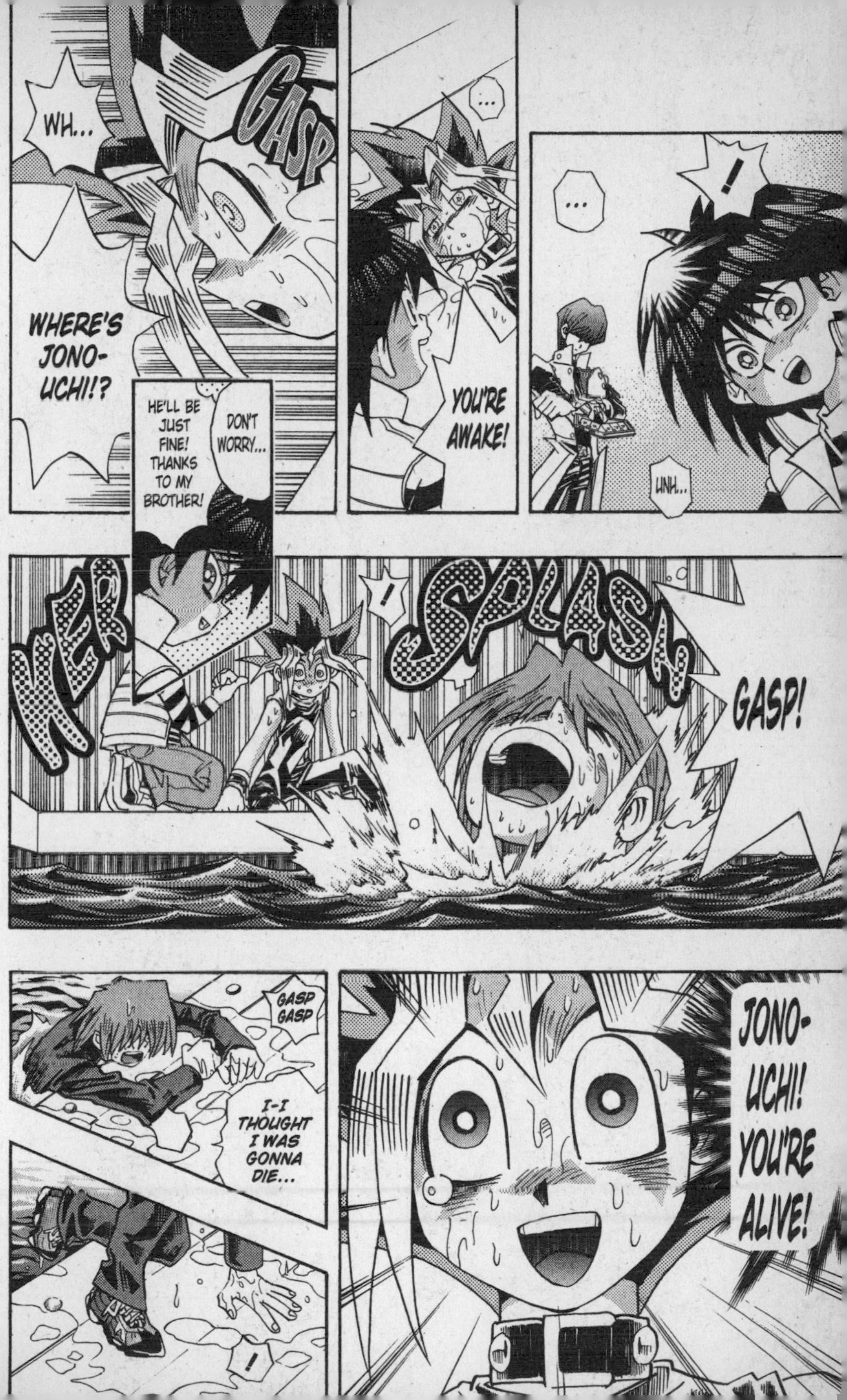
!
...
UNH...
...
YOU'RE AWAKE!
WH...
GASP
WHERE'S JONO-UCHI!?
DON'T WORRY...
HE'LL BE JUST FINE! THANKS TO MY BROTHER!
SPLASH
KER
!
GASP!
JONO-UCHI! YOU'RE ALIVE!
GASP GASP
I-I THOUGHT I WAS GONNA DIE...
!

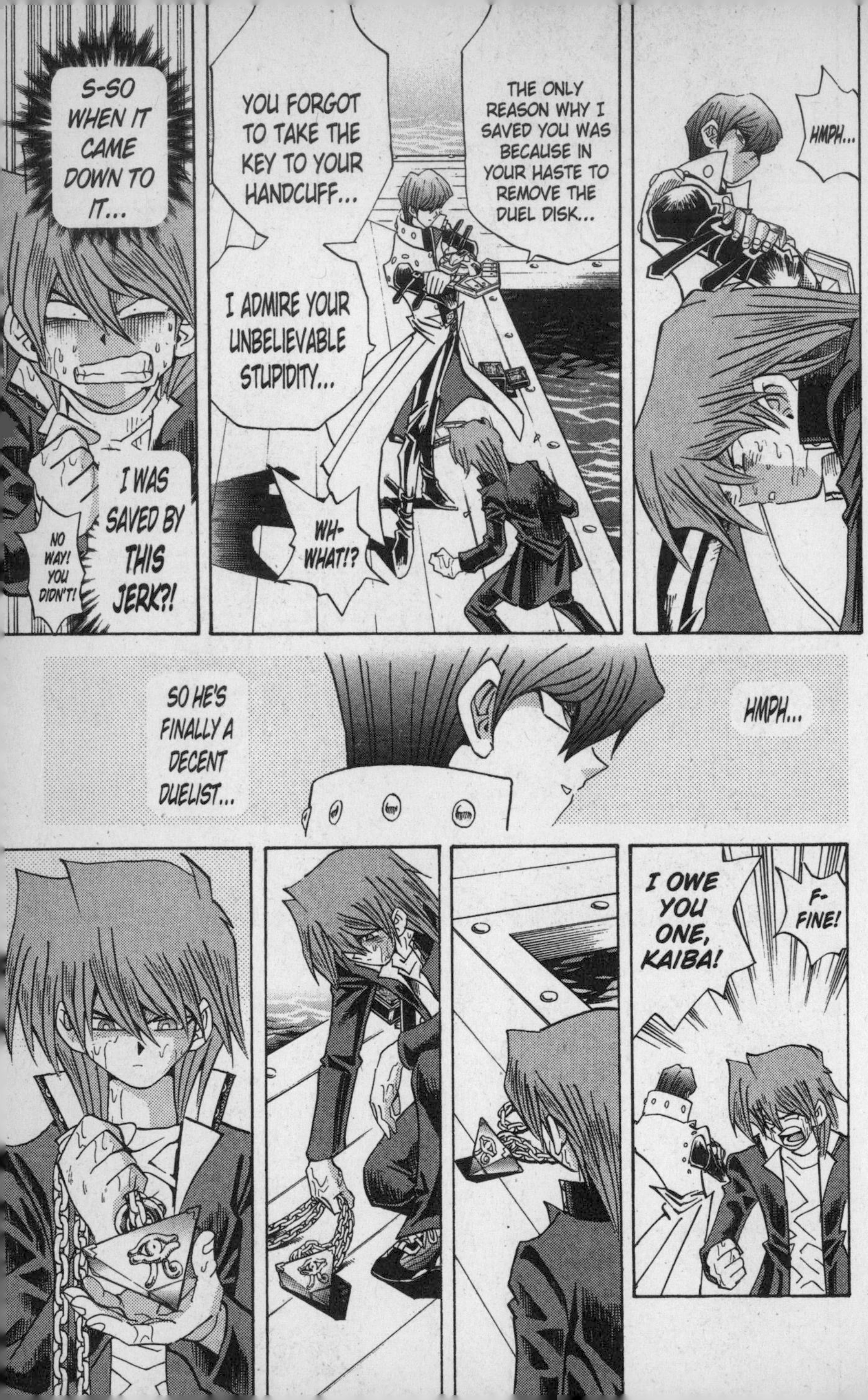
HMPH...
THE ONLY REASON WHY I SAVED YOU WAS BECAUSE IN YOUR HASTE TO REMOVE THE DUEL DISK...
YOU FORGOT TO TAKE THE KEY TO YOUR HANDCUFF...
I ADMIRE YOUR UNBELIEVABLE STUPIDITY...
WH- WHAT!?
S-SO WHEN IT CAME DOWN TO IT...
I WAS SAVED BY THIS JERK?!
NO WAY! YOU DIDN'T!
HMPH...
SO HE'S FINALLY A DECENT DUELIST...
F- FINE!
I OWE YOU ONE, KAIBA!

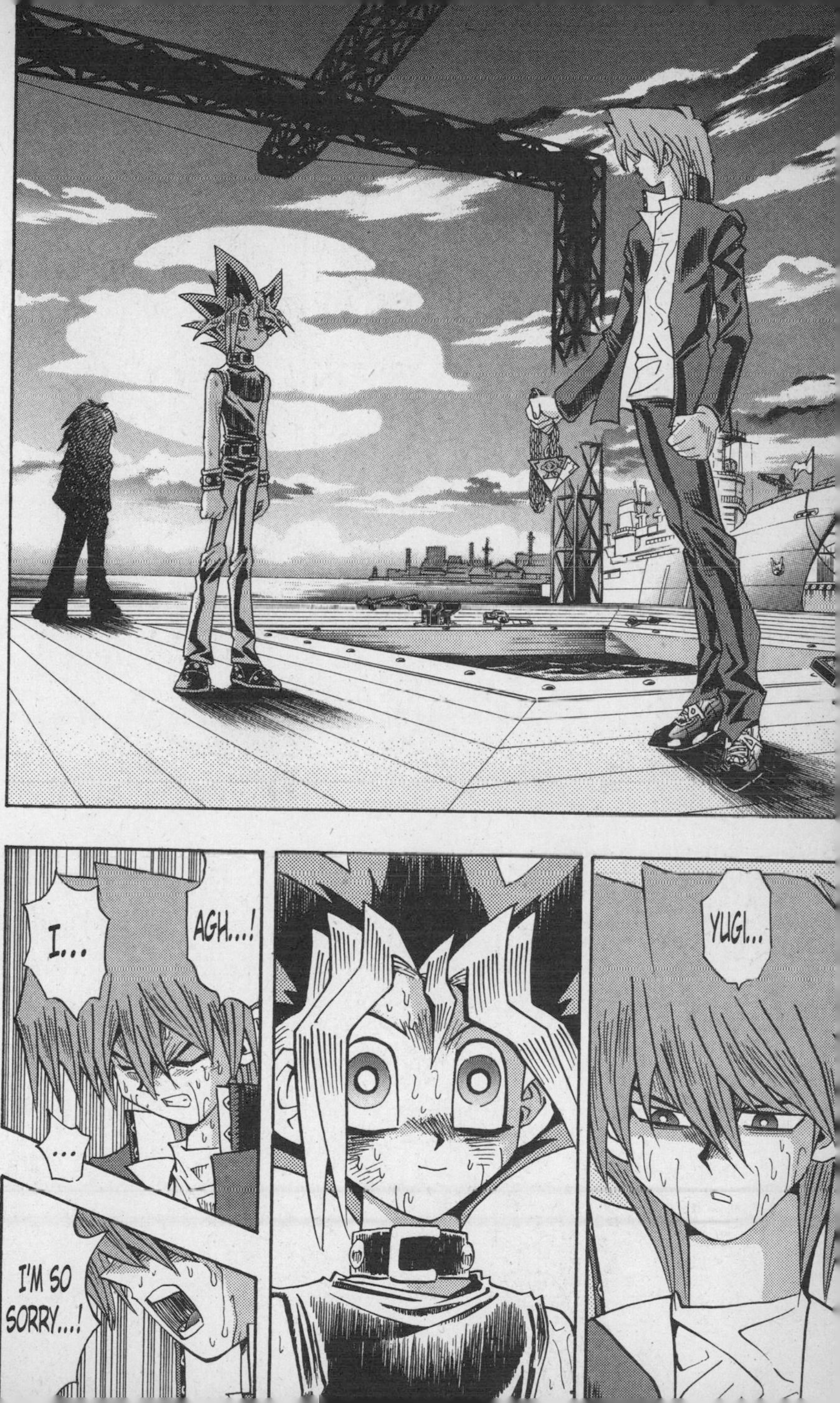
YUGI...
AGH...!
I...
...
I'M SO SORRY...!

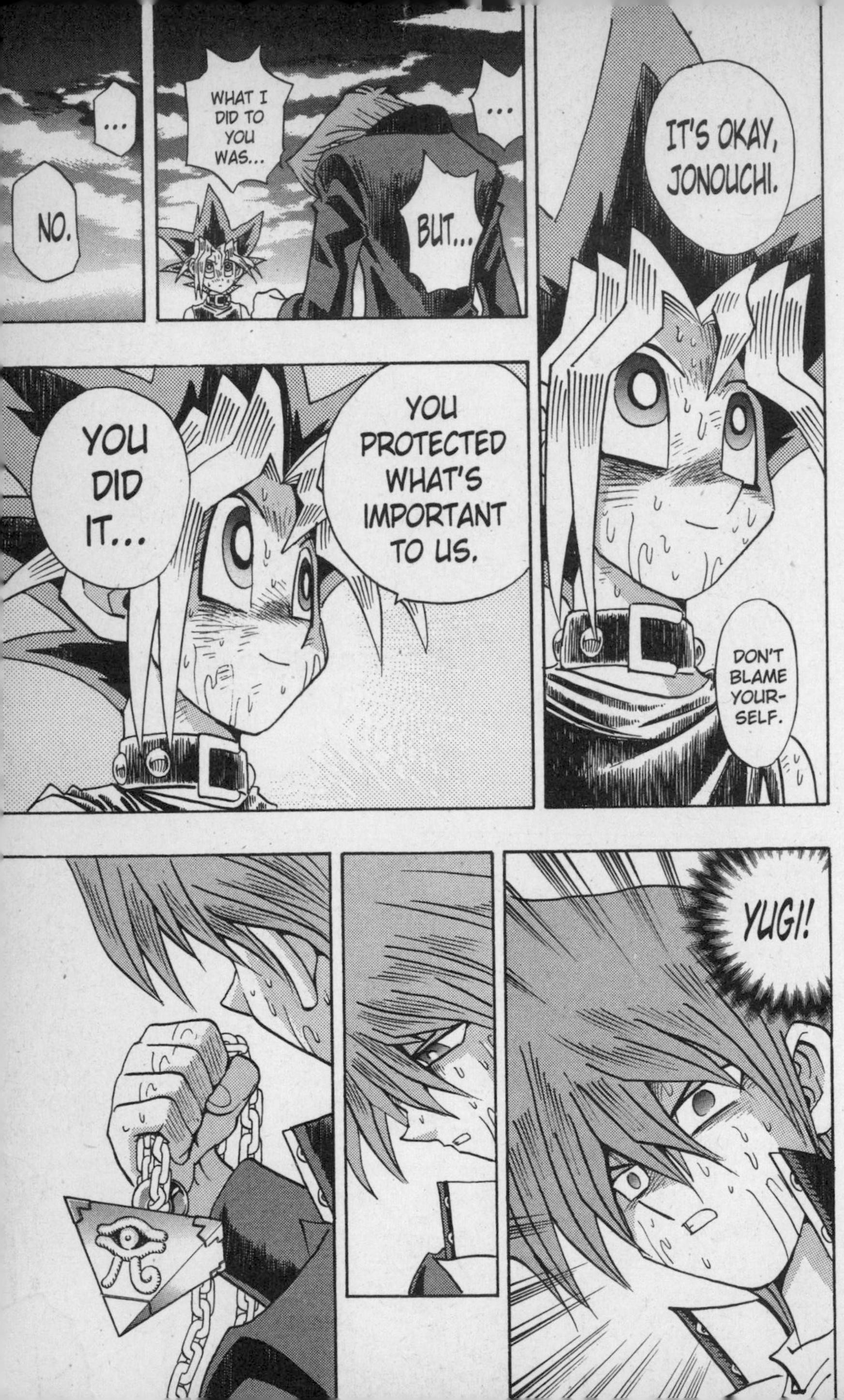
IT'S OKAY, JONOUCHI.
DON'T BLAME YOURSELF.
...
WHAT I DID TO YOU WAS...
BUT...
...
NO.
YOU PROTECTED WHAT'S IMPORTANT TO US.
YOU DID IT...
YUGI!

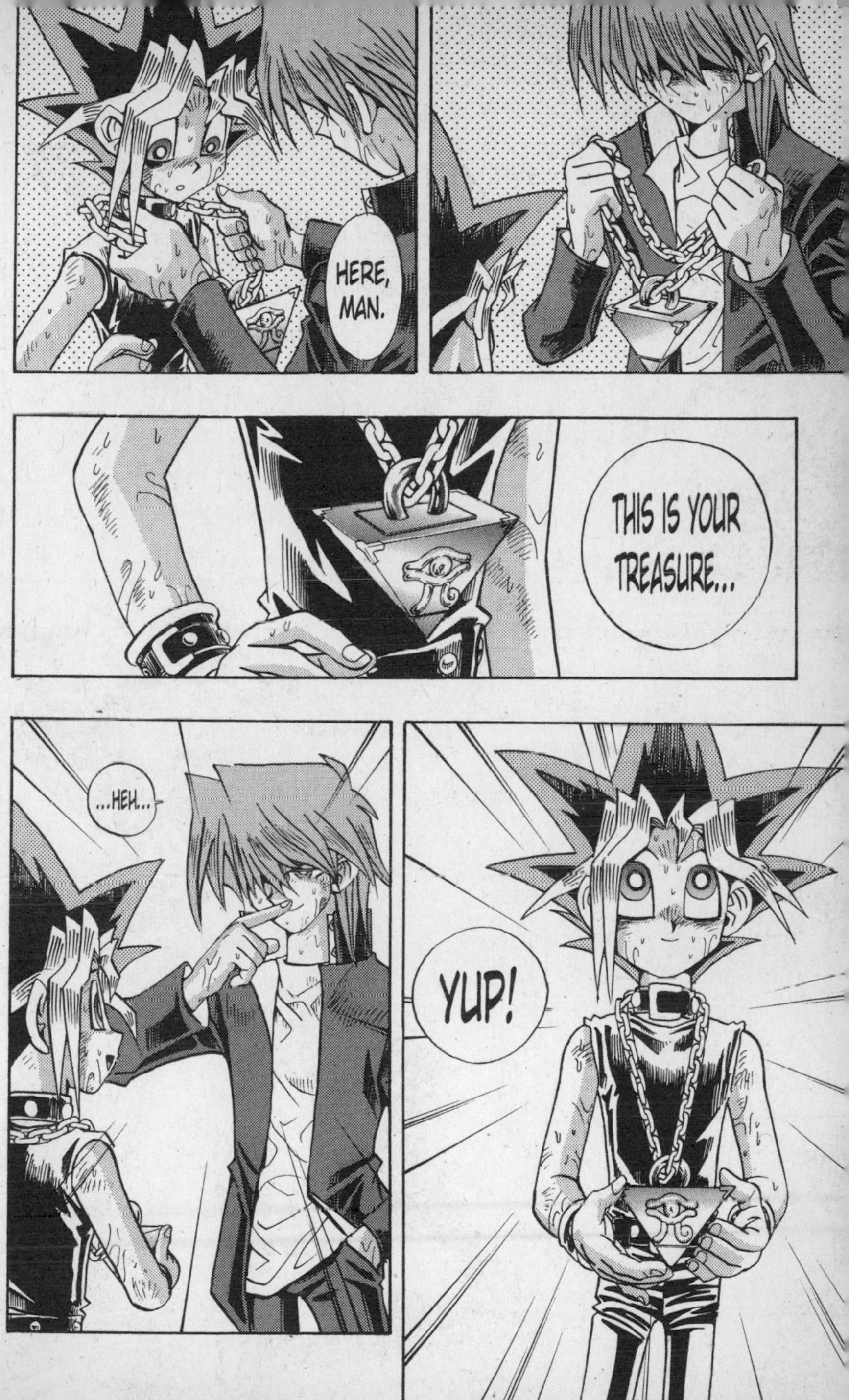
HERE, MAN.
THIS IS YOUR TREASURE...
YUP!
...HEH...

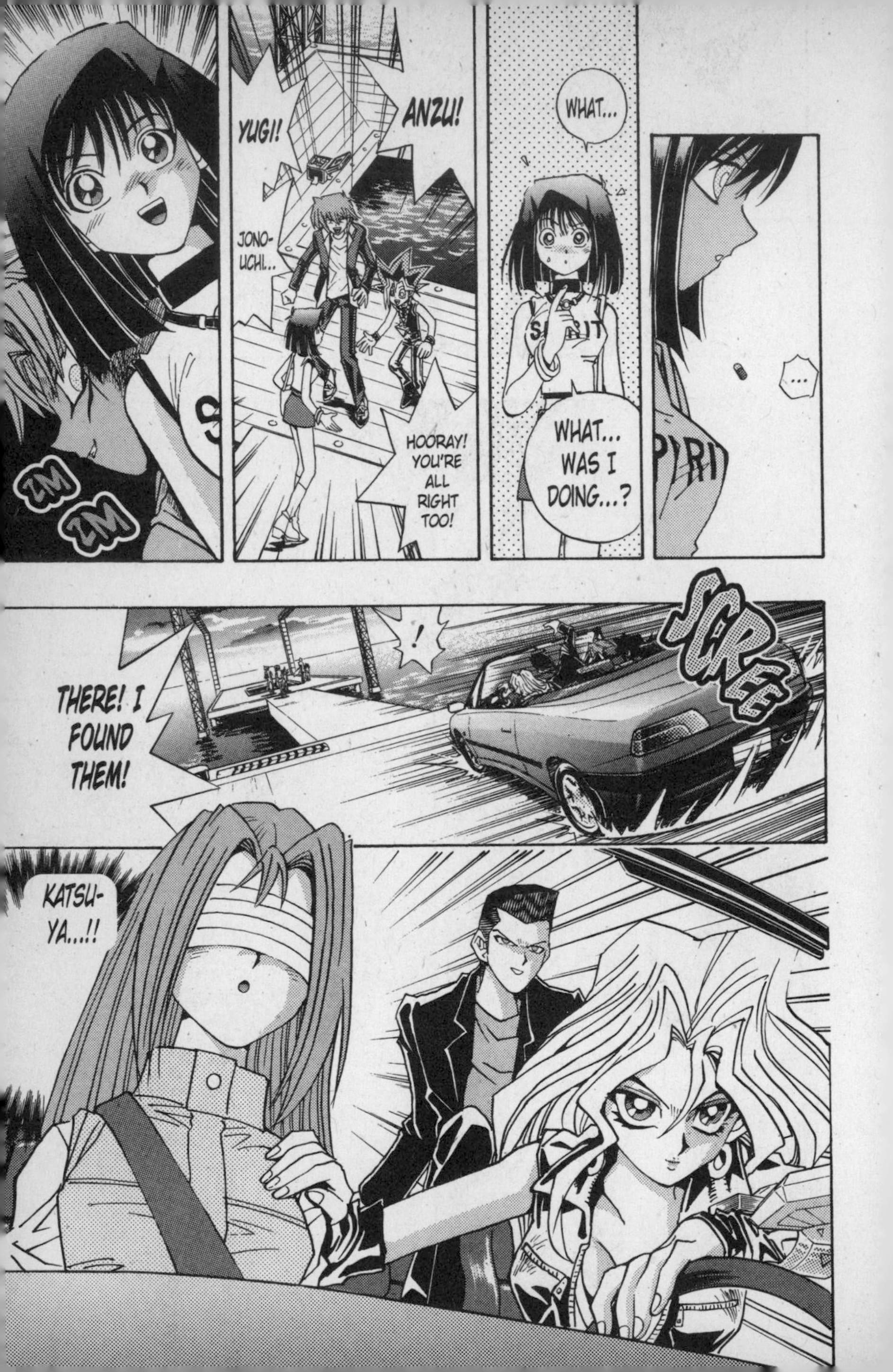
...
WHAT...
WHAT... WAS I DOING...?
ANZU!
YUGI!
JONO-UCHI...
HOORAY! YOU'RE ALL RIGHT TOO!
SCREE
!
THERE! I FOUND THEM!
KATSU-YA...!!

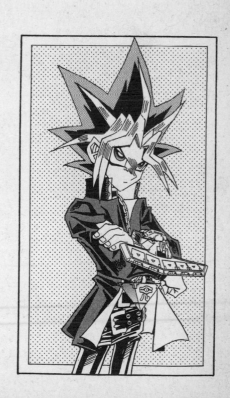

Duel 141: The Courage to See

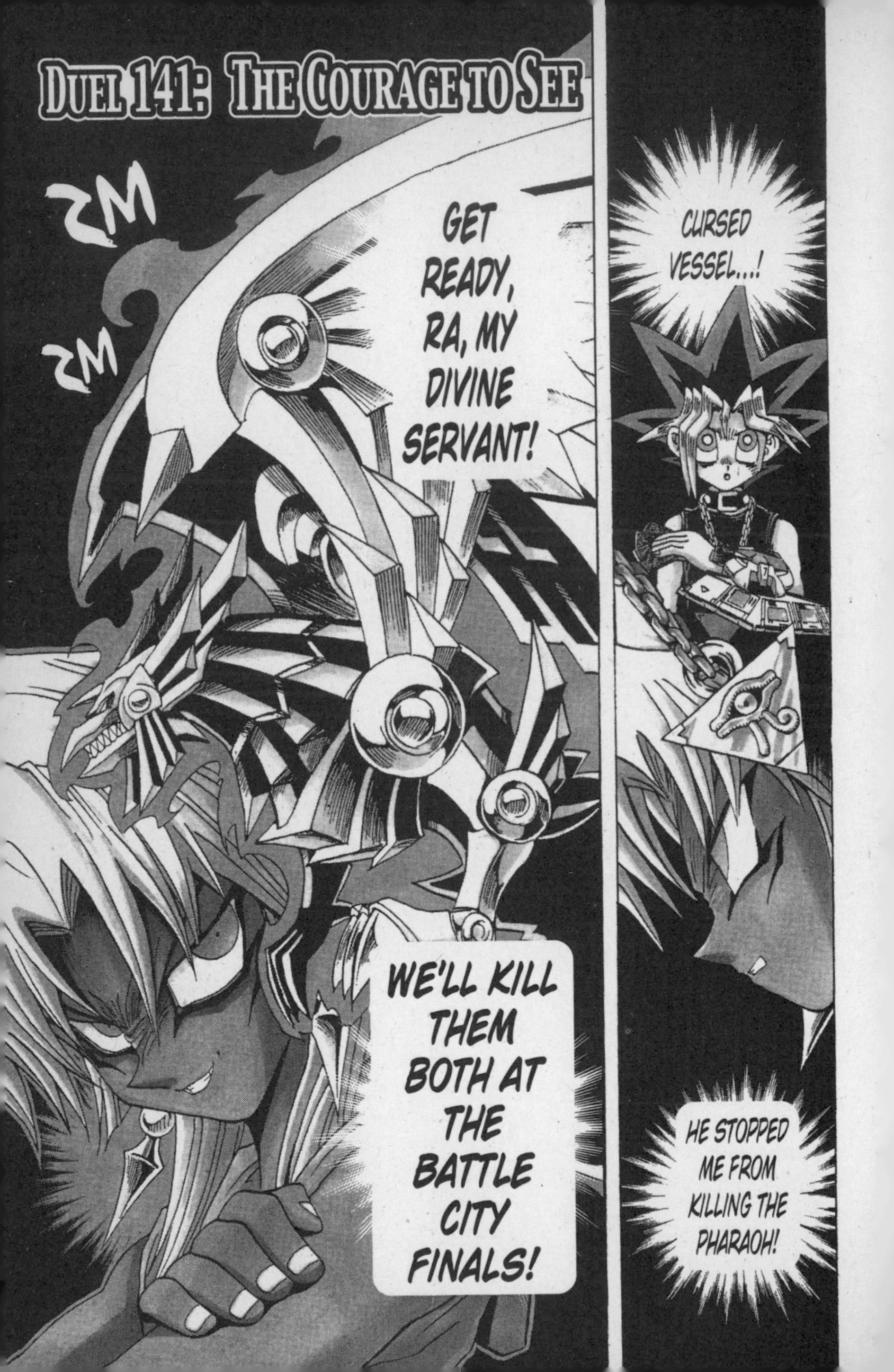
CURSED VESSEL...!
HE STOPPED ME FROM KILLING THE PHARAOH!
GET READY, RA, MY DIVINE SERVANT!
WE'LL KILL THEM BOTH AT THE BATTLE CITY FINALS!

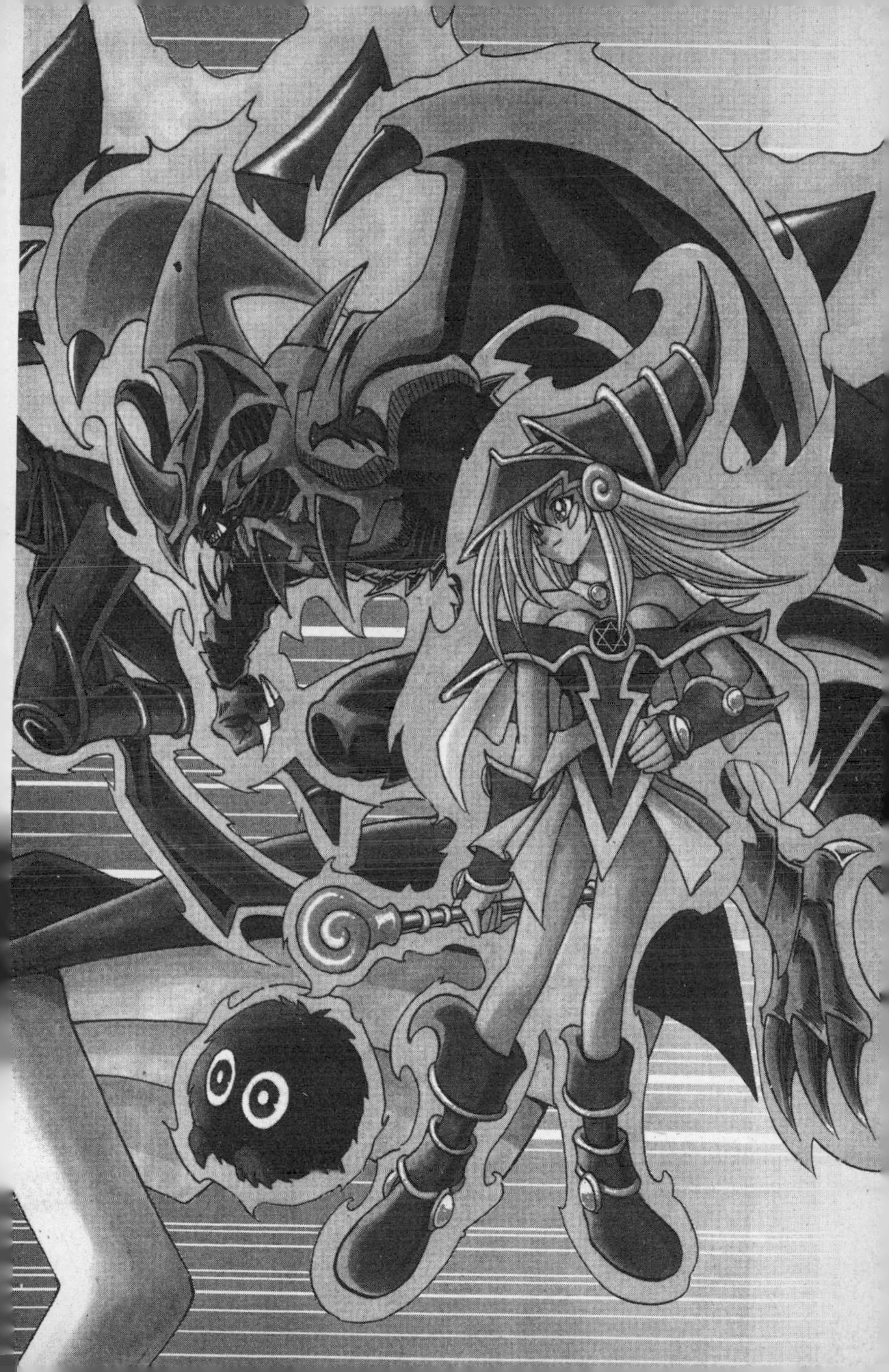

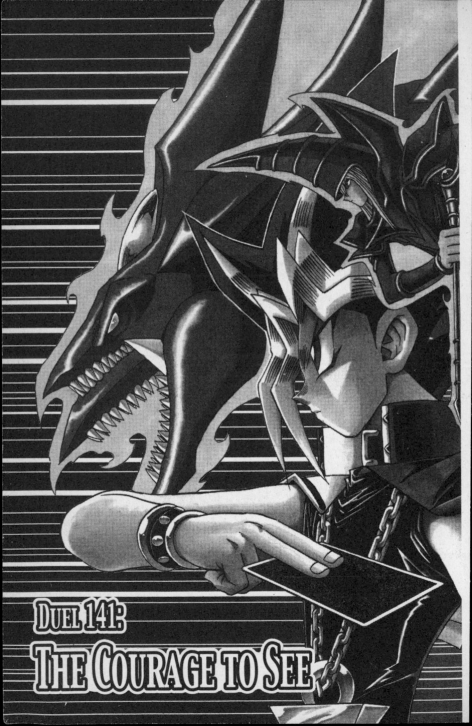

DUEL 141:
THE COURAGE TO SEE

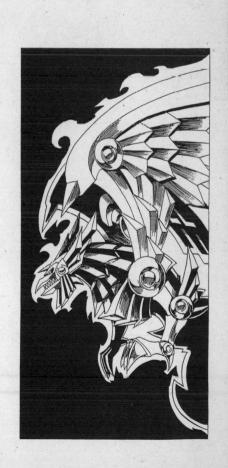

READ THIS WAY

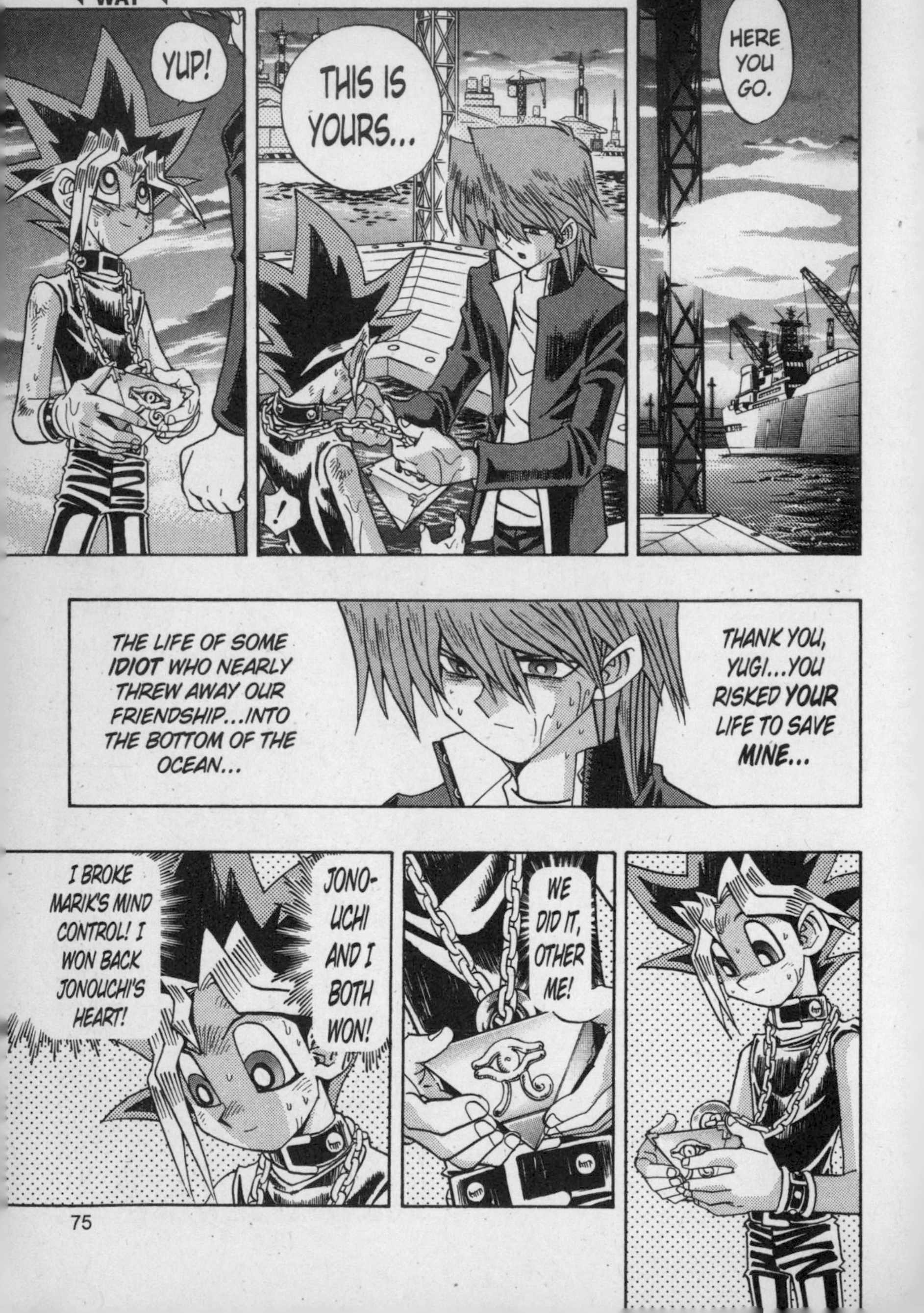
HERE YOU GO.
THIS IS YOURS...
!
YUP!
THANK YOU, YUGI...YOU RISKED YOUR LIFE TO SAVE MINE...
THE LIFE OF SOME IDIOT WHO NEARLY THREW AWAY OUR FRIENDSHIP...INTO THE BOTTOM OF THE OCEAN...
WE DID IT, OTHER ME!
JONOUCHI AND I BOTH WON!
I BROKE MARIK'S MIND CONTROL! I WON BACK JONOUCHI'S HEART!

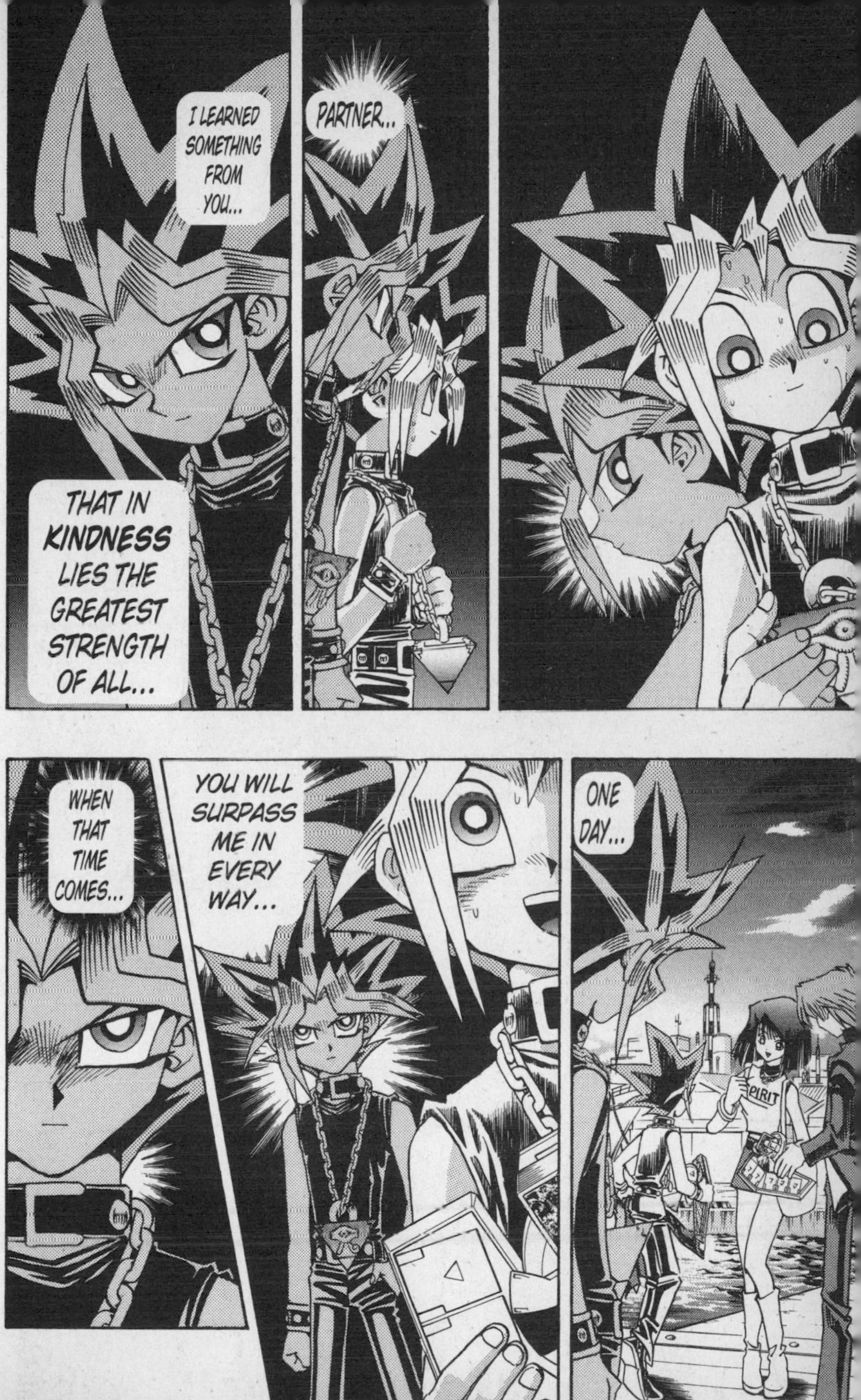
PARTNER...
I LEARNED SOMETHING FROM YOU...
THAT IN KINDNESS LIES THE GREATEST STRENGTH OF ALL...
ONE DAY...
YOU WILL SURPASS ME IN EVERY WAY...
WHEN THAT TIME COMES...

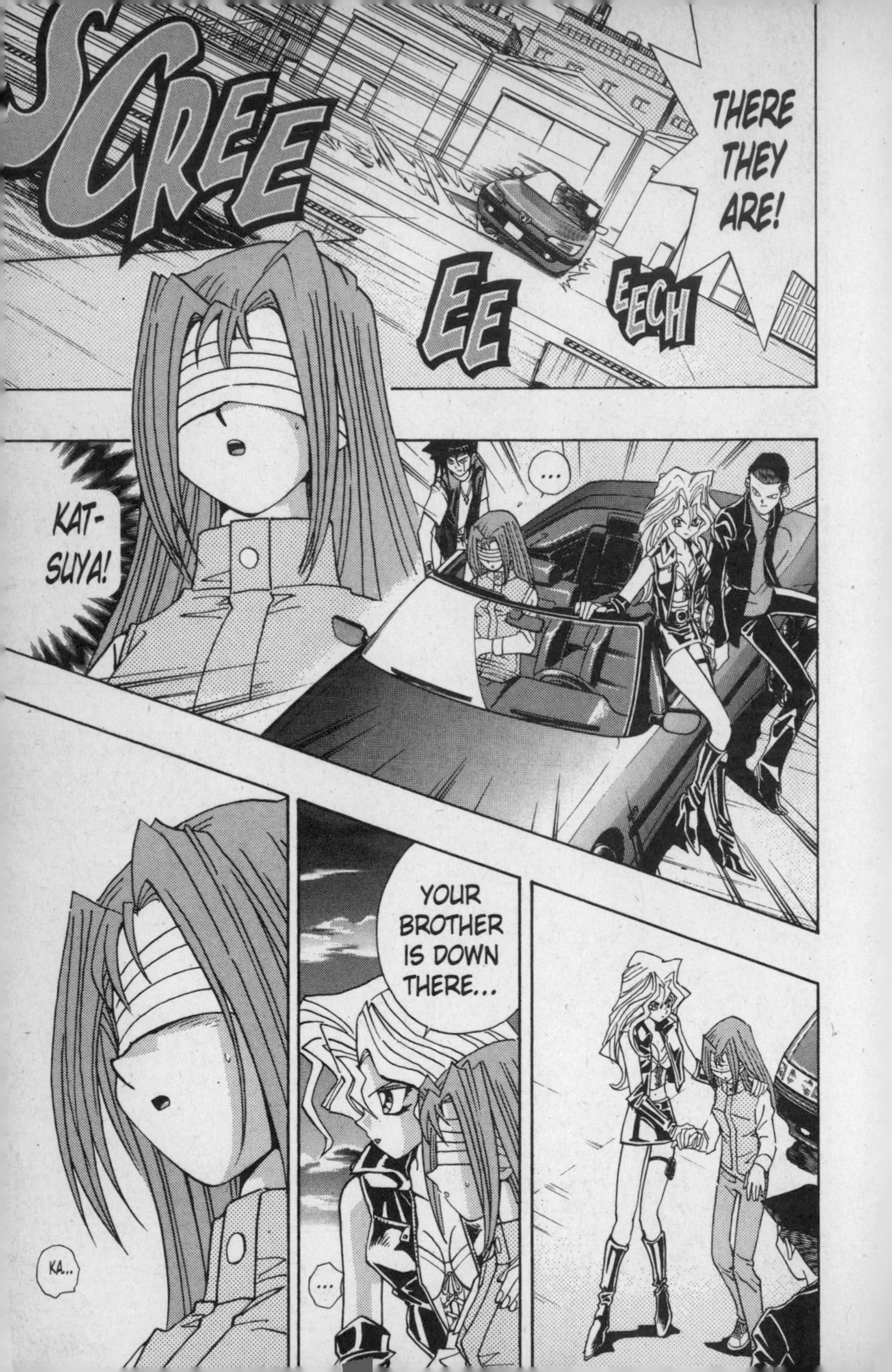
THERE THEY ARE!
SCREE
EE
EECH
...
KAT-SUYA!
YOUR BROTHER IS DOWN THERE...
...
KA...

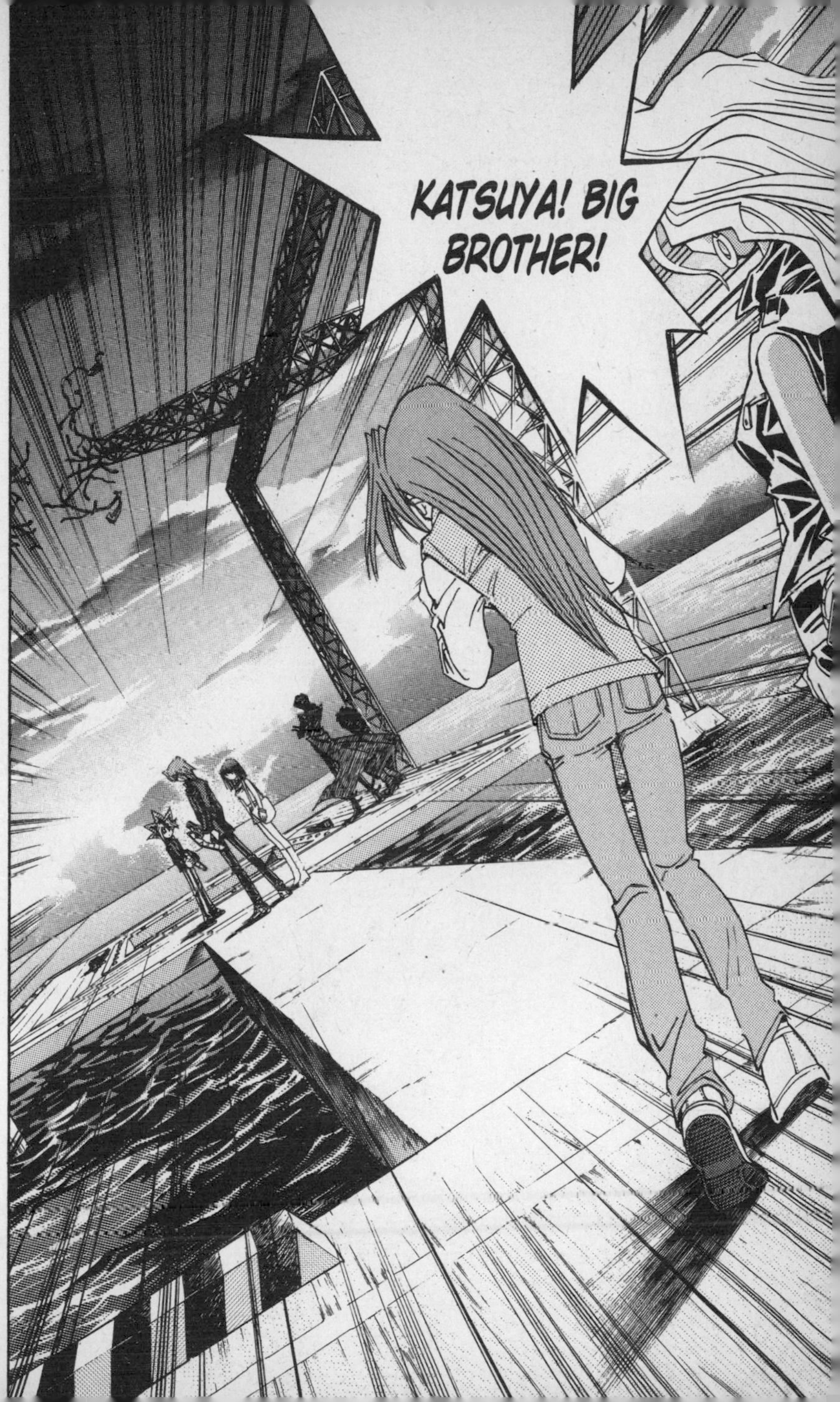
KATSUYA! BIG BROTHER!

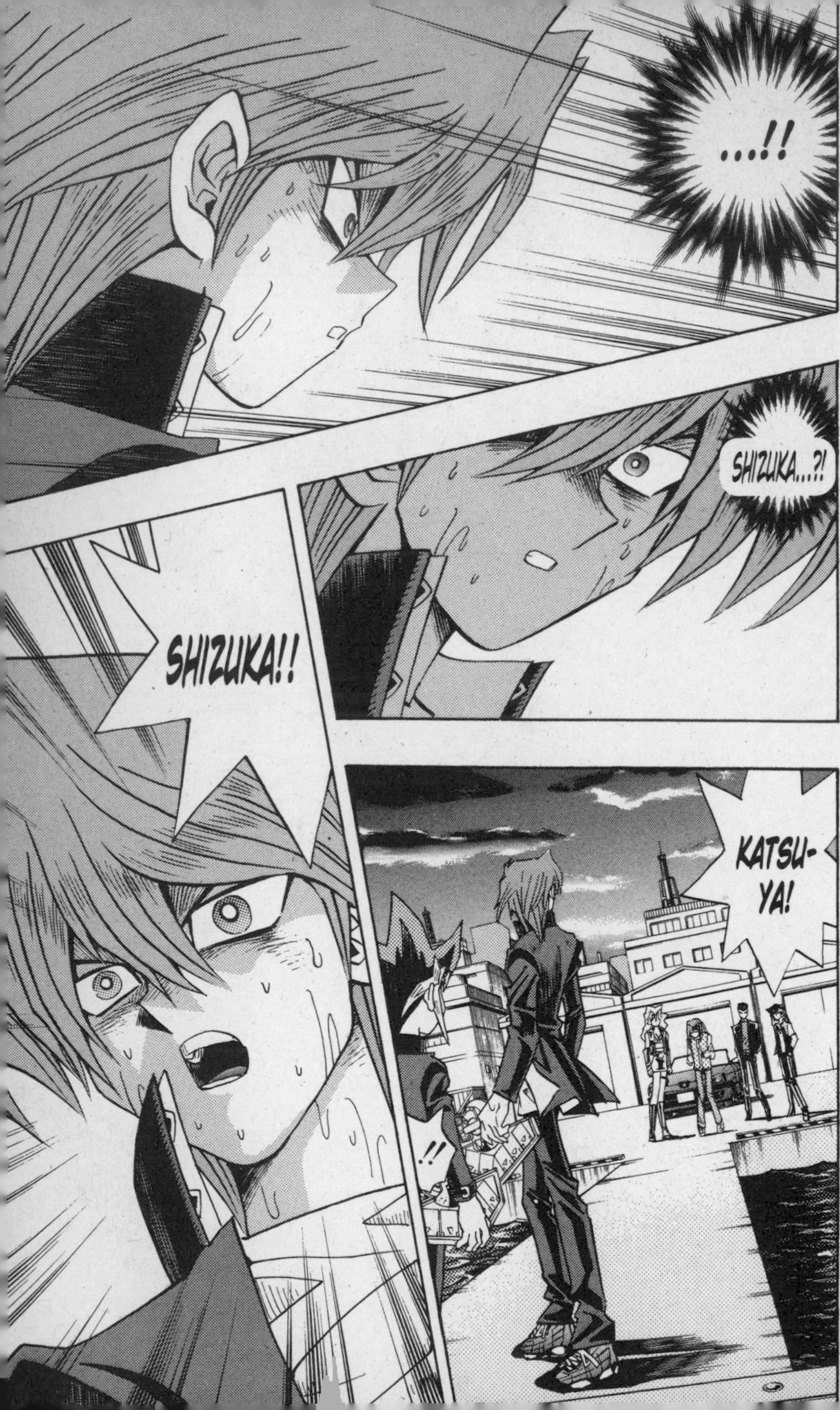
...!!
SHIZUKA...?!
SHIZUKA!!
KATSU-YA!
!!

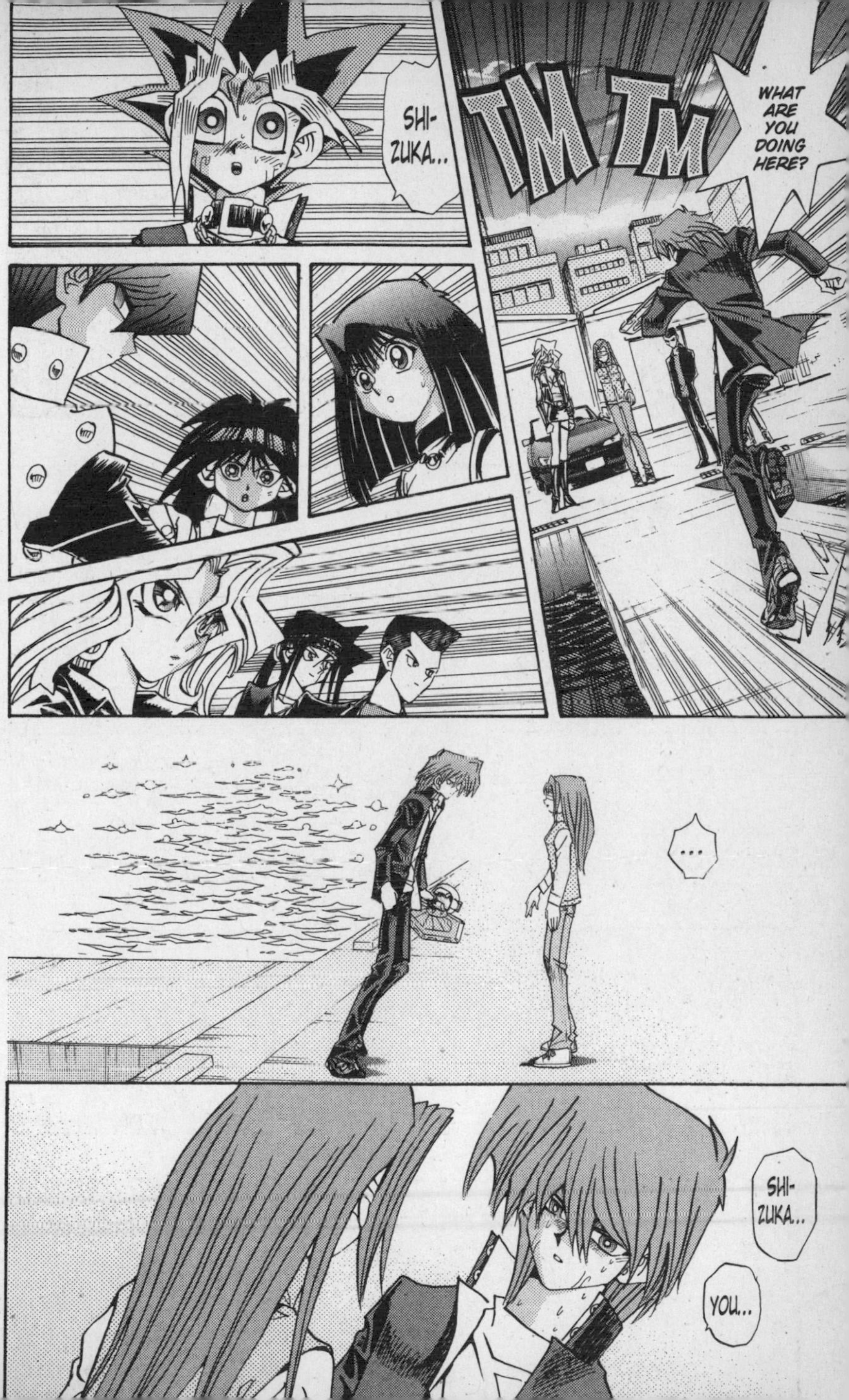
TM TM
WHAT ARE YOU DOING HERE?
SHI-ZUKA...
...
SHI-ZUKA...
YOU...

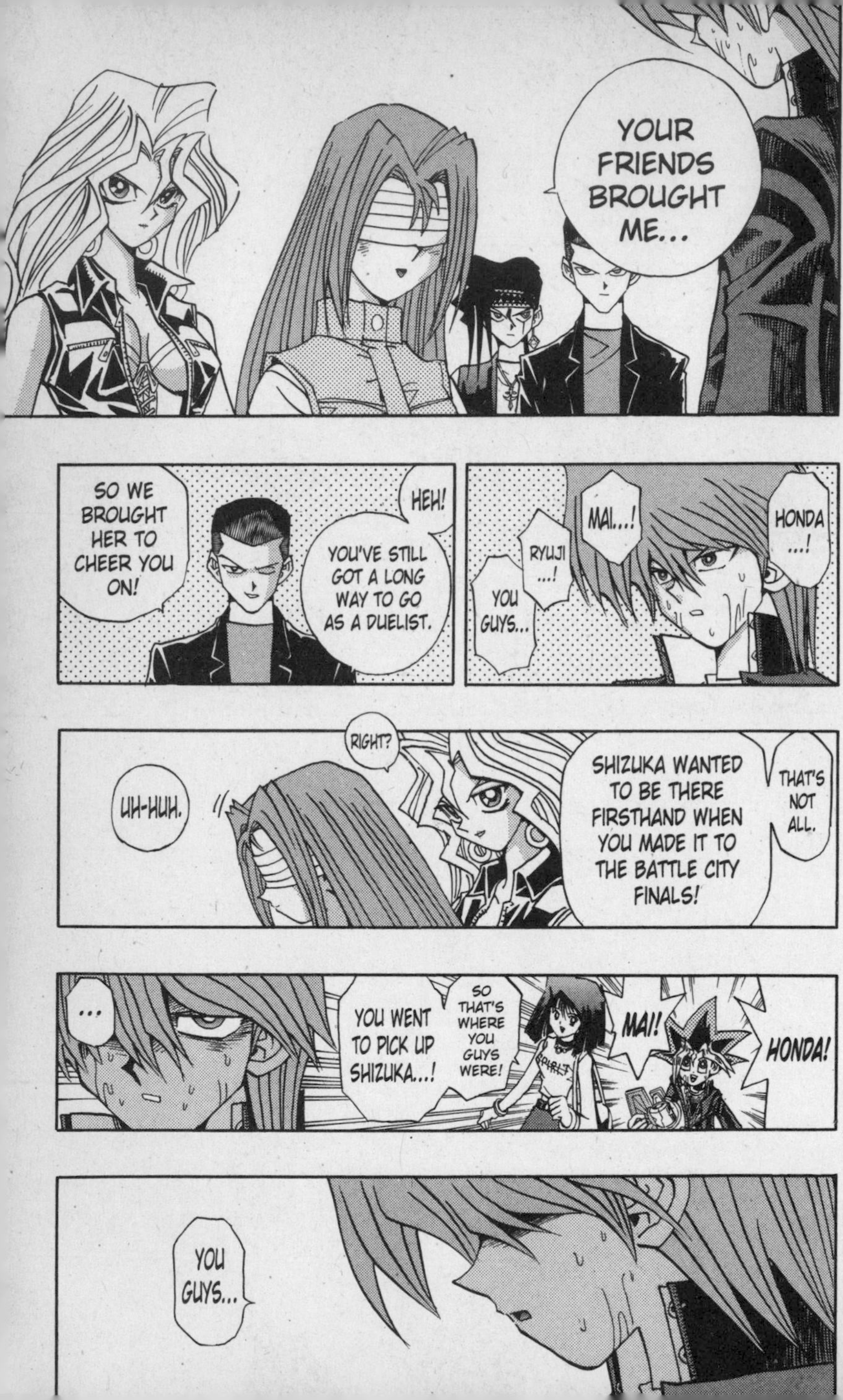
YOUR FRIENDS BROUGHT ME...
HONDA ...!
MAI...!
RYUJI ...!
YOU GUYS...
HEH!
YOU'VE STILL GOT A LONG WAY TO GO AS A DUELIST.
SO WE BROUGHT HER TO CHEER YOU ON!
THAT'S NOT ALL.
SHIZUKA WANTED TO BE THERE FIRSTHAND WHEN YOU MADE IT TO THE BATTLE CITY FINALS!
RIGHT?
UH-HUH.
HONDA!
MAI!
SO THAT'S WHERE YOU GUYS WERE!
YOU WENT TO PICK UP SHIZUKA...!
...
YOU GUYS...

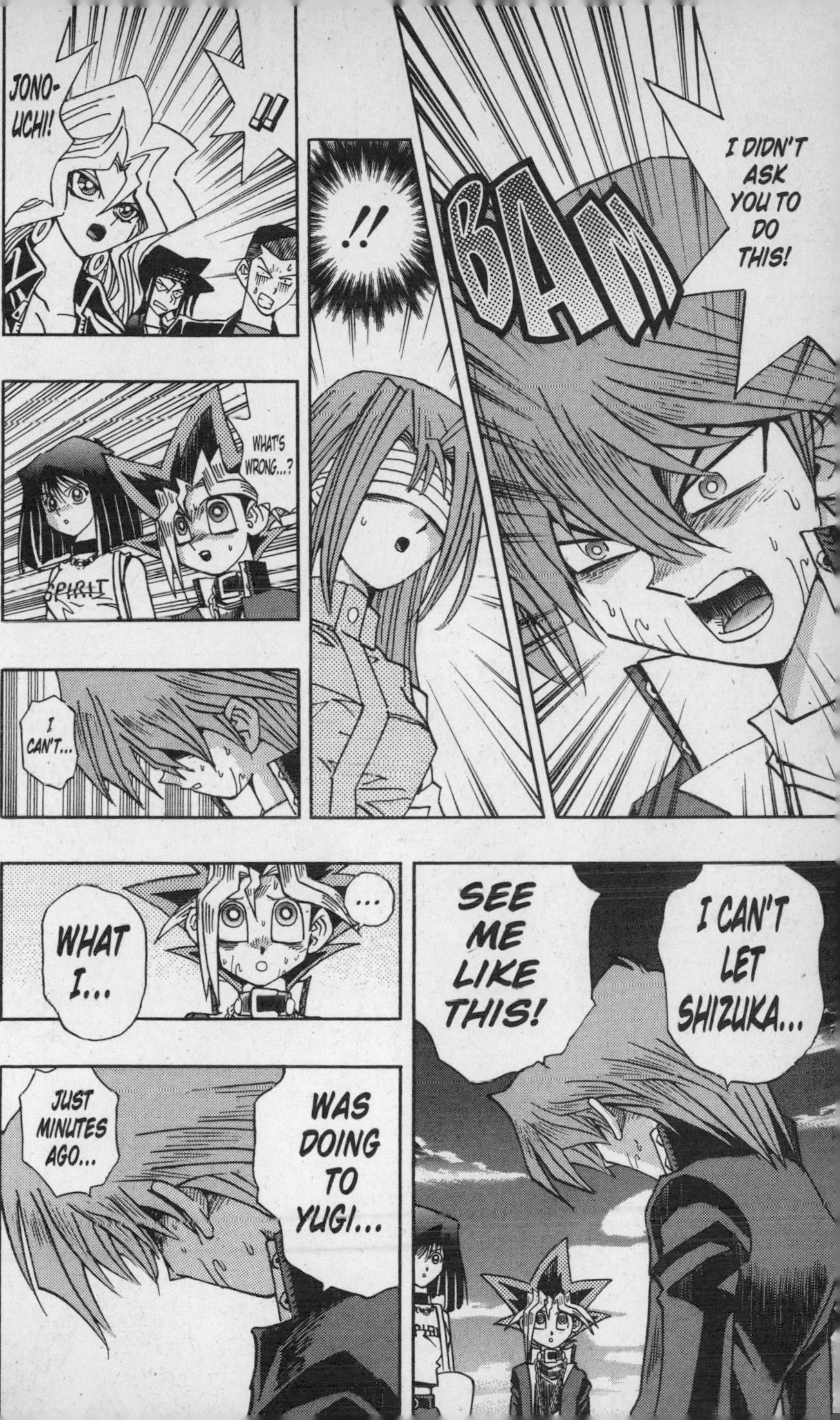
BAM
I DIDN'T ASK YOU TO DO THIS!
!!
JONO-UCHI!
!!
WHAT'S WRONG...?
I CAN'T...
I CAN'T LET SHIZUKA...
SEE ME LIKE THIS!
...
WHAT I...
JUST MINUTES AGO...
WAS DOING TO YUGI...

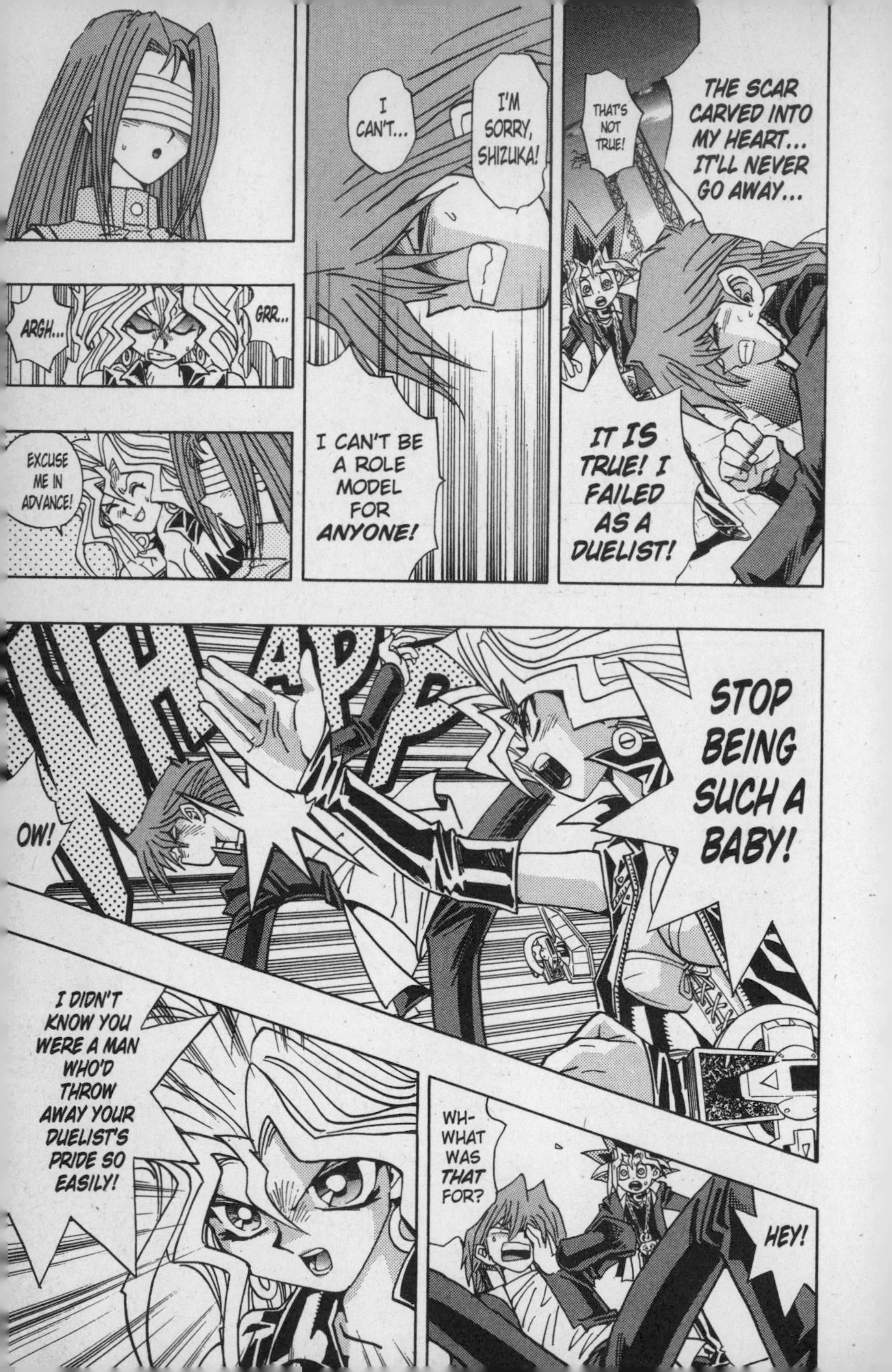
THE SCAR CARVED INTO MY HEART... IT'LL NEVER GO AWAY...
THAT'S NOT TRUE!
IT IS TRUE! I FAILED AS A DUELIST!
I'M SORRY, SHIZUKA!
I CAN'T...
I CAN'T BE A ROLE MODEL FOR ANYONE!
GRR...
ARGH...
EXCUSE ME IN ADVANCE!
STOP BEING SUCH A BABY!
OW!
HEY!
WH- WHAT WAS THAT FOR?
I DIDN'T KNOW YOU WERE A MAN WHO'D THROW AWAY YOUR DUELIST'S PRIDE SO EASILY!

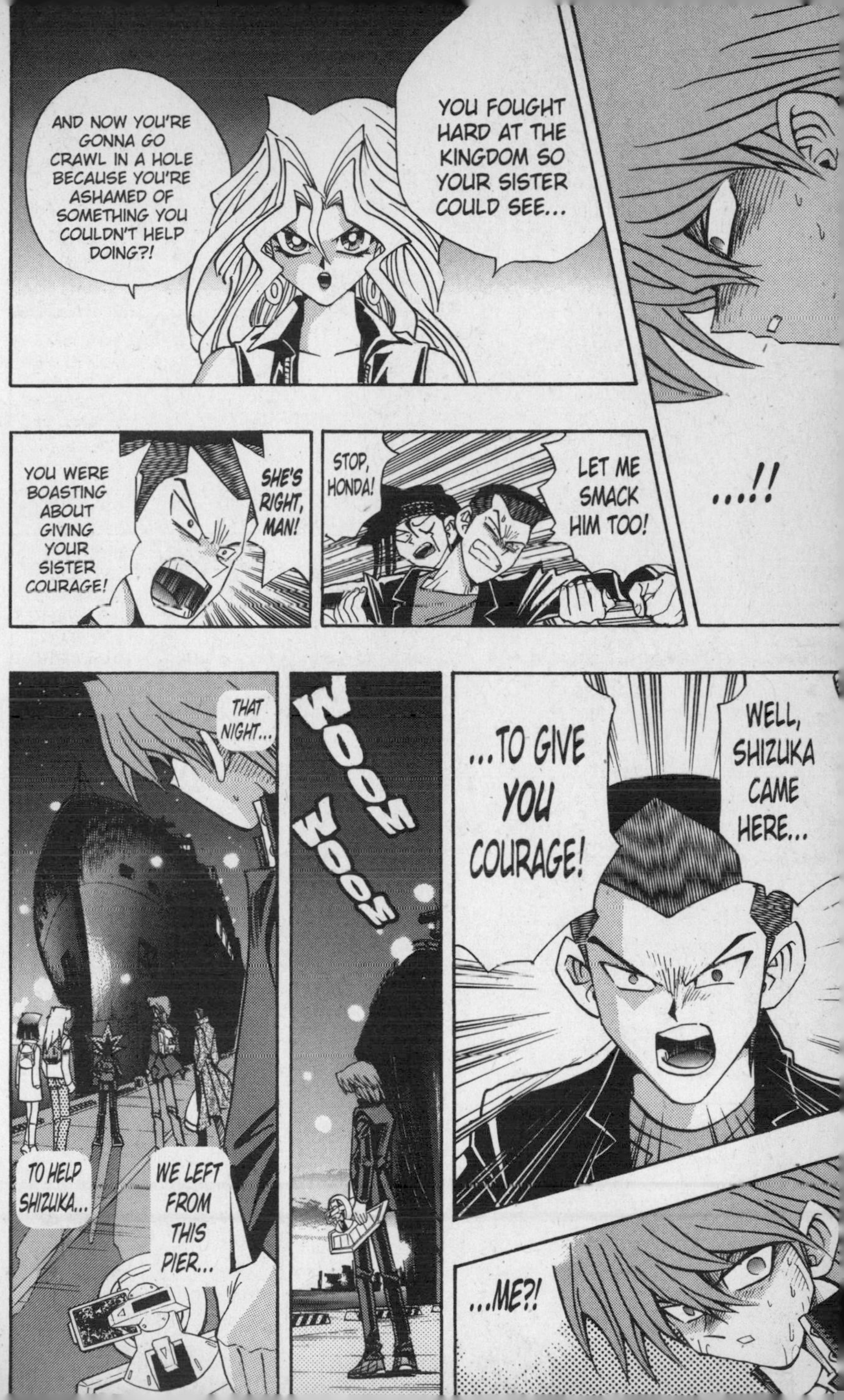
...!!
YOU FOUGHT HARD AT THE KINGDOM SO YOUR SISTER COULD SEE...
AND NOW YOU'RE GONNA GO CRAWL IN A HOLE BECAUSE YOU'RE ASHAMED OF SOMETHING YOU COULDN'T HELP DOING?!
LET ME SMACK HIM TOO!
STOP, HONDA!
SHE'S RIGHT, MAN!
YOU WERE BOASTING ABOUT GIVING YOUR SISTER COURAGE!
WELL, SHIZUKA CAME HERE...
...TO GIVE YOU COURAGE!
...ME?!
WOOM WOOM
THAT NIGHT...
WE LEFT FROM THIS PIER...
TO HELP SHIZUKA...

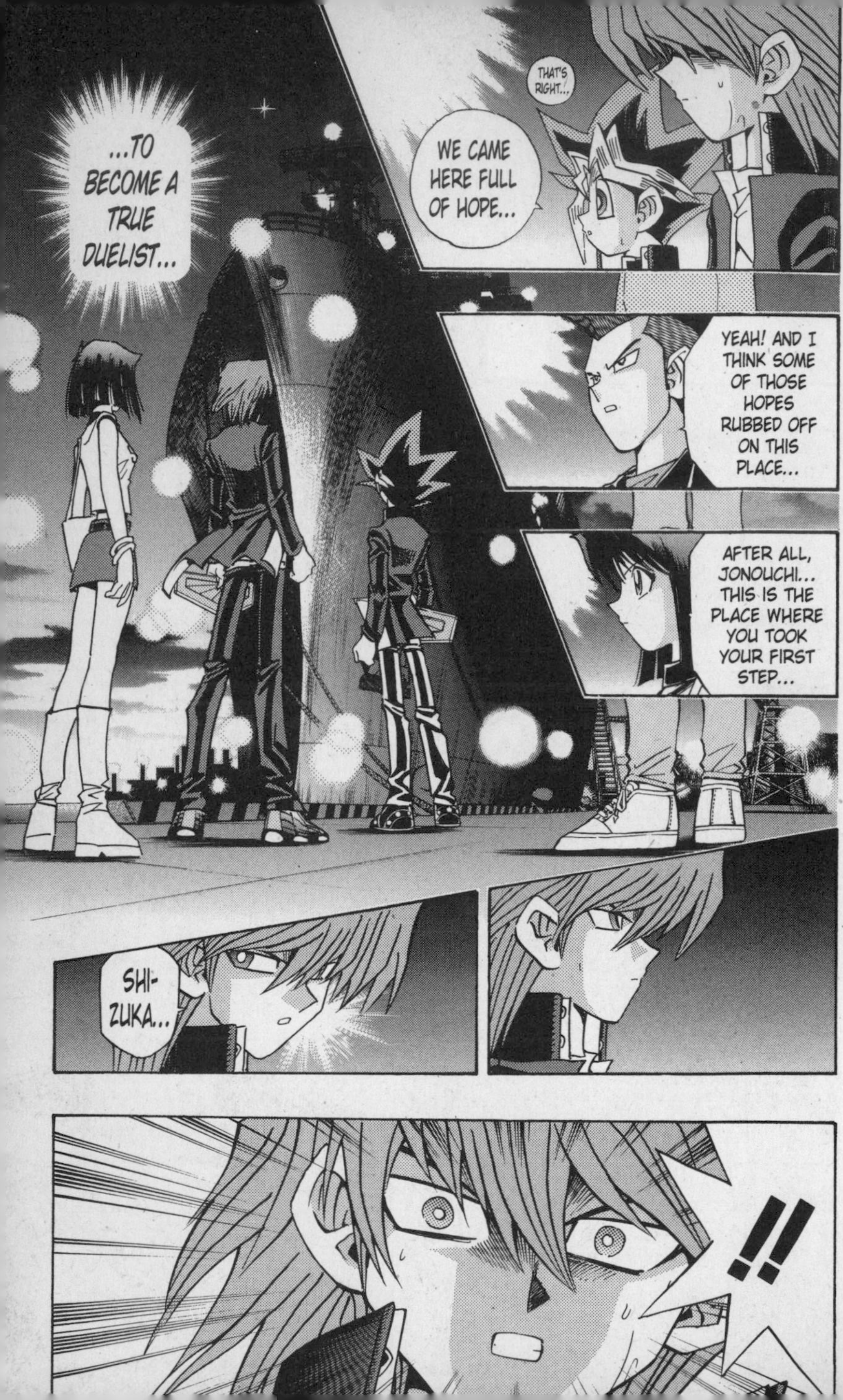

THAT'S RIGHT...
WE CAME HERE FULL OF HOPE...
YEAH! AND I THINK SOME OF THOSE HOPES RUBBED OFF ON THIS PLACE...
AFTER ALL, JONOUCHI... THIS IS THE PLACE WHERE YOU TOOK YOUR FIRST STEP...
...TO BECOME A TRUE DUELIST...
SHI-ZUKA...
!!

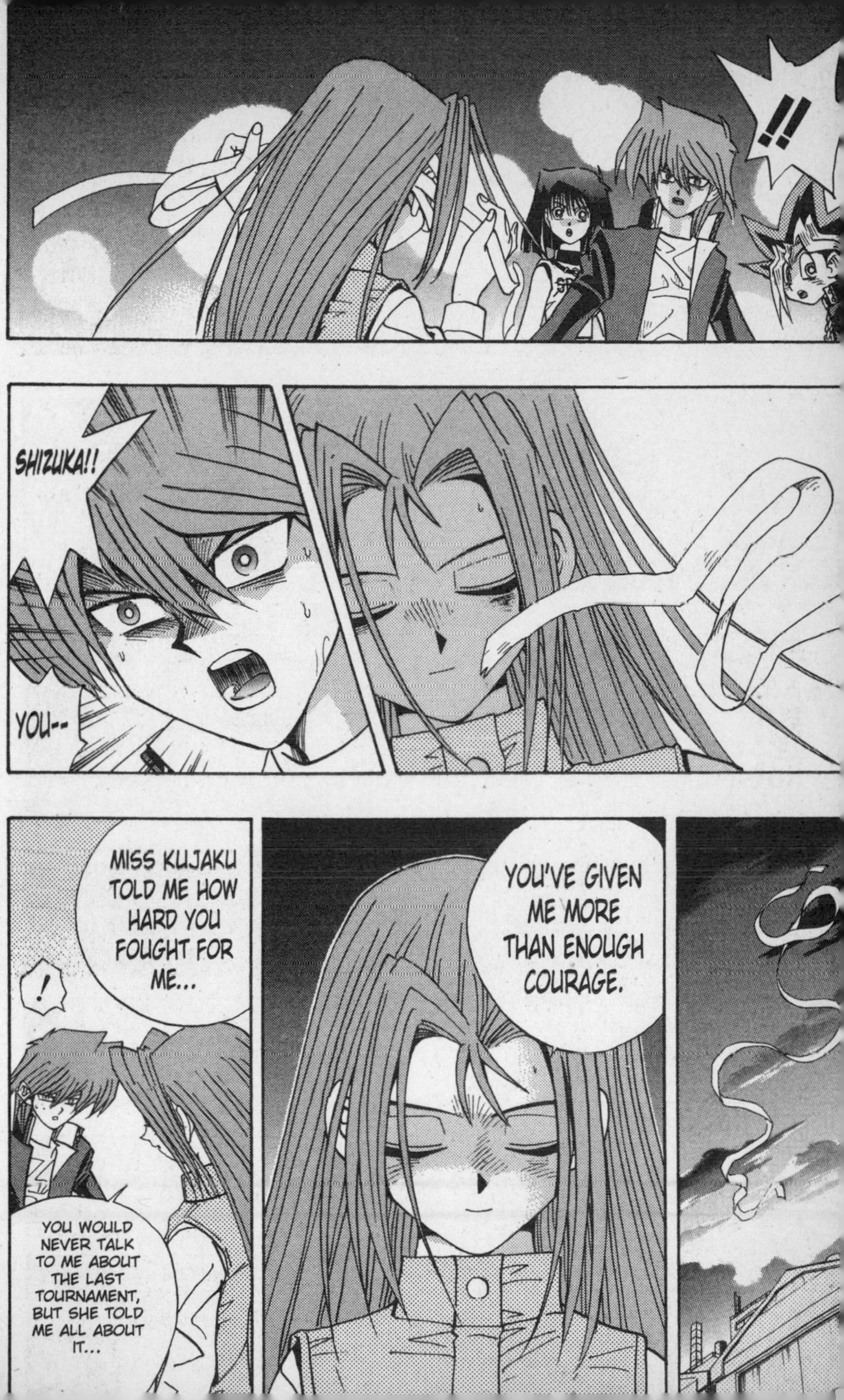
!!
SHIZUKA!!
YOU--
YOU'VE GIVEN ME MORE THAN ENOUGH COURAGE.
MISS KUJAKU TOLD ME HOW HARD YOU FOUGHT FOR ME...
!
YOU WOULD NEVER TALK TO ME ABOUT THE LAST TOURNAMENT, BUT SHE TOLD ME ALL ABOUT IT...

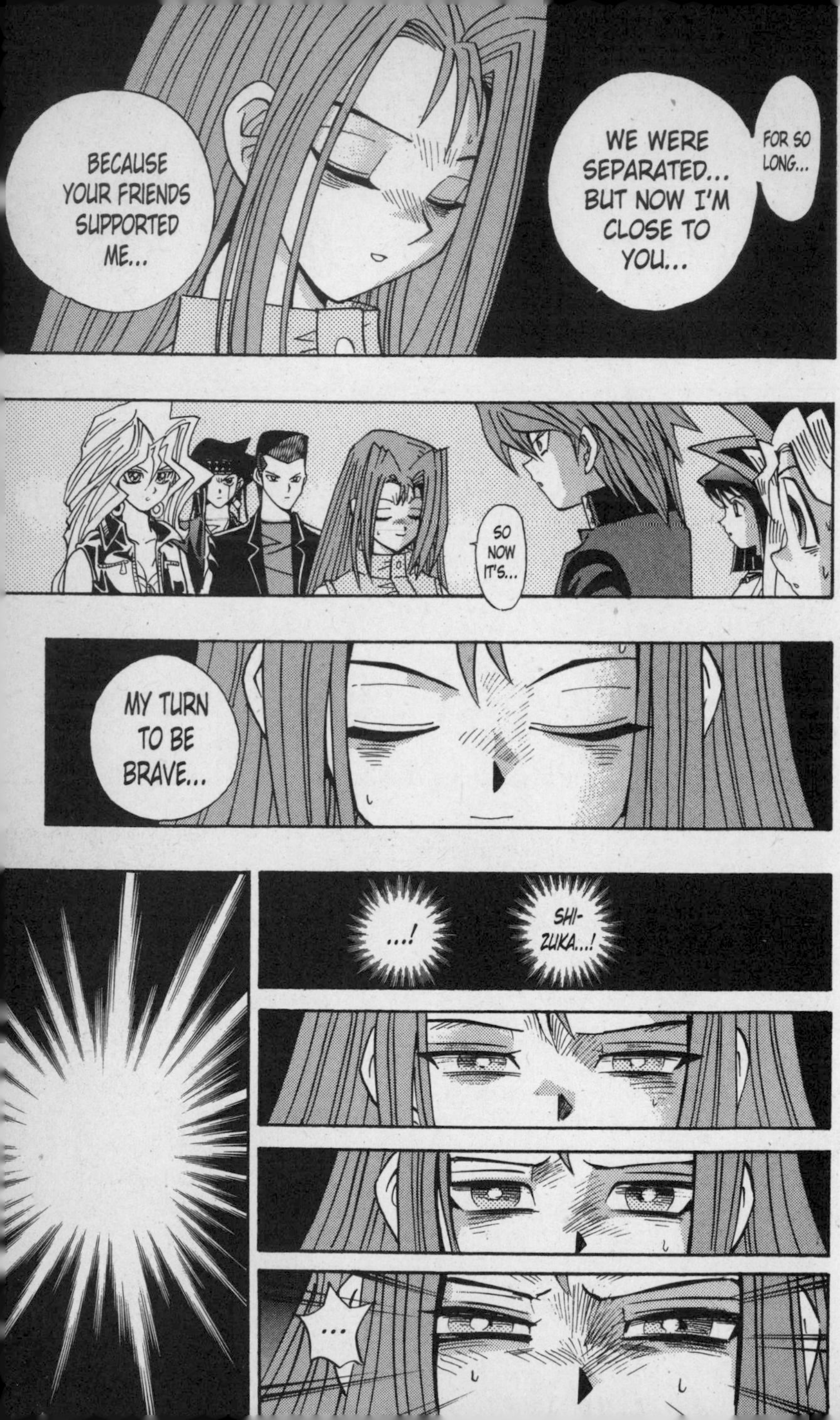

FOR SO LONG...
WE WERE SEPARATED... BUT NOW I'M CLOSE TO YOU...
BECAUSE YOUR FRIENDS SUPPORTED ME...
SO NOW IT'S...
MY TURN TO BE BRAVE...
SHI-ZUKA...!
...!
...

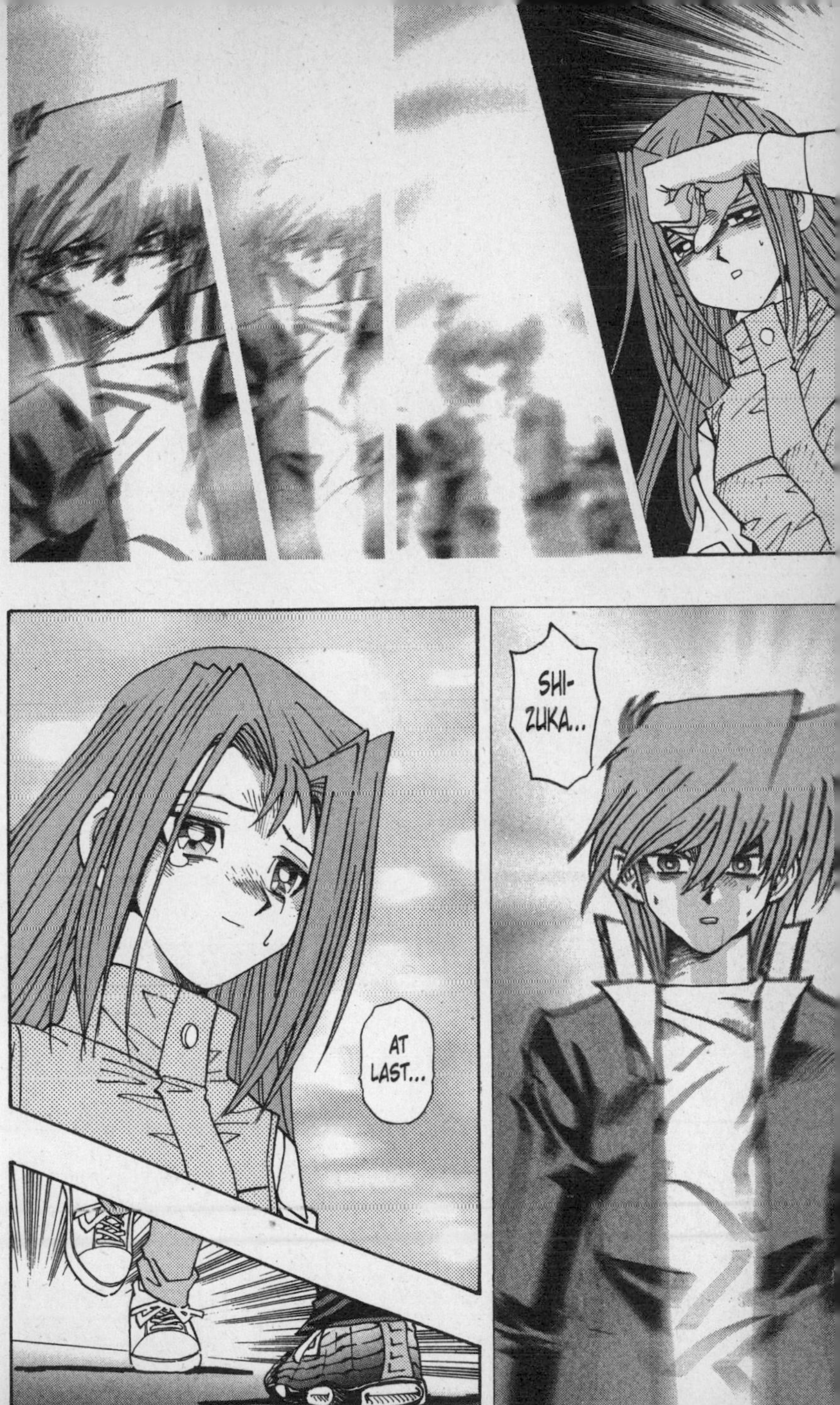
SHI-
ZUKA...
AT
LAST...

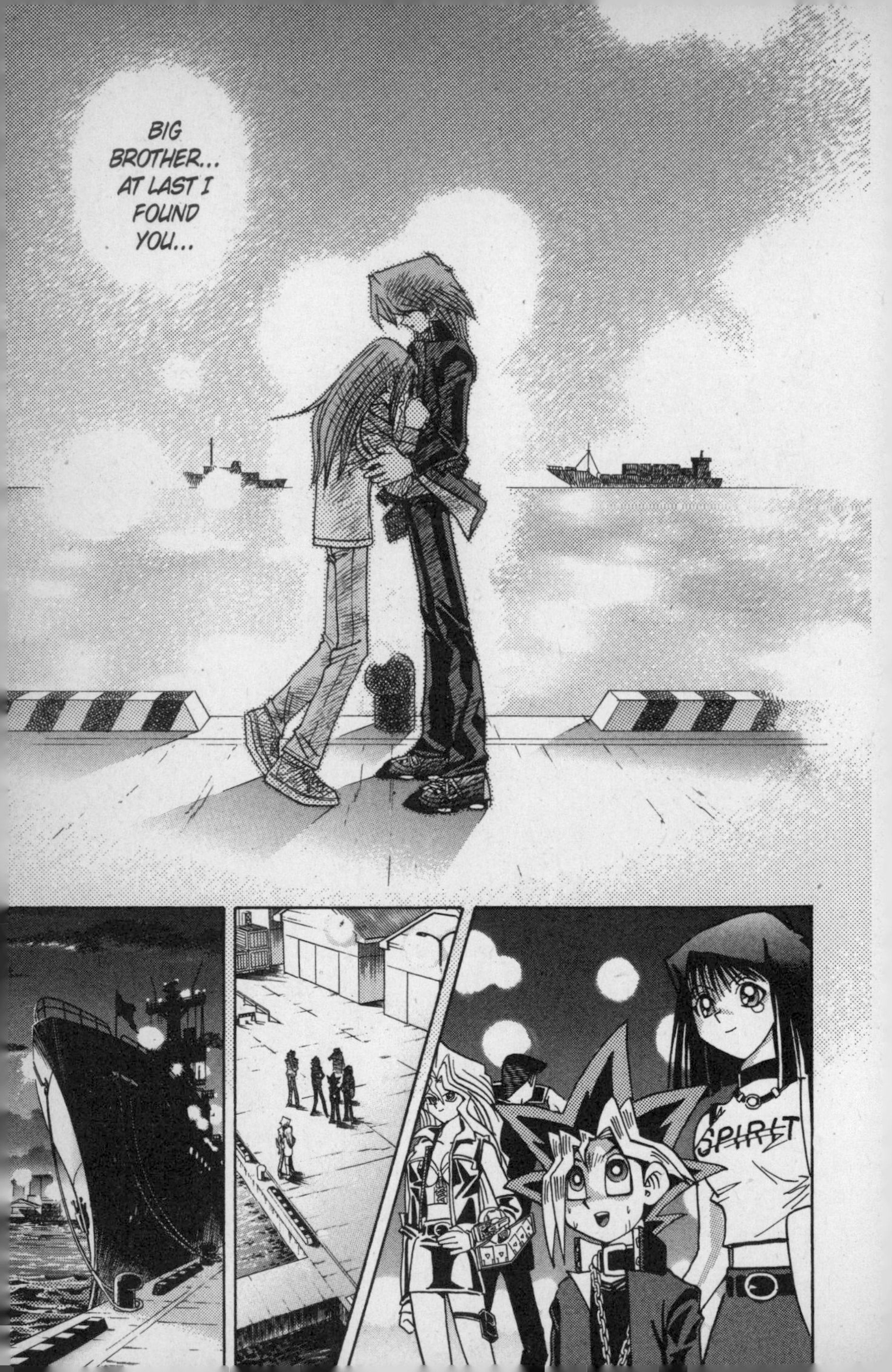
BIG BROTHER... AT LAST I FOUND YOU...
SPIRIT

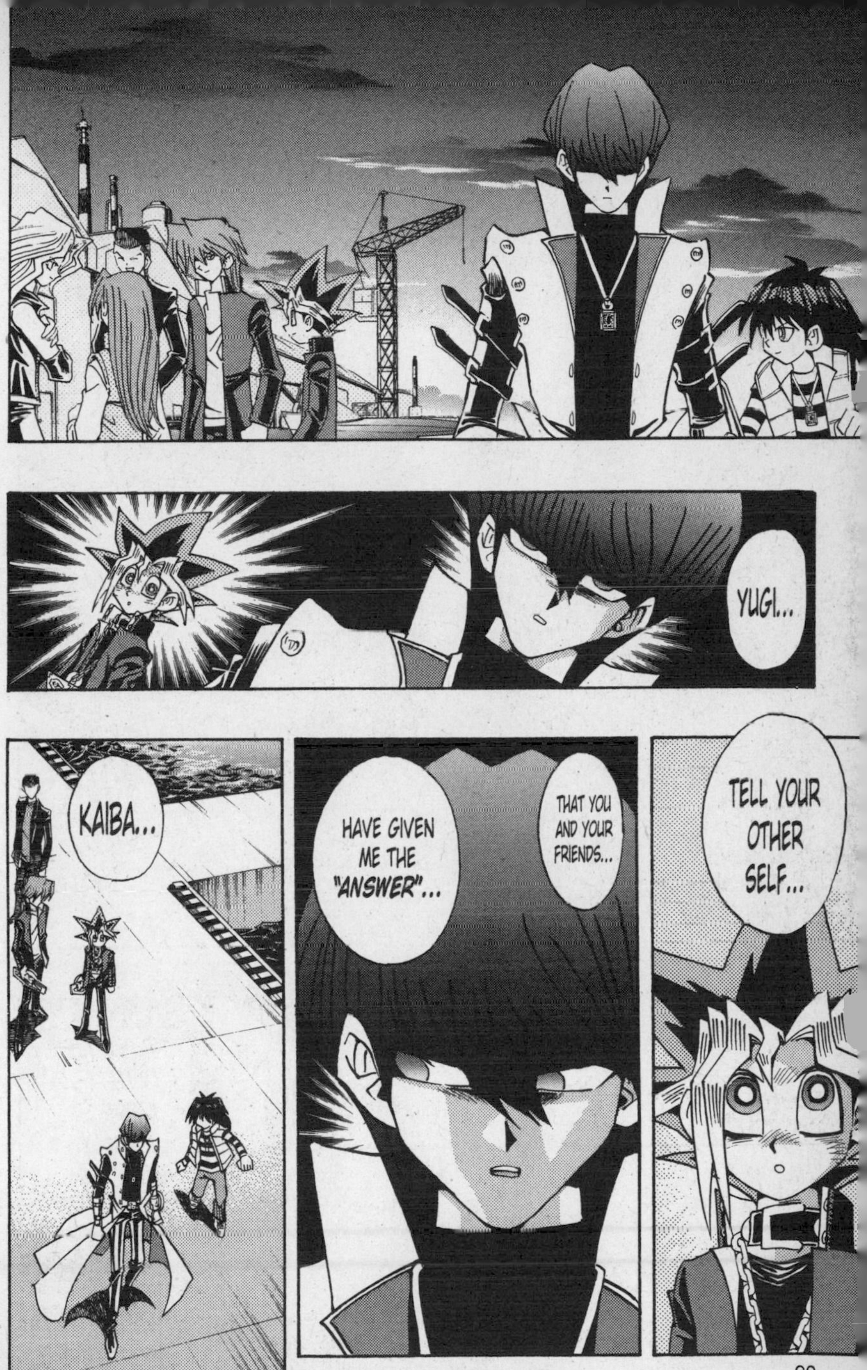
YUGI...
TELL YOUR OTHER SELF...
THAT YOU AND YOUR FRIENDS...
HAVE GIVEN ME THE "ANSWER"...
KAIBA...

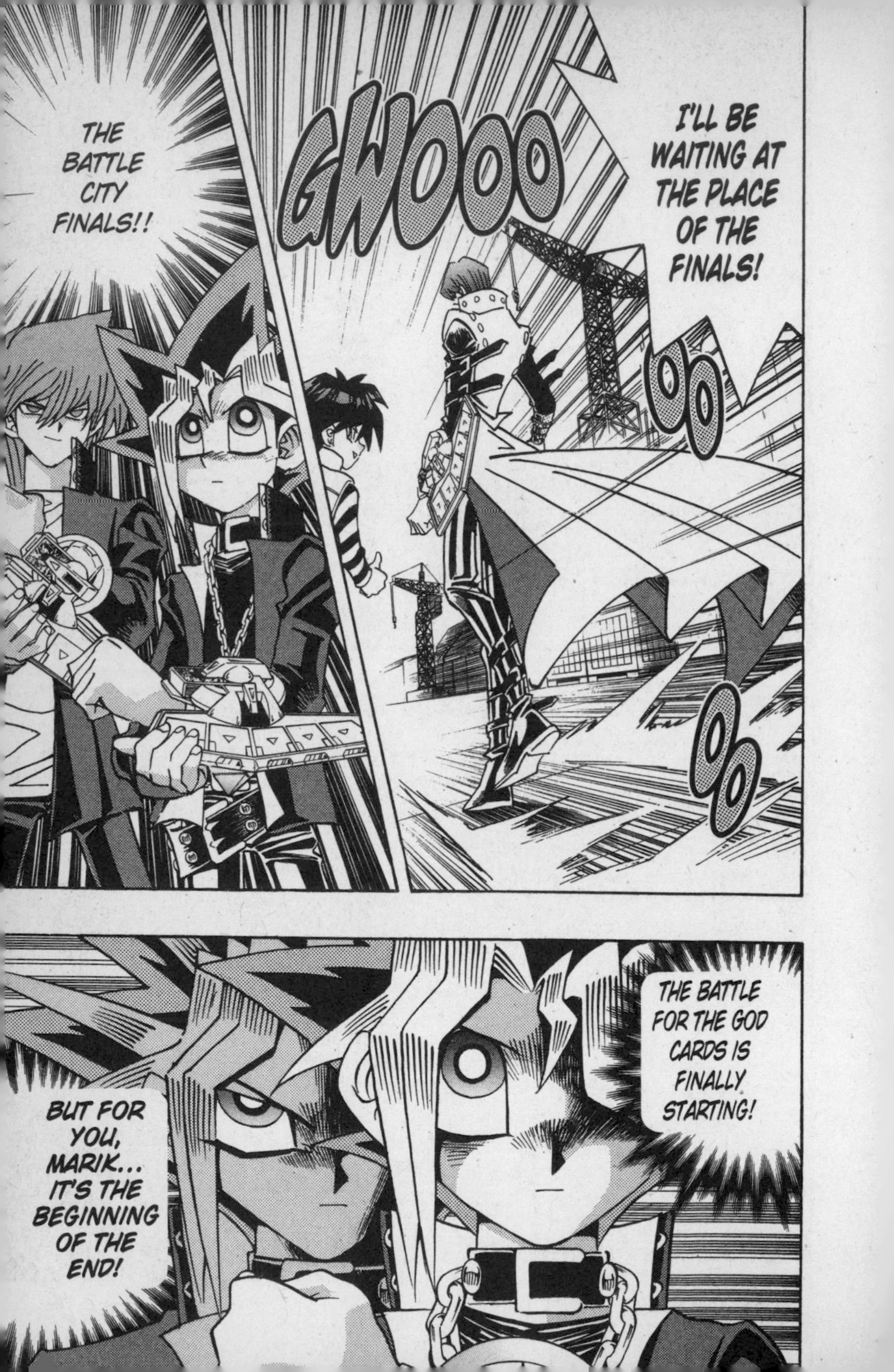
I'LL BE WAITING AT THE PLACE OF THE FINALS!
GWOOO
OO
OO
THE BATTLE CITY FINALS!!
THE BATTLE FOR THE GOD CARDS IS FINALLY STARTING!
BUT FOR YOU, MARIK... IT'S THE BEGINNING OF THE END!

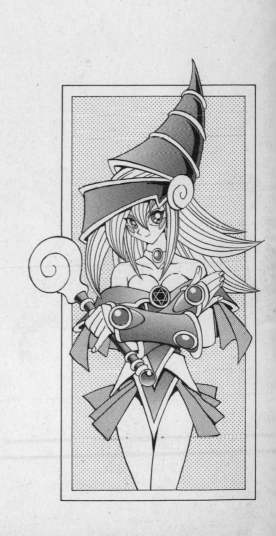

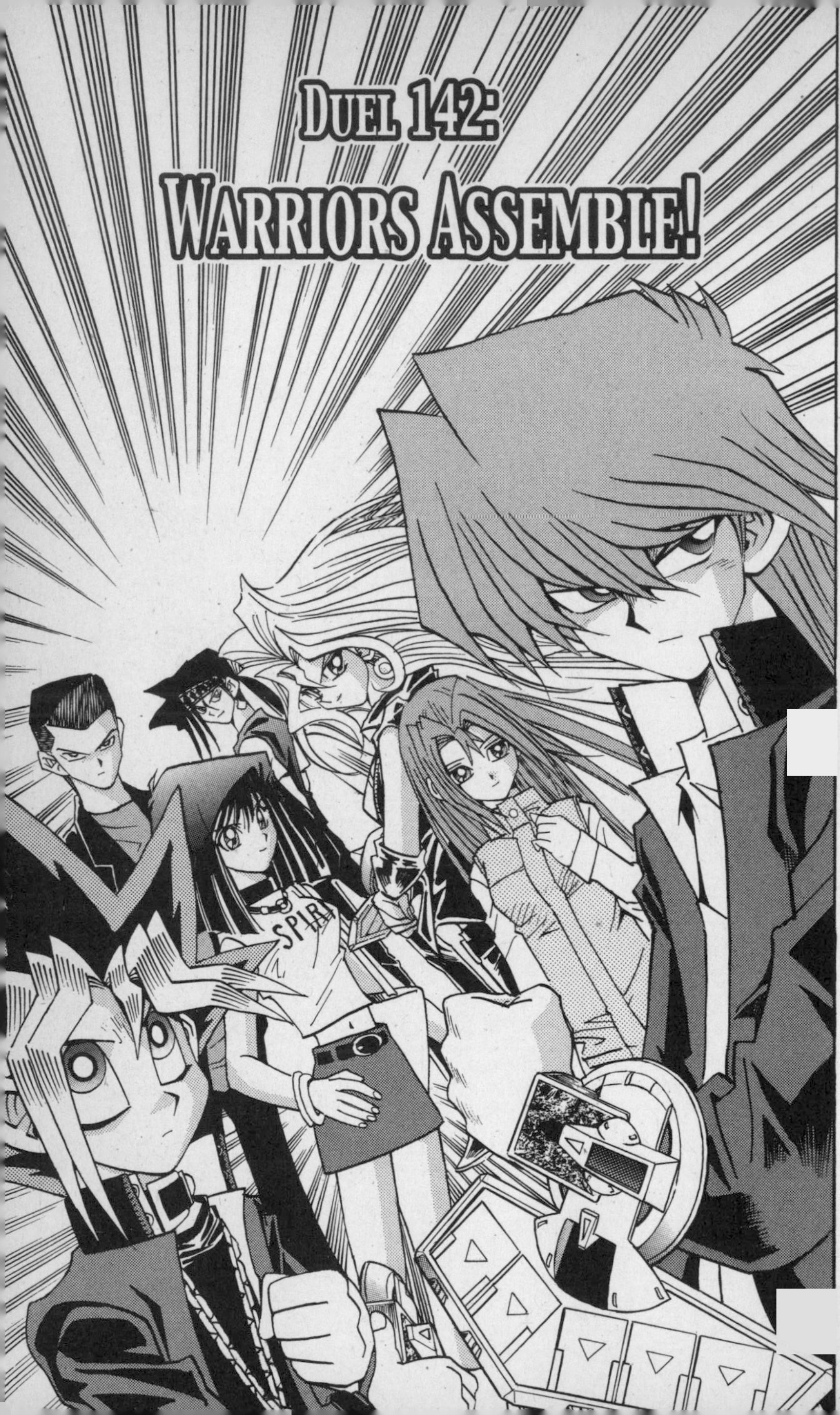
DUEL 142:
WARRIORS ASSEMBLE!
SPIR

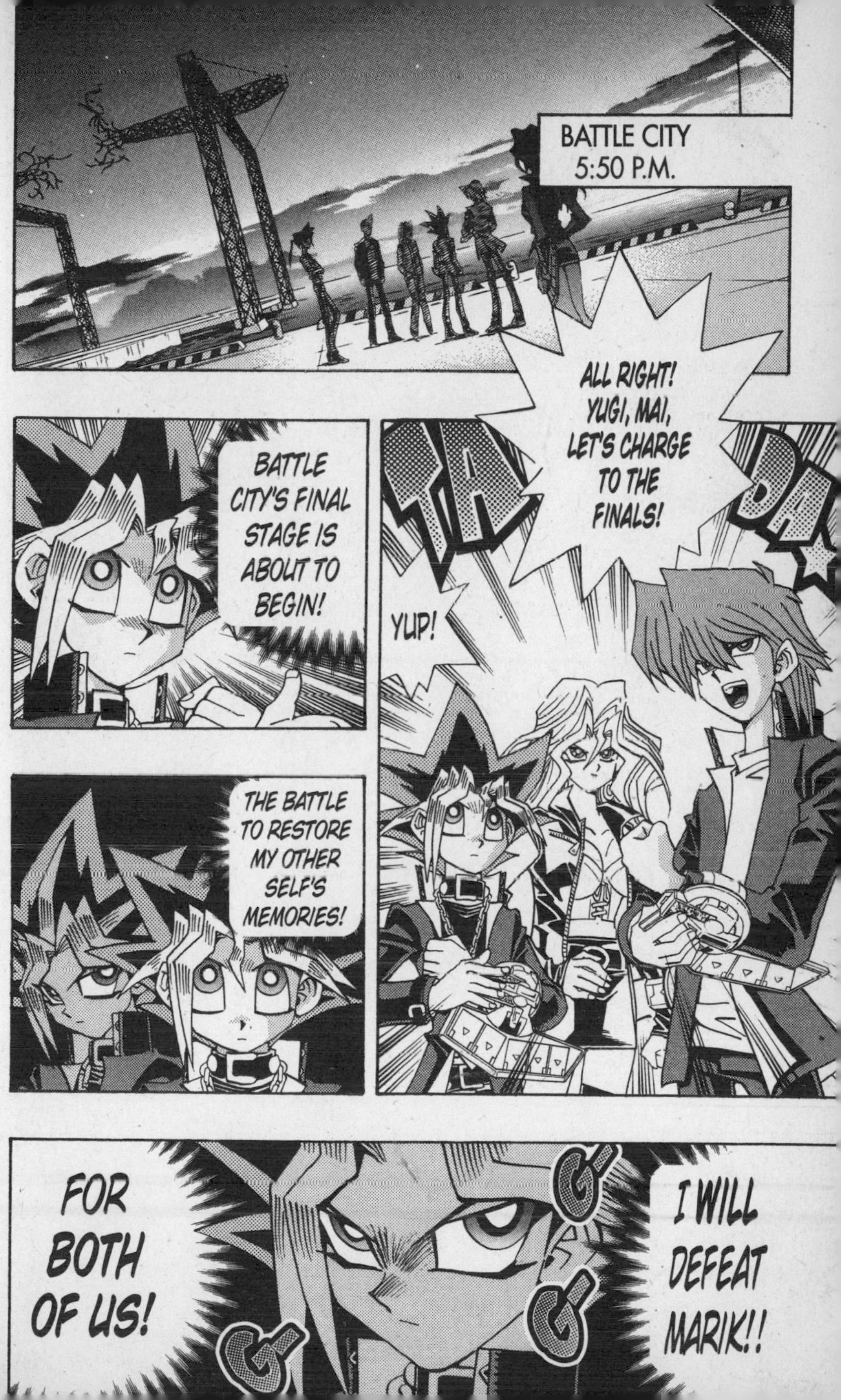
BATTLE CITY 5:50 P.M.
ALL RIGHT! YUGI, MAI, LET'S CHARGE TO THE FINALS!
TA
DA
YUP!
BATTLE CITY'S FINAL STAGE IS ABOUT TO BEGIN!
THE BATTLE TO RESTORE MY OTHER SELF'S MEMORIES!
I WILL DEFEAT MARIK!!
FOR BOTH OF US!

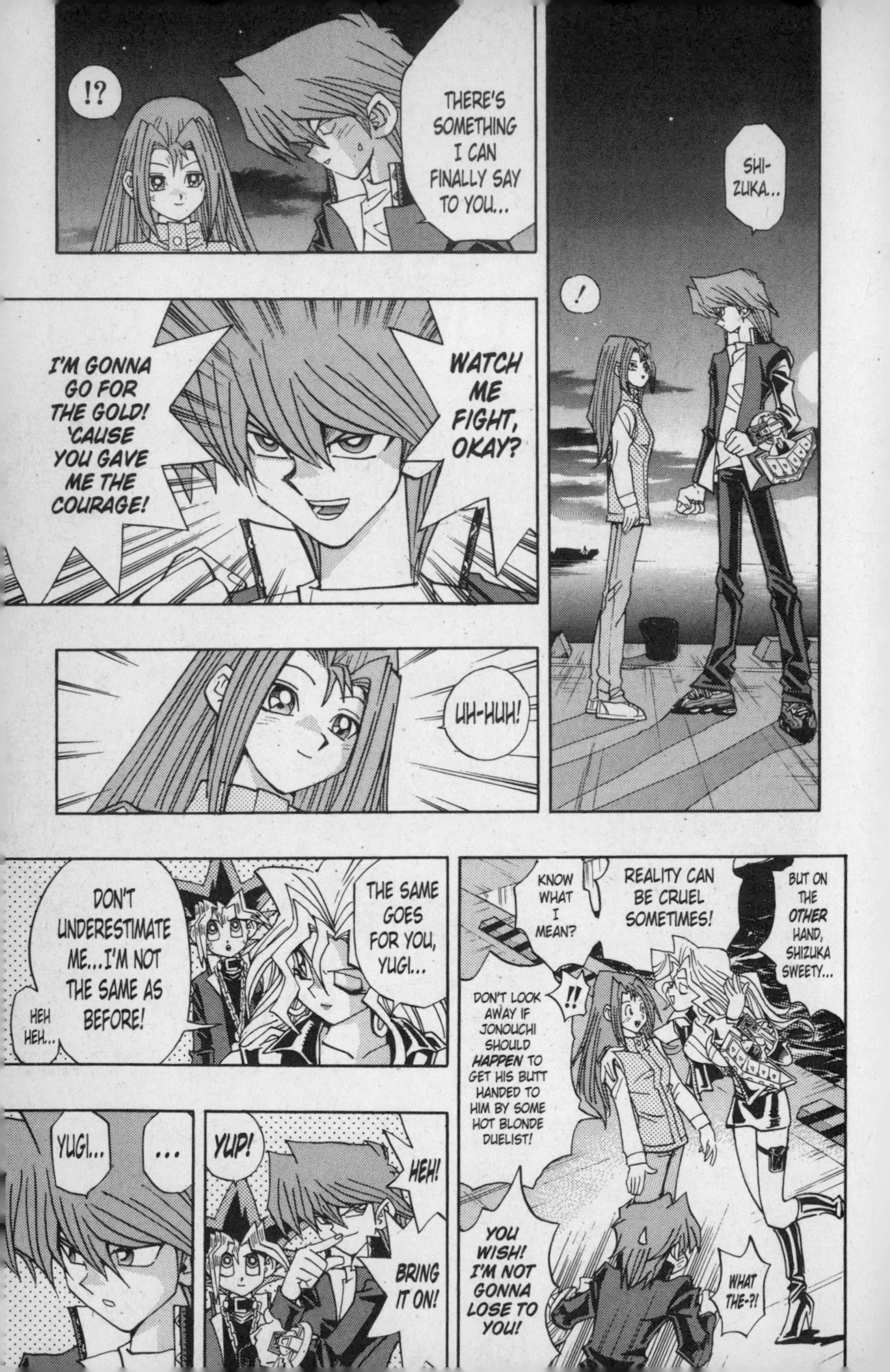

SHI-ZUKA...
!
THERE'S SOMETHING I CAN FINALLY SAY TO YOU...
!?
WATCH ME FIGHT, OKAY?
I'M GONNA GO FOR THE GOLD! 'CAUSE YOU GAVE ME THE COURAGE!
UH-HUH!
BUT ON THE OTHER HAND, SHIZUKA SWEETY...
REALITY CAN BE CRUEL SOMETIMES!
KNOW WHAT I MEAN?
!!
DON'T LOOK AWAY IF JONOUCHI SHOULD HAPPEN TO GET HIS BUTT HANDED TO HIM BY SOME HOT BLONDE DUELIST!
WHAT THE-?!
YOU WISH! I'M NOT GONNA LOSE TO YOU!
THE SAME GOES FOR YOU, YUGI...
DON'T UNDERESTIMATE ME...I'M NOT THE SAME AS BEFORE!
HEH HEH...
YUP!
HEH!
BRING IT ON!
...
YUGI...

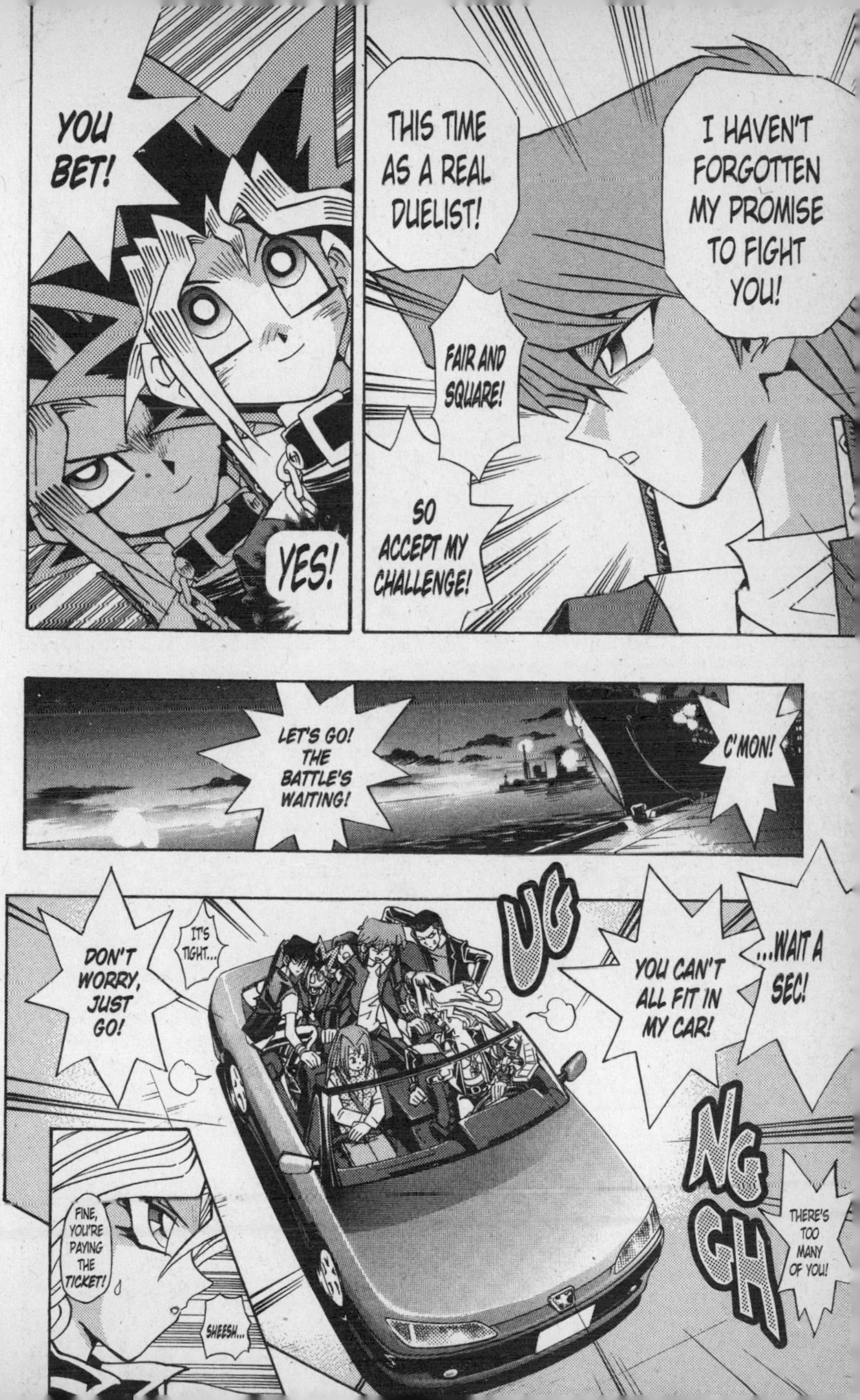
I HAVEN'T FORGOTTEN MY PROMISE TO FIGHT YOU!
THIS TIME AS A REAL DUELIST!
FAIR AND SQUARE!
SO ACCEPT MY CHALLENGE!
YOU BET!
YES!
C'MON!
LET'S GO! THE BATTLE'S WAITING!
...WAIT A SEC!
YOU CAN'T ALL FIT IN MY CAR!
UG
NG GH
THERE'S TOO MANY OF YOU!
IT'S TIGHT...
DON'T WORRY, JUST GO!
FINE, YOU'RE PAYING THE TICKET!
SHEESH...

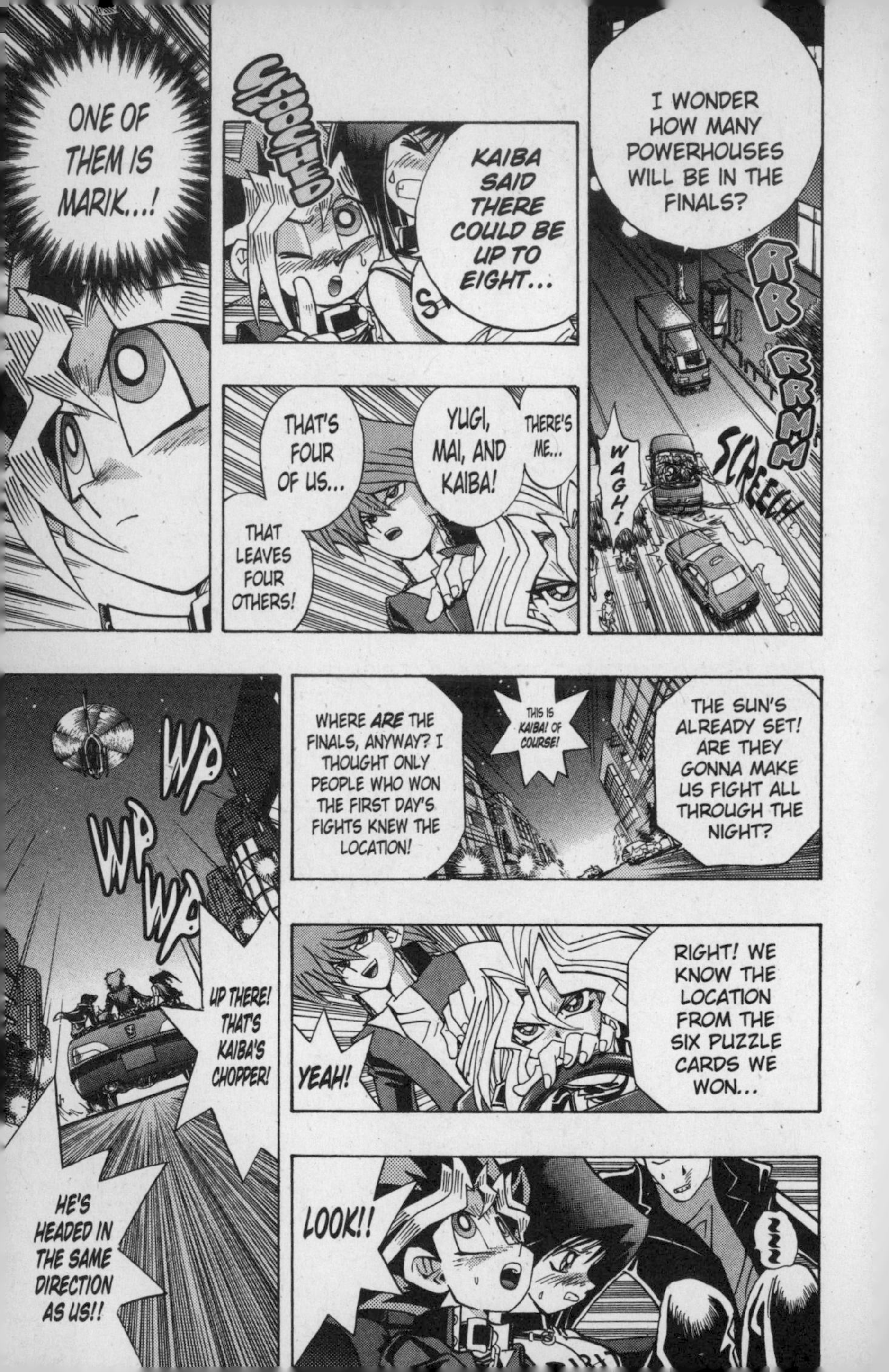
I WONDER HOW MANY POWERHOUSES WILL BE IN THE FINALS?
RR RRMM
SCREECH
WAGH!
SHOCKED
KAIBA SAID THERE COULD BE UP TO EIGHT...
THERE'S ME...
YUGI, MAI, AND KAIBA!
THAT'S FOUR OF US...
THAT LEAVES FOUR OTHERS!
ONE OF THEM IS MARIK...!
THE SUN'S ALREADY SET! ARE THEY GONNA MAKE US FIGHT ALL THROUGH THE NIGHT?
THIS IS KAIBA! OF COURSE!
WHERE *ARE* THE FINALS, ANYWAY? I THOUGHT ONLY PEOPLE WHO WON THE FIRST DAY'S FIGHTS KNEW THE LOCATION!
RIGHT! WE KNOW THE LOCATION FROM THE SIX PUZZLE CARDS WE WON...
YEAH!
LOOK!!
WP WP WP WP
UP THERE! THAT'S KAIBA'S CHOPPER!
HE'S HEADED IN THE SAME DIRECTION AS US!!

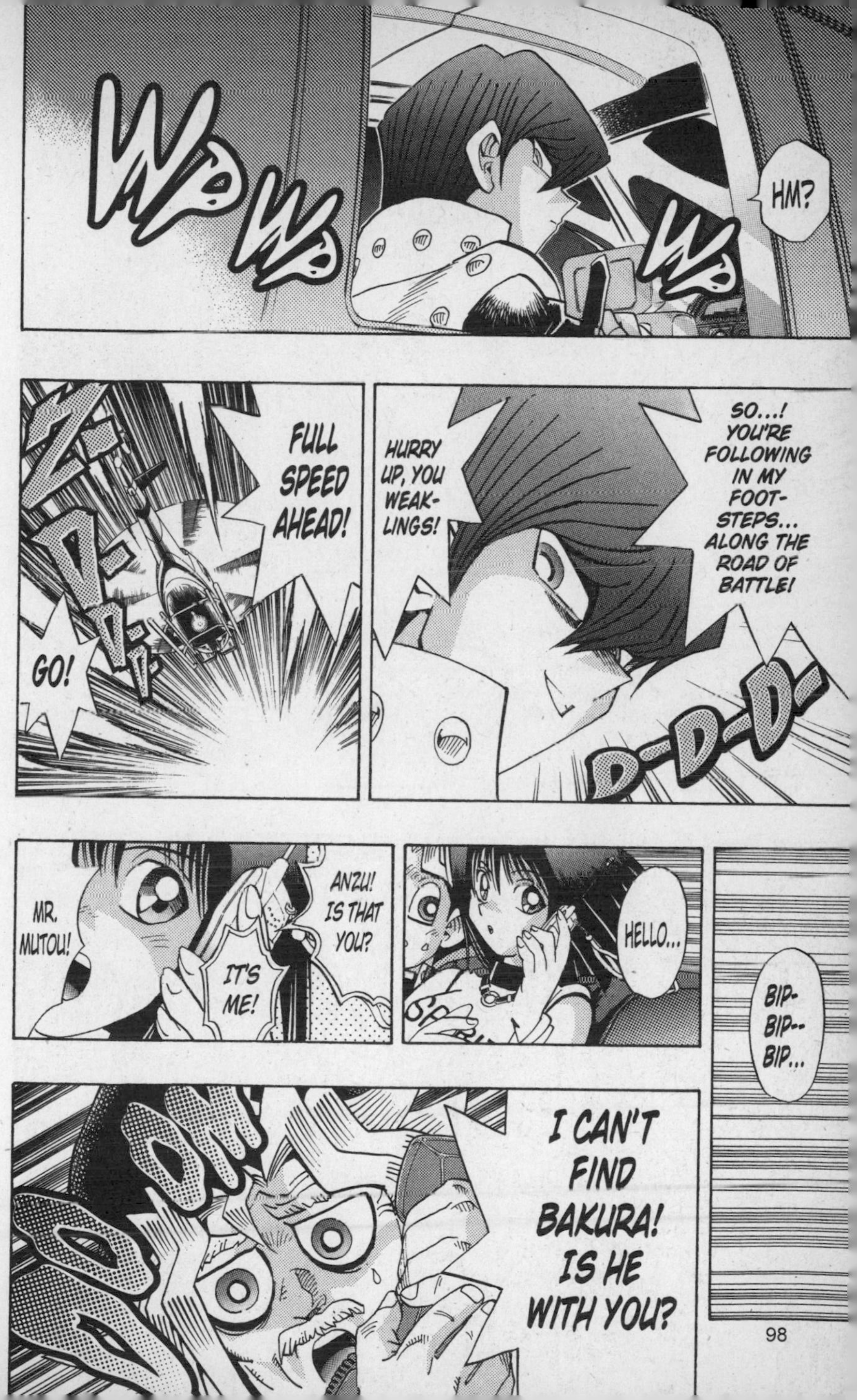
HM?
WP
WP WP
SO...! YOU'RE FOLLOWING IN MY FOOT-STEPS... ALONG THE ROAD OF BATTLE!
HURRY UP, YOU WEAK-LINGS!
D-D-D-D-
FULL SPEED AHEAD!
GO!
BIP-BIP--BIP...
HELLO...
ANZU! IS THAT YOU?
IT'S ME!
MR. MUTOU!
I CAN'T FIND BAKURA! IS HE WITH YOU?

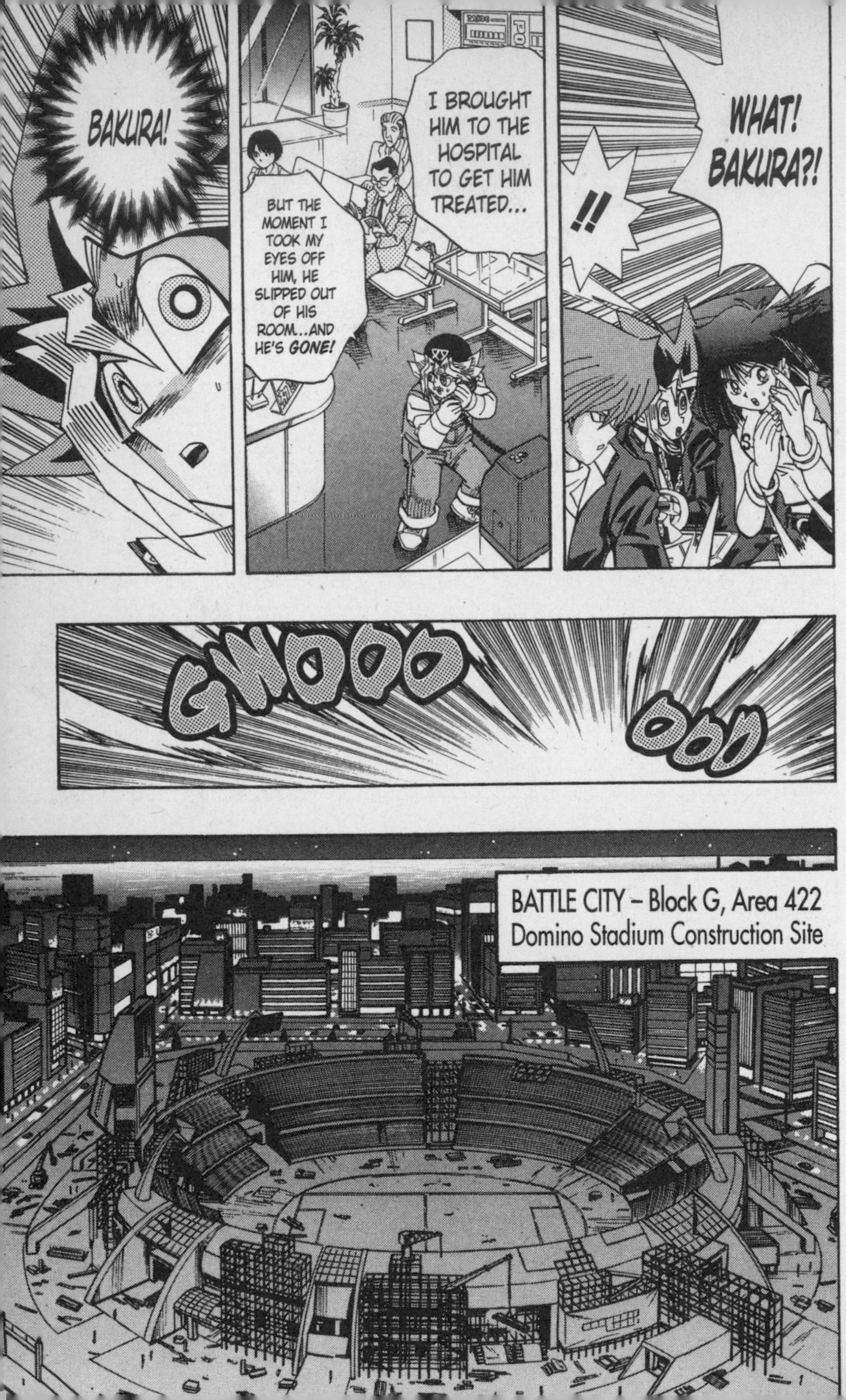
WHAT! BAKURA?!
!!
I BROUGHT HIM TO THE HOSPITAL TO GET HIM TREATED...
BUT THE MOMENT I TOOK MY EYES OFF HIM, HE SLIPPED OUT OF HIS ROOM...AND HE'S GONE!
BAKURA!
GWOOO
OOO
BATTLE CITY – Block G, Area 422
Domino Stadium Construction Site

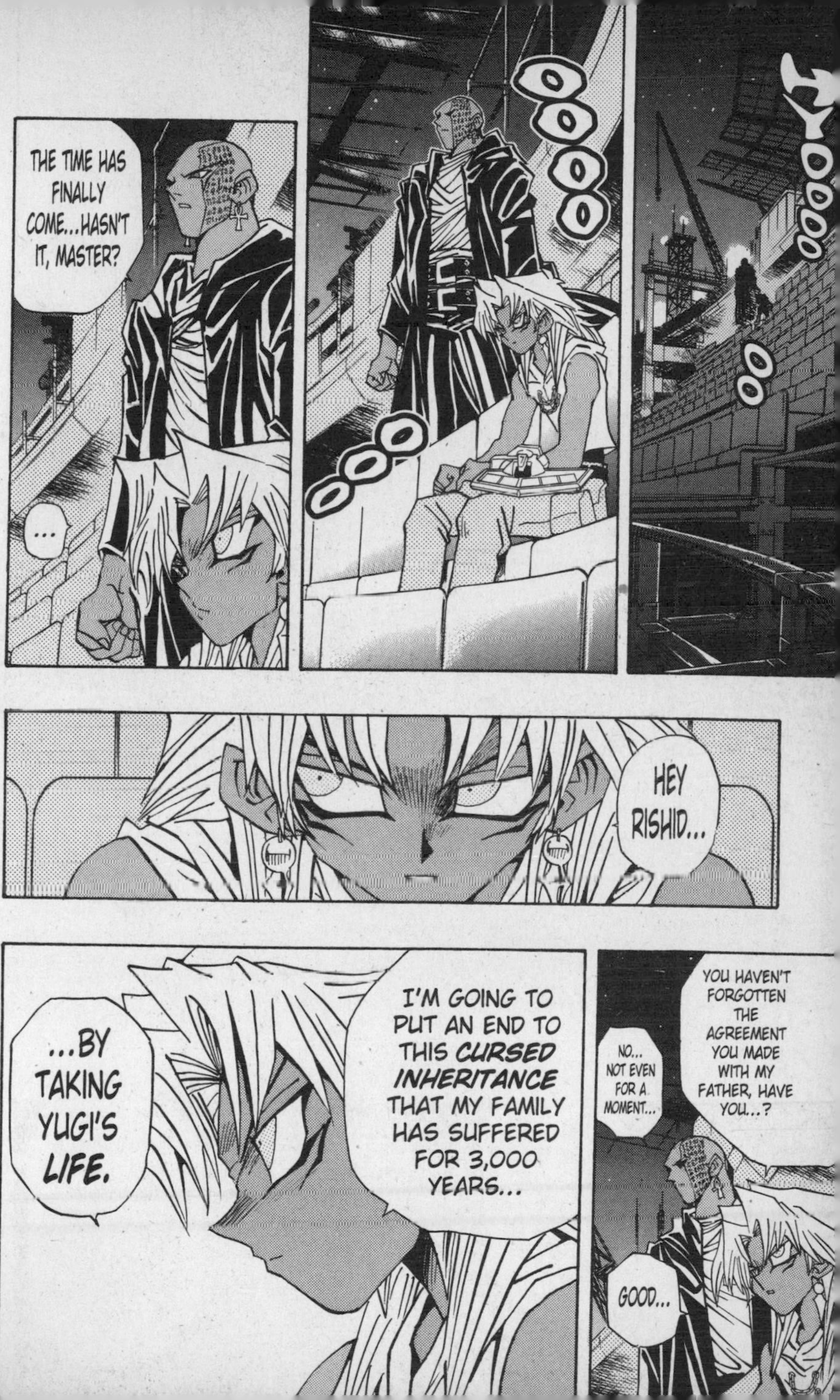
THE TIME HAS FINALLY COME...HASN'T IT, MASTER?
...
HEY RISHID...
YOU HAVEN'T FORGOTTEN THE AGREEMENT YOU MADE WITH MY FATHER, HAVE YOU...?
NO... NOT EVEN FOR A MOMENT...
GOOD...
I'M GOING TO PUT AN END TO THIS *CURSED INHERITANCE* THAT MY FAMILY HAS SUFFERED FOR 3,000 YEARS...
...BY TAKING YUGI'S *LIFE.*

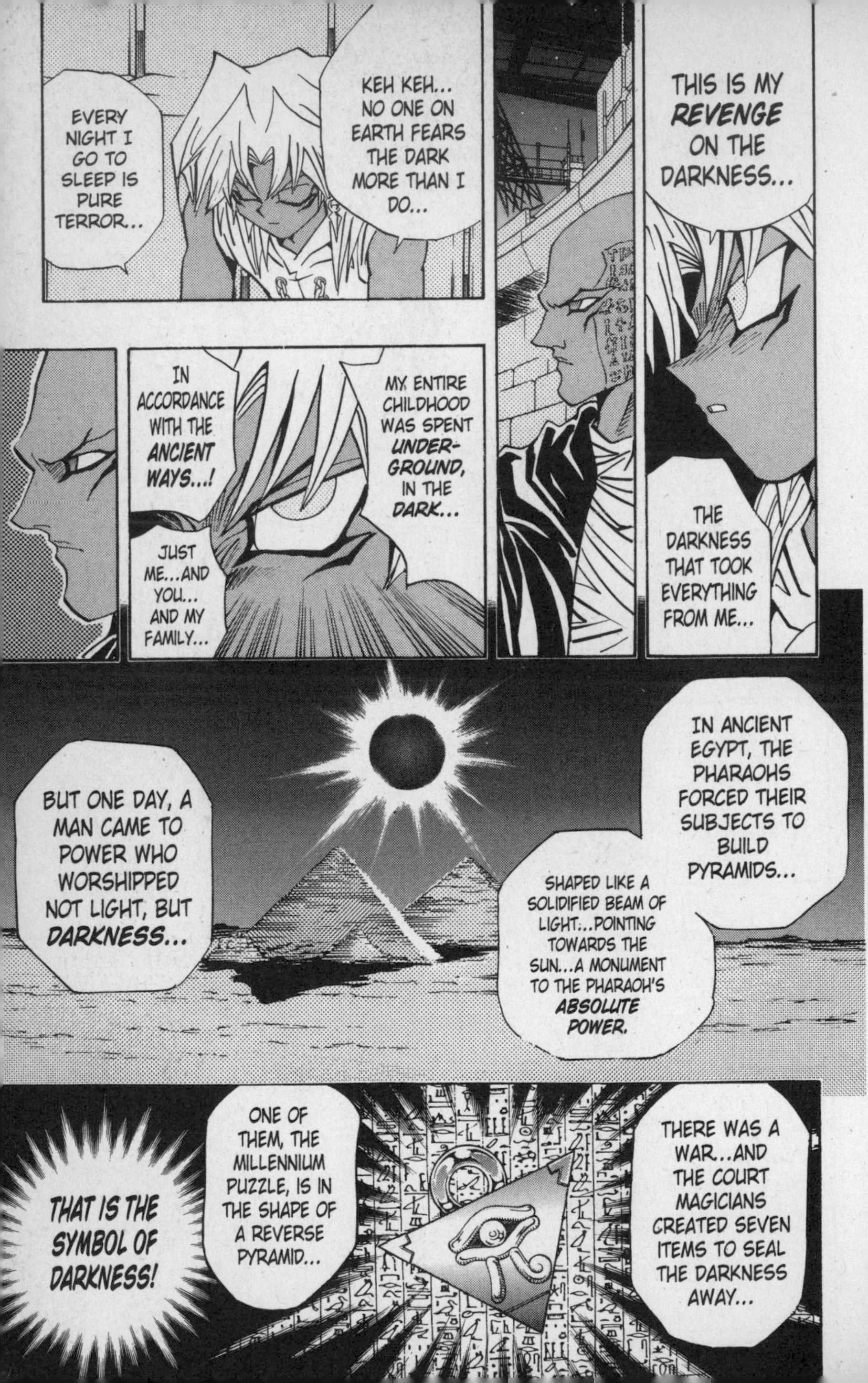
THIS IS MY REVENGE ON THE DARKNESS...
THE DARKNESS THAT TOOK EVERYTHING FROM ME...
KEH KEH... NO ONE ON EARTH FEARS THE DARK MORE THAN I DO...
EVERY NIGHT I GO TO SLEEP IS PURE TERROR...
MY ENTIRE CHILDHOOD WAS SPENT UNDERGROUND, IN THE DARK...
IN ACCORDANCE WITH THE ANCIENT WAYS...!
JUST ME...AND YOU... AND MY FAMILY...
IN ANCIENT EGYPT, THE PHARAOHS FORCED THEIR SUBJECTS TO BUILD PYRAMIDS...
SHAPED LIKE A SOLIDIFIED BEAM OF LIGHT...POINTING TOWARDS THE SUN...A MONUMENT TO THE PHARAOH'S ABSOLUTE POWER.
BUT ONE DAY, A MAN CAME TO POWER WHO WORSHIPPED NOT LIGHT, BUT DARKNESS...
THERE WAS A WAR...AND THE COURT MAGICIANS CREATED SEVEN ITEMS TO SEAL THE DARKNESS AWAY...
ONE OF THEM, THE MILLENNIUM PUZZLE, IS IN THE SHAPE OF A REVERSE PYRAMID...
THAT IS THE SYMBOL OF DARKNESS!

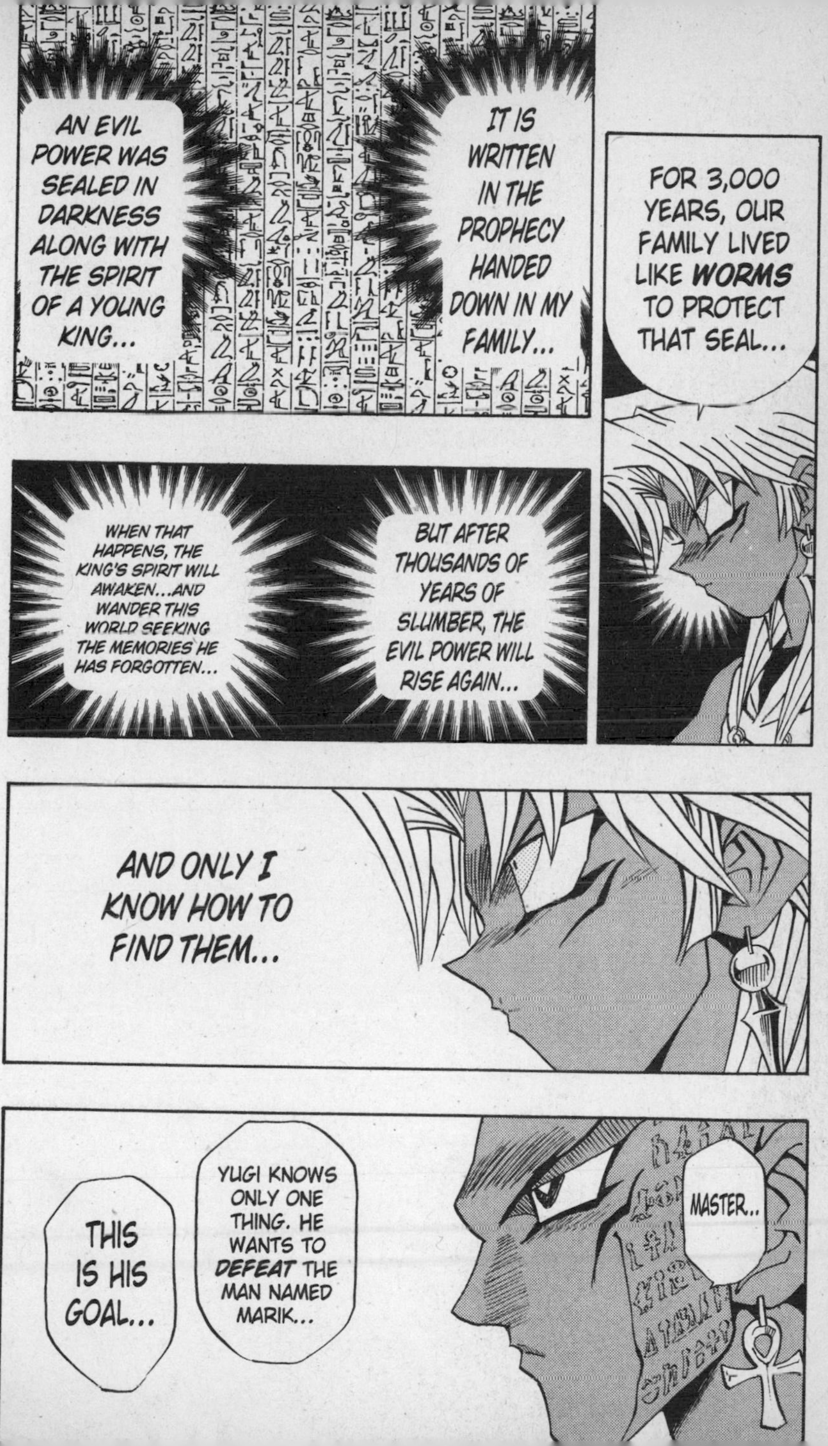

FOR 3,000 YEARS, OUR FAMILY LIVED LIKE **WORMS** TO PROTECT THAT SEAL...
IT IS WRITTEN IN THE PROPHECY HANDED DOWN IN MY FAMILY...
AN EVIL POWER WAS SEALED IN DARKNESS ALONG WITH THE SPIRIT OF A YOUNG KING...
BUT AFTER THOUSANDS OF YEARS OF SLUMBER, THE EVIL POWER WILL RISE AGAIN...
WHEN THAT HAPPENS, THE KING'S SPIRIT WILL AWAKEN...AND WANDER THIS WORLD SEEKING THE MEMORIES HE HAS FORGOTTEN...
AND ONLY I KNOW HOW TO FIND THEM...
MASTER...
YUGI KNOWS ONLY ONE THING. HE WANTS TO **DEFEAT** THE MAN NAMED MARIK...
THIS IS HIS GOAL...

READ THIS WAY

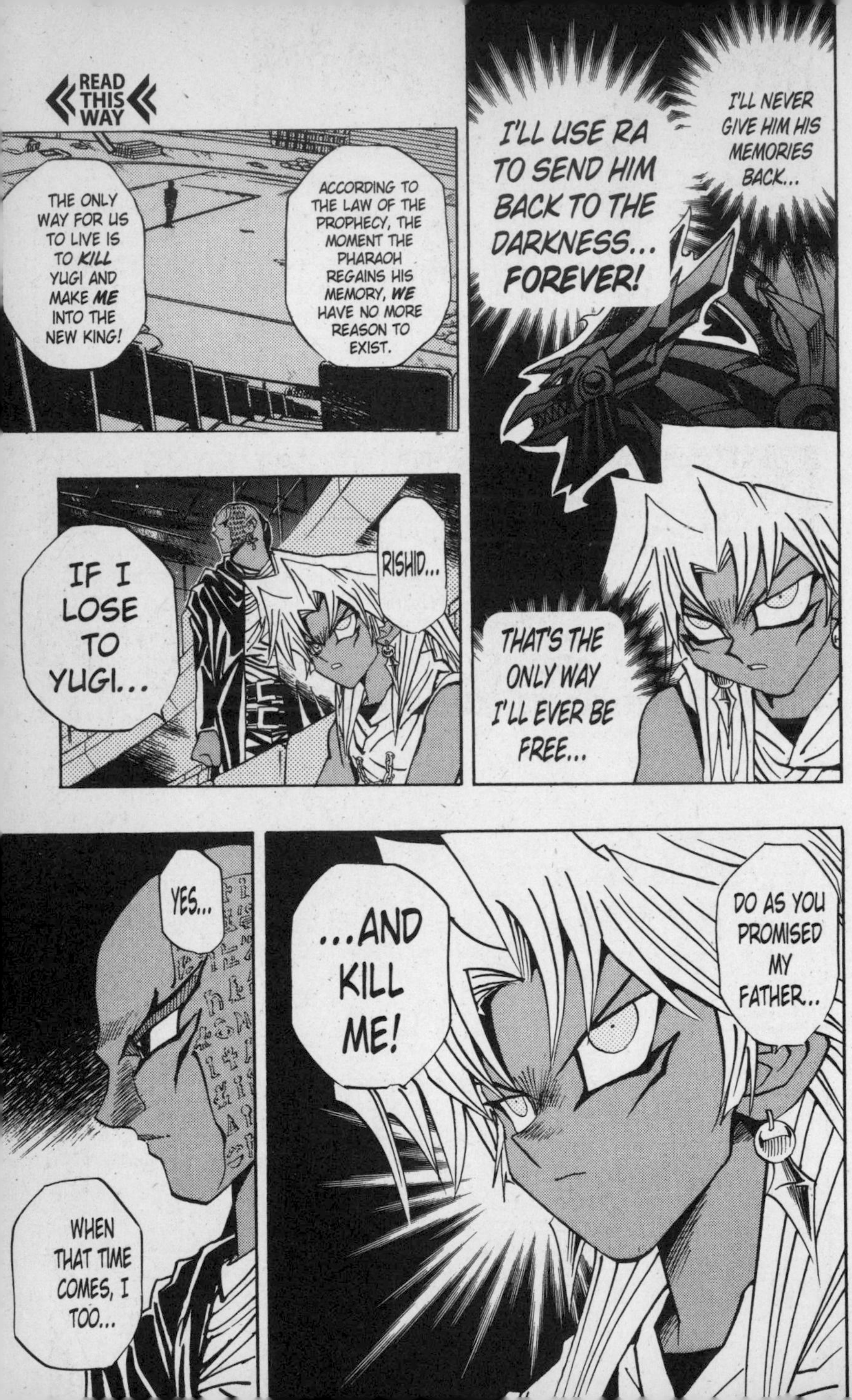

I'LL NEVER GIVE HIM HIS MEMORIES BACK...
I'LL USE RA TO SEND HIM BACK TO THE DARKNESS... FOREVER!
ACCORDING TO THE LAW OF THE PROPHECY, THE MOMENT THE PHARAOH REGAINS HIS MEMORY, WE HAVE NO MORE REASON TO EXIST.
THE ONLY WAY FOR US TO LIVE IS TO KILL YUGI AND MAKE ME INTO THE NEW KING!
THAT'S THE ONLY WAY I'LL EVER BE FREE...
RISHID...
IF I LOSE TO YUGI...
DO AS YOU PROMISED MY FATHER...
...AND KILL ME!
YES...
WHEN THAT TIME COMES, I TOO...

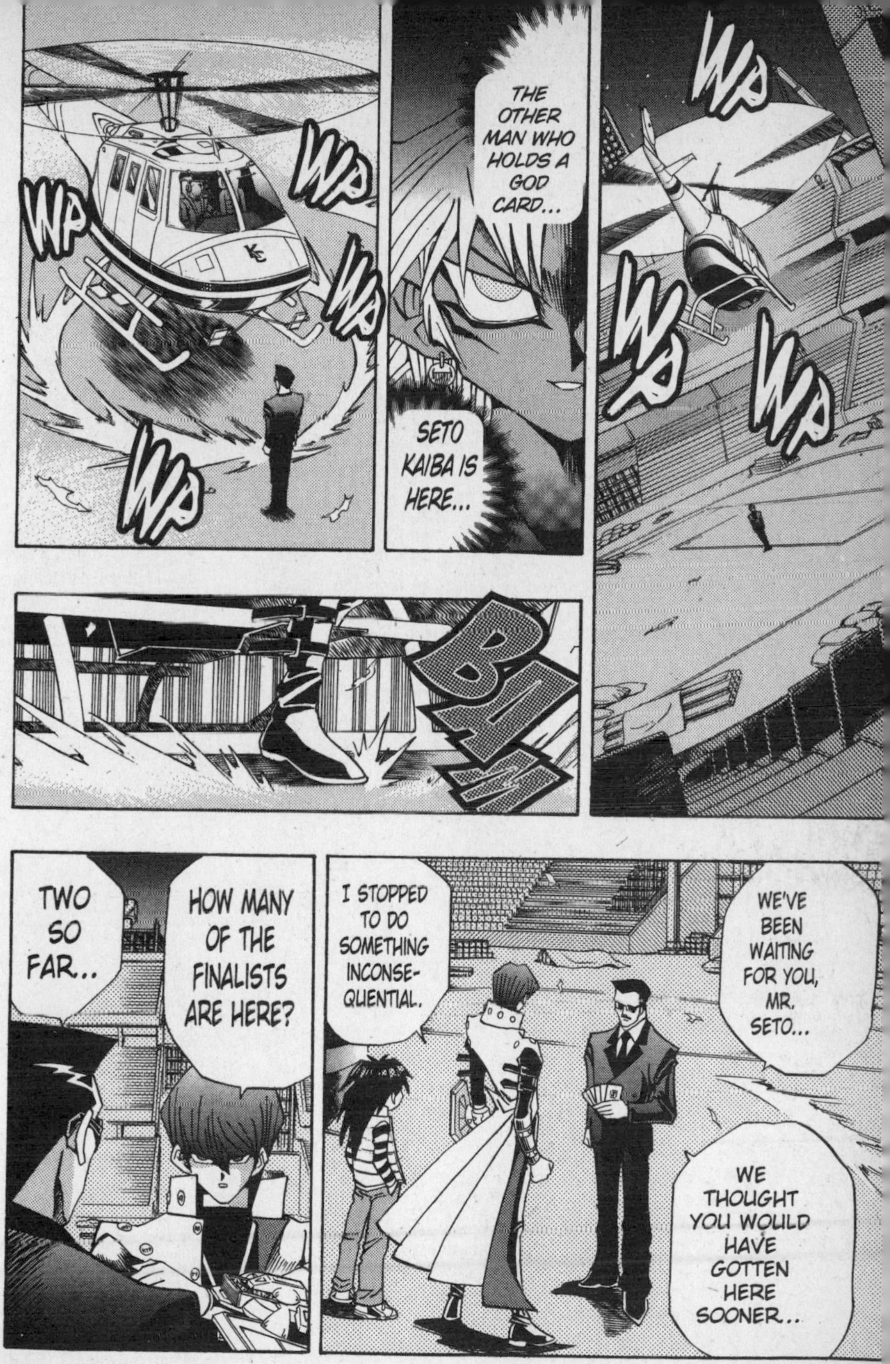
WP
WP
WP
WP
THE OTHER MAN WHO HOLDS A GOD CARD...
SETO KAIBA IS HERE...
WP
WP
WP
WP
BAM
WE'VE BEEN WAITING FOR YOU, MR. SETO...
WE THOUGHT YOU WOULD HAVE GOTTEN HERE SOONER...
I STOPPED TO DO SOMETHING INCONSE-QUENTIAL.
HOW MANY OF THE FINALISTS ARE HERE?
TWO SO FAR...

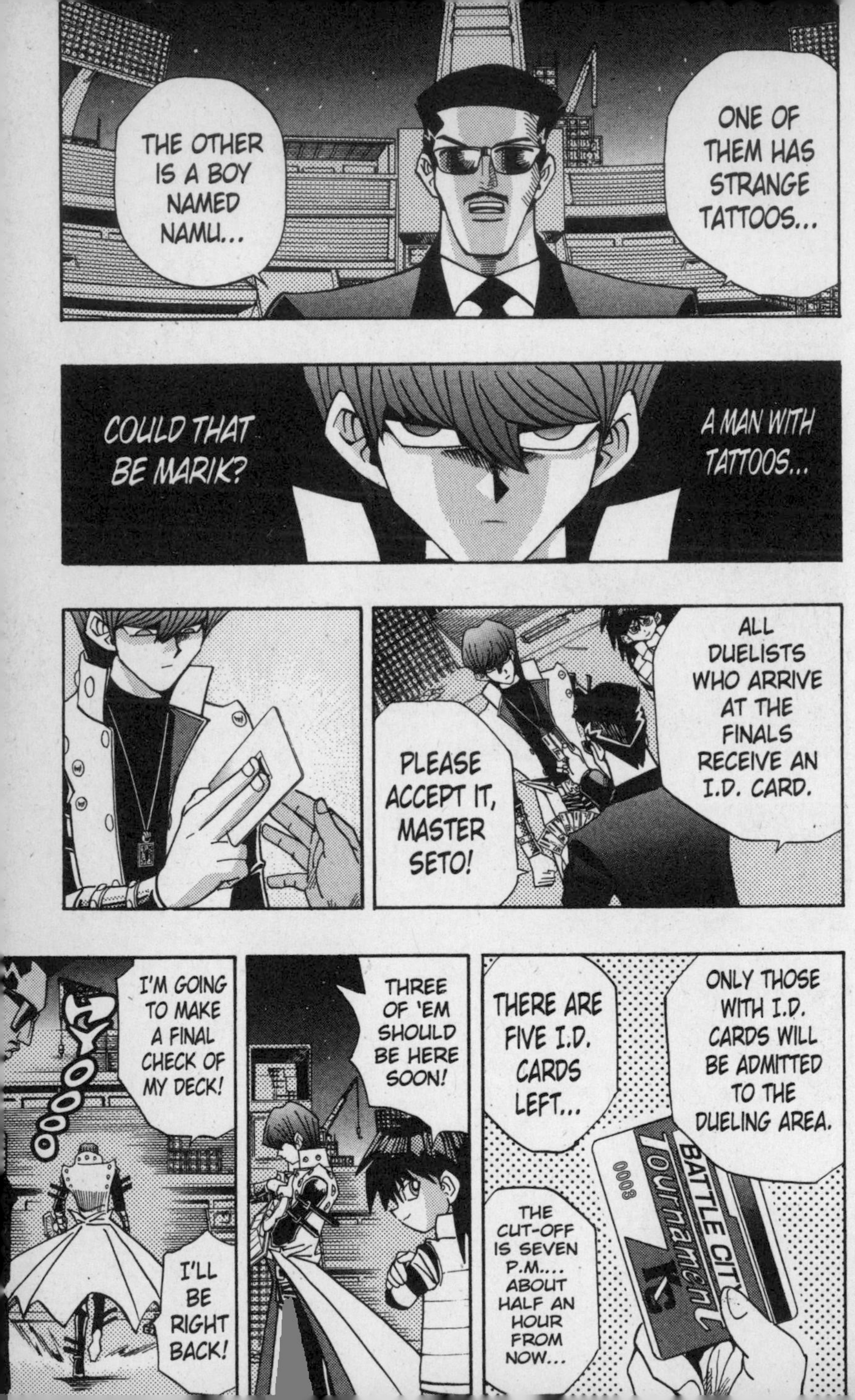
ONE OF THEM HAS STRANGE TATTOOS...
THE OTHER IS A BOY NAMED NAMU...
A MAN WITH TATTOOS...
COULD THAT BE MARIK?
ALL DUELISTS WHO ARRIVE AT THE FINALS RECEIVE AN I.D. CARD.
PLEASE ACCEPT IT, MASTER SETO!
ONLY THOSE WITH I.D. CARDS WILL BE ADMITTED TO THE DUELING AREA.
THERE ARE FIVE I.D. CARDS LEFT...
THE CUT-OFF IS SEVEN P.M.... ABOUT HALF AN HOUR FROM NOW...
BATTLE CITY
Tournament
0003
KC
THREE OF 'EM SHOULD BE HERE SOON!
I'M GOING TO MAKE A FINAL CHECK OF MY DECK!
I'LL BE RIGHT BACK!

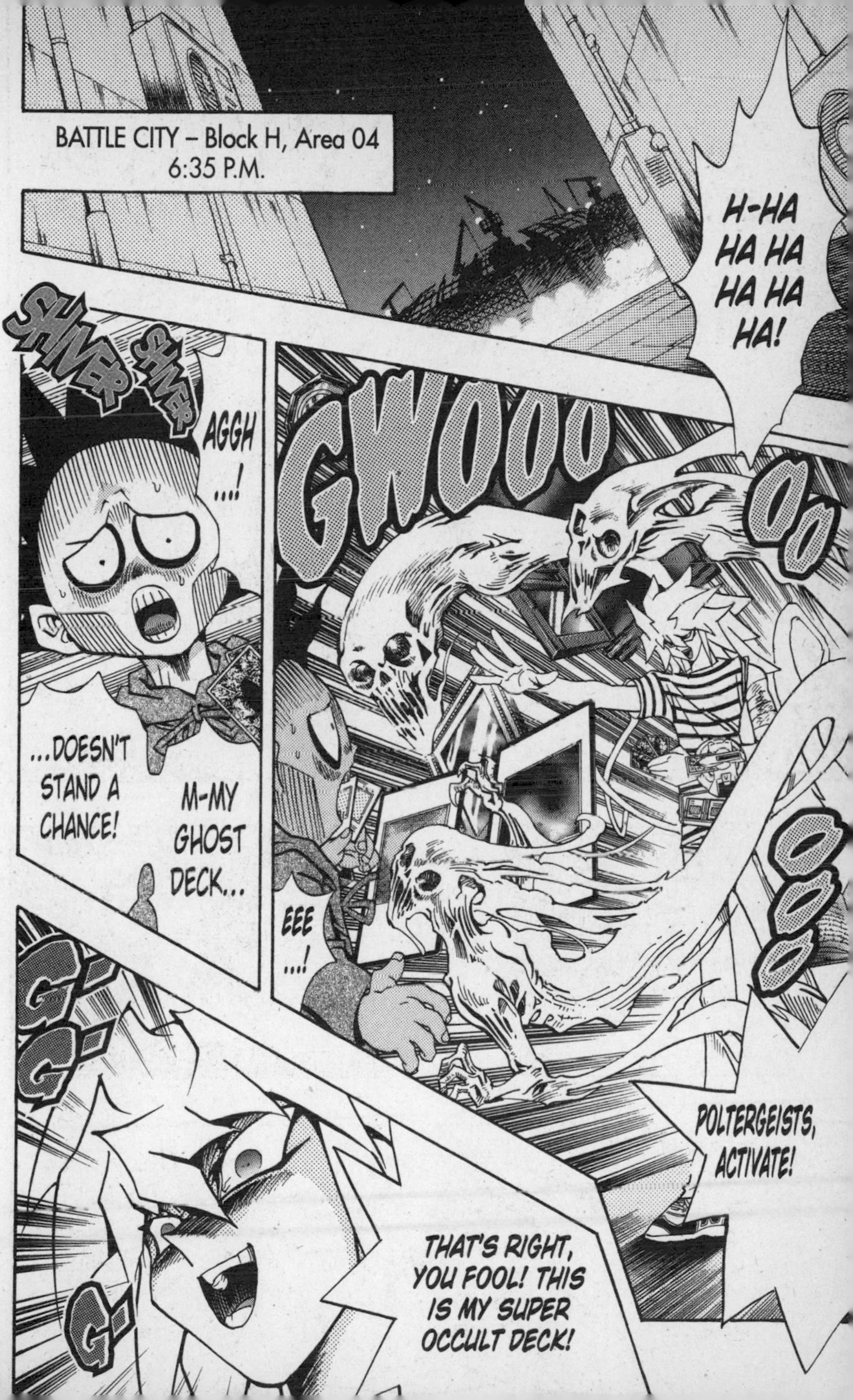
BATTLE CITY – Block H, Area 04
6:35 P.M.
H-HA HA HA HA HA HA HA!
GWOOOOOOOOOO
EEE ...!
POLTERGEISTS, ACTIVATE!
SHIVER SHIVER
AGGH ...!
M-MY GHOST DECK...
...DOESN'T STAND A CHANCE!
G G G G
THAT'S RIGHT, YOU FOOL! THIS IS MY SUPER OCCULT DECK!

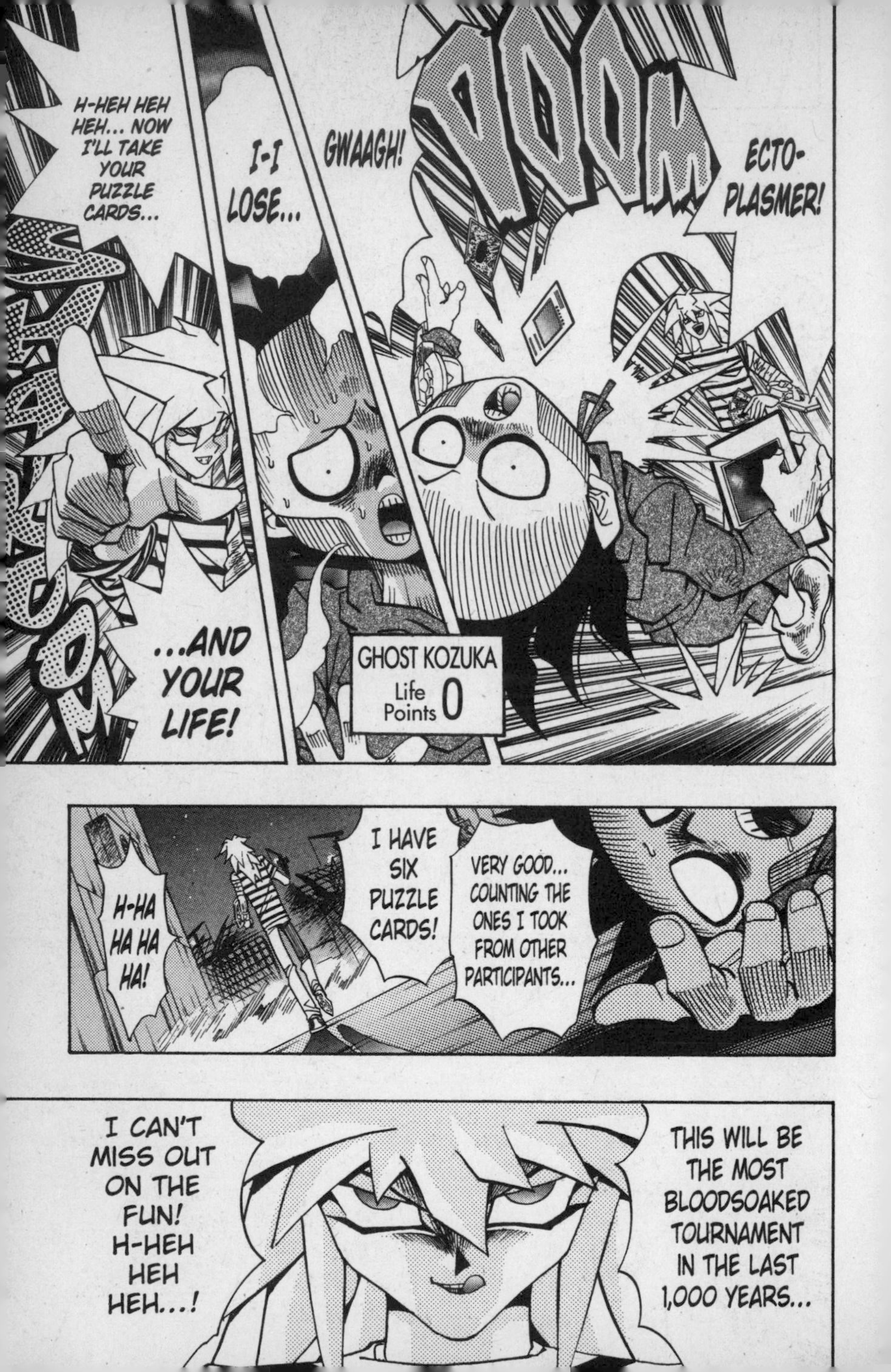
DOOM
ECTO-PLASMER!
GHOST KOZUKA
Life Points 0
GWAAGH!
I-I LOSE...
H-HEH HEH HEH... NOW I'LL TAKE YOUR PUZZLE CARDS...
...AND YOUR LIFE!
VERY GOOD... COUNTING THE ONES I TOOK FROM OTHER PARTICIPANTS...
I HAVE SIX PUZZLE CARDS!
H-HA HA HA HA!
THIS WILL BE THE MOST BLOODSOAKED TOURNAMENT IN THE LAST 1,000 YEARS...
I CAN'T MISS OUT ON THE FUN! H-HEH HEH HEH...!

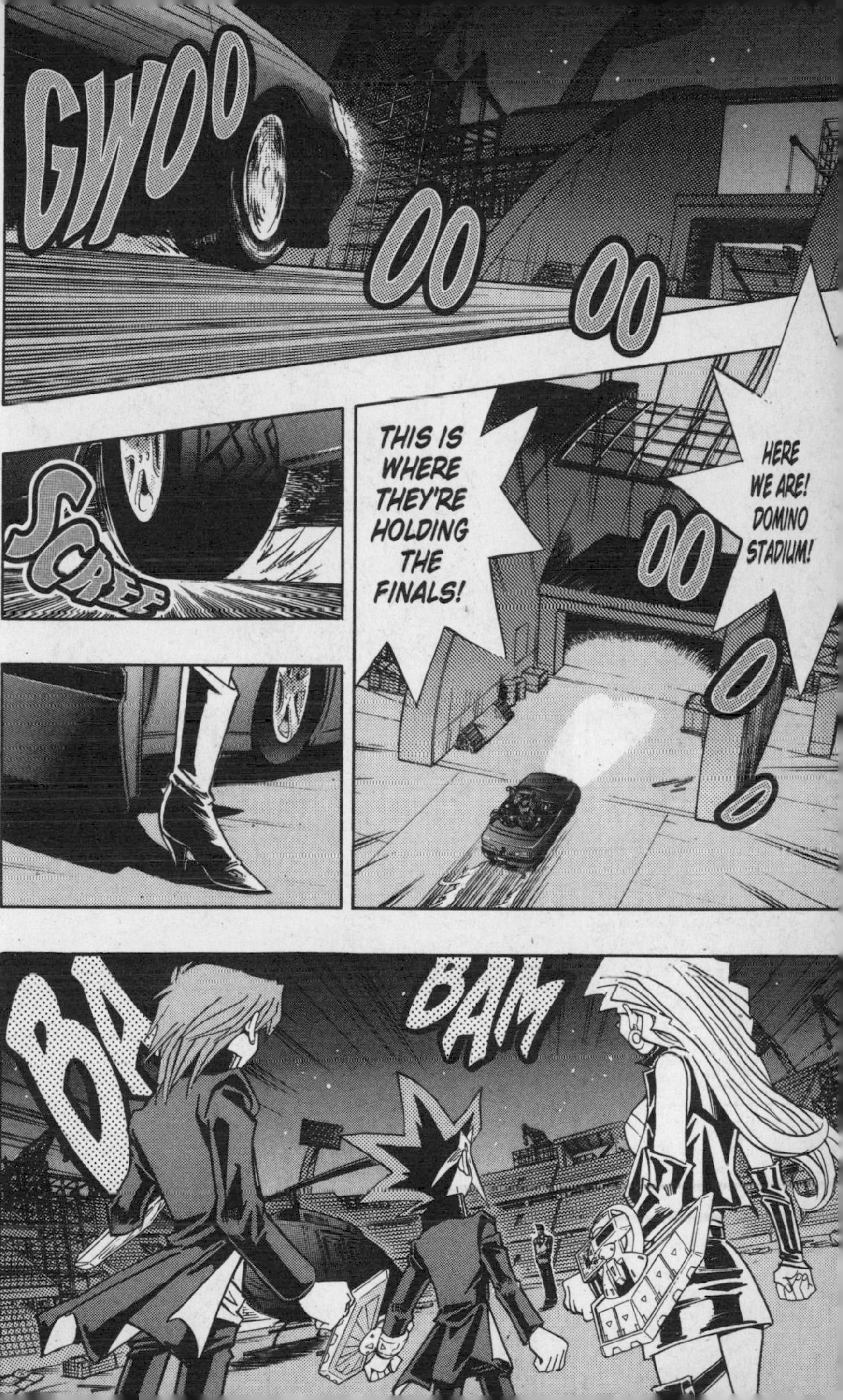
GWOO
OO
OO
HERE WE ARE! DOMINO STADIUM!
THIS IS WHERE THEY'RE HOLDING THE FINALS!
OO
O
O
SCREE
BAM
BA

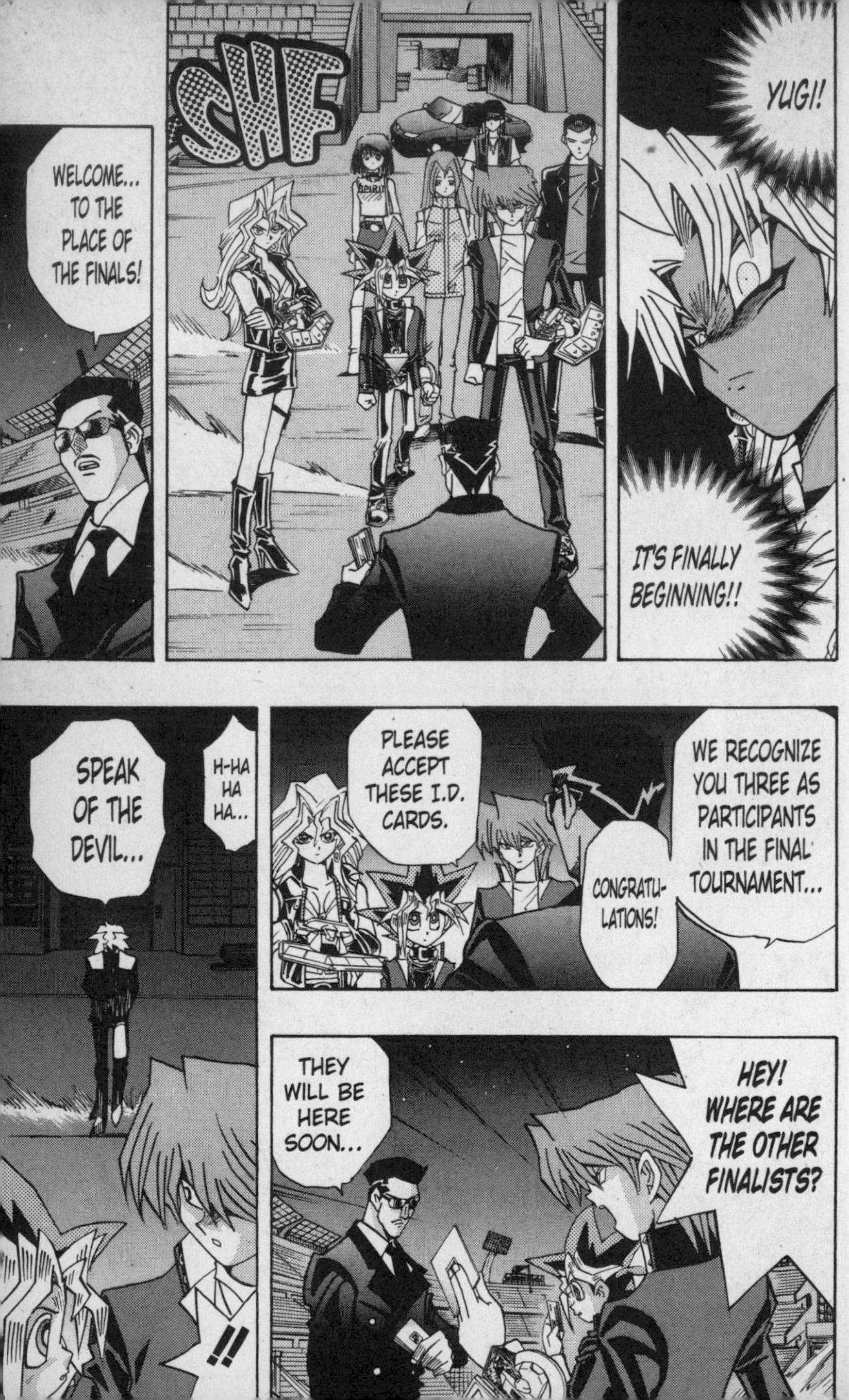
YUGI!
IT'S FINALLY BEGINNING!!
SHF
WELCOME... TO THE PLACE OF THE FINALS!
WE RECOGNIZE YOU THREE AS PARTICIPANTS IN THE FINAL TOURNAMENT...
CONGRATULATIONS!
PLEASE ACCEPT THESE I.D. CARDS.
HEY! WHERE ARE THE OTHER FINALISTS?
THEY WILL BE HERE SOON...
H-HA HA HA...
SPEAK OF THE DEVIL...
!!

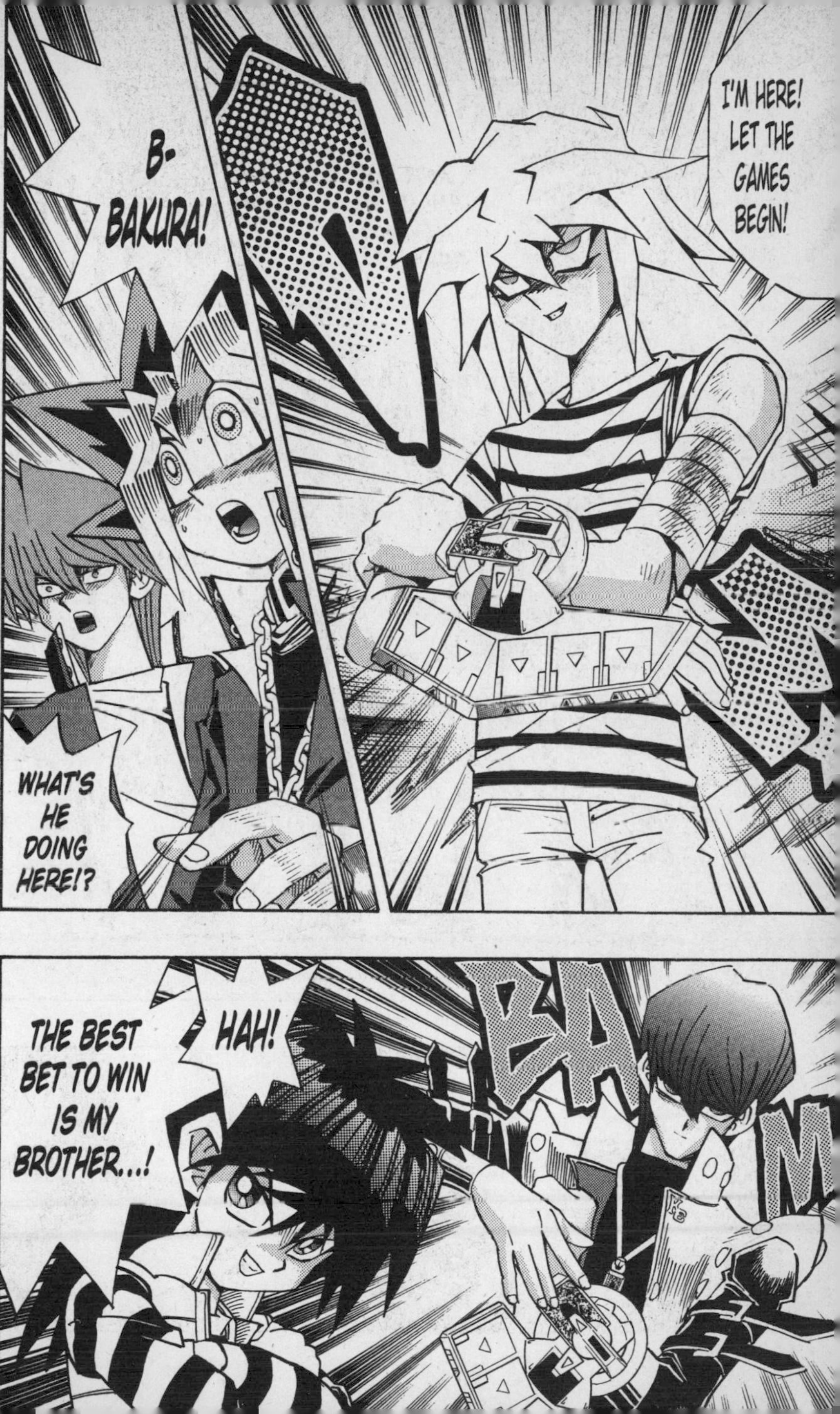
I'M HERE! LET THE GAMES BEGIN!
B-BAKURA!
WHAT'S HE DOING HERE!?
HAH!
THE BEST BET TO WIN IS MY BROTHER...!

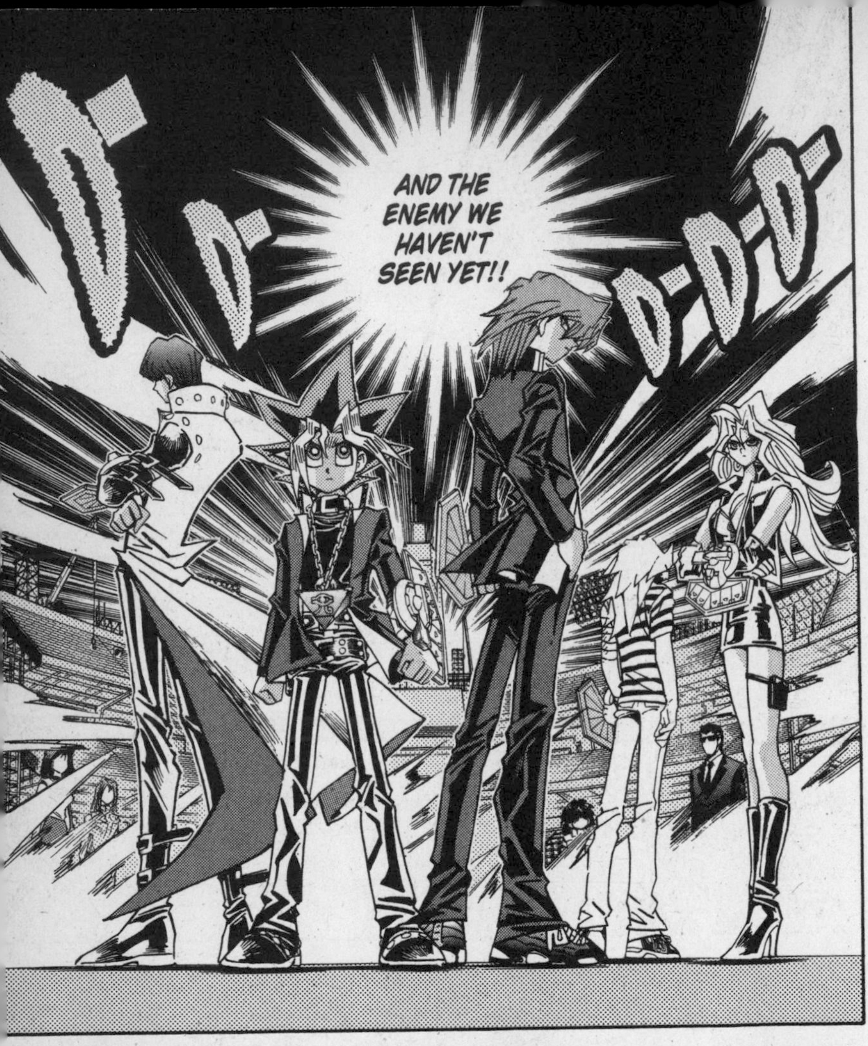
AND THE ENEMY WE HAVEN'T SEEN YET!!

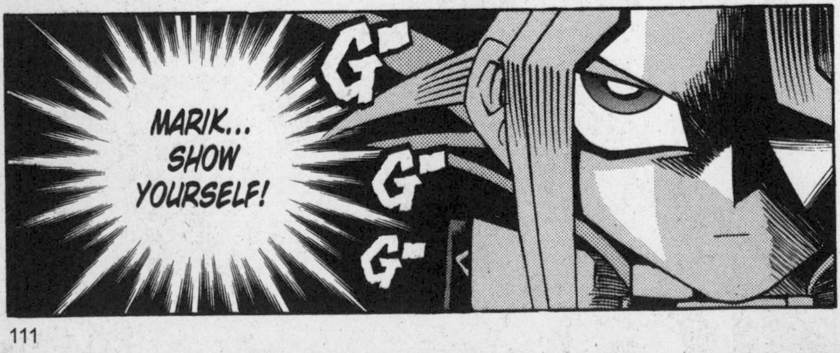
MARIK... SHOW YOURSELF!
G-
G-
G-

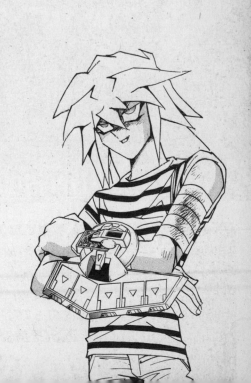

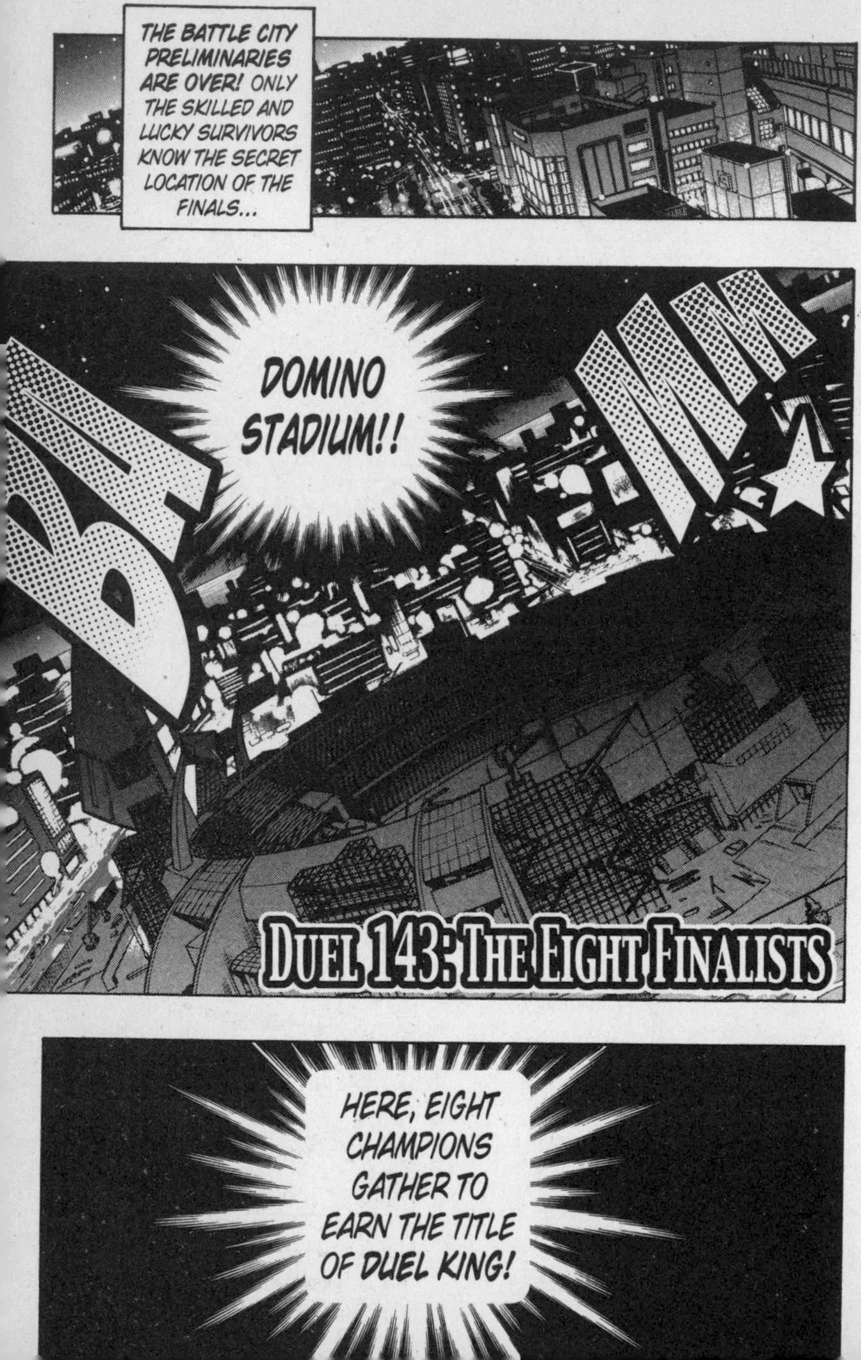
THE BATTLE CITY PRELIMINARIES ARE OVER! ONLY THE SKILLED AND LUCKY SURVIVORS KNOW THE SECRET LOCATION OF THE FINALS...
DOMINO STADIUM!!
DUEL 143: THE EIGHT FINALISTS
HERE, EIGHT CHAMPIONS GATHER TO EARN THE TITLE OF DUEL KING!

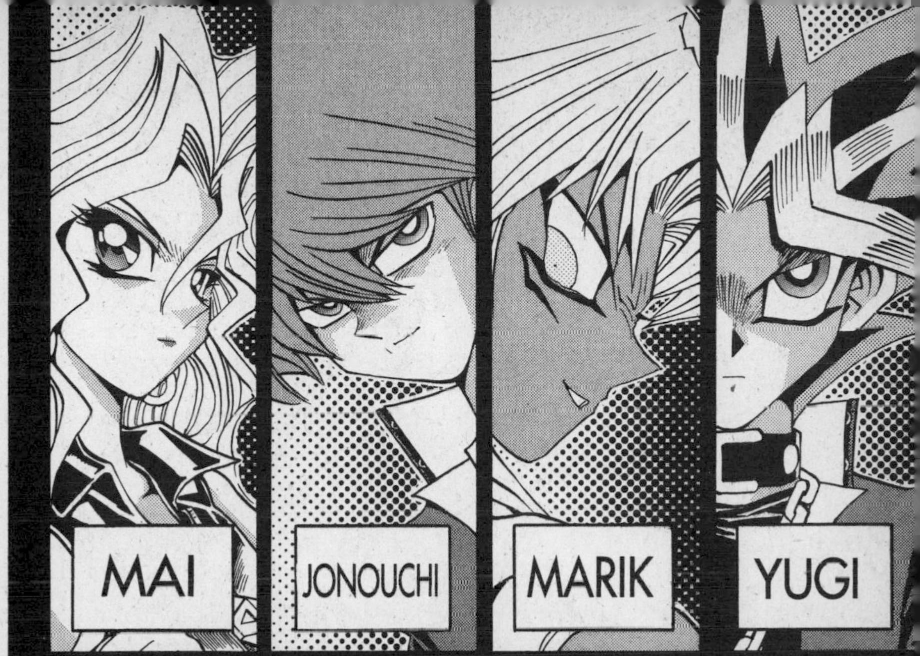
YUGI
MARIK
JONOUCHI
MAI

DUEL 143: THE EIGHT FINALISTS

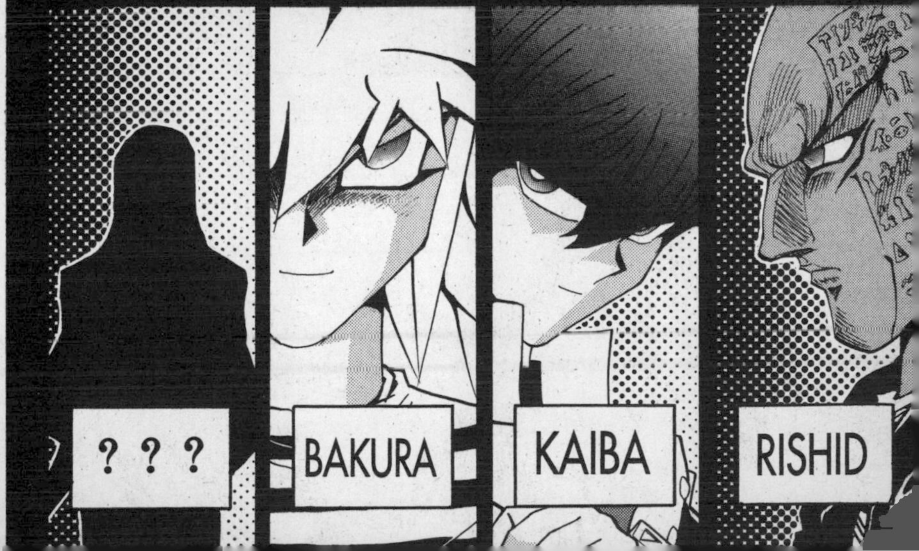
RISHID
KAIBA
BAKURA
???

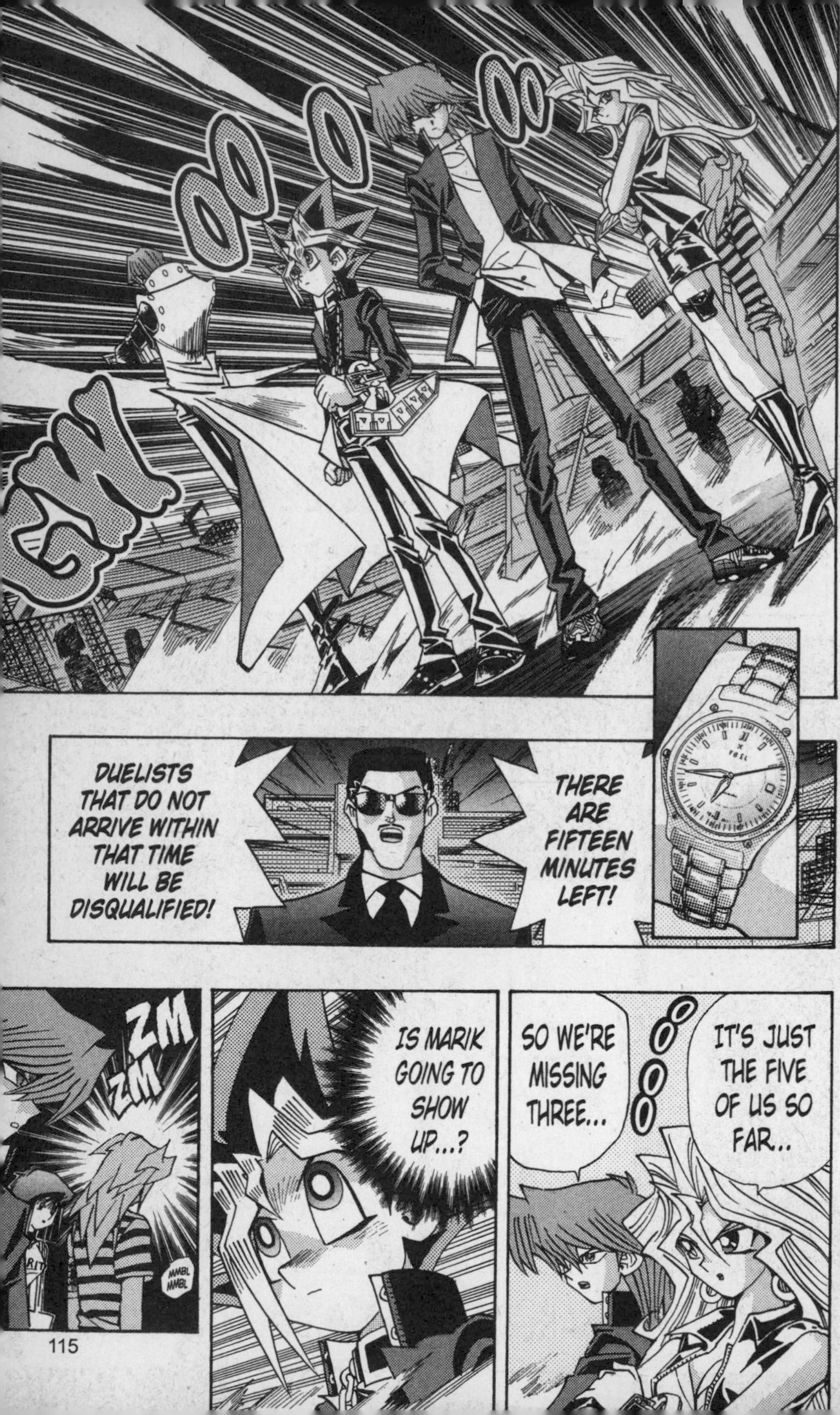
THERE ARE FIFTEEN MINUTES LEFT!
DUELISTS THAT DO NOT ARRIVE WITHIN THAT TIME WILL BE DISQUALIFIED!
IT'S JUST THE FIVE OF US SO FAR...
SO WE'RE MISSING THREE...
IS MARIK GOING TO SHOW UP...?
ZM ZM
MMBL MMBL

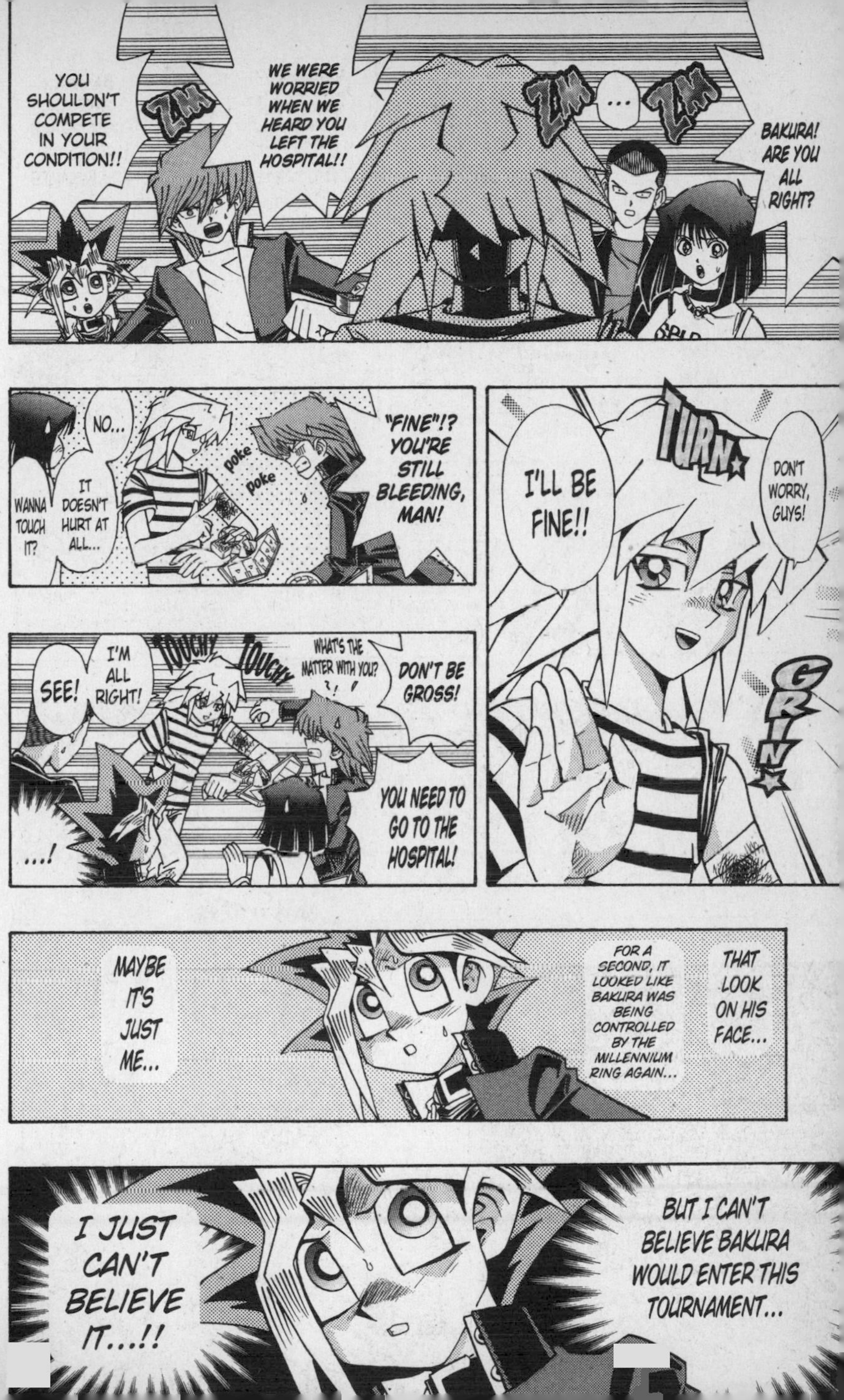
BAKURA! ARE YOU ALL RIGHT?
ZM
...
ZM
WE WERE WORRIED WHEN WE HEARD YOU LEFT THE HOSPITAL!!
ZM
YOU SHOULDN'T COMPETE IN YOUR CONDITION!!
TURN
DON'T WORRY, GUYS!
I'LL BE FINE!!
GRIN
"FINE"!? YOU'RE STILL BLEEDING, MAN!
poke
poke
NO...
IT DOESN'T HURT AT ALL...
WANNA TOUCH IT?
WHAT'S THE MATTER WITH YOU?
DON'T BE GROSS!
TOUCHY
TOUCHY
I'M ALL RIGHT!
SEE!
YOU NEED TO GO TO THE HOSPITAL!
...!
THAT LOOK ON HIS FACE...
FOR A SECOND, IT LOOKED LIKE BAKURA WAS BEING CONTROLLED BY THE MILLENNIUM RING AGAIN...
MAYBE IT'S JUST ME...
BUT I CAN'T BELIEVE BAKURA WOULD ENTER THIS TOURNAMENT...
I JUST CAN'T BELIEVE IT...!!

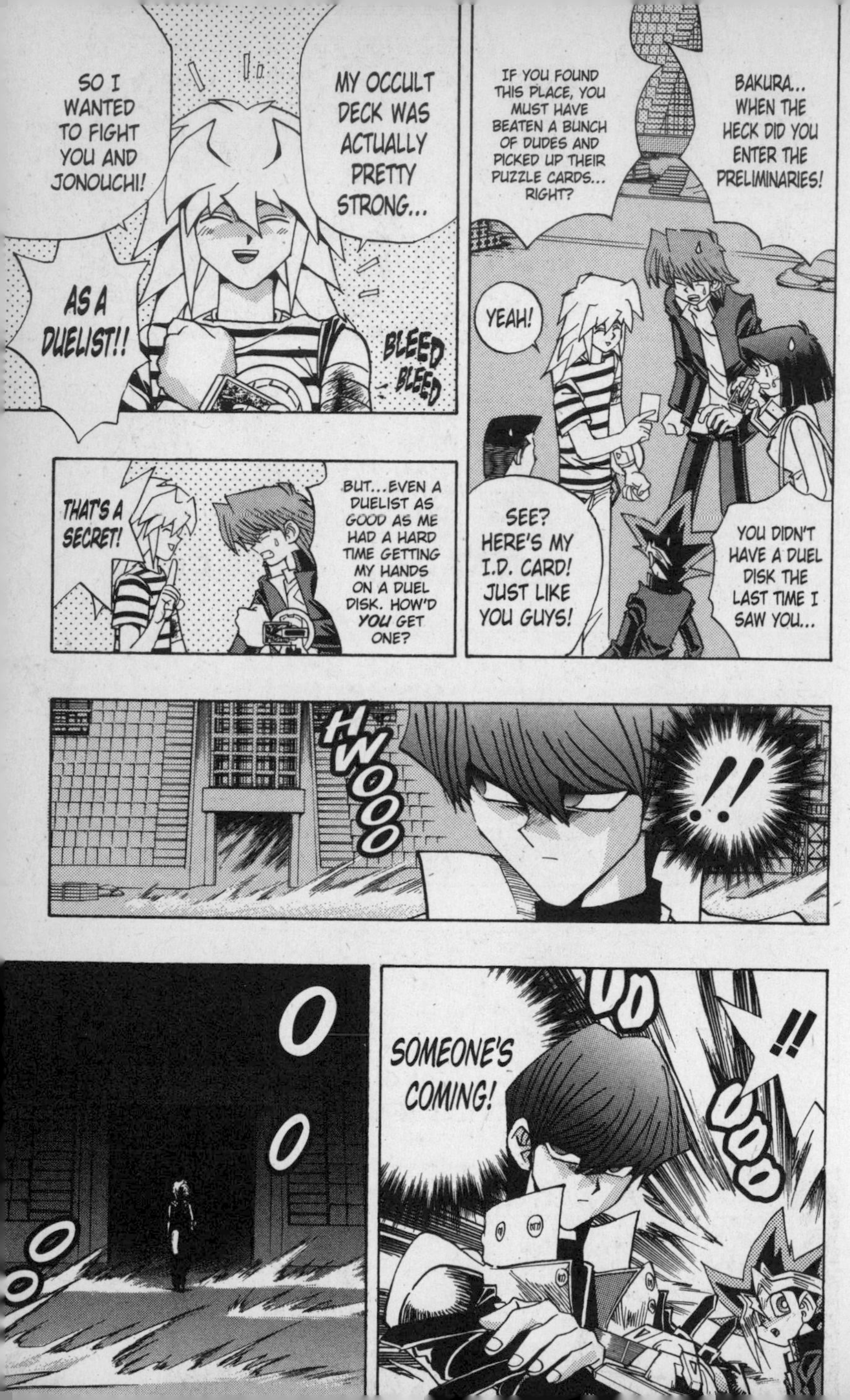
BAKURA... WHEN THE HECK DID YOU ENTER THE PRELIMINARIES!
IF YOU FOUND THIS PLACE, YOU MUST HAVE BEATEN A BUNCH OF DUDES AND PICKED UP THEIR PUZZLE CARDS... RIGHT?
YEAH!
YOU DIDN'T HAVE A DUEL DISK THE LAST TIME I SAW YOU...
SEE? HERE'S MY I.D. CARD! JUST LIKE YOU GUYS!
MY OCCULT DECK WAS ACTUALLY PRETTY STRONG...
SO I WANTED TO FIGHT YOU AND JONOUCHI!
AS A DUELIST!!
BLEED BLEED
BUT...EVEN A DUELIST AS GOOD AS ME HAD A HARD TIME GETTING MY HANDS ON A DUEL DISK. HOW'D *YOU* GET ONE?
THAT'S A SECRET!
!!
HWOOO
!!
SOMEONE'S COMING!
OOO
O O OO

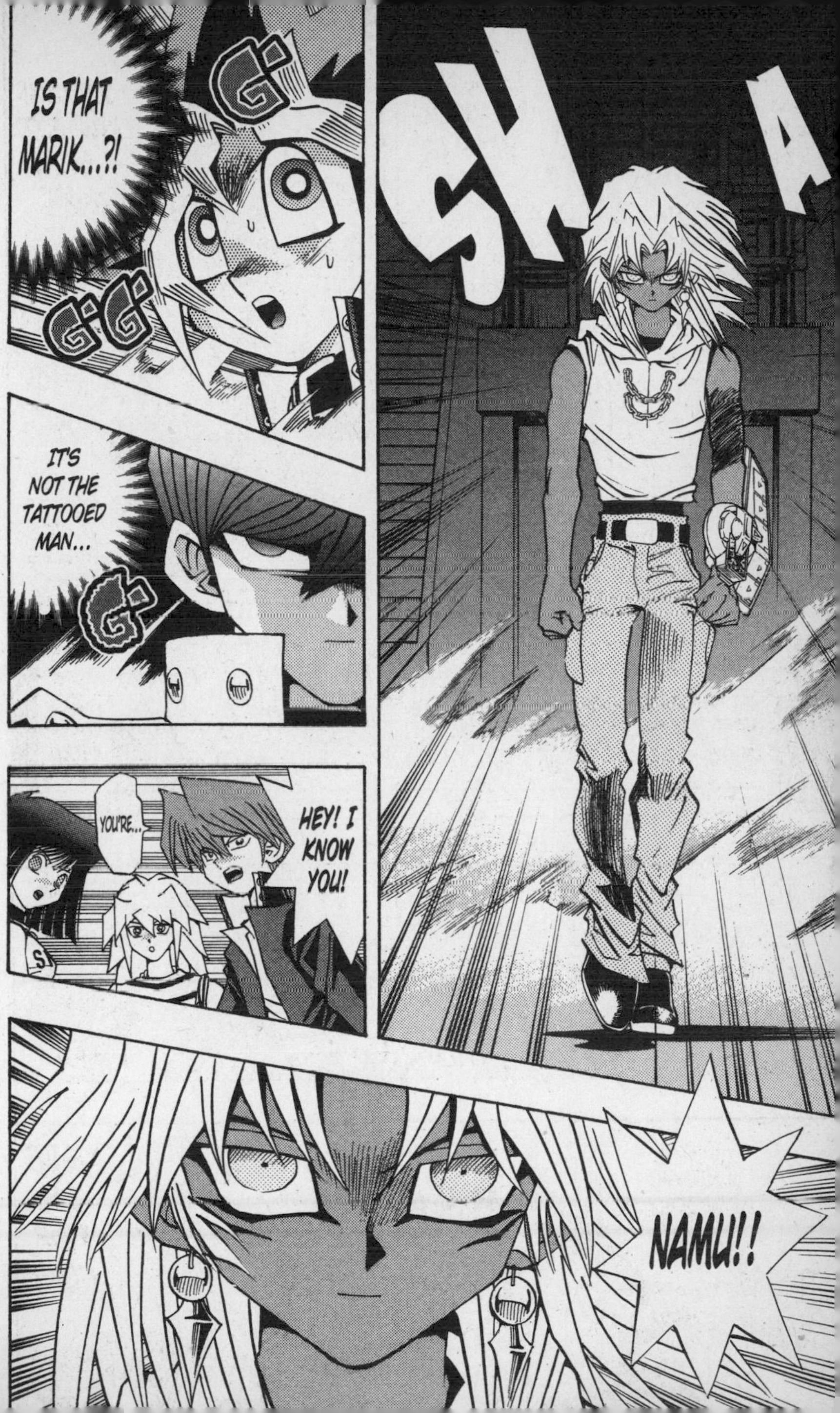
SH A
G
IS THAT MARIK...?!
G G
IT'S NOT THE TATTOOED MAN...
G
HEY! I KNOW YOU!
YOU'RE...
NAMU!!

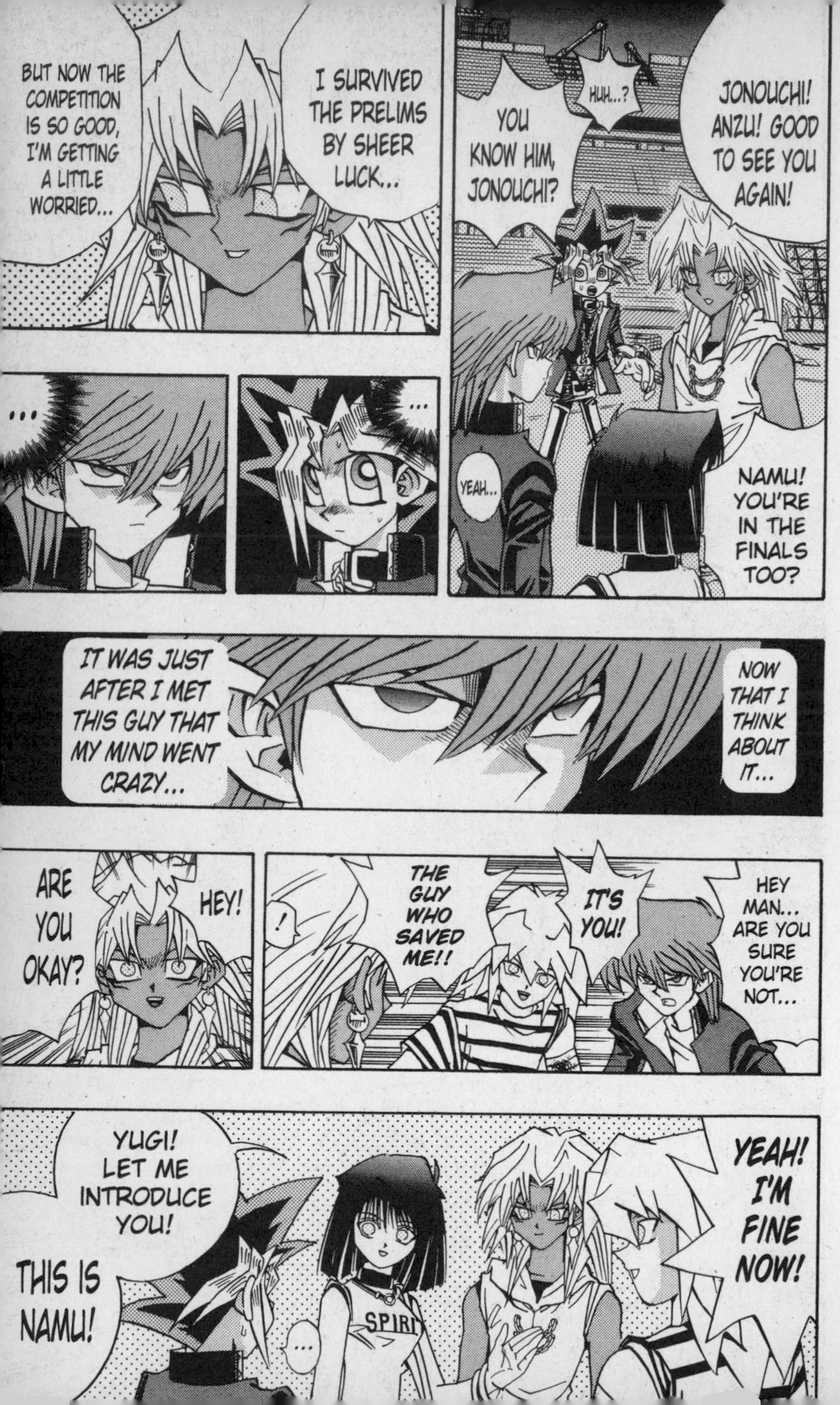
JONOUCHI! ANZU! GOOD TO SEE YOU AGAIN!
HUH...?
YOU KNOW HIM, JONOUCHI?
YEAH...
NAMU! YOU'RE IN THE FINALS TOO?
I SURVIVED THE PRELIMS BY SHEER LUCK...
BUT NOW THE COMPETITION IS SO GOOD, I'M GETTING A LITTLE WORRIED...
...
...
NOW THAT I THINK ABOUT IT...
IT WAS JUST AFTER I MET THIS GUY THAT MY MIND WENT CRAZY...
HEY MAN... ARE YOU SURE YOU'RE NOT...
IT'S YOU!
THE GUY WHO SAVED ME!!
!
HEY!
ARE YOU OKAY?
YEAH! I'M FINE NOW!
...
SPIRI
YUGI! LET ME INTRODUCE YOU!
THIS IS NAMU!

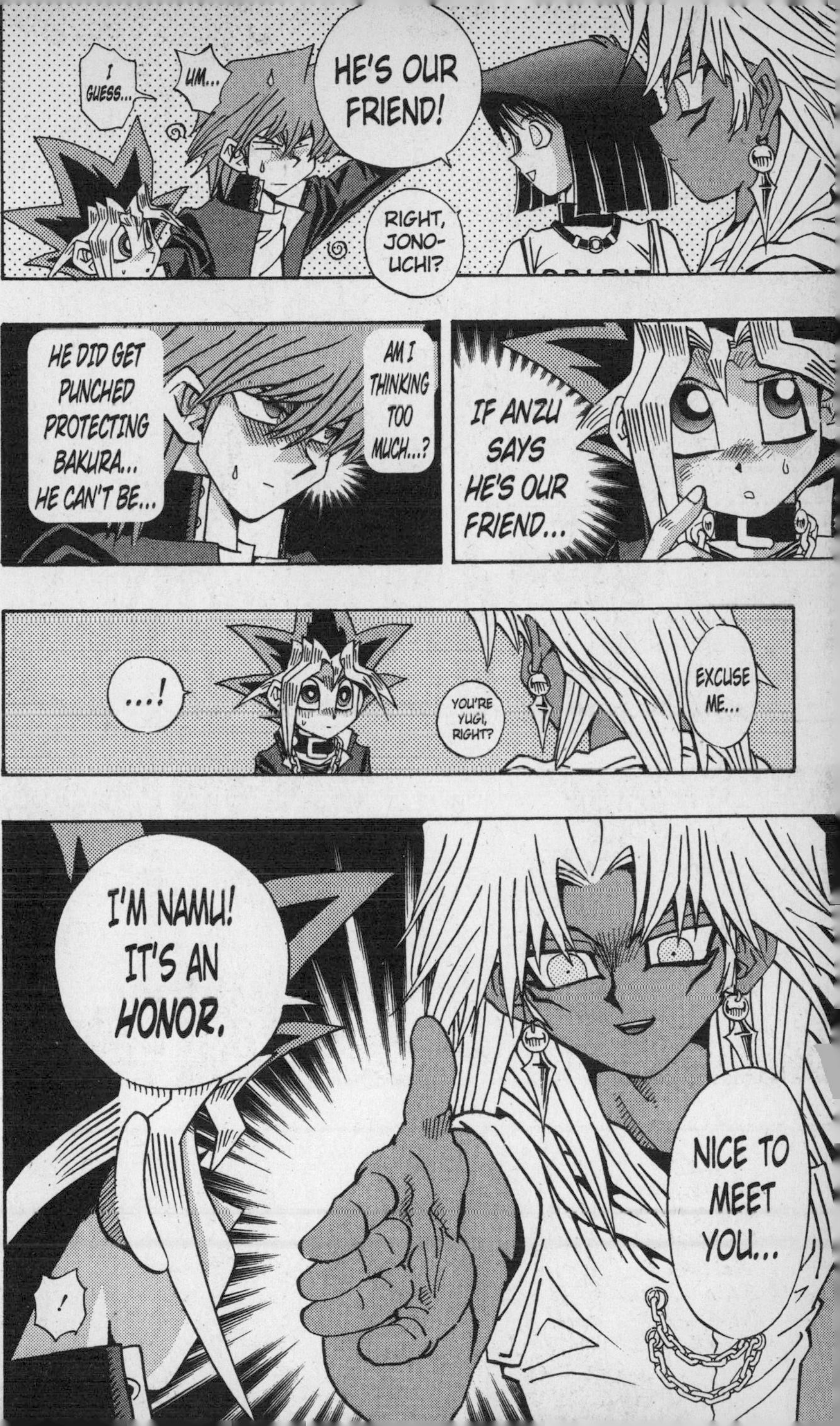
HE'S OUR FRIEND!
RIGHT, JONO-UCHI?
UM...
I GUESS...
IF ANZU SAYS HE'S OUR FRIEND...
AM I THINKING TOO MUCH...?
HE DID GET PUNCHED PROTECTING BAKURA... HE CAN'T BE...
EXCUSE ME...
YOU'RE YUGI, RIGHT?
...!
NICE TO MEET YOU...
I'M NAMU! IT'S AN HONOR.
!

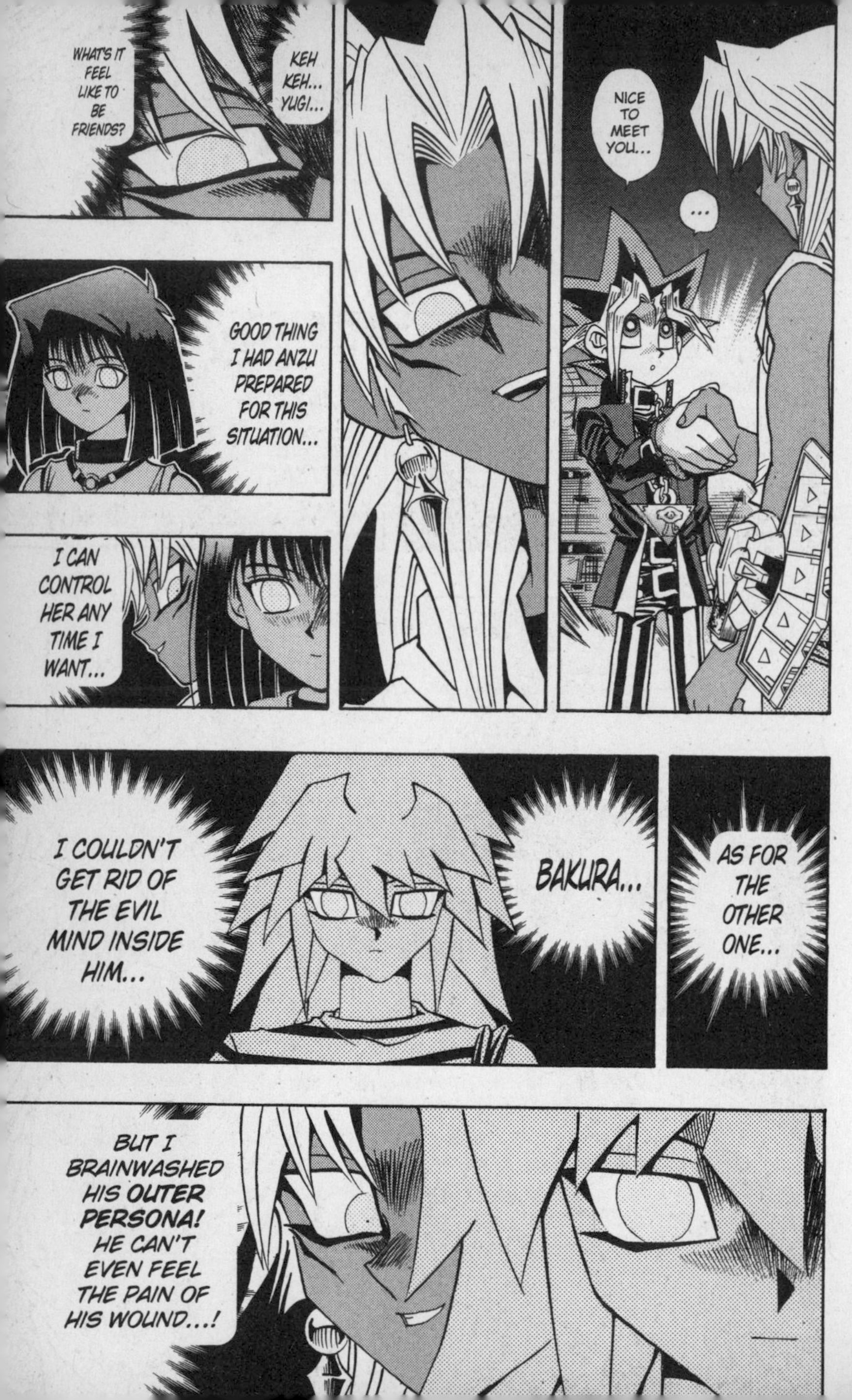
NICE TO MEET YOU...
...
KEH KEH... YUGI...
WHAT'S IT FEEL LIKE TO BE FRIENDS?
GOOD THING I HAD ANZU PREPARED FOR THIS SITUATION...
I CAN CONTROL HER ANY TIME I WANT...
AS FOR THE OTHER ONE...
BAKURA...
I COULDN'T GET RID OF THE EVIL MIND INSIDE HIM...
BUT I BRAINWASHED HIS OUTER PERSONA! HE CAN'T EVEN FEEL THE PAIN OF HIS WOUND...!

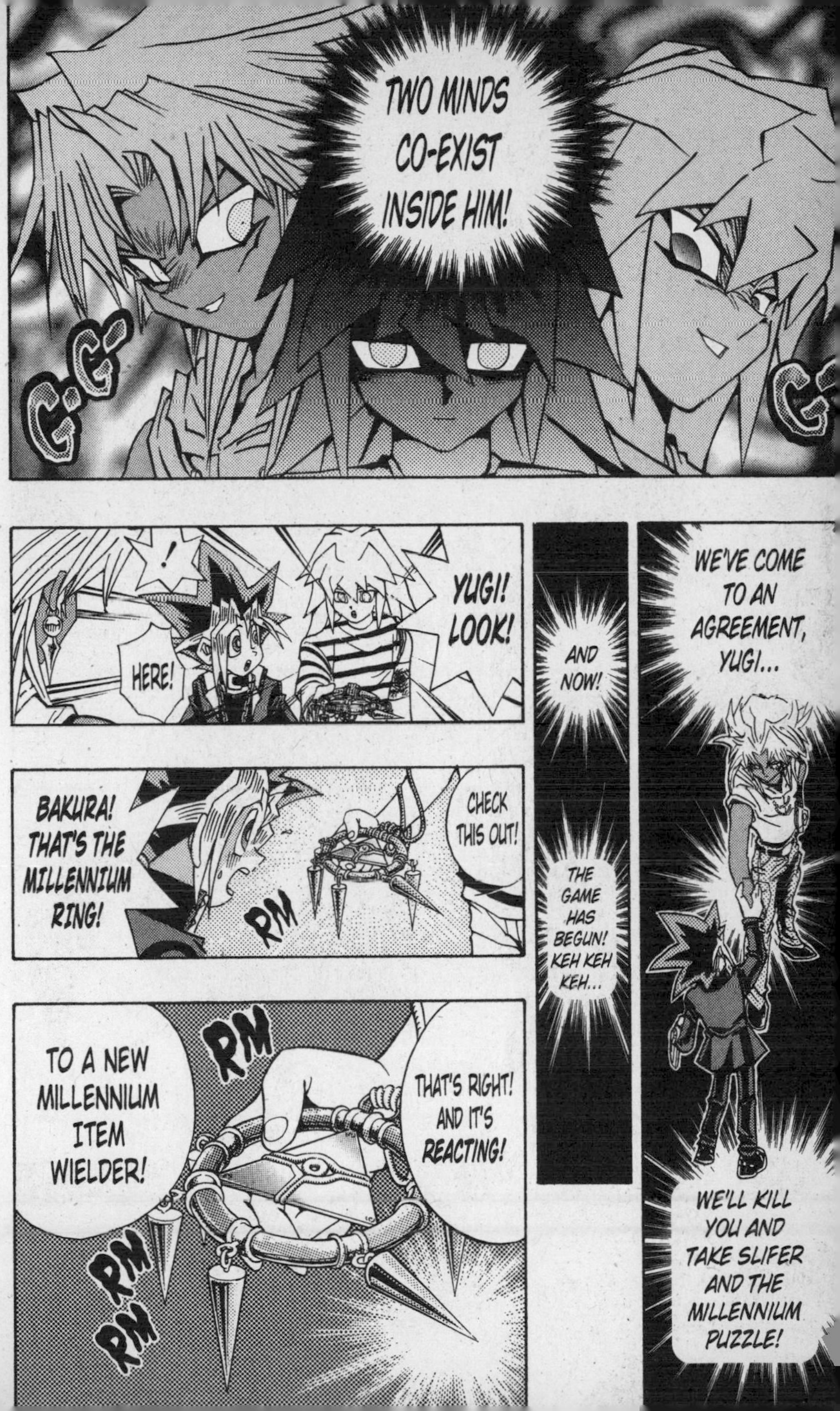
G-
TWO MINDS CO-EXIST INSIDE HIM!
G-G-
WE'VE COME TO AN AGREEMENT, YUGI...
WE'LL KILL YOU AND TAKE SLIFER AND THE MILLENNIUM PUZZLE!
AND NOW!
THE GAME HAS BEGUN! KEH KEH KEH...
YUGI! LOOK!
!
HERE!
CHECK THIS OUT!
BAKURA! THAT'S THE MILLENNIUM RING!
RM
THAT'S RIGHT! AND IT'S REACTING!
RM
TO A NEW MILLENNIUM ITEM WIELDER!
RM RM

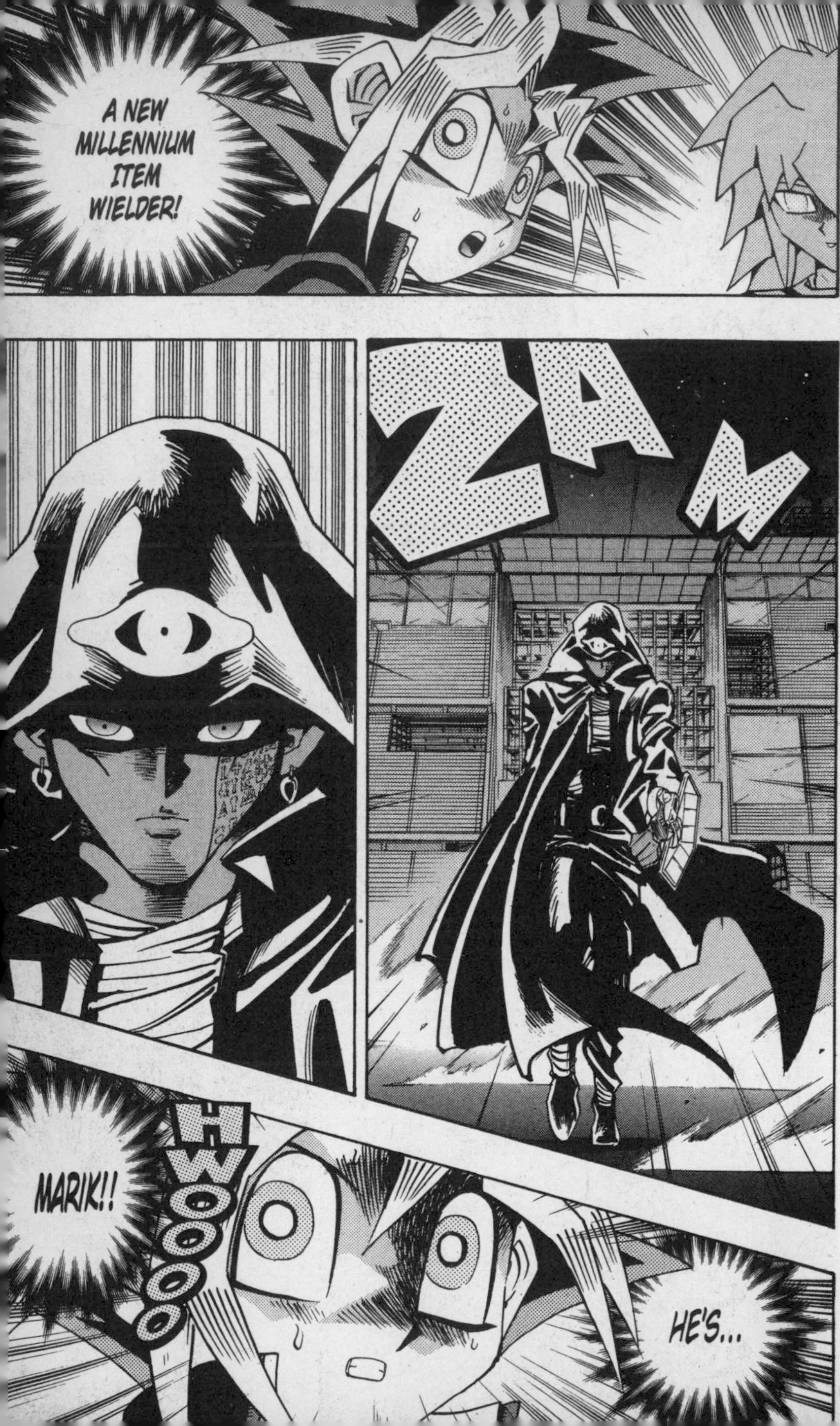
A NEW MILLENNIUM ITEM WIELDER!
ZAM
HE'S...
HWOOOO
MARIK!!

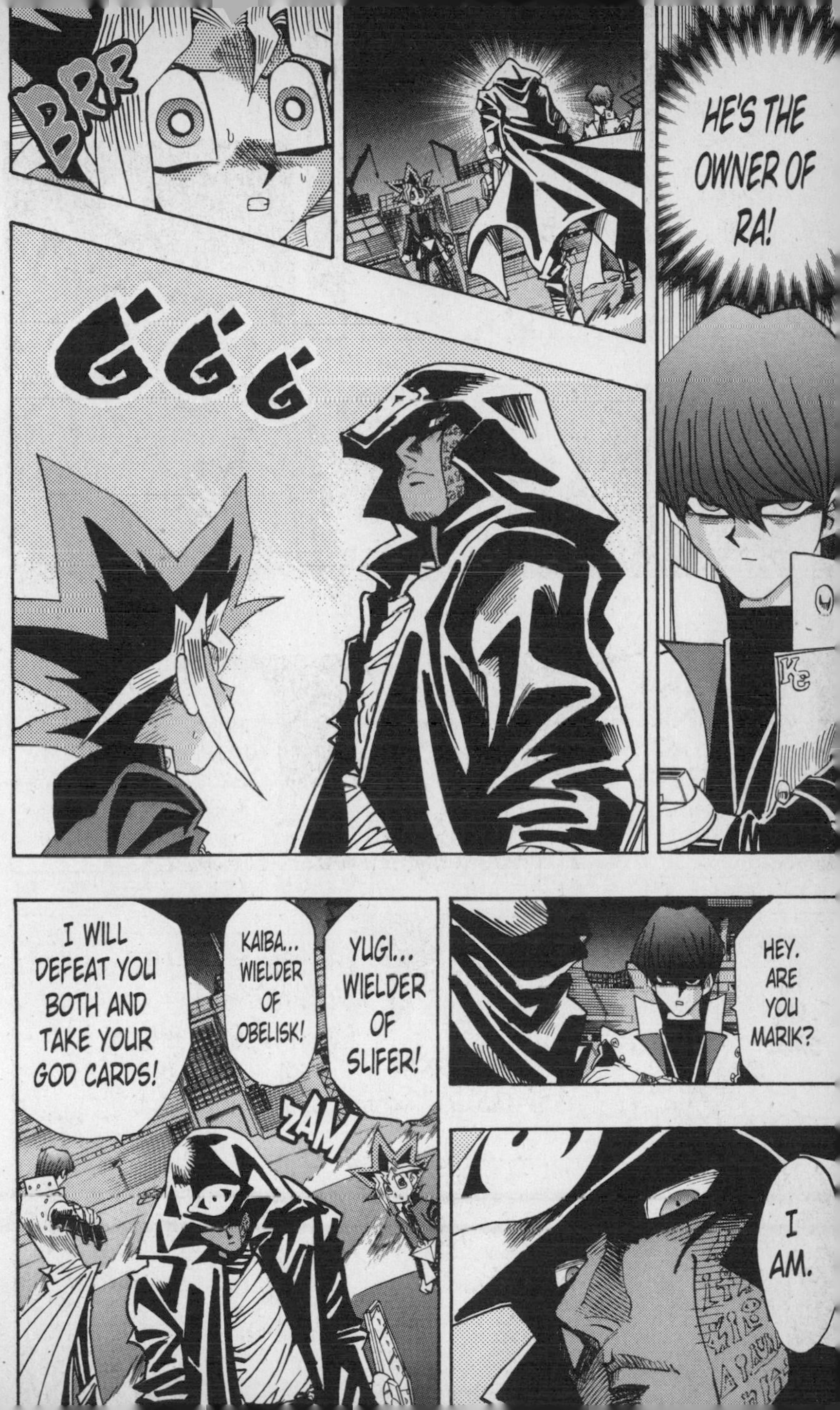
HE'S THE OWNER OF RA!
BRR
GGG
HEY. ARE YOU MARIK?
I AM.
YUGI... WIELDER OF SLIFER!
KAIBA... WIELDER OF OBELISK!
I WILL DEFEAT YOU BOTH AND TAKE YOUR GOD CARDS!
ZAM

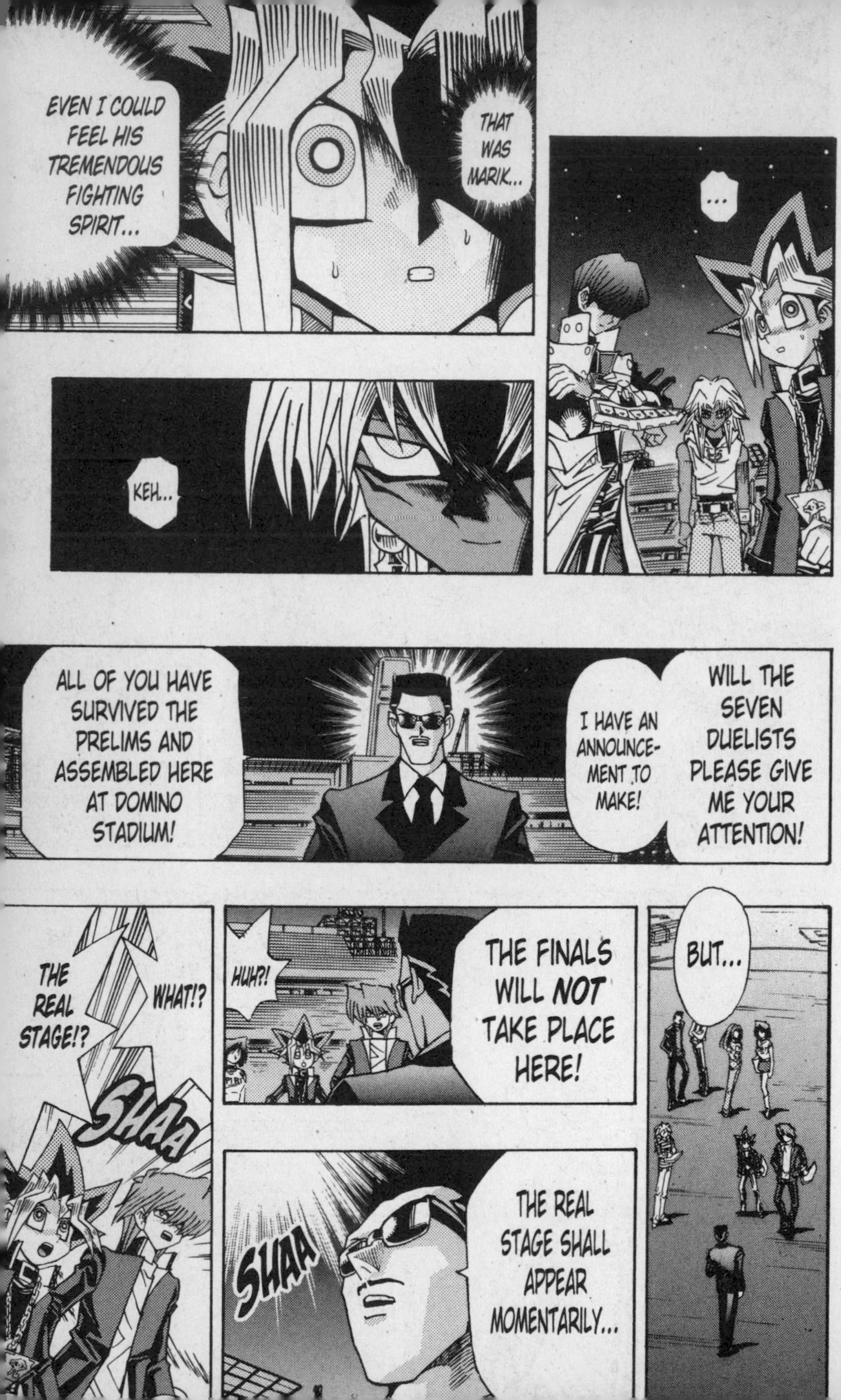
...
THAT WAS MARIK...
EVEN I COULD FEEL HIS TREMENDOUS FIGHTING SPIRIT...
KEH...
WILL THE SEVEN DUELISTS PLEASE GIVE ME YOUR ATTENTION!
I HAVE AN ANNOUNCEMENT TO MAKE!
ALL OF YOU HAVE SURVIVED THE PRELIMS AND ASSEMBLED HERE AT DOMINO STADIUM!
BUT...
THE FINALS WILL **NOT** TAKE PLACE HERE!
HUH?!
THE REAL STAGE SHALL APPEAR MOMENTARILY...
SHAA
WHAT!?
THE REAL STAGE!?
SHAA

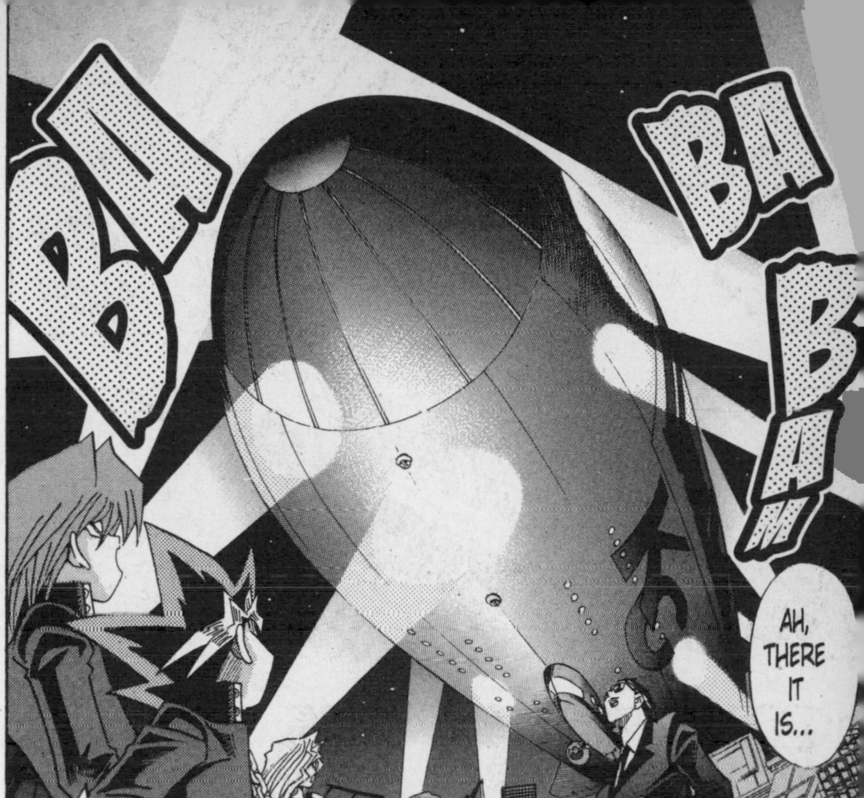
BA
BA!
AH, THERE IT IS...
BA
!!

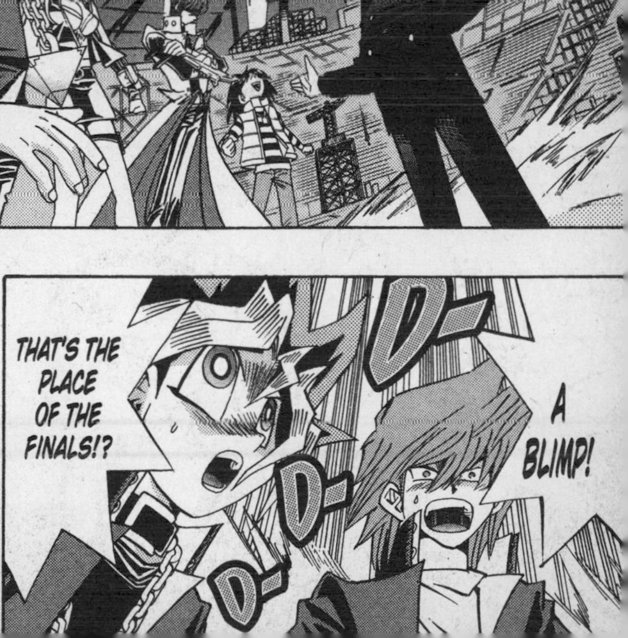
A BLIMP!
THAT'S THE PLACE OF THE FINALS!?

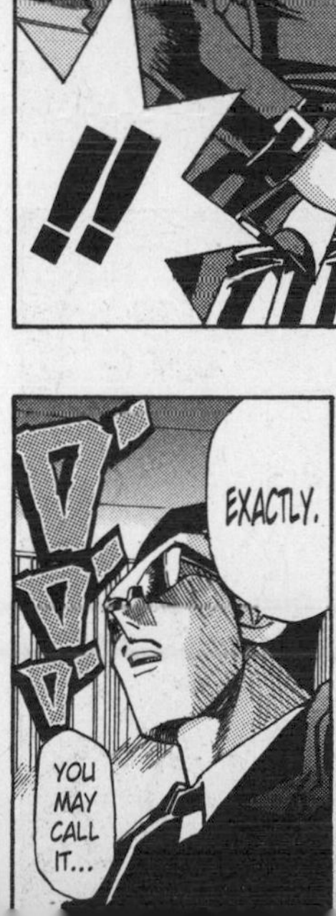
EXACTLY.
YOU MAY CALL IT...

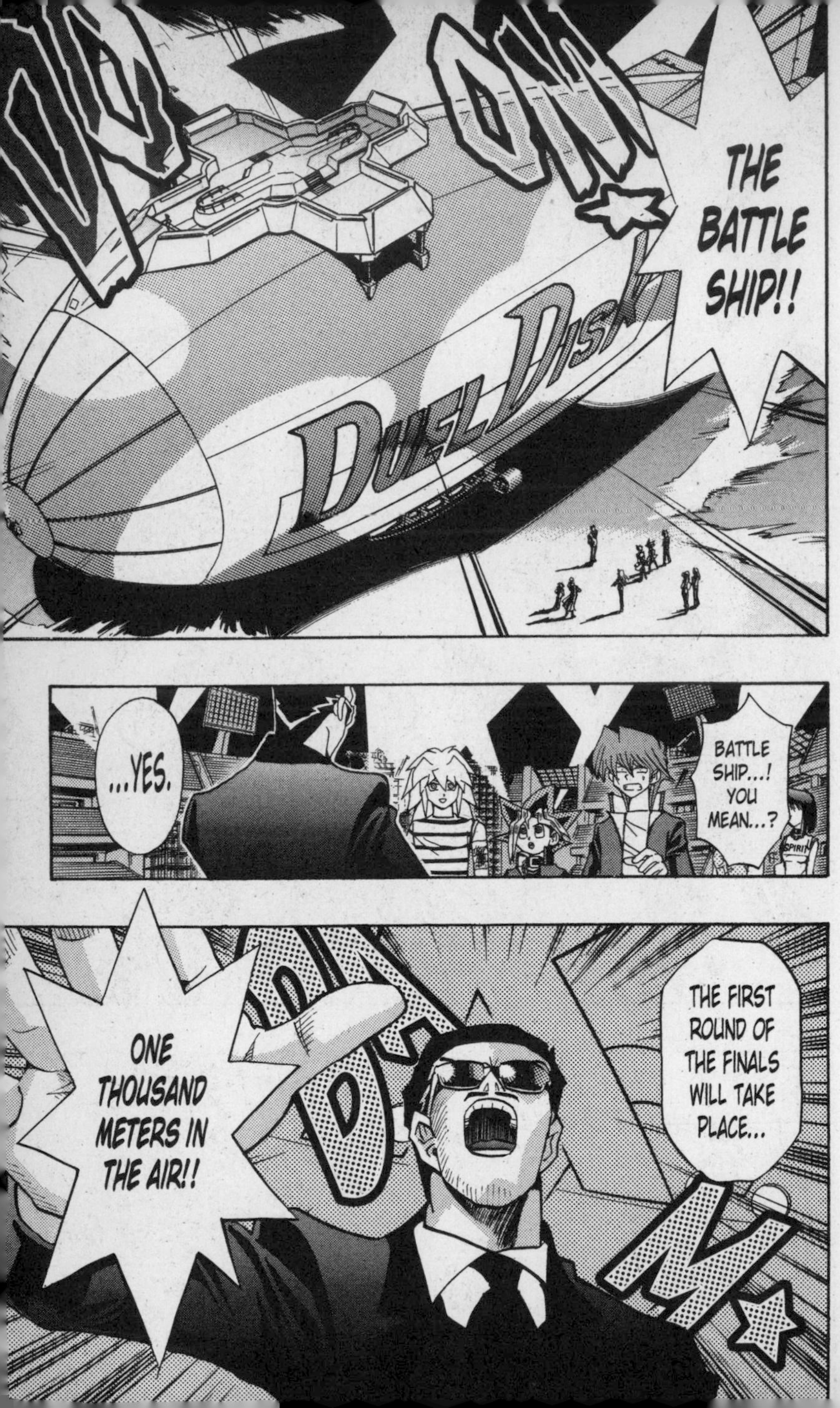
THE BATTLE SHIP!!
DUEL DISK
BATTLE SHIP...! YOU MEAN...?
...YES.
SPIRIT
THE FIRST ROUND OF THE FINALS WILL TAKE PLACE...
ONE THOUSAND METERS IN THE AIR!!

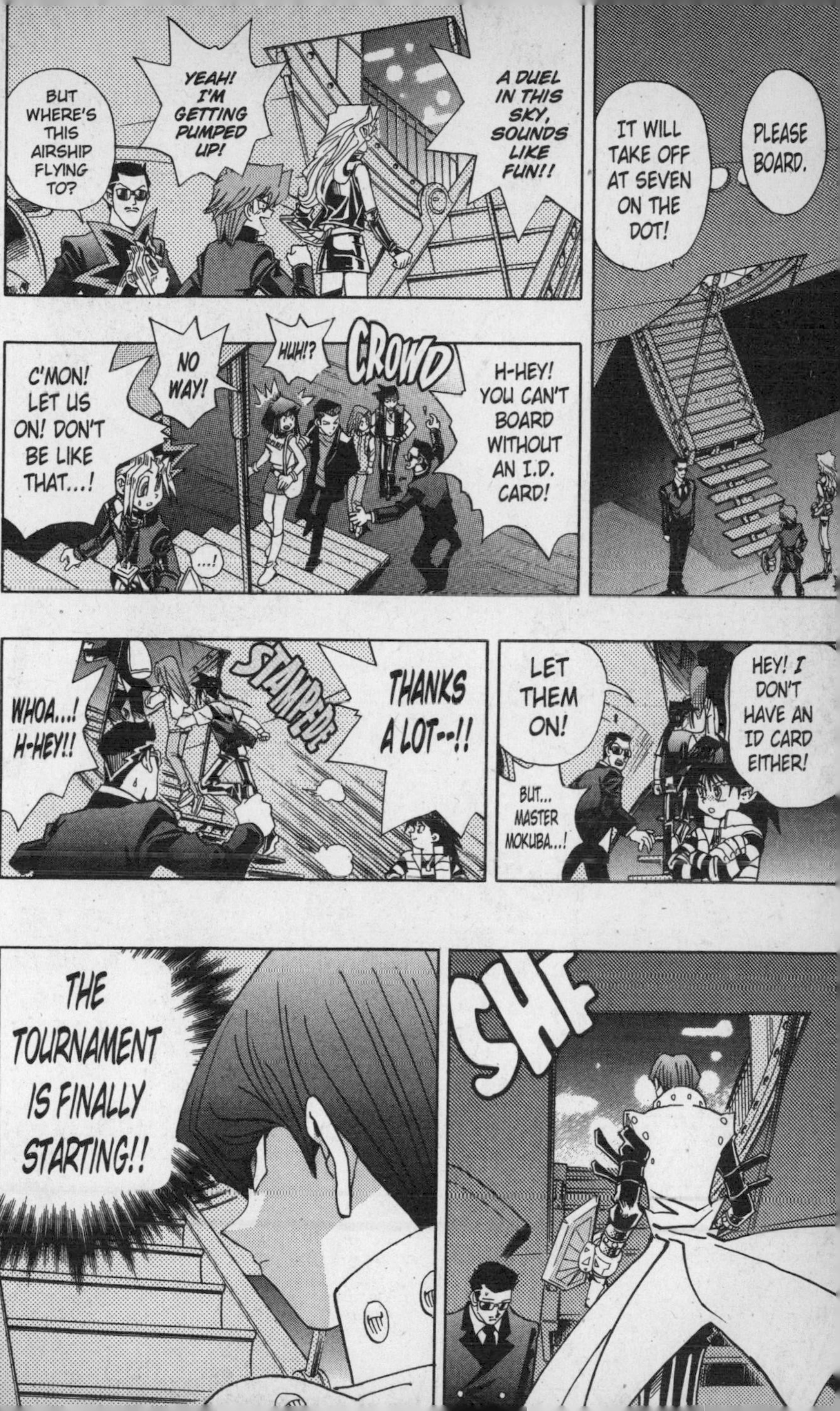
PLEASE BOARD.
IT WILL TAKE OFF AT SEVEN ON THE DOT!
A DUEL IN THIS SKY, SOUNDS LIKE FUN!!
YEAH! I'M GETTING PUMPED UP!
BUT WHERE'S THIS AIRSHIP FLYING TO?
H-HEY! YOU CAN'T BOARD WITHOUT AN I.D. CARD!
CROWD
HUH!?
NO WAY!
C'MON! LET US ON! DON'T BE LIKE THAT...!
...!
HEY! I DON'T HAVE AN ID CARD EITHER!
LET THEM ON!
BUT... MASTER MOKUBA...!
THANKS A LOT--!!
STAMPEDE
WHOA...! H-HEY!!
SHF
THE TOURNAMENT IS FINALLY STARTING!!

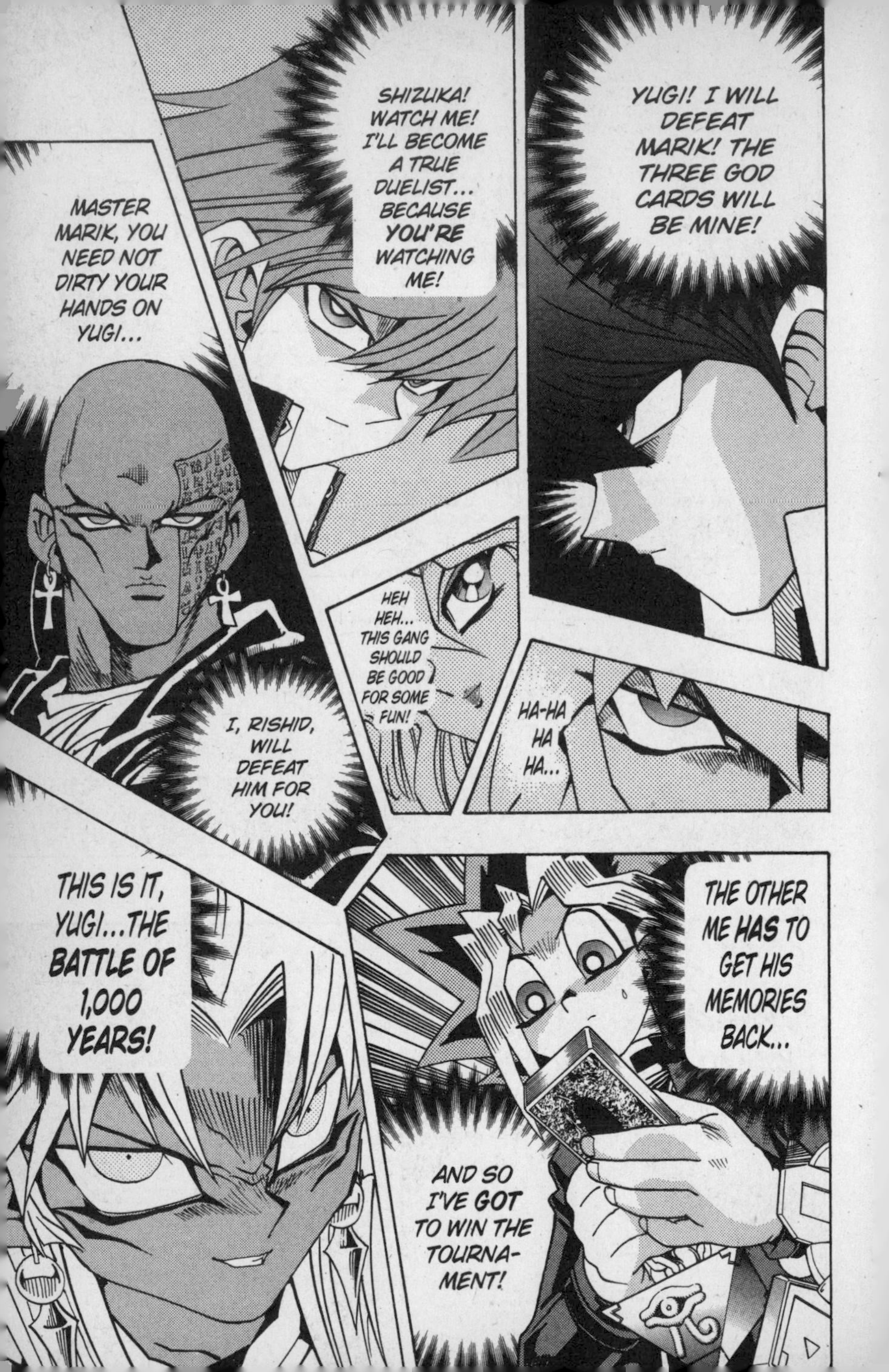

YUGI! I WILL DEFEAT MARIK! THE THREE GOD CARDS WILL BE MINE!
SHIZUKA! WATCH ME! I'LL BECOME A TRUE DUELIST... BECAUSE YOU'RE WATCHING ME!
HA-HA HA HA...
HEH HEH... THIS GANG SHOULD BE GOOD FOR SOME FUN!
MASTER MARIK, YOU NEED NOT DIRTY YOUR HANDS ON YUGI...
I, RISHID, WILL DEFEAT HIM FOR YOU!
THE OTHER ME HAS TO GET HIS MEMORIES BACK...
AND SO I'VE GOT TO WIN THE TOURNA-MENT!
THIS IS IT, YUGI...THE BATTLE OF 1,000 YEARS!

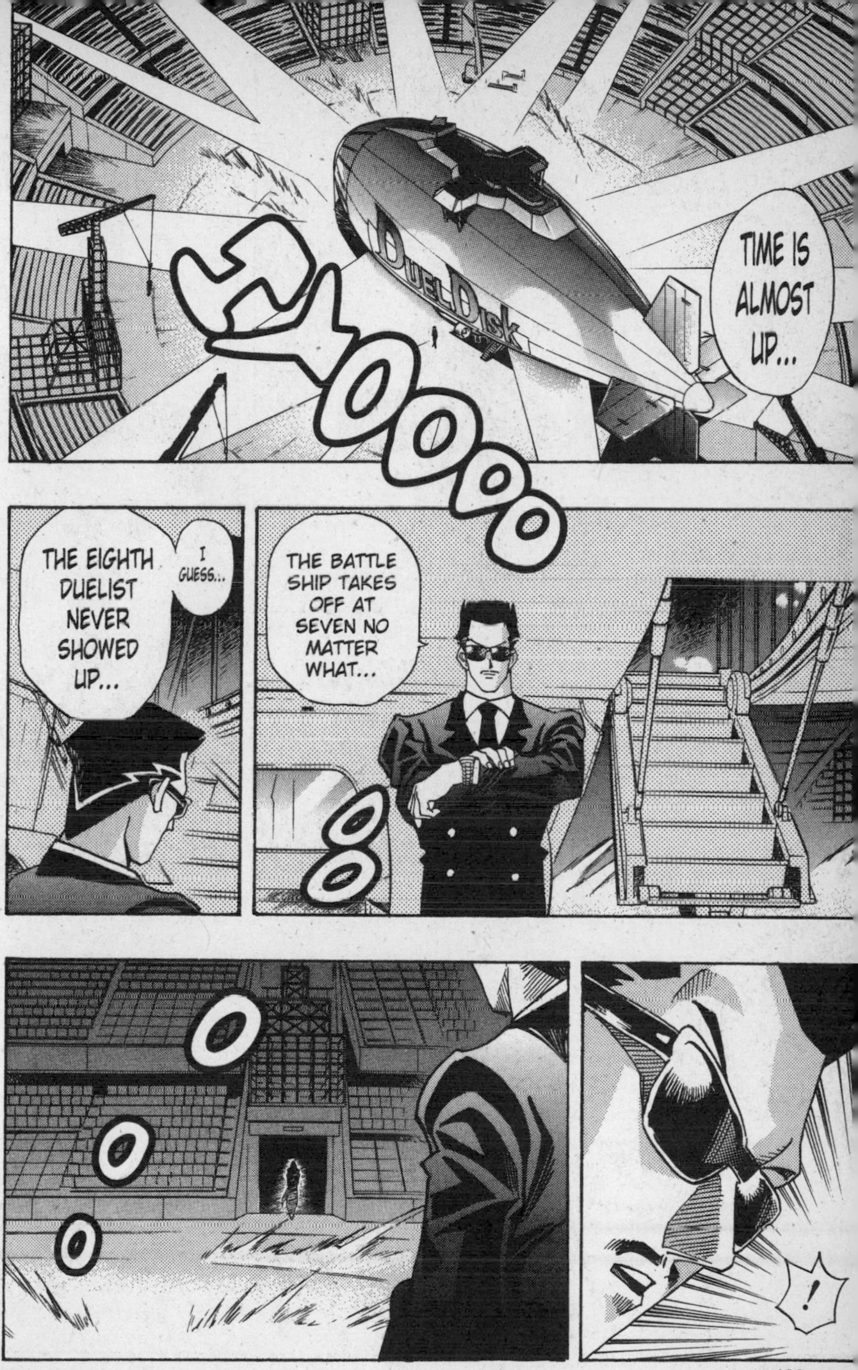
TIME IS ALMOST UP...
THE BATTLE SHIP TAKES OFF AT SEVEN NO MATTER WHAT...
THE EIGHTH DUELIST NEVER SHOWED UP...
I GUESS...
!

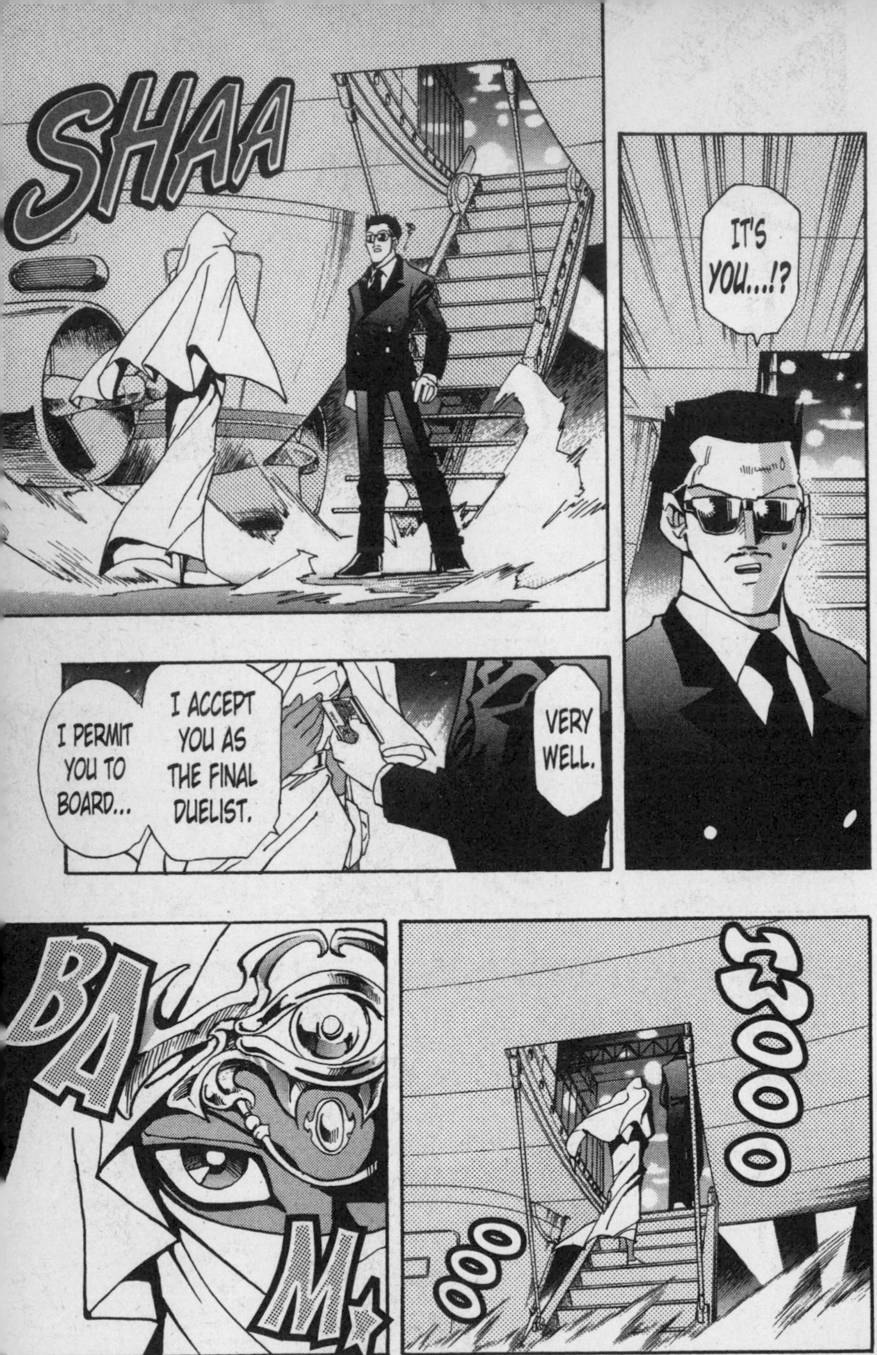
IT'S YOU...!?
SHAA
VERY WELL.
I ACCEPT YOU AS THE FINAL DUELIST.
I PERMIT YOU TO BOARD...
ZOOOO
OOO
BAM

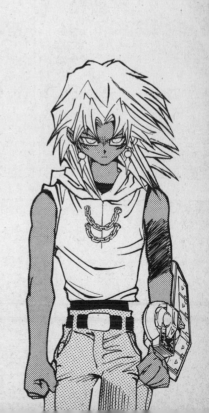

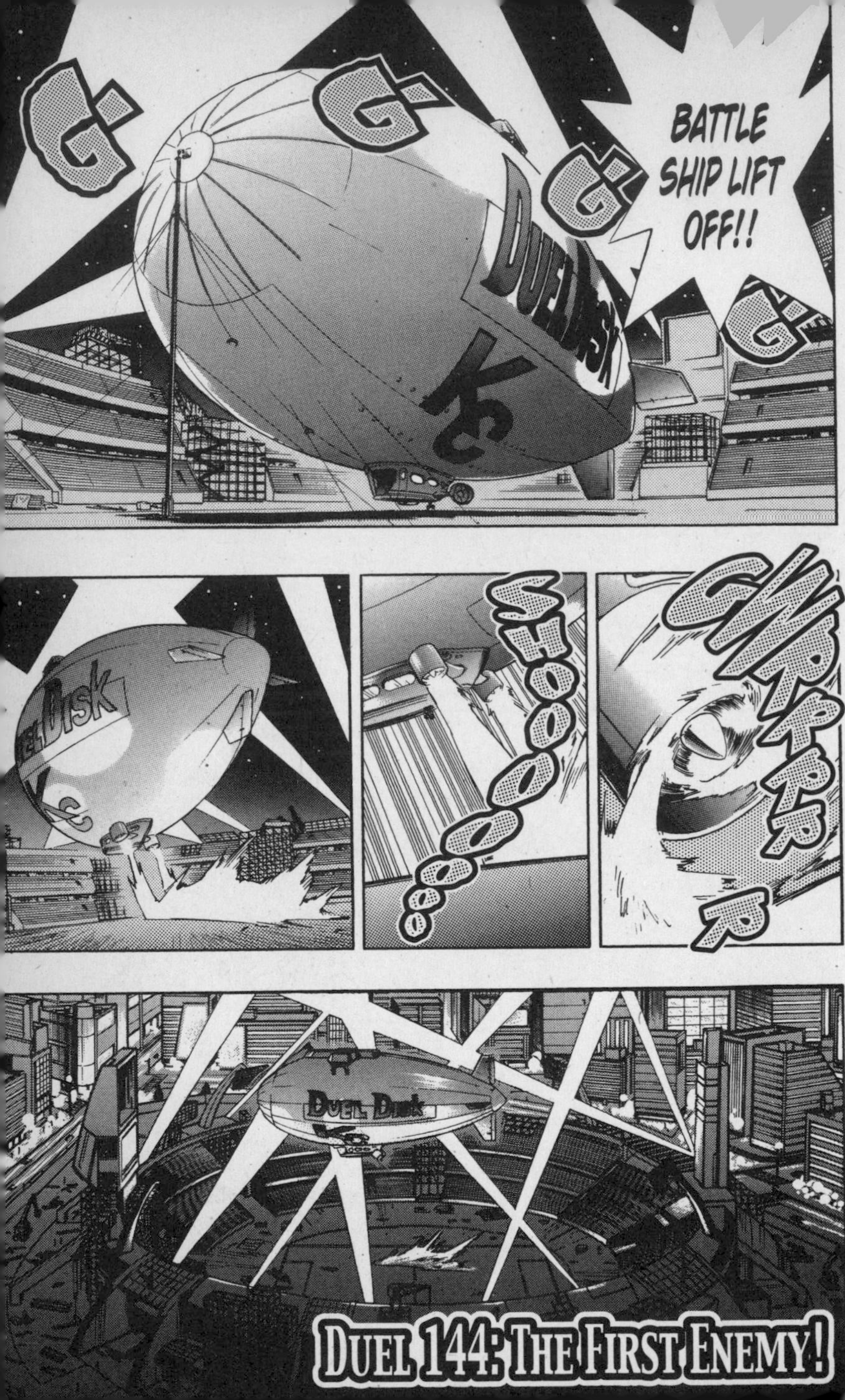
G G G G
BATTLE SHIP LIFT OFF!!
DUEL DISK
KC
GWRRRRR
SHOOOO...
DUEL DISK
DUEL 144: THE FIRST ENEMY!

DUEL 144: THE FIRST ENEMY!

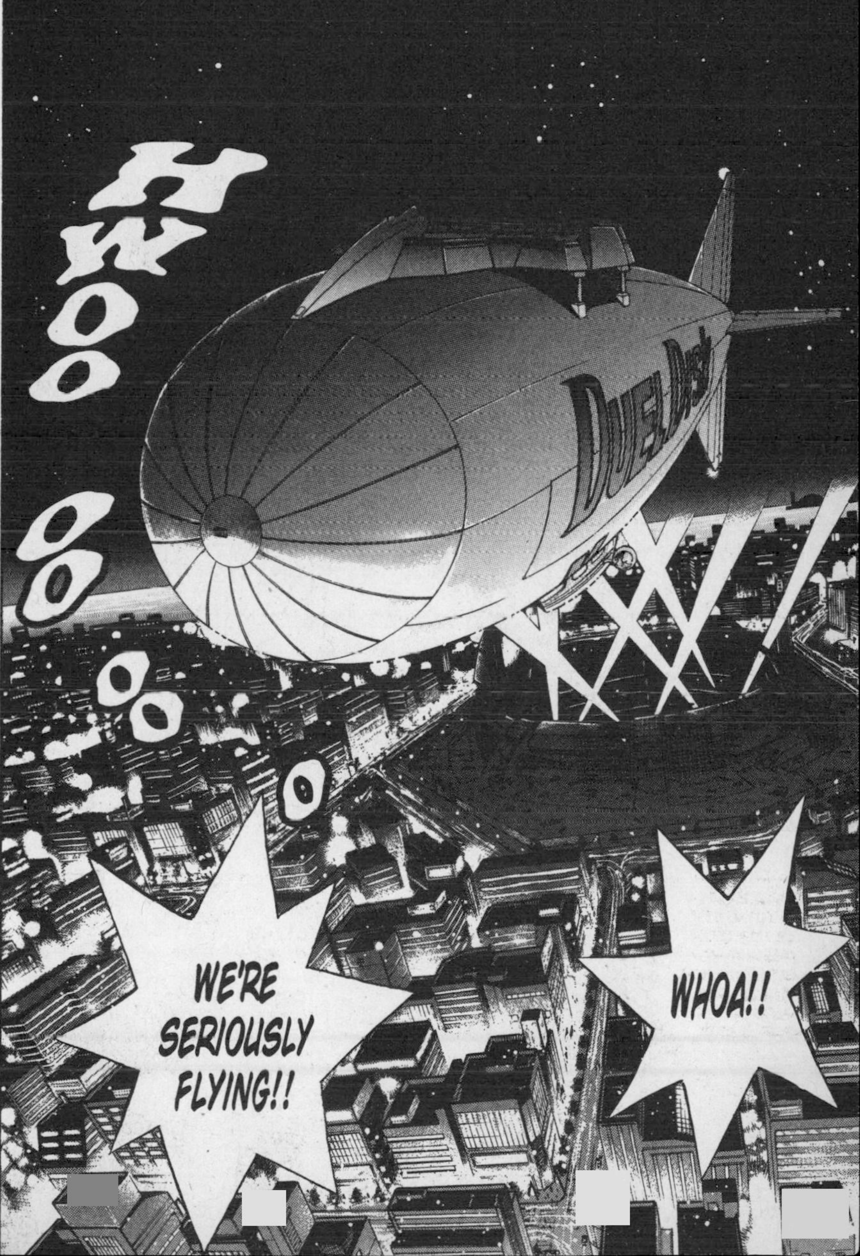

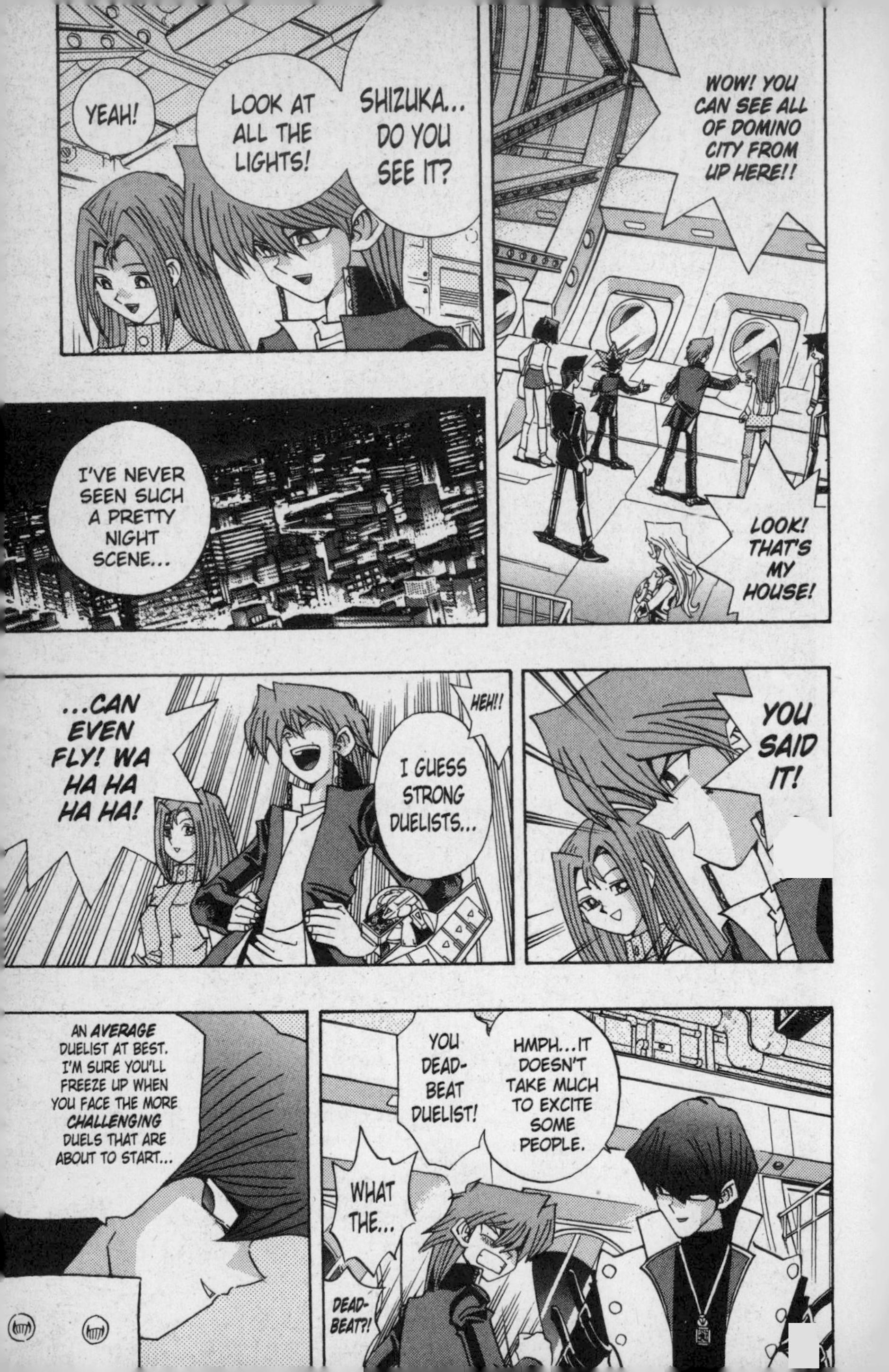
WOW! YOU CAN SEE ALL OF DOMINO CITY FROM UP HERE!!
LOOK! THAT'S MY HOUSE!
SHIZUKA... DO YOU SEE IT?
LOOK AT ALL THE LIGHTS!
YEAH!
I'VE NEVER SEEN SUCH A PRETTY NIGHT SCENE...
YOU SAID IT!
HEH!!
I GUESS STRONG DUELISTS...
...CAN EVEN FLY! WA HA HA HA HA!
HMPH...IT DOESN'T TAKE MUCH TO EXCITE SOME PEOPLE.
YOU DEAD-BEAT DUELIST!
WHAT THE...
DEAD-BEAT?!
AN AVERAGE DUELIST AT BEST. I'M SURE YOU'LL FREEZE UP WHEN YOU FACE THE MORE CHALLENGING DUELS THAT ARE ABOUT TO START...

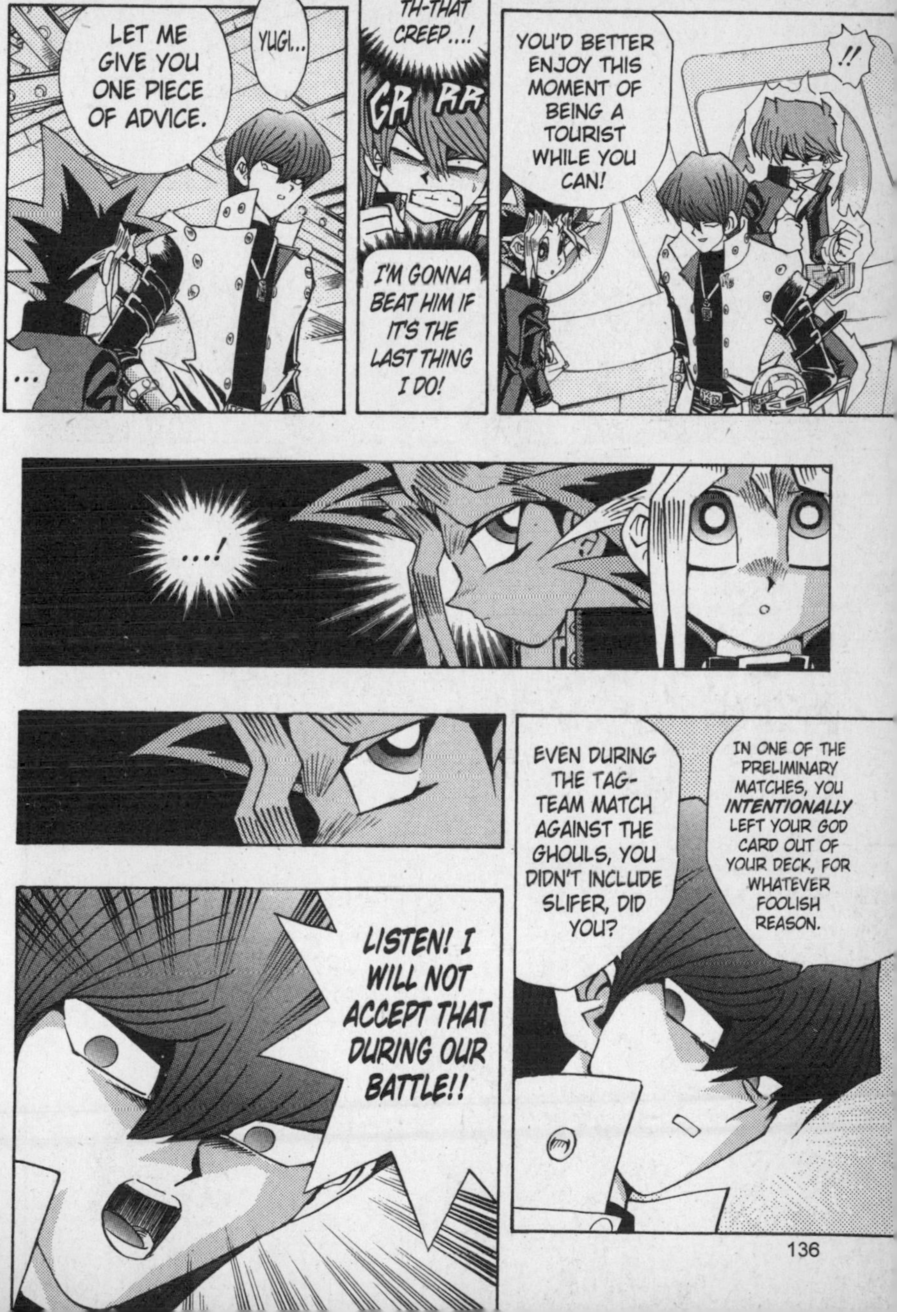
YOU'D BETTER ENJOY THIS MOMENT OF BEING A TOURIST WHILE YOU CAN!
!!
TH-THAT CREEP...!
GR RR
I'M GONNA BEAT HIM IF IT'S THE LAST THING I DO!
YUGI...
LET ME GIVE YOU ONE PIECE OF ADVICE.
...
...!
IN ONE OF THE PRELIMINARY MATCHES, YOU *INTENTIONALLY* LEFT YOUR GOD CARD OUT OF YOUR DECK, FOR WHATEVER FOOLISH REASON.
EVEN DURING THE TAG-TEAM MATCH AGAINST THE GHOULS, YOU DIDN'T INCLUDE SLIFER, DID YOU?
LISTEN! I WILL NOT ACCEPT THAT DURING OUR BATTLE!!

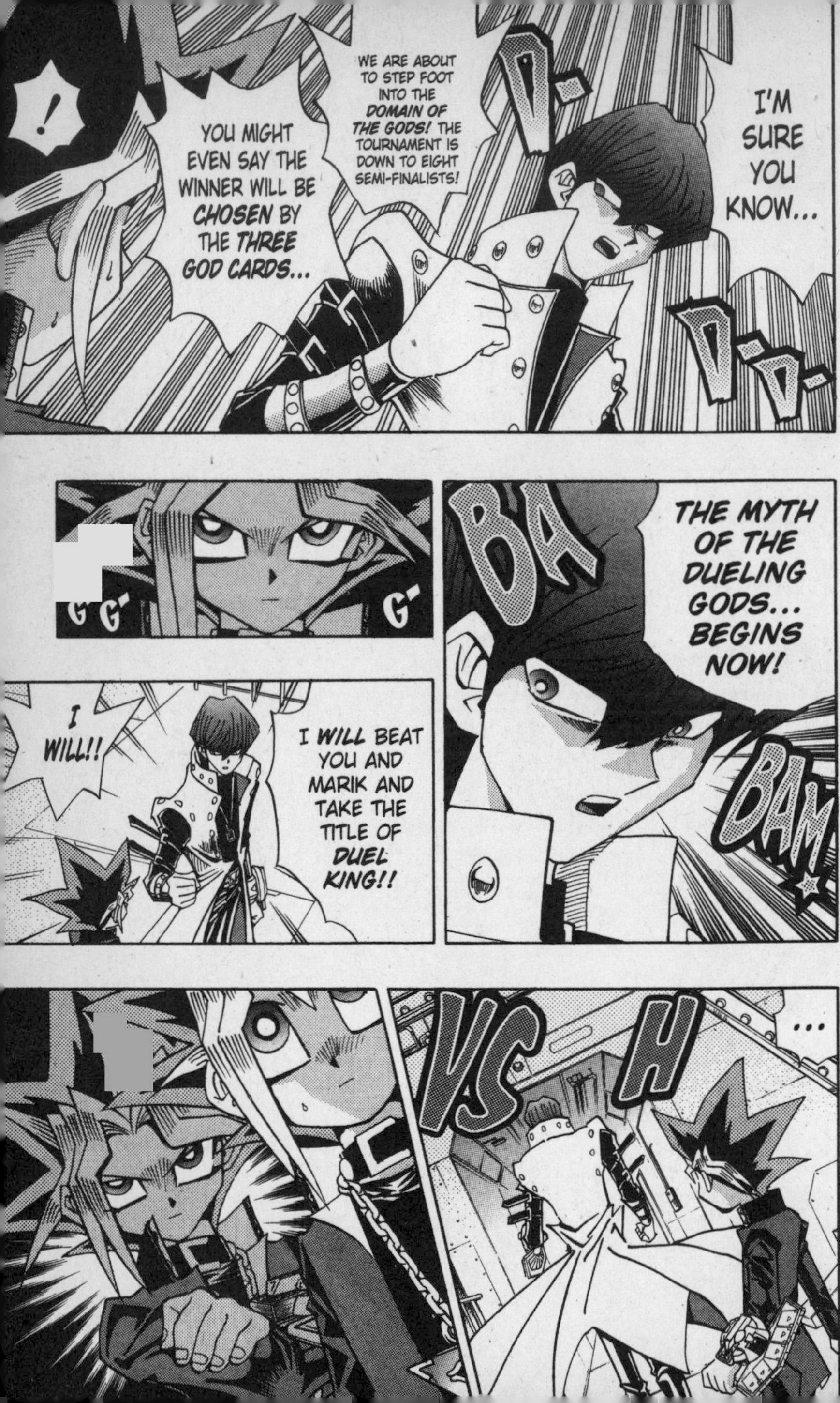
I'M SURE YOU KNOW...
D-
WE ARE ABOUT TO STEP FOOT INTO THE DOMAIN OF THE GODS! THE TOURNAMENT IS DOWN TO EIGHT SEMI-FINALISTS!
YOU MIGHT EVEN SAY THE WINNER WILL BE CHOSEN BY THE THREE GOD CARDS...
!
D-D-
BA
THE MYTH OF THE DUELING GODS... BEGINS NOW!
BAM
G G- G-
I WILL BEAT YOU AND MARIK AND TAKE THE TITLE OF DUEL KING!!
I WILL!!
...
H
VS

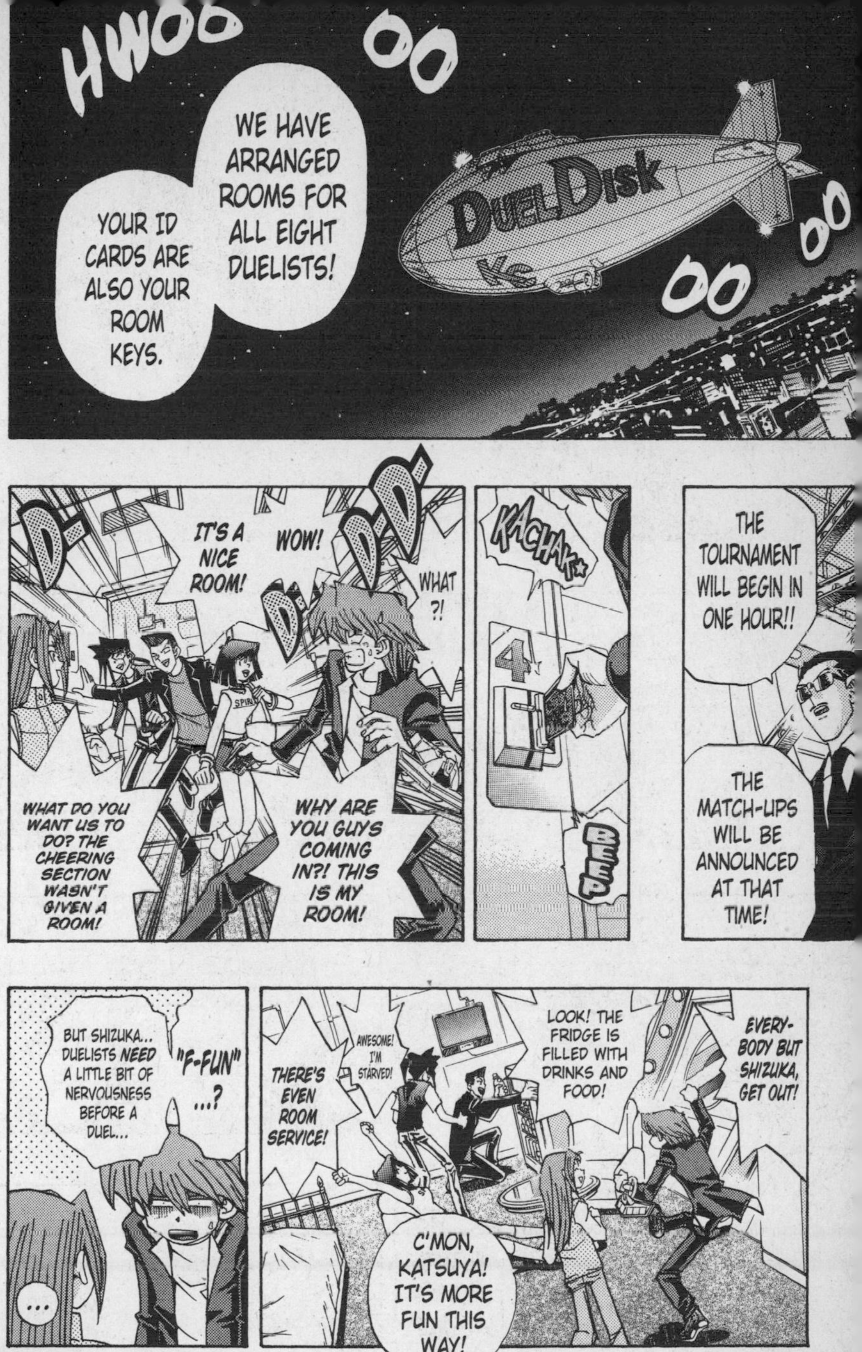
HWOO OO OO OO
DuelDisk
KC
WE HAVE ARRANGED ROOMS FOR ALL EIGHT DUELISTS!
YOUR ID CARDS ARE ALSO YOUR ROOM KEYS.
THE TOURNAMENT WILL BEGIN IN ONE HOUR!!
THE MATCH-UPS WILL BE ANNOUNCED AT THAT TIME!
KACHAK☆
4
BEEP
D-D-D-
D-
WOW!
IT'S A NICE ROOM!
WHAT?!
WHY ARE YOU GUYS COMING IN?! THIS IS MY ROOM!
WHAT DO YOU WANT US TO DO? THE CHEERING SECTION WASN'T GIVEN A ROOM!
EVERYBODY BUT SHIZUKA, GET OUT!
LOOK! THE FRIDGE IS FILLED WITH DRINKS AND FOOD!
AWESOME! I'M STARVED!
THERE'S EVEN ROOM SERVICE!
C'MON, KATSUYA! IT'S MORE FUN THIS WAY!
"F-FUN" ...?
BUT SHIZUKA... DUELISTS NEED A LITTLE BIT OF NERVOUSNESS BEFORE A DUEL...
...

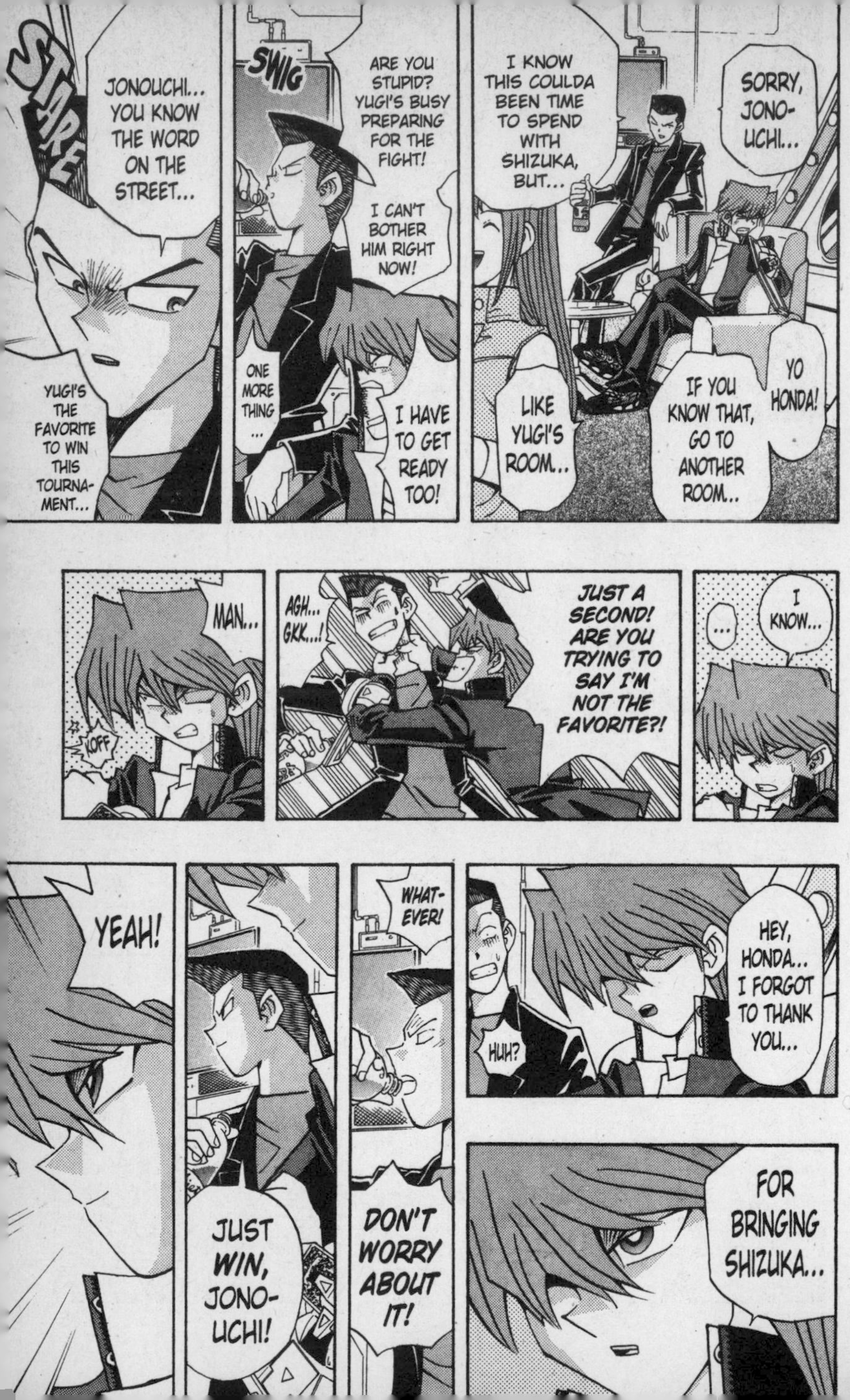
SORRY, JONO-UCHI...
I KNOW THIS COULDA BEEN TIME TO SPEND WITH SHIZUKA, BUT...
YO HONDA!
IF YOU KNOW THAT, GO TO ANOTHER ROOM...
LIKE YUGI'S ROOM...
SWIG
ARE YOU STUPID? YUGI'S BUSY PREPARING FOR THE FIGHT!
I CAN'T BOTHER HIM RIGHT NOW!
I HAVE TO GET READY TOO!
ONE MORE THING ...
STARE
JONOUCHI... YOU KNOW THE WORD ON THE STREET...
YUGI'S THE FAVORITE TO WIN THIS TOURNA-MENT...
I KNOW...
...
JUST A SECOND! ARE YOU TRYING TO SAY I'M NOT THE FAVORITE?!
AGH... GKK...!
MAN...
KOFF
HEY, HONDA... I FORGOT TO THANK YOU...
HUH?
FOR BRINGING SHIZUKA...
WHAT-EVER!
DON'T WORRY ABOUT IT!
JUST WIN, JONO-UCHI!
YEAH!

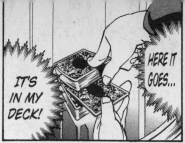

IT'S IN MY DECK!

HERE IT GOES...

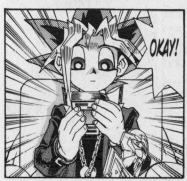

OKAY!

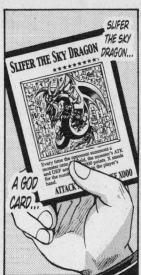

SLIFER THE SKY DRAGON...

SLIFER THE SKY DRAGON

Every time the opponent summons a monster onto the field, the monster's ATK and DEF increase X000 points. X stands for the number of cards in the player's hand.

ATTACK X000   DEFENSE X000

A GOD CARD...

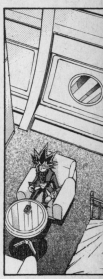

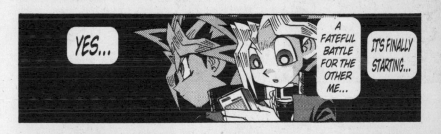

YES...

A FATEFUL BATTLE FOR THE OTHER ME...

IT'S FINALLY STARTING...

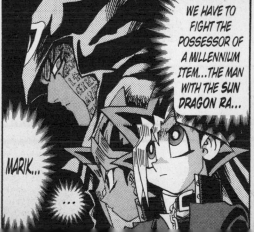

WE HAVE TO FIGHT THE POSSESSOR OF A MILLENNIUM ITEM...THE MAN WITH THE SUN DRAGON RA...

MARIK...

...

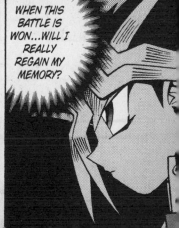

WHEN THIS BATTLE IS WON...WILL I REALLY REGAIN MY MEMORY?

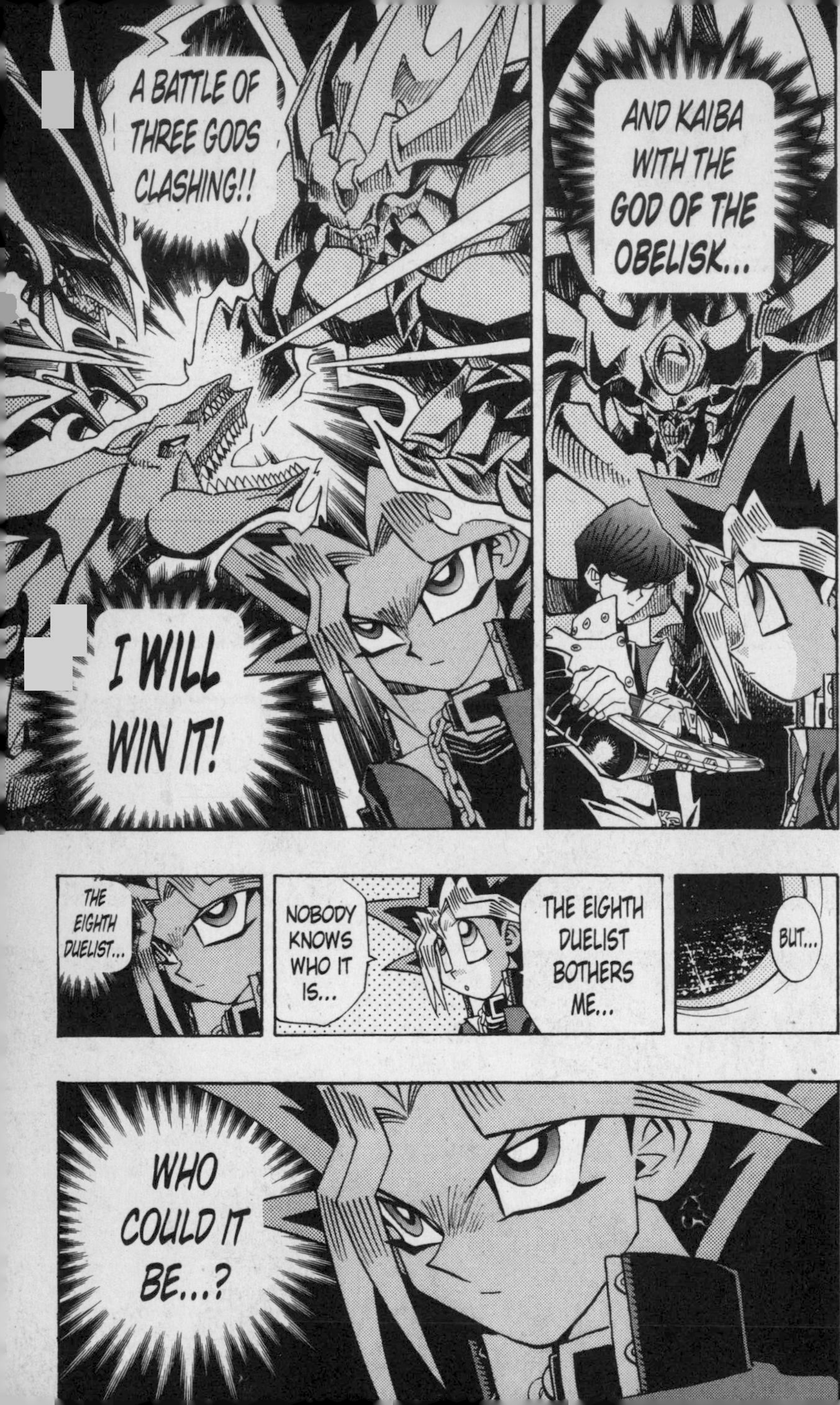
AND KAIBA WITH THE GOD OF THE OBELISK...
A BATTLE OF THREE GODS CLASHING!!
I WILL WIN IT!
BUT...
THE EIGHTH DUELIST BOTHERS ME...
NOBODY KNOWS WHO IT IS...
THE EIGHTH DUELIST...
WHO COULD IT BE...?

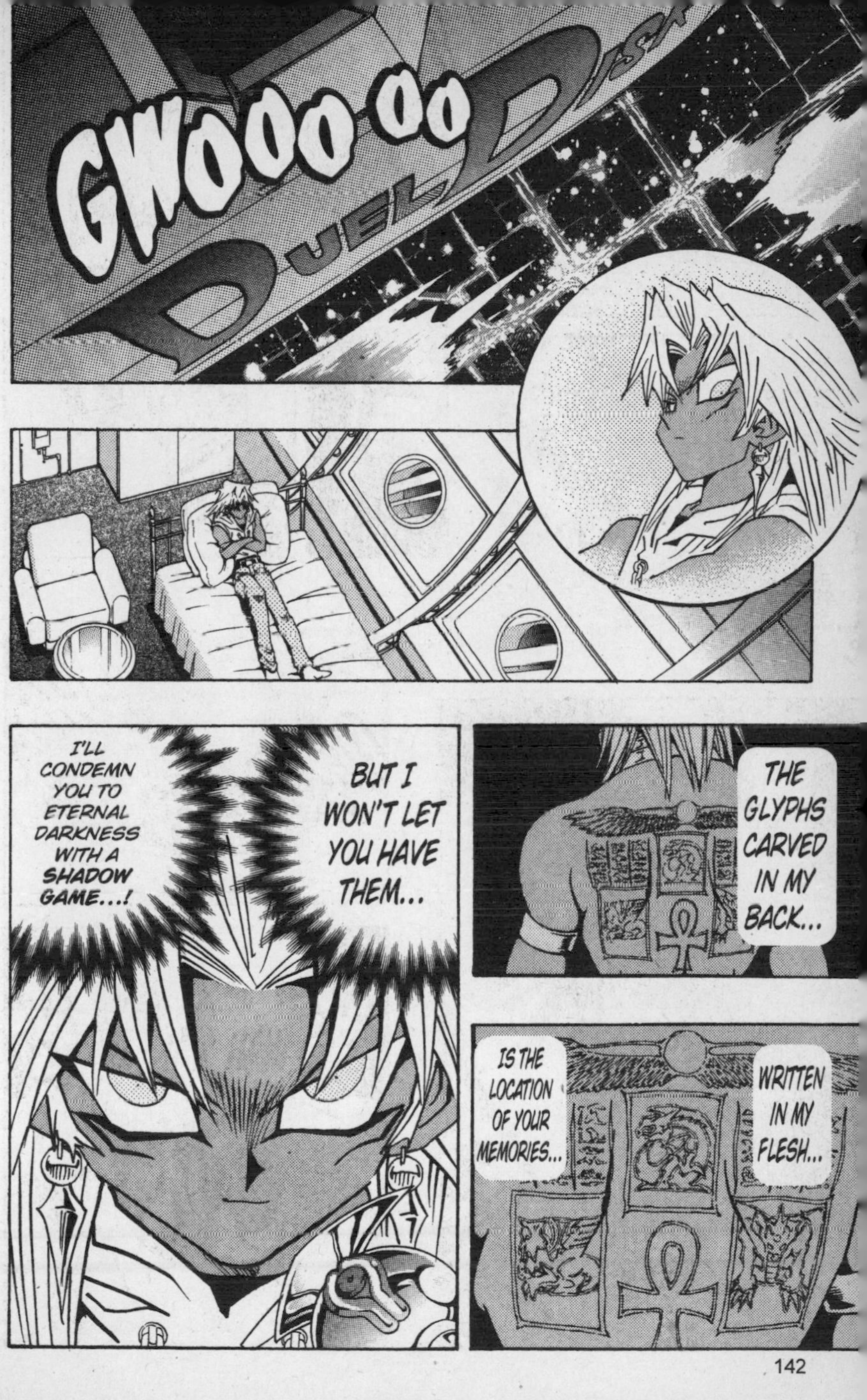
GWOOO OO
THE GLYPHS CARVED IN MY BACK...
WRITTEN IN MY FLESH...
IS THE LOCATION OF YOUR MEMORIES...
BUT I WON'T LET YOU HAVE THEM...
I'LL CONDEMN YOU TO ETERNAL DARKNESS WITH A SHADOW GAME...!

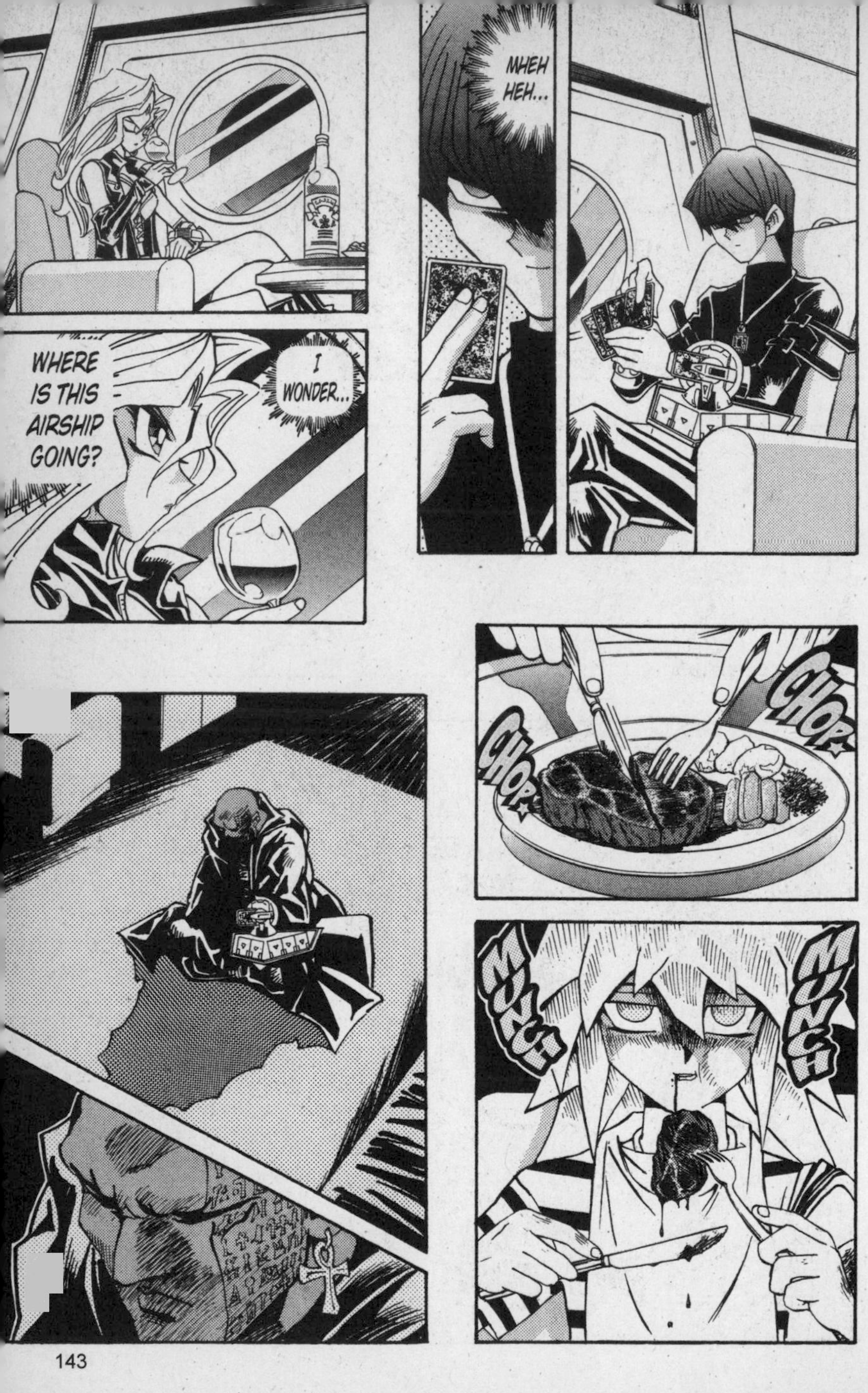
MHEH HEH...
I WONDER...
WHERE IS THIS AIRSHIP GOING?
CHOP
CHOP
MUNCH
MUNCH

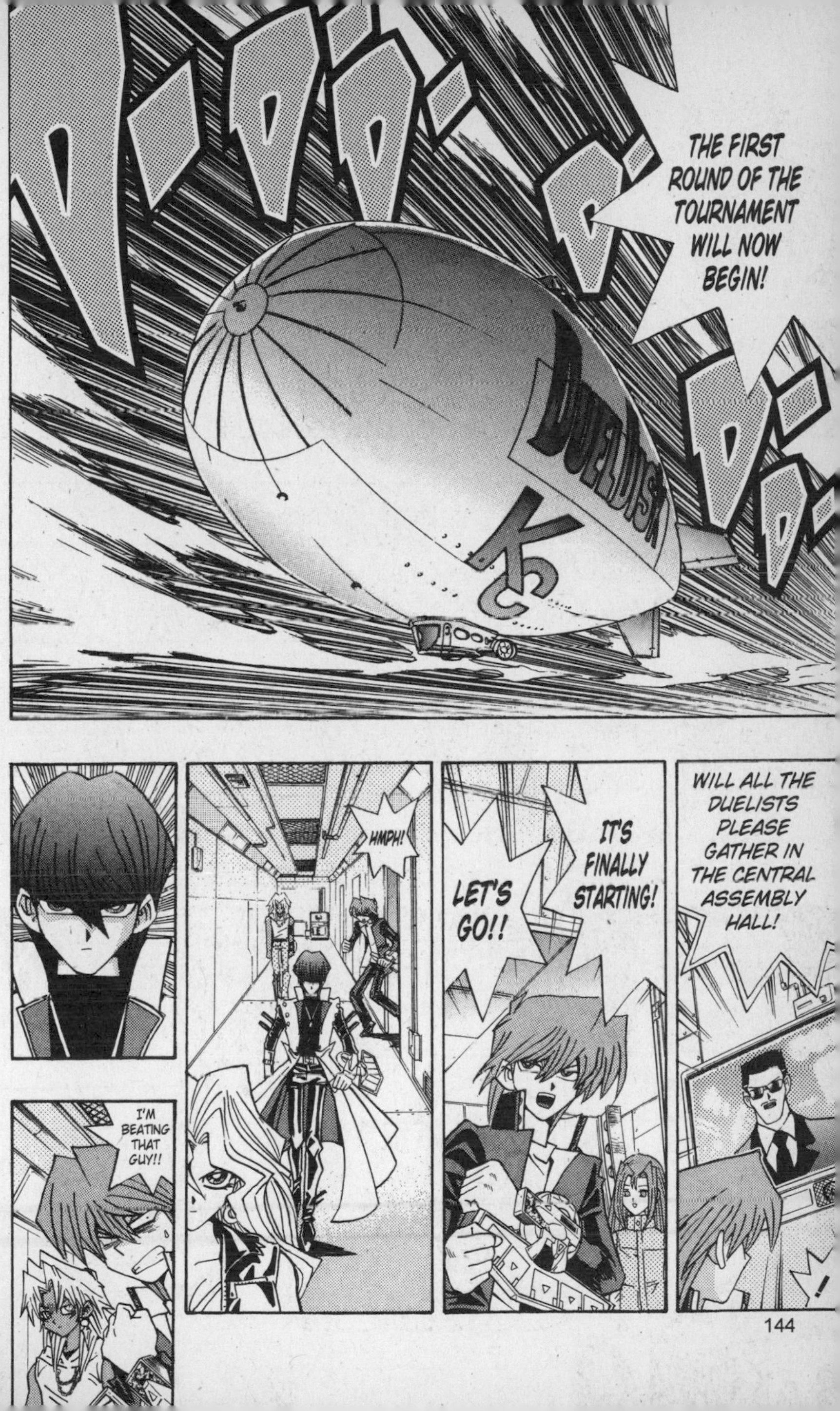
THE FIRST ROUND OF THE TOURNAMENT WILL NOW BEGIN!
WILL ALL THE DUELISTS PLEASE GATHER IN THE CENTRAL ASSEMBLY HALL!
!
IT'S FINALLY STARTING!
LET'S GO!!
HMPH!
I'M BEATING THAT GUY!!

READ THIS WAY

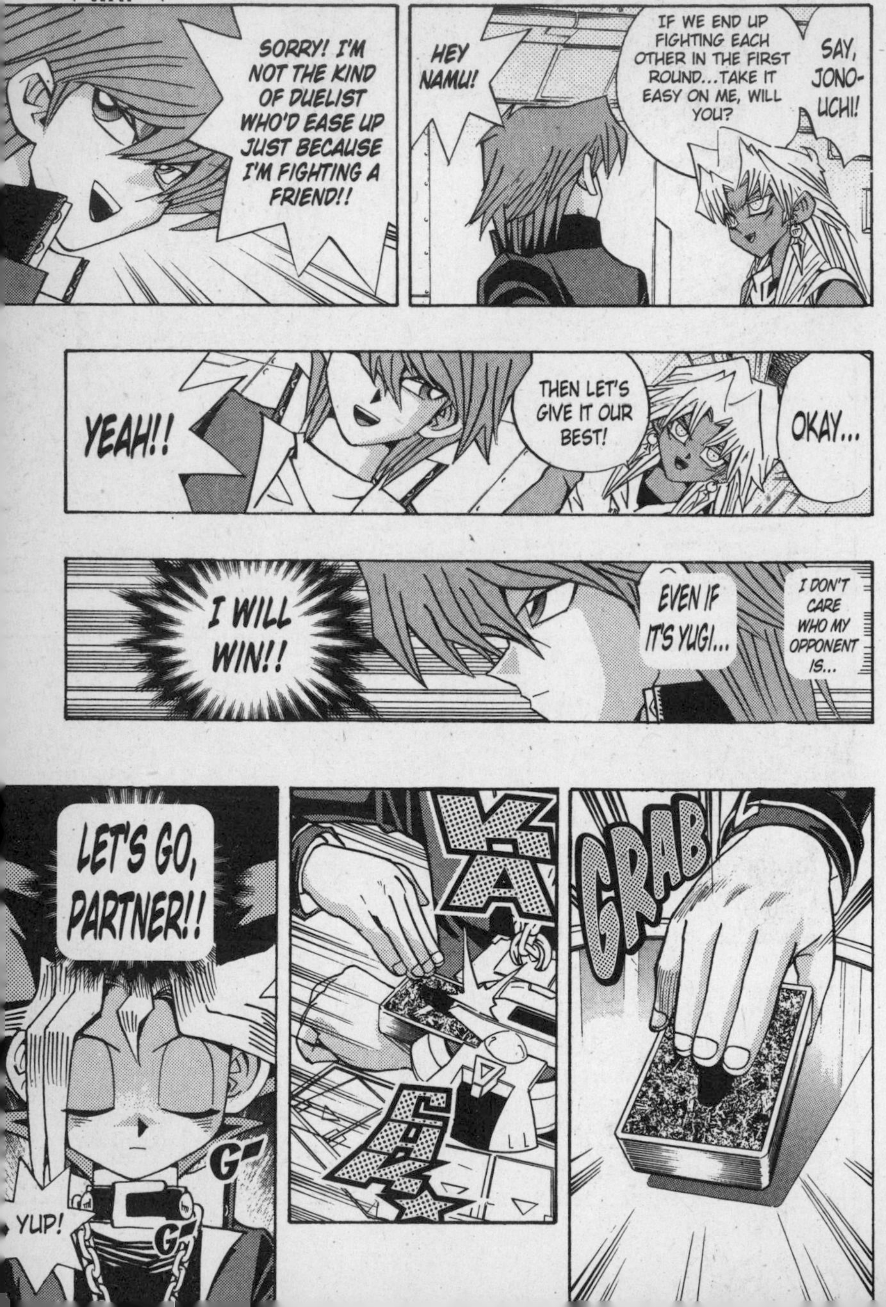
SAY, JONO-UCHI!
IF WE END UP FIGHTING EACH OTHER IN THE FIRST ROUND...TAKE IT EASY ON ME, WILL YOU?
HEY NAMU!
SORRY! I'M NOT THE KIND OF DUELIST WHO'D EASE UP JUST BECAUSE I'M FIGHTING A FRIEND!!
OKAY...
THEN LET'S GIVE IT OUR BEST!
YEAH!!
I DON'T CARE WHO MY OPPONENT IS...
EVEN IF IT'S YUGI...
I WILL WIN!!
GRAB
KA
LET'S GO, PARTNER!!
YUP!

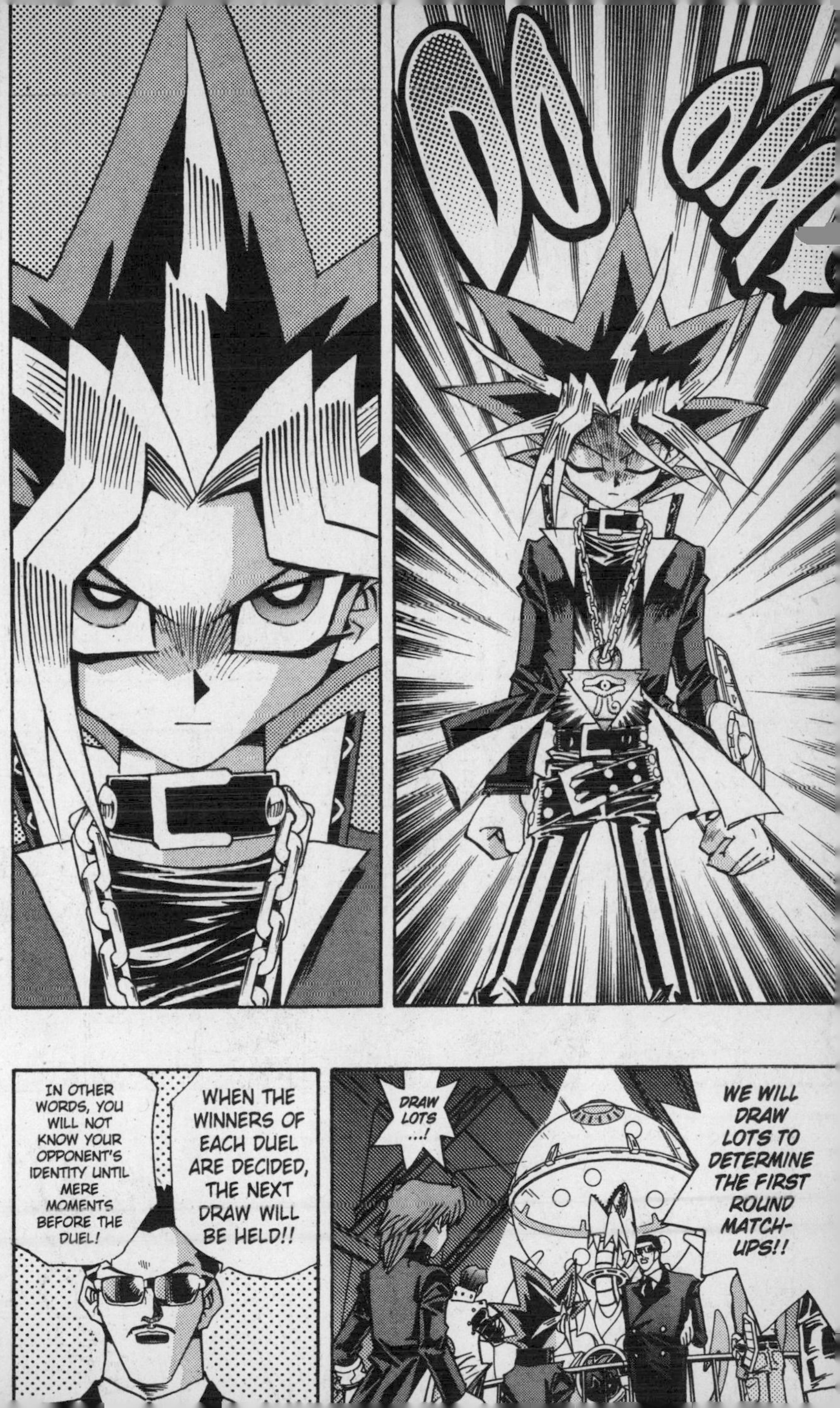
OO OH
WE WILL DRAW LOTS TO DETERMINE THE FIRST ROUND MATCH-UPS!!
DRAW LOTS ...!
WHEN THE WINNERS OF EACH DUEL ARE DECIDED, THE NEXT DRAW WILL BE HELD!!
IN OTHER WORDS, YOU WILL NOT KNOW YOUR OPPONENT'S IDENTITY UNTIL MERE MOMENTS BEFORE THE DUEL!

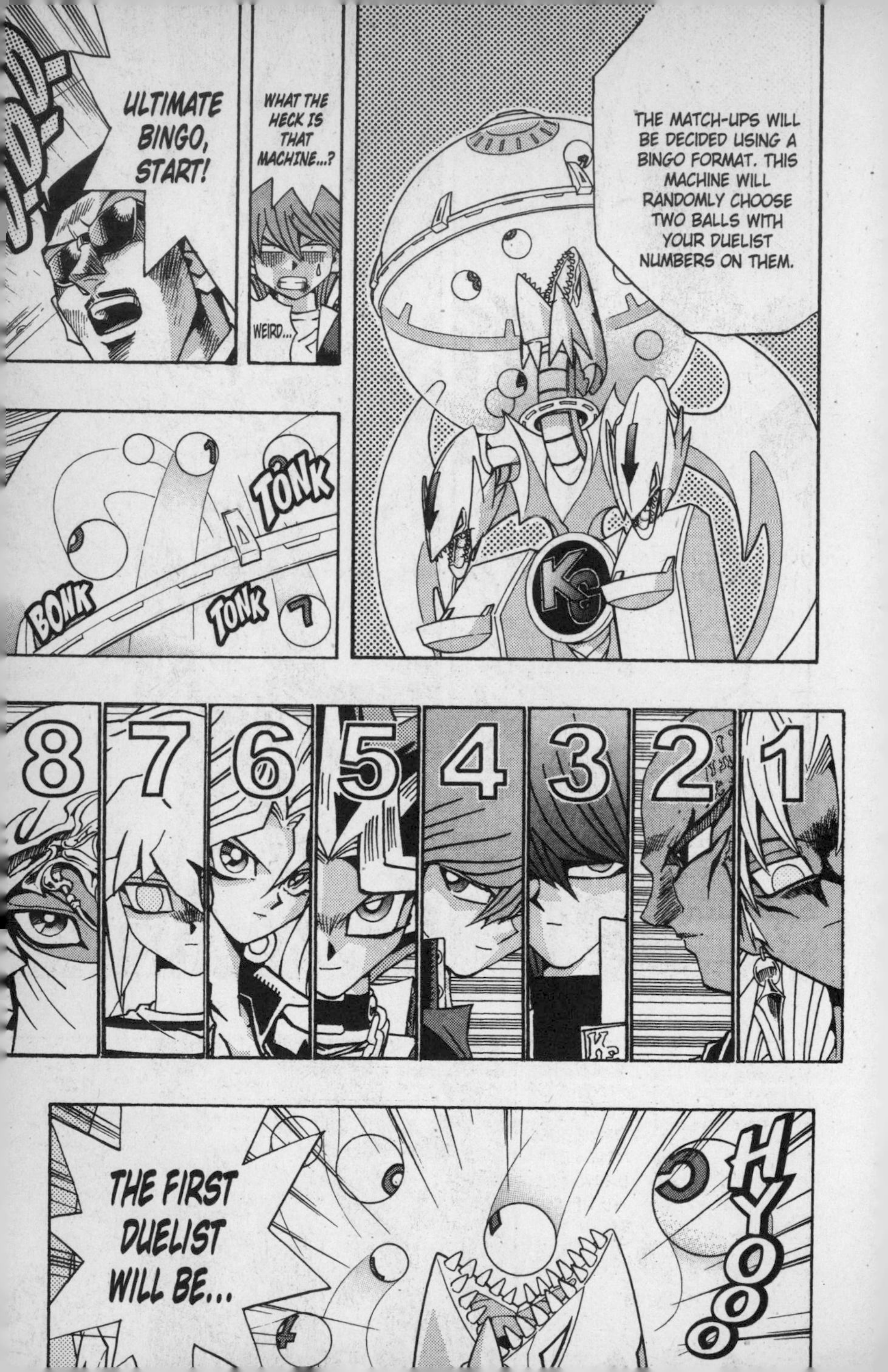

THE MATCH-UPS WILL BE DECIDED USING A BINGO FORMAT. THIS MACHINE WILL RANDOMLY CHOOSE TWO BALLS WITH YOUR DUELIST NUMBERS ON THEM.
WHAT THE HECK IS THAT MACHINE...?
WEIRD...
ULTIMATE BINGO, START!
TONK
TONK
BONK
1
2
3
4
5
6
7
8
HYOOOO
THE FIRST DUELIST WILL BE...

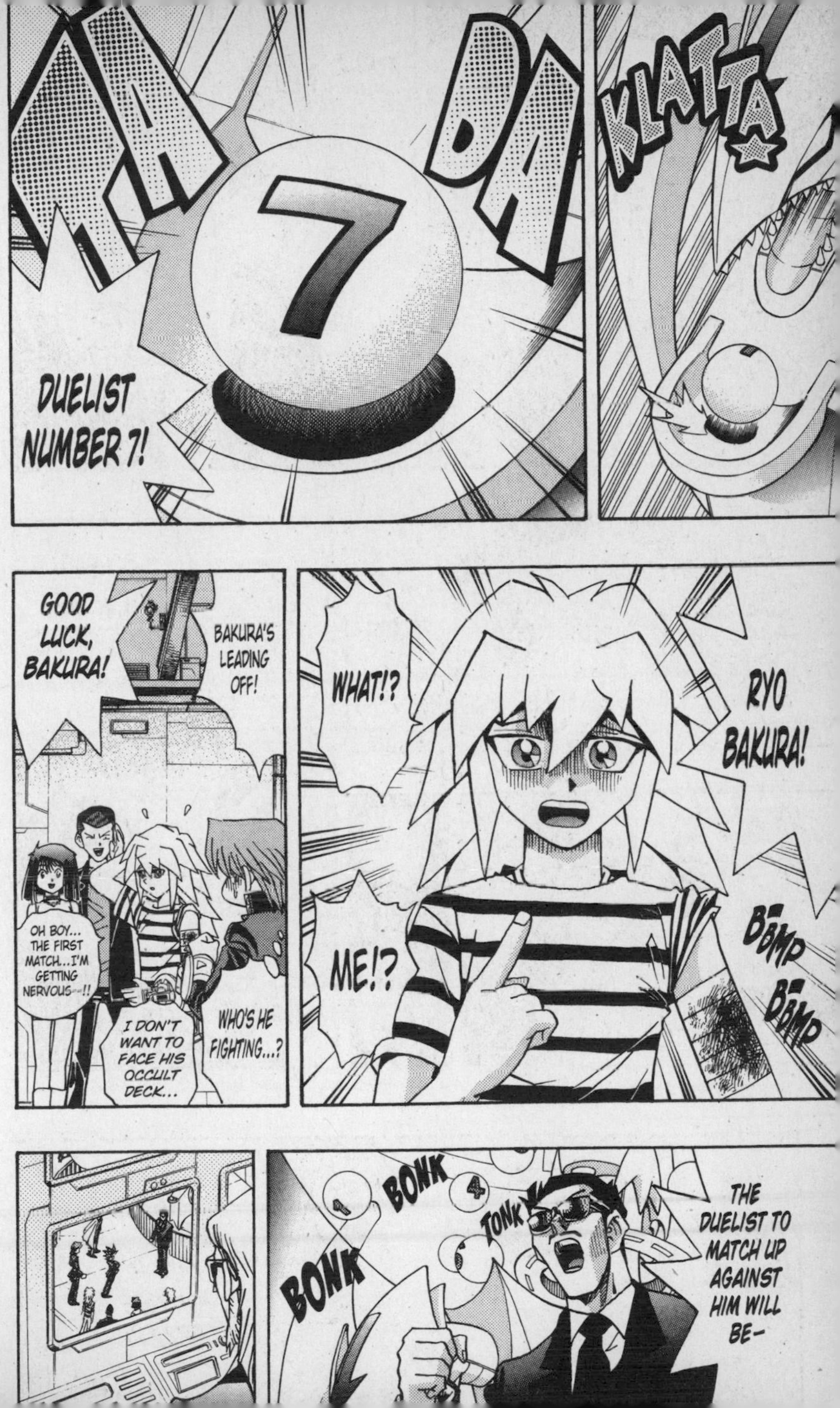
KLATTA
DA
7
DUELIST NUMBER 7!
RYO BAKURA!
WHAT!?
ME!?
B-BMP
B-BMP
BAKURA'S LEADING OFF!
GOOD LUCK, BAKURA!
WHO'S HE FIGHTING...?
I DON'T WANT TO FACE HIS OCCULT DECK...
OH BOY... THE FIRST MATCH...I'M GETTING NERVOUS--!!
THE DUELIST TO MATCH UP AGAINST HIM WILL BE-
TONK
BONK
BONK

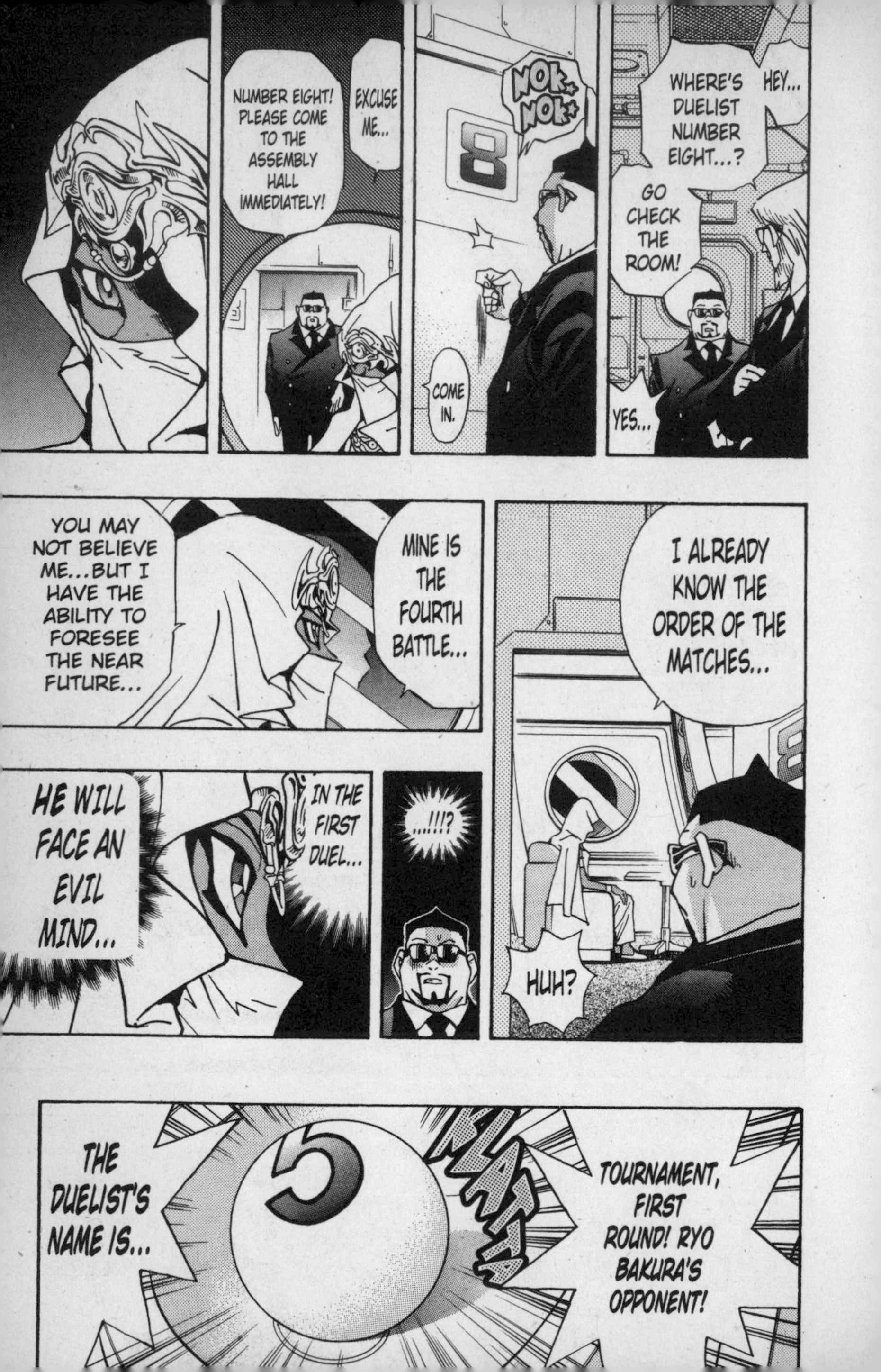
HEY...
WHERE'S DUELIST NUMBER EIGHT...?
GO CHECK THE ROOM!
YES...
NOK NOK
COME IN.
EXCUSE ME...
NUMBER EIGHT! PLEASE COME TO THE ASSEMBLY HALL IMMEDIATELY!
I ALREADY KNOW THE ORDER OF THE MATCHES...
HUH?
MINE IS THE FOURTH BATTLE...
YOU MAY NOT BELIEVE ME...BUT I HAVE THE ABILITY TO FORESEE THE NEAR FUTURE...
...!!!?
IN THE FIRST DUEL...
HE WILL FACE AN EVIL MIND...
TOURNAMENT, FIRST ROUND! RYO BAKURA'S OPPONENT!
THE DUELIST'S NAME IS...

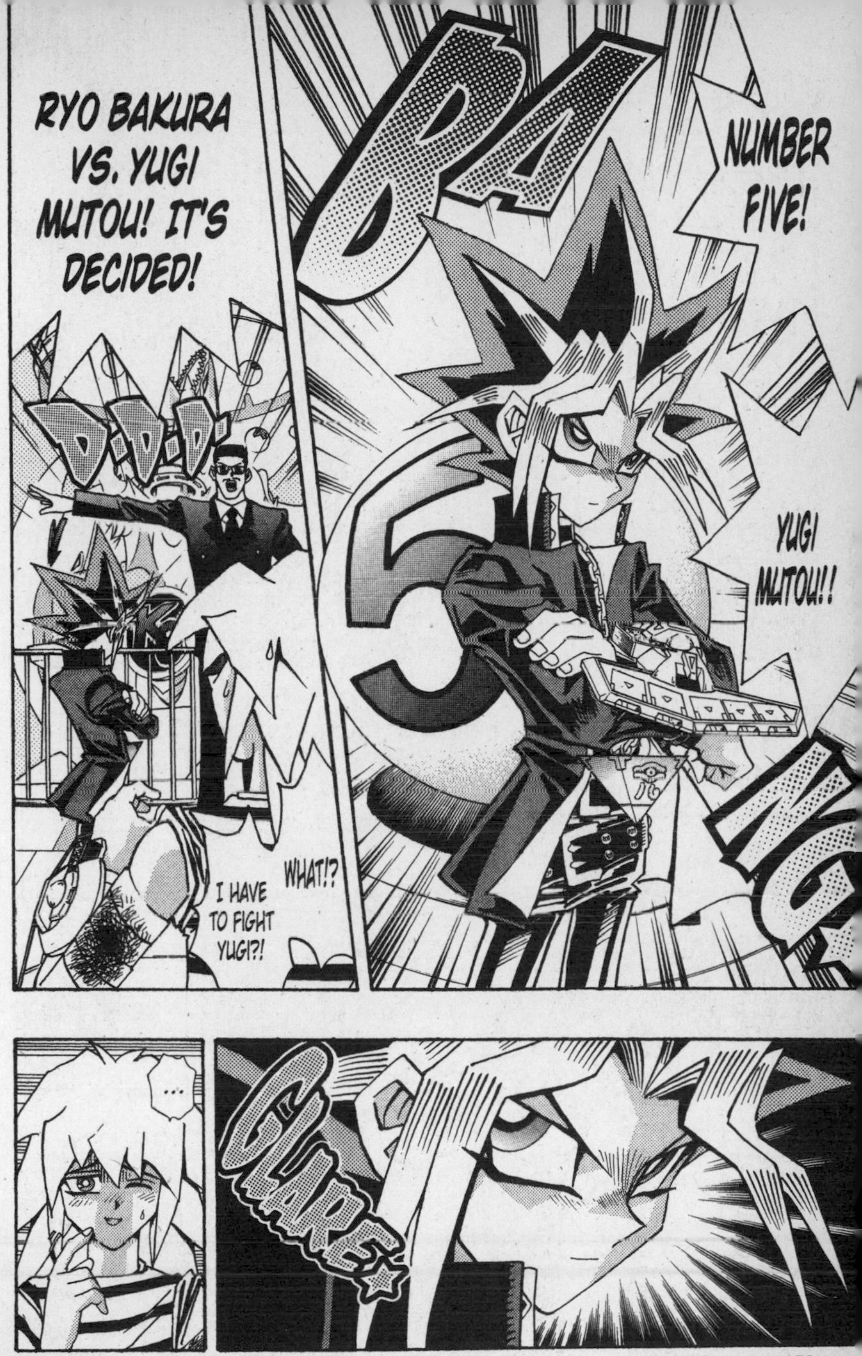
NUMBER FIVE!
BA
YUGI MUTOU!!
NG
RYO BAKURA VS. YUGI MUTOU! IT'S DECIDED!
D-D-D
WHAT!?
I HAVE TO FIGHT YUGI?!
GLARE
...

READ THIS WAY

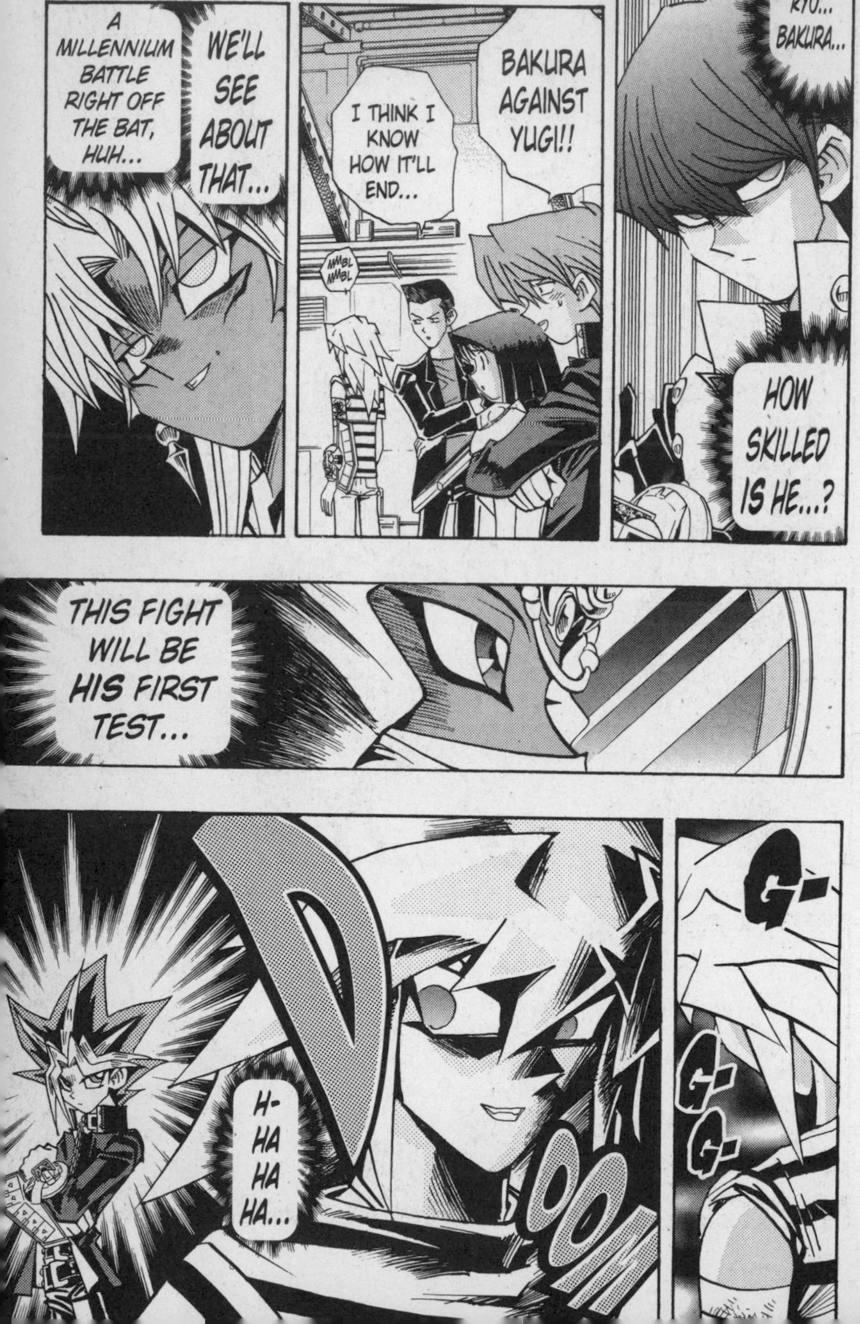
RYO... BAKURA...
HOW SKILLED IS HE...?
BAKURA AGAINST YUGI!!
I THINK I KNOW HOW IT'LL END...
MMBL MMBL
WE'LL SEE ABOUT THAT...
A MILLENNIUM BATTLE RIGHT OFF THE BAT, HUH...
THIS FIGHT WILL BE HIS FIRST TEST...
G-
G-
G-
G-
H-HA HA HA...

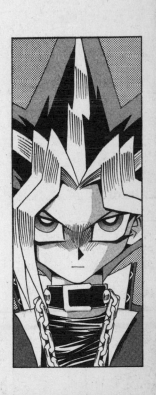

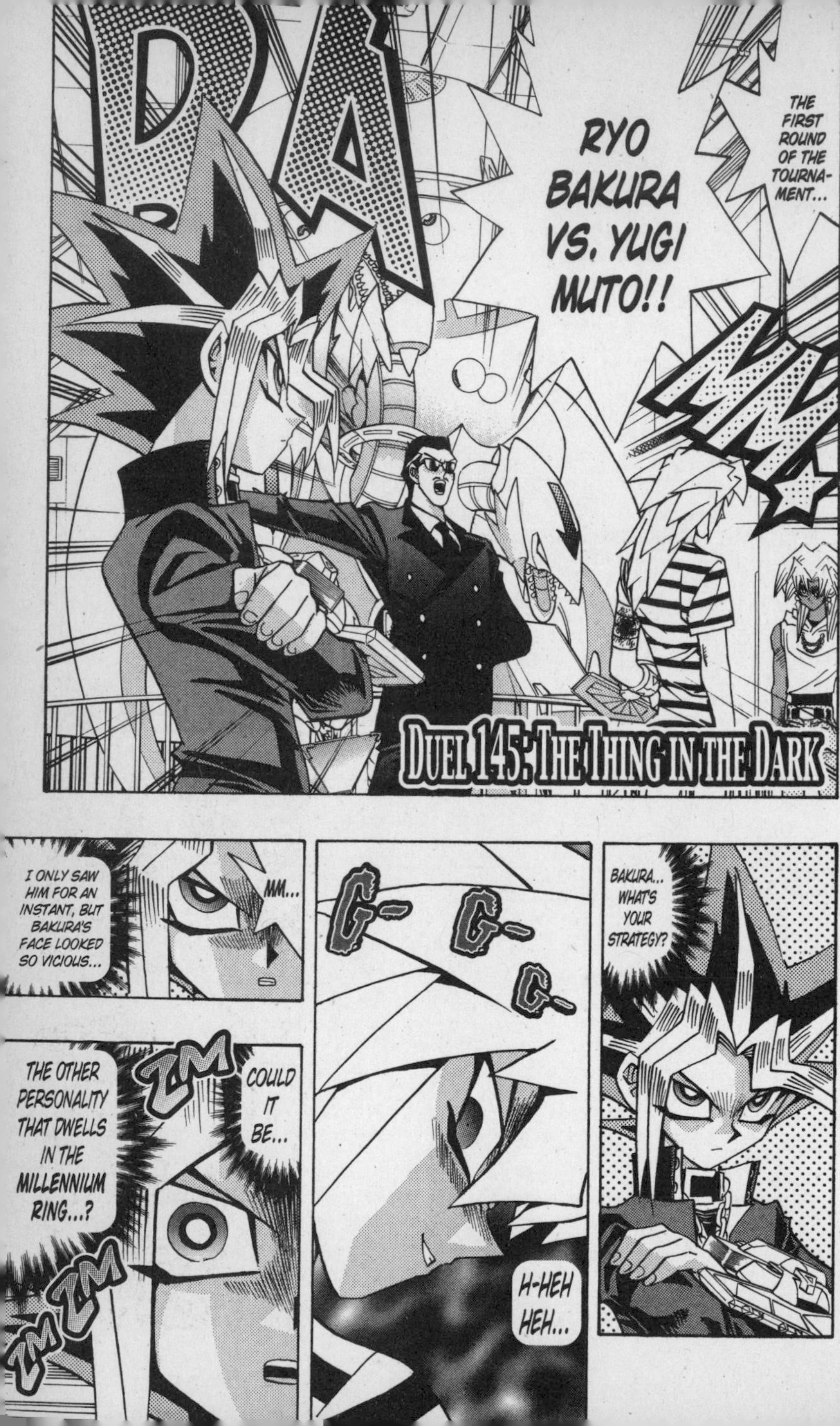
THE FIRST ROUND OF THE TOURNAMENT...
RYO BAKURA VS. YUGI MUTO!!
DA
MM
DUEL 145: THE THING IN THE DARK
BAKURA... WHAT'S YOUR STRATEGY?
G- G- G-
H-HEH HEH...
MM...
I ONLY SAW HIM FOR AN INSTANT, BUT BAKURA'S FACE LOOKED SO VICIOUS...
COULD IT BE...
ZM
THE OTHER PERSONALITY THAT DWELLS IN THE MILLENNIUM RING...?
ZM ZM

Duel 145: The Thing in the Dark

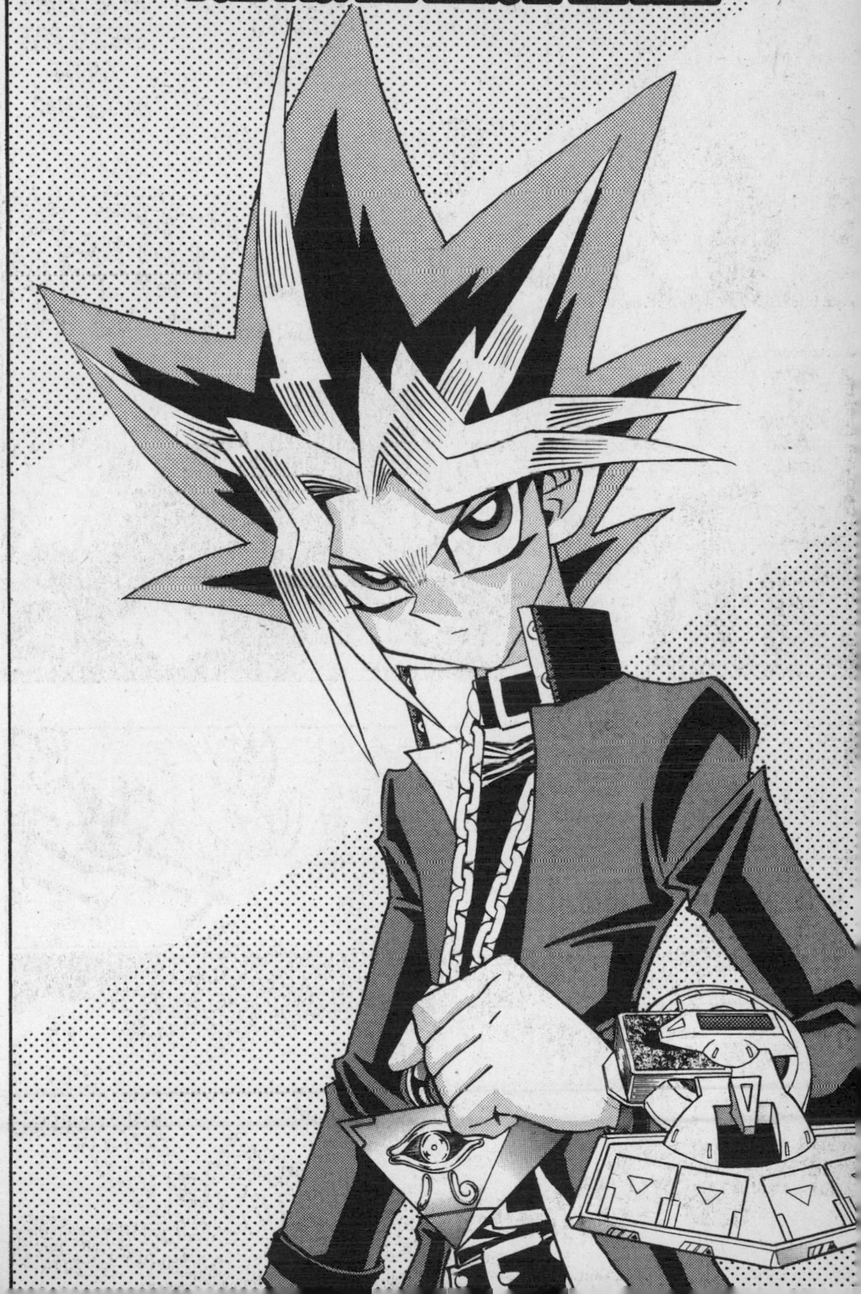

READ THIS WAY

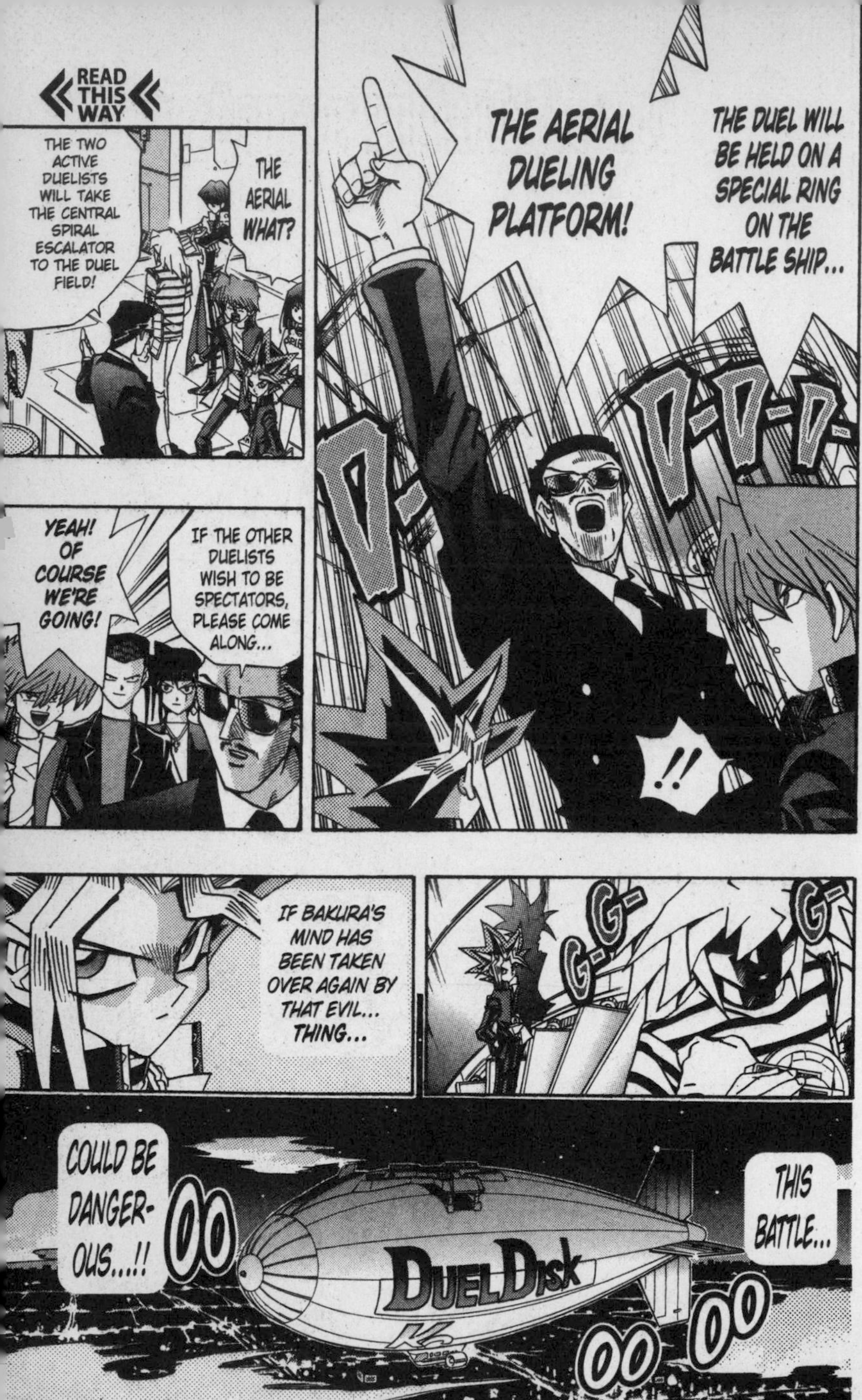
THE DUEL WILL BE HELD ON A SPECIAL RING ON THE BATTLE SHIP...
THE AERIAL DUELING PLATFORM!
D-D-D-
D-
!!
THE AERIAL WHAT?
THE TWO ACTIVE DUELISTS WILL TAKE THE CENTRAL SPIRAL ESCALATOR TO THE DUEL FIELD!
IF THE OTHER DUELISTS WISH TO BE SPECTATORS, PLEASE COME ALONG...
YEAH! OF COURSE WE'RE GOING!
G-G-
G-
IF BAKURA'S MIND HAS BEEN TAKEN OVER AGAIN BY THAT EVIL... THING...
THIS BATTLE...
OO
OO
DUEL DISK
OO
COULD BE DANGER-OUS...!!

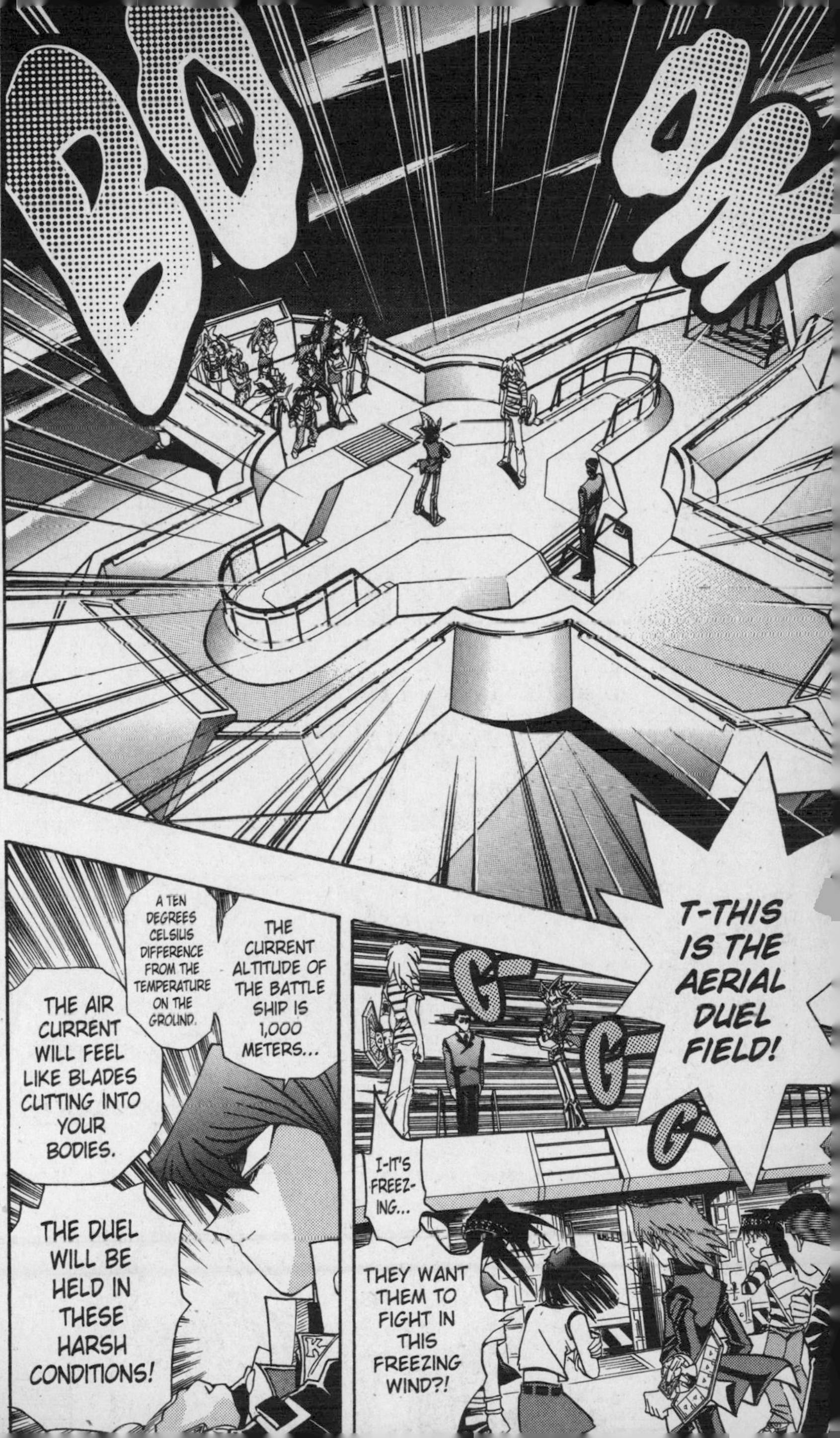
BOOM
T-THIS IS THE AERIAL DUEL FIELD!
G- G- G
I-IT'S FREEZ-ING...
THEY WANT THEM TO FIGHT IN THIS FREEZING WIND?!
THE CURRENT ALTITUDE OF THE BATTLE SHIP IS 1,000 METERS...
A TEN DEGREES CELSIUS DIFFERENCE FROM THE TEMPERATURE ON THE GROUND.
THE AIR CURRENT WILL FEEL LIKE BLADES CUTTING INTO YOUR BODIES.
THE DUEL WILL BE HELD IN THESE HARSH CONDITIONS!

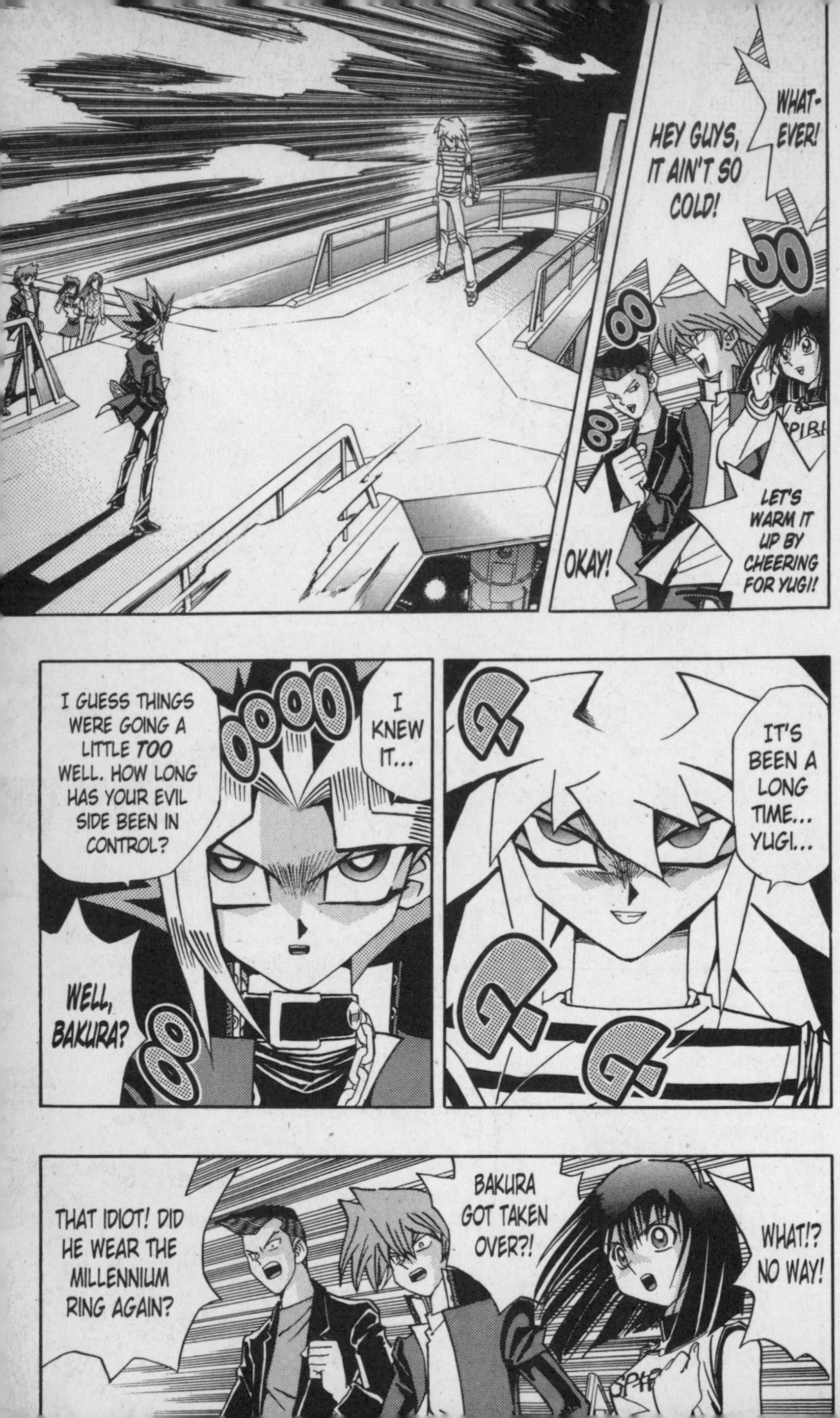
WHAT-EVER!
HEY GUYS, IT AIN'T SO COLD!
LET'S WARM IT UP BY CHEERING FOR YUGI!
OKAY!
IT'S BEEN A LONG TIME... YUGI...
I KNEW IT...
I GUESS THINGS WERE GOING A LITTLE TOO WELL. HOW LONG HAS YOUR EVIL SIDE BEEN IN CONTROL?
WELL, BAKURA?
WHAT!? NO WAY!
BAKURA GOT TAKEN OVER?!
THAT IDIOT! DID HE WEAR THE MILLENNIUM RING AGAIN?

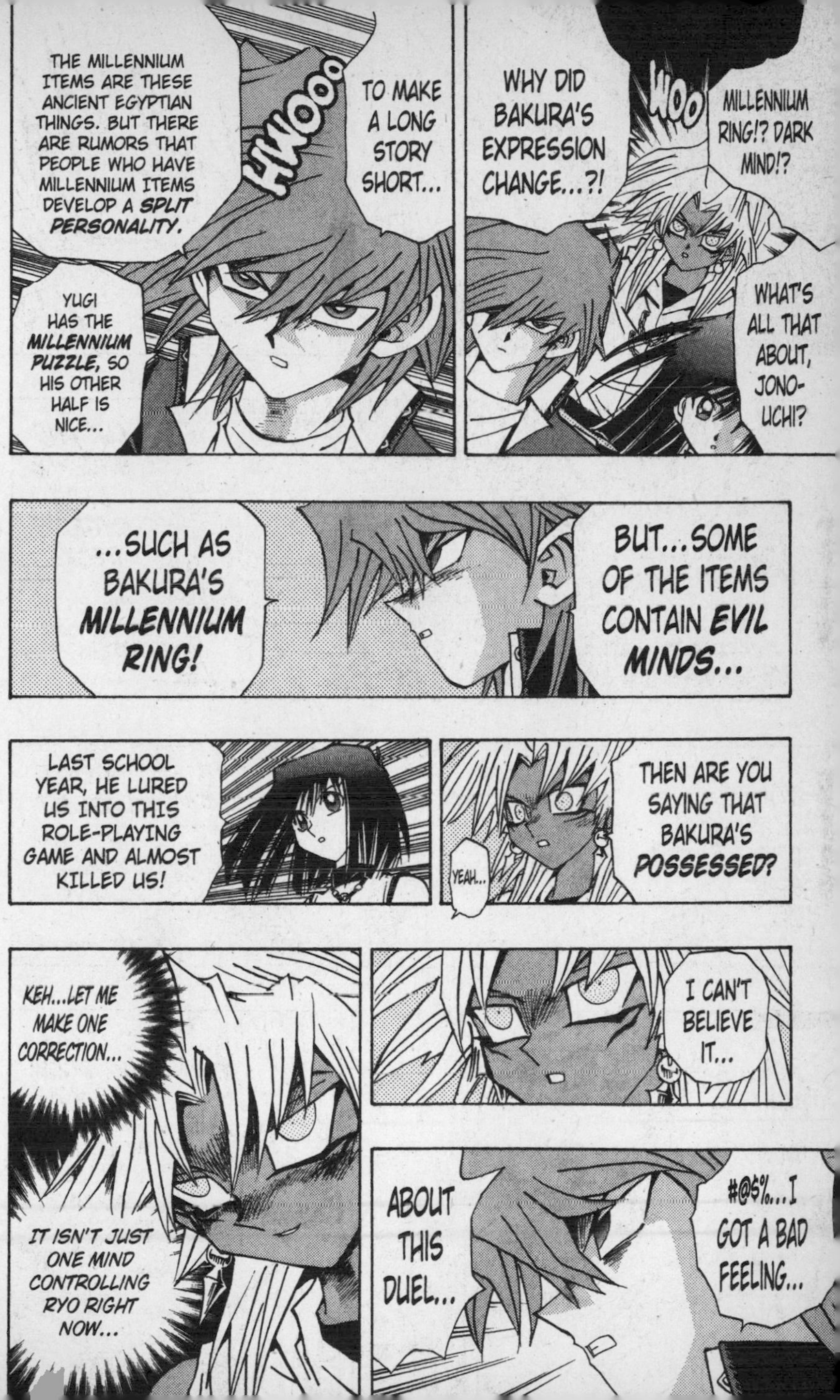
MILLENNIUM RING!? DARK MIND!?
WOO
WHY DID BAKURA'S EXPRESSION CHANGE...?!
WHAT'S ALL THAT ABOUT, JONO-UCHI?
TO MAKE A LONG STORY SHORT...
HWOOO
THE MILLENNIUM ITEMS ARE THESE ANCIENT EGYPTIAN THINGS. BUT THERE ARE RUMORS THAT PEOPLE WHO HAVE MILLENNIUM ITEMS DEVELOP A SPLIT PERSONALITY.
YUGI HAS THE MILLENNIUM PUZZLE, SO HIS OTHER HALF IS NICE...
BUT...SOME OF THE ITEMS CONTAIN EVIL MINDS...
...SUCH AS BAKURA'S MILLENNIUM RING!
THEN ARE YOU SAYING THAT BAKURA'S POSSESSED?
YEAH...
LAST SCHOOL YEAR, HE LURED US INTO THIS ROLE-PLAYING GAME AND ALMOST KILLED US!
I CAN'T BELIEVE IT...
#@$%...I GOT A BAD FEELING...
ABOUT THIS DUEL...
KEH...LET ME MAKE ONE CORRECTION...
IT ISN'T JUST ONE MIND CONTROLLING RYO RIGHT NOW...

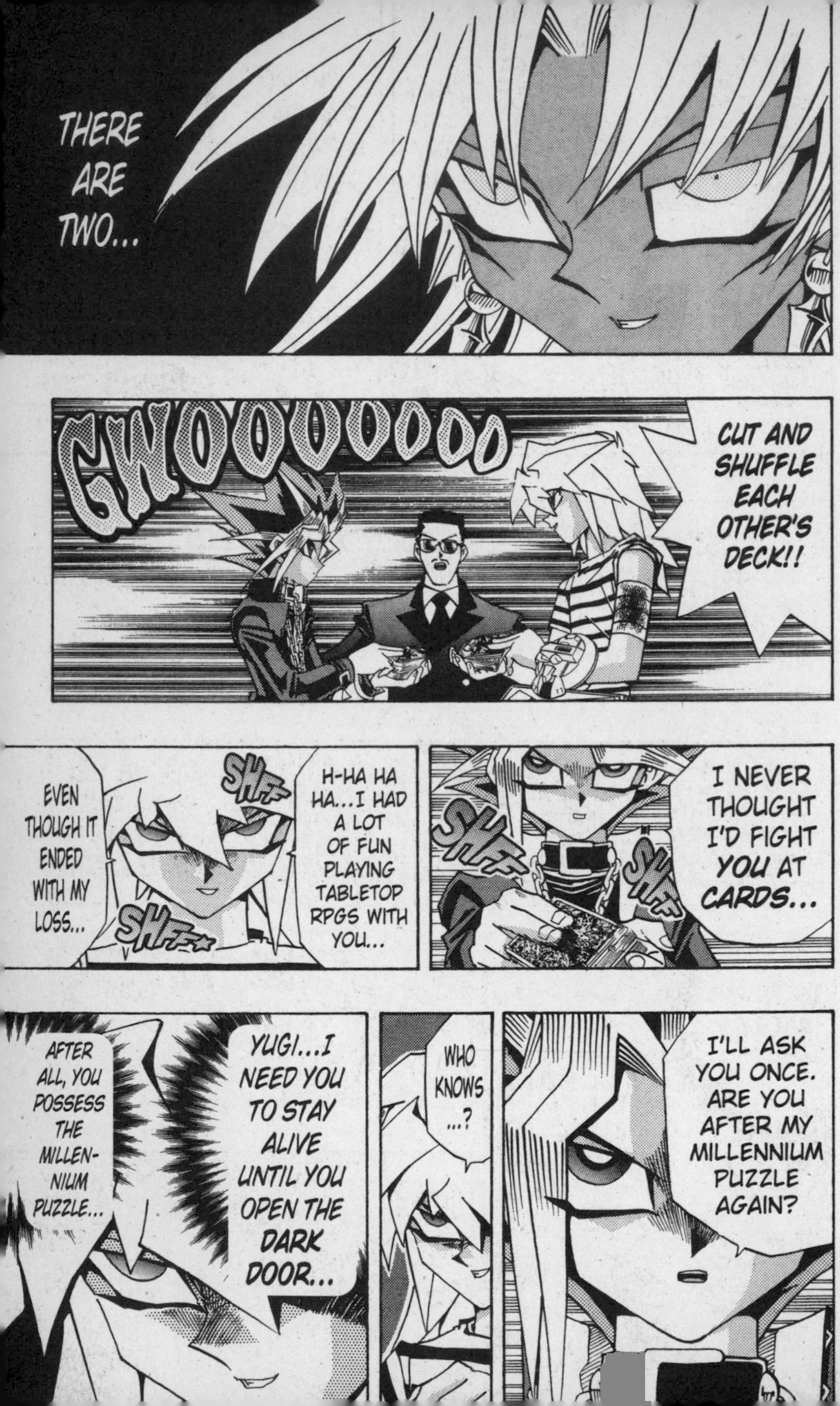
THERE ARE TWO...
CUT AND SHUFFLE EACH OTHER'S DECK!!
GWOOOOOOO
I NEVER THOUGHT I'D FIGHT YOU AT CARDS...
SHFF
SHFF
H-HA HA HA...I HAD A LOT OF FUN PLAYING TABLETOP RPGS WITH YOU...
SHFF
EVEN THOUGH IT ENDED WITH MY LOSS...
SHFF
I'LL ASK YOU ONCE. ARE YOU AFTER MY MILLENNIUM PUZZLE AGAIN?
WHO KNOWS...?
YUGI...I NEED YOU TO STAY ALIVE UNTIL YOU OPEN THE DARK DOOR...
AFTER ALL, YOU POSSESS THE MILLEN-NIUM PUZZLE...

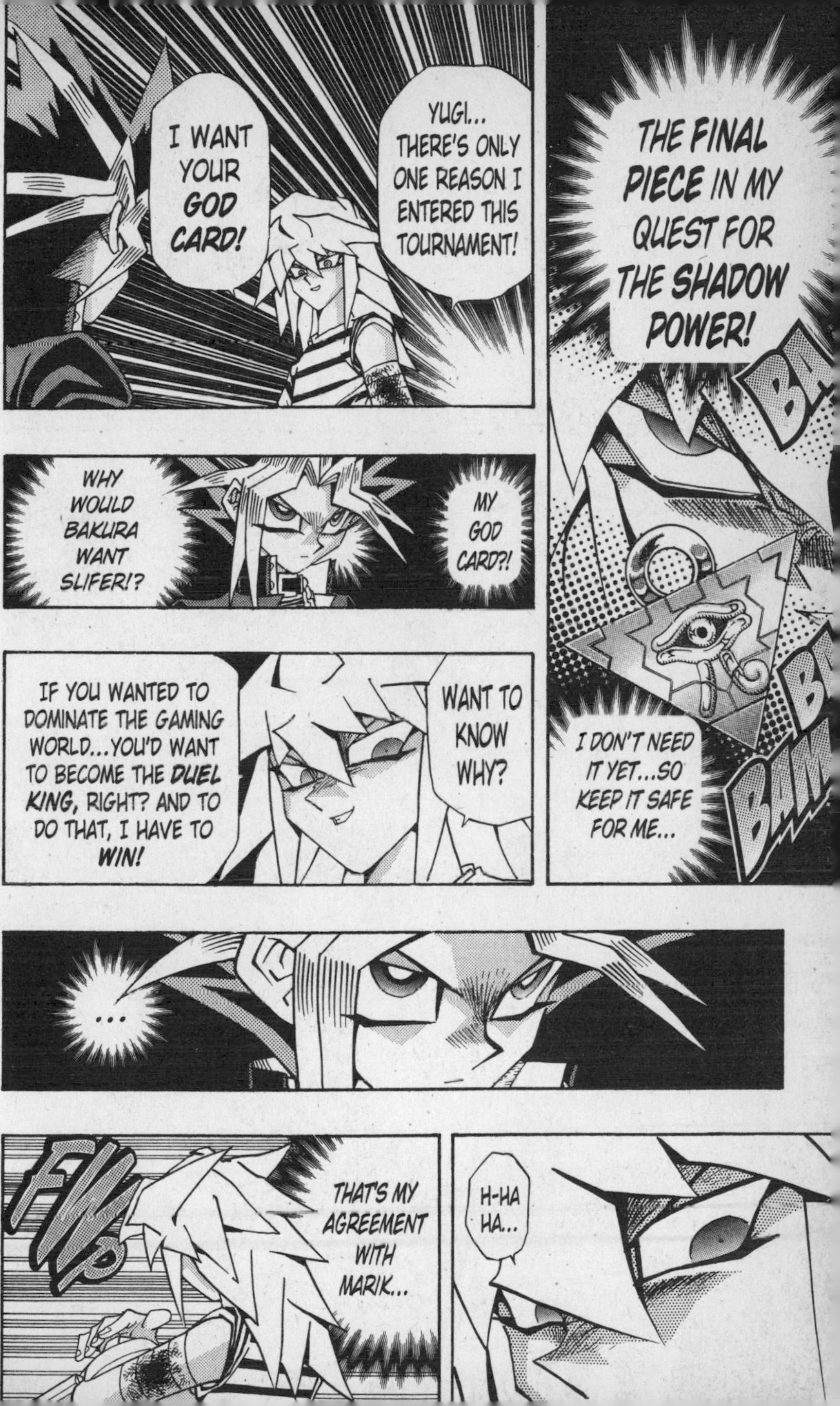
THE FINAL PIECE IN MY QUEST FOR THE SHADOW POWER!
I DON'T NEED IT YET...SO KEEP IT SAFE FOR ME...
YUGI... THERE'S ONLY ONE REASON I ENTERED THIS TOURNAMENT!
I WANT YOUR GOD CARD!
MY GOD CARD?!
WHY WOULD BAKURA WANT SLIFER!?
WANT TO KNOW WHY?
IF YOU WANTED TO DOMINATE THE GAMING WORLD...YOU'D WANT TO BECOME THE DUEL KING, RIGHT? AND TO DO THAT, I HAVE TO WIN!
...
H-HA HA...
THAT'S MY AGREEMENT WITH MARIK...

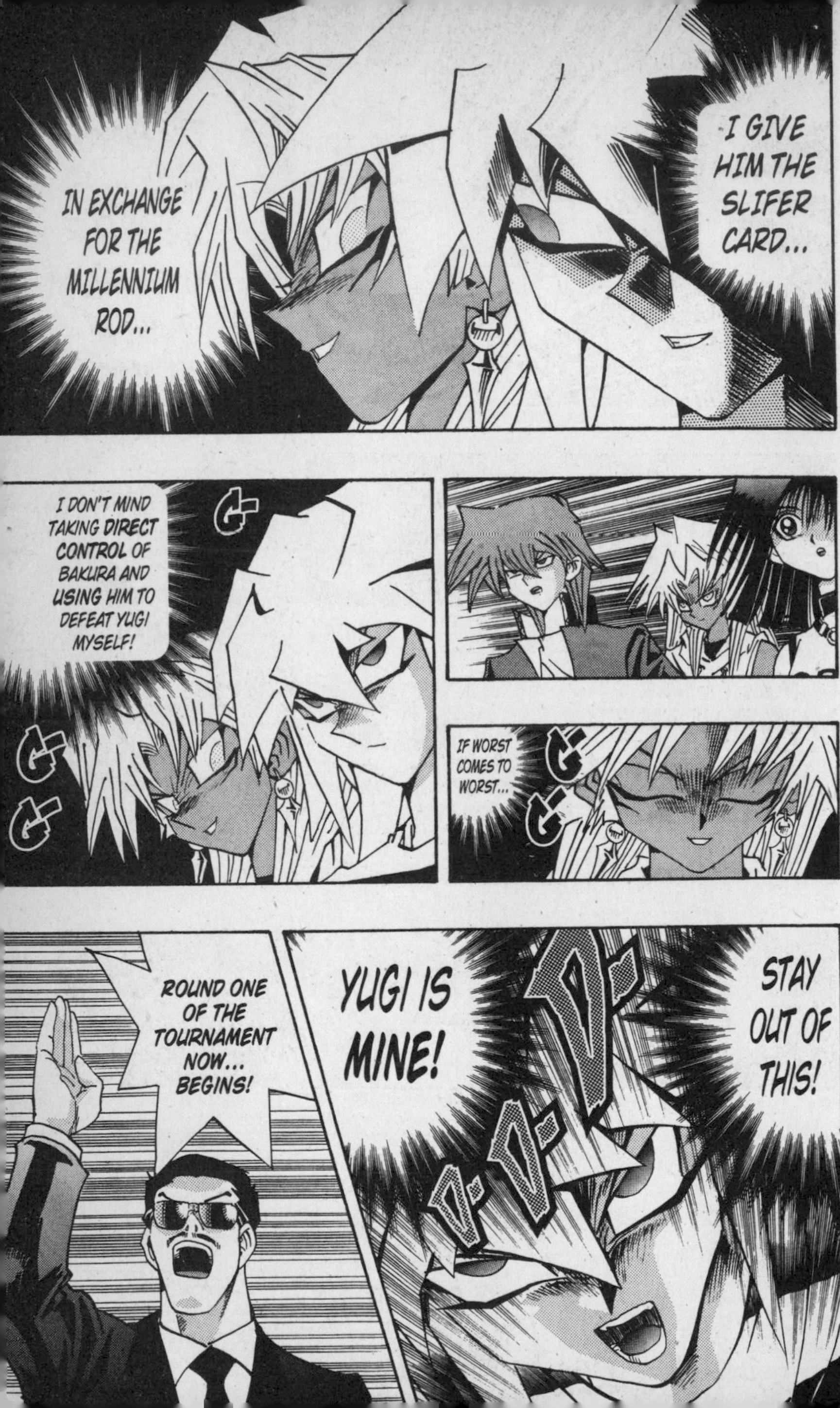
I GIVE HIM THE SLIFER CARD...
IN EXCHANGE FOR THE MILLENNIUM ROD...
IF WORST COMES TO WORST...
I DON'T MIND TAKING DIRECT CONTROL OF BAKURA AND USING HIM TO DEFEAT YUGI MYSELF!
STAY OUT OF THIS!
YUGI IS MINE!
ROUND ONE OF THE TOURNAMENT NOW... BEGINS!

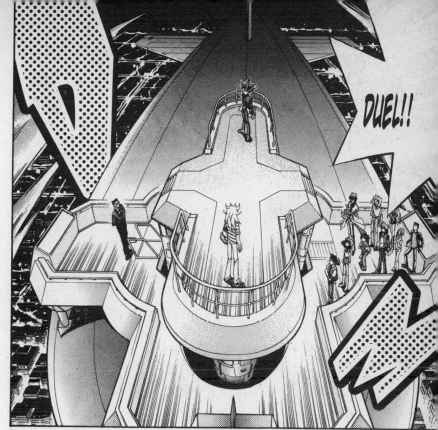

DUEL!!

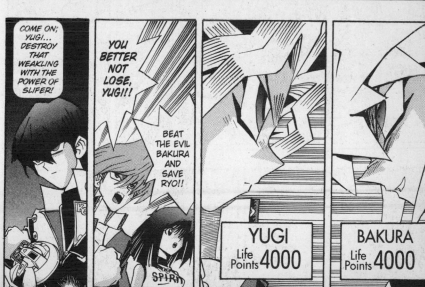

COME ON, YUGI... DESTROY THAT WEAKLING WITH THE POWER OF SLIFER!

YOU BETTER NOT LOSE, YUGI!!!

BEAT THE EVIL BAKURA AND SAVE RYO!!

YUGI Life Points	BAKURA Life Points
4000	4000

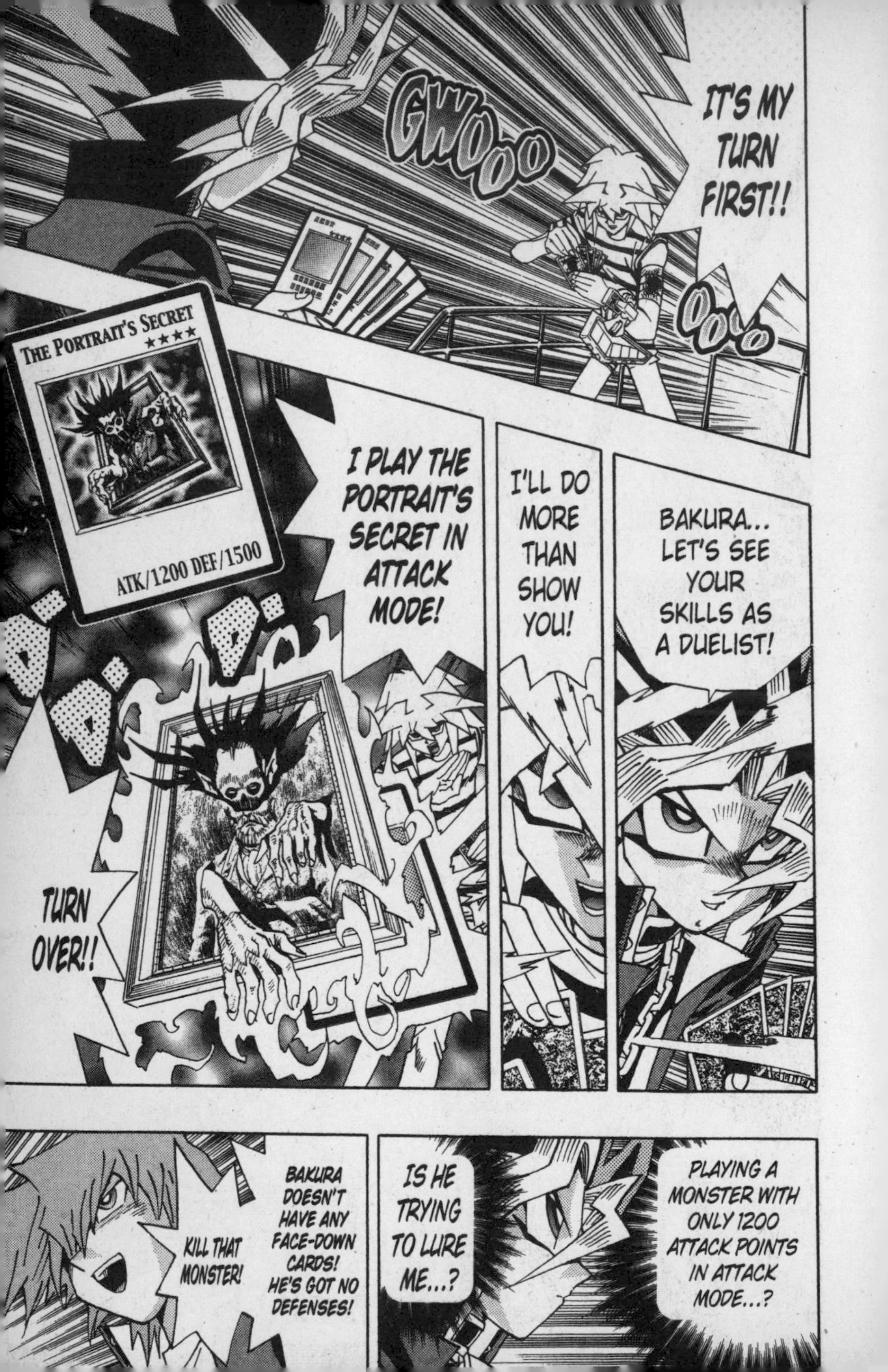
IT'S MY TURN FIRST!!
GWOOOO
OOOO
BAKURA... LET'S SEE YOUR SKILLS AS A DUELIST!
I'LL DO MORE THAN SHOW YOU!
I PLAY THE PORTRAIT'S SECRET IN ATTACK MODE!
THE PORTRAIT'S SECRET ★★★★
ATK/1200 DEF/1500
TURN OVER!!
PLAYING A MONSTER WITH ONLY 1200 ATTACK POINTS IN ATTACK MODE...?
IS HE TRYING TO LURE ME...?
BAKURA DOESN'T HAVE ANY FACE-DOWN CARDS! HE'S GOT NO DEFENSES!
KILL THAT MONSTER!

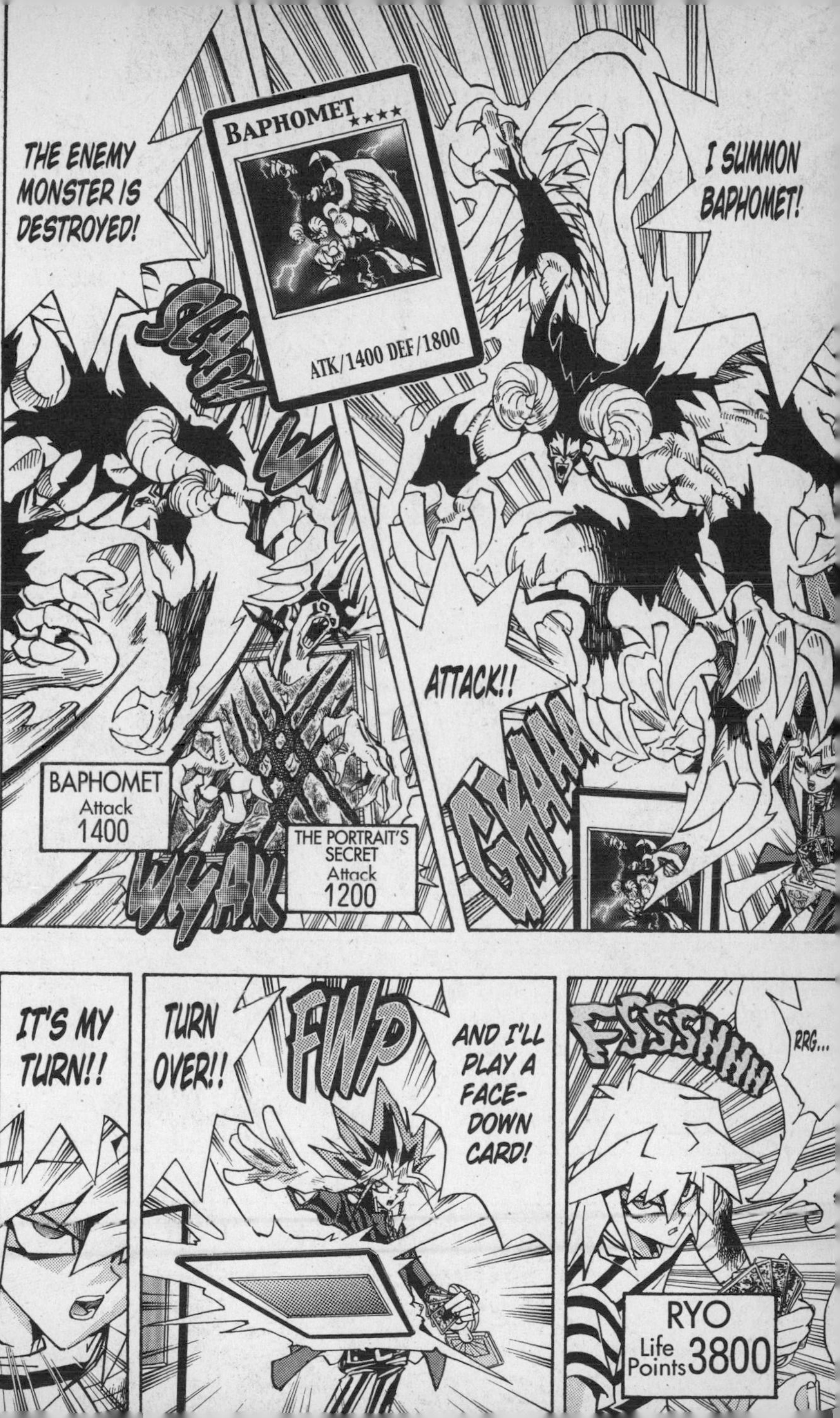
I SUMMON BAPHOMET!
BAPHOMET ★★★★
ATK/1400 DEF/1800
ATTACK!!
GWAA
THE ENEMY MONSTER IS DESTROYED!
SLASH
WHAK
BAPHOMET Attack 1400
THE PORTRAIT'S SECRET Attack 1200
FSSSHHH
RRG...
RYO Life Points 3800
AND I'LL PLAY A FACE-DOWN CARD!
FWP
TURN OVER!!
IT'S MY TURN!!

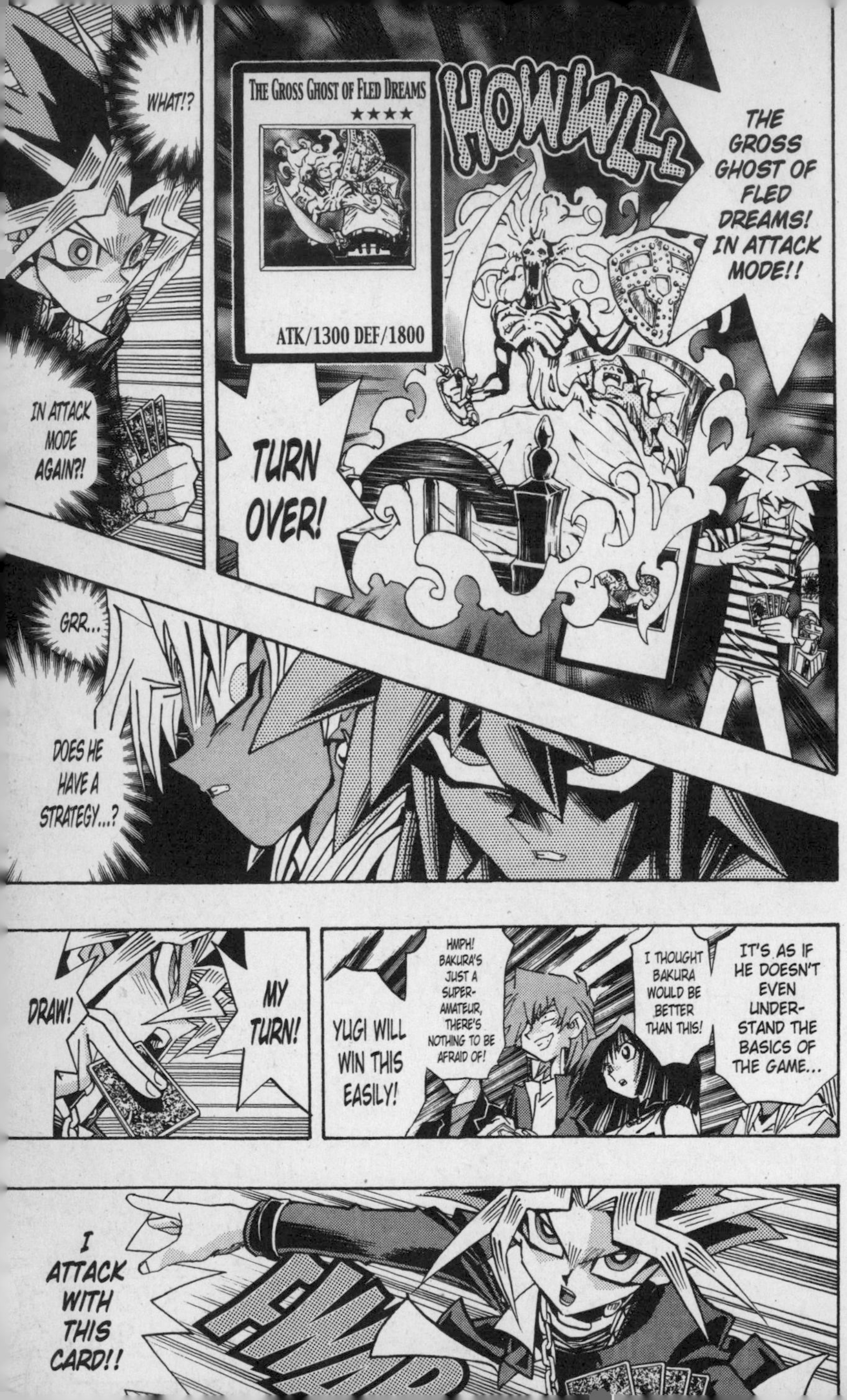
The Gross Ghost of Fled Dreams
★★★★
ATK/1300 DEF/1800
HOWWLL
THE GROSS GHOST OF FLED DREAMS! IN ATTACK MODE!!
TURN OVER!
WHAT!?
IN ATTACK MODE AGAIN?!
GRR...
DOES HE HAVE A STRATEGY...?
IT'S AS IF HE DOESN'T EVEN UNDERSTAND THE BASICS OF THE GAME...
I THOUGHT BAKURA WOULD BE BETTER THAN THIS!
HMPH! BAKURA'S JUST A SUPER-AMATEUR, THERE'S NOTHING TO BE AFRAID OF!
YUGI WILL WIN THIS EASILY!
MY TURN!
DRAW!
I ATTACK WITH THIS CARD!!

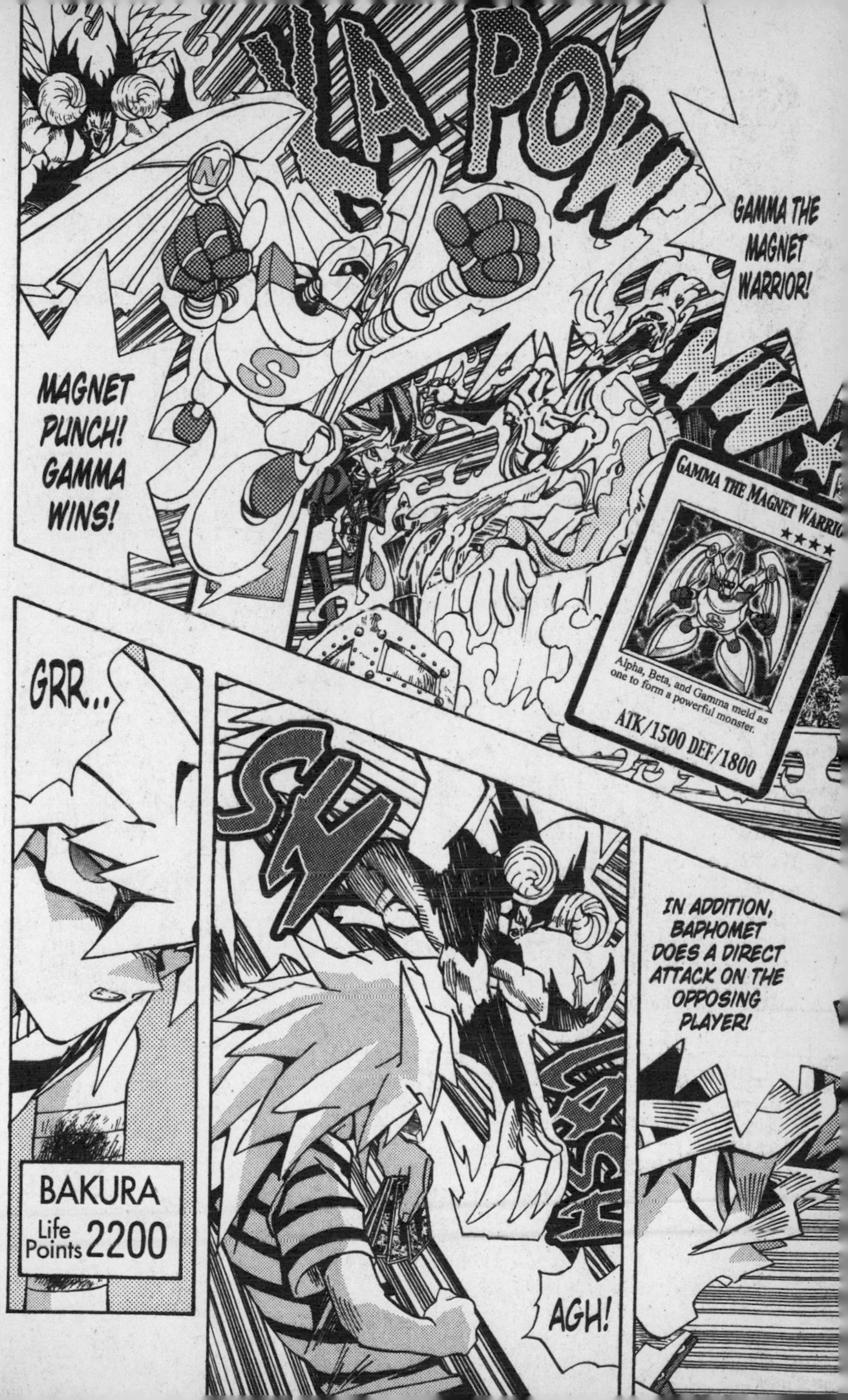

KA POW
GAMMA THE MAGNET WARRIOR!
MAGNET PUNCH! GAMMA WINS!
Gamma the Magnet Warrior
Alpha, Beta, and Gamma meld as one to form a powerful monster.
ATK/1500 DEF/1800
IN ADDITION, BAPHOMET DOES A DIRECT ATTACK ON THE OPPOSING PLAYER!
AGH!
GRR..
BAKURA
Life Points 2200

READ THIS WAY

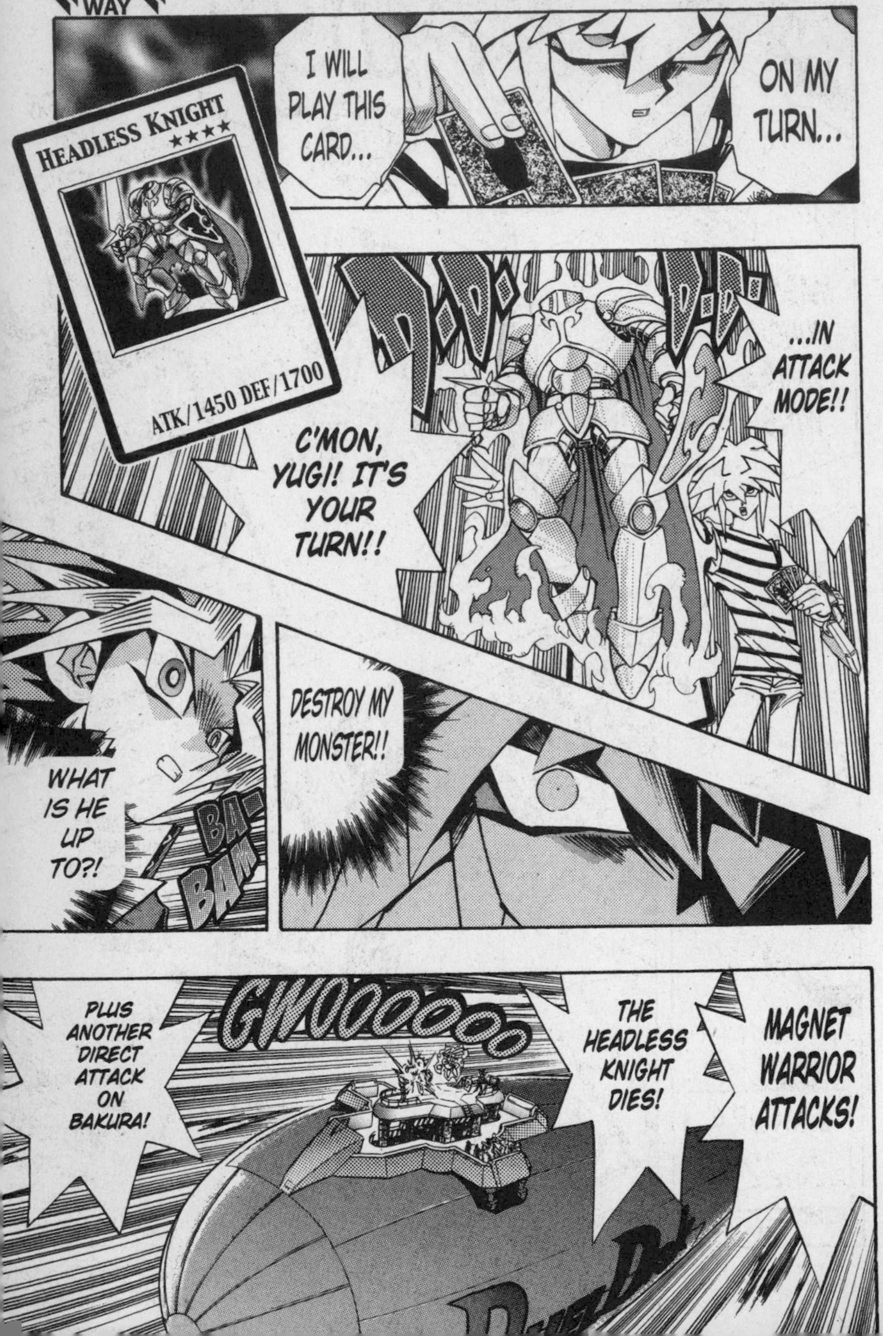
ON MY TURN...
I WILL PLAY THIS CARD...
HEADLESS KNIGHT ★★★★
ATK/1450 DEF/1700
...IN ATTACK MODE!!
C'MON, YUGI! IT'S YOUR TURN!!
DESTROY MY MONSTER!!
WHAT IS HE UP TO?!
BA-BAM
MAGNET WARRIOR ATTACKS!
THE HEADLESS KNIGHT DIES!
GWOOOOOOO
PLUS ANOTHER DIRECT ATTACK ON BAKURA!

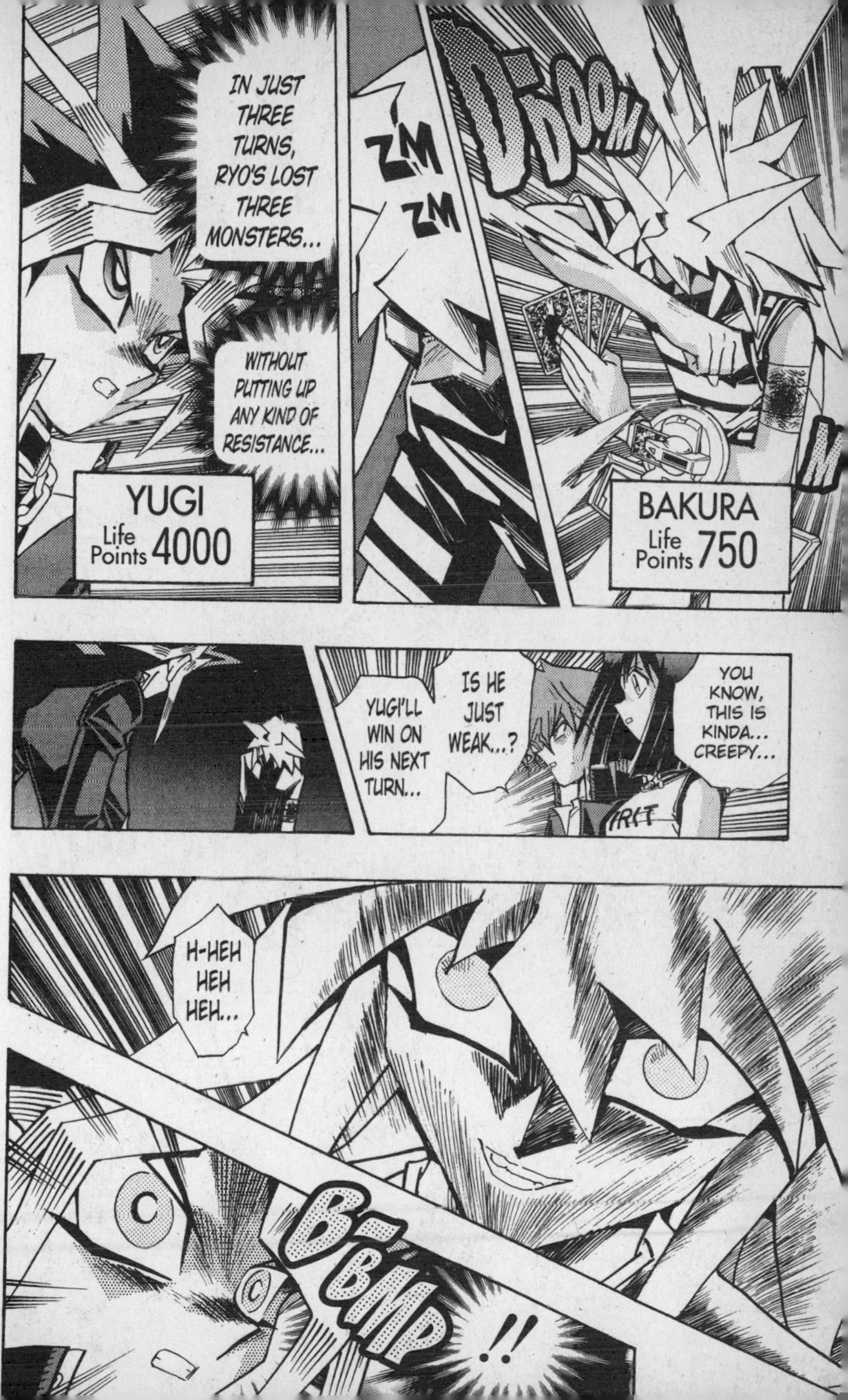
D-DOOM
BAKURA Life Points 750
ZM ZM
IN JUST THREE TURNS, RYO'S LOST THREE MONSTERS...
WITHOUT PUTTING UP ANY KIND OF RESISTANCE...
YUGI Life Points 4000
YOU KNOW, THIS IS KINDA... CREEPY...
IS HE JUST WEAK...?
YUGI'LL WIN ON HIS NEXT TURN...
H-HEH HEH HEH...
B-BMP !!

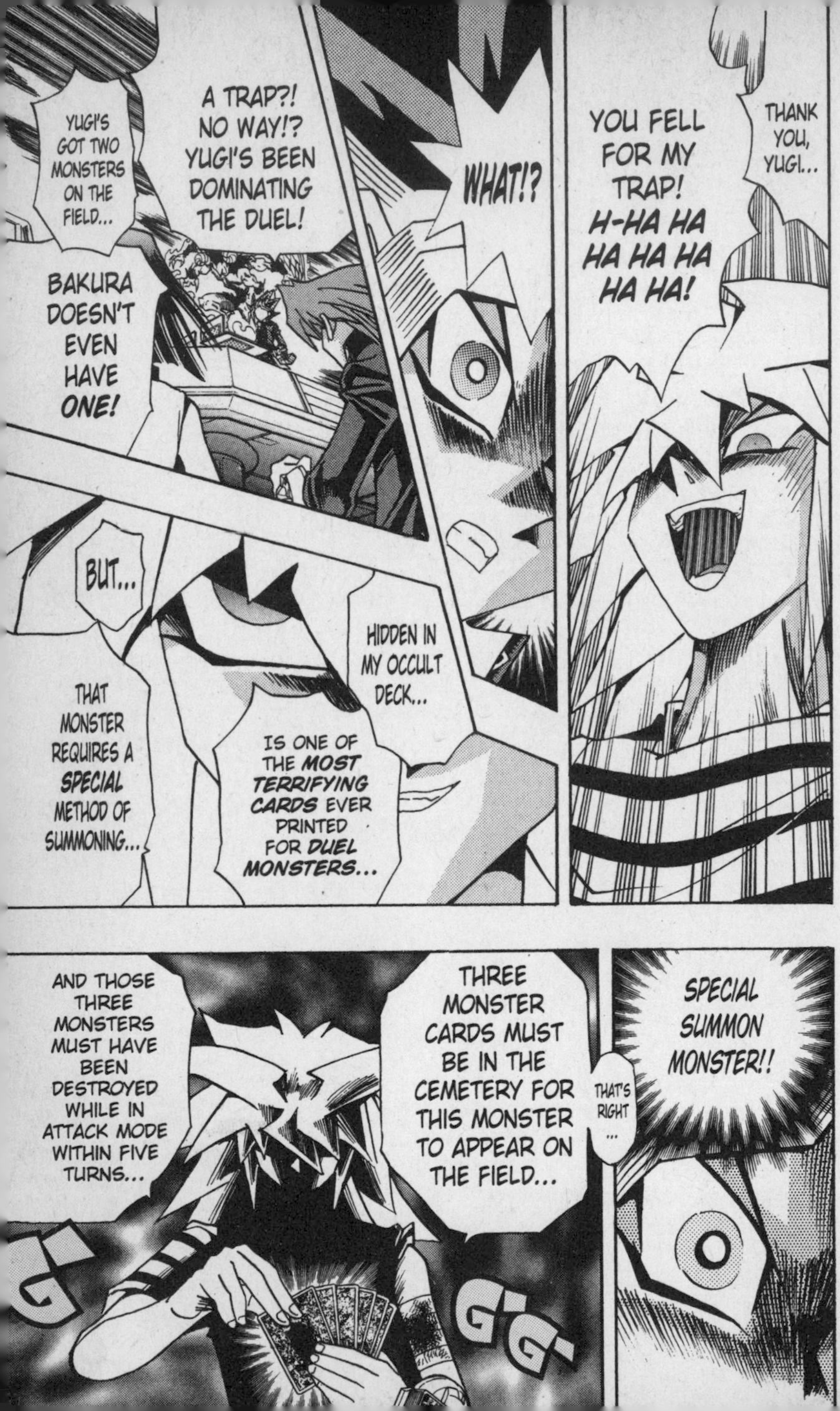

THANK YOU, YUGI...
YOU FELL FOR MY TRAP! *H-HA HA HA HA HA HA HA!*
WHAT!?
A TRAP?! NO WAY!? YUGI'S BEEN DOMINATING THE DUEL!
YUGI'S GOT TWO MONSTERS ON THE FIELD...
BAKURA DOESN'T EVEN HAVE *ONE!*
BUT...
HIDDEN IN MY OCCULT DECK...
IS ONE OF THE *MOST TERRIFYING CARDS* EVER PRINTED FOR *DUEL MONSTERS...*
THAT MONSTER REQUIRES A *SPECIAL* METHOD OF SUMMONING...
SPECIAL SUMMON MONSTER!!
THAT'S RIGHT...
THREE MONSTER CARDS MUST BE IN THE CEMETERY FOR THIS MONSTER TO APPEAR ON THE FIELD...
AND THOSE THREE MONSTERS MUST HAVE BEEN DESTROYED WHILE IN ATTACK MODE WITHIN FIVE TURNS...

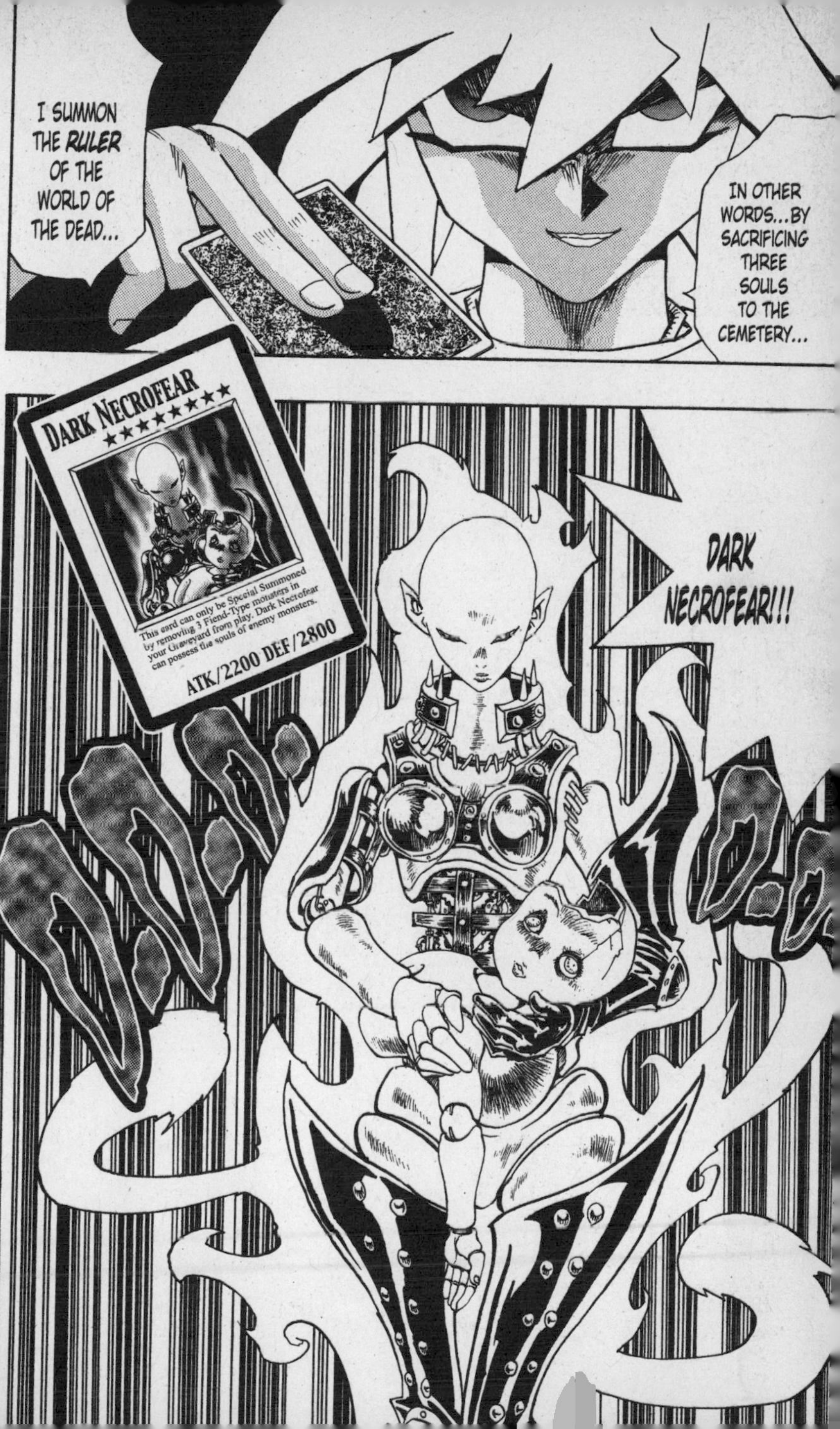
IN OTHER WORDS...BY SACRIFICING THREE SOULS TO THE CEMETERY...
I SUMMON THE RULER OF THE WORLD OF THE DEAD...
DARK NECROFEAR!!!
DARK NECROFEAR
This card can only be Special Summoned by removing 3 Fiend-Type monsters in your Graveyard from play. Dark Necrofear can possess the souls of enemy monsters.
ATK/2200 DEF/2800

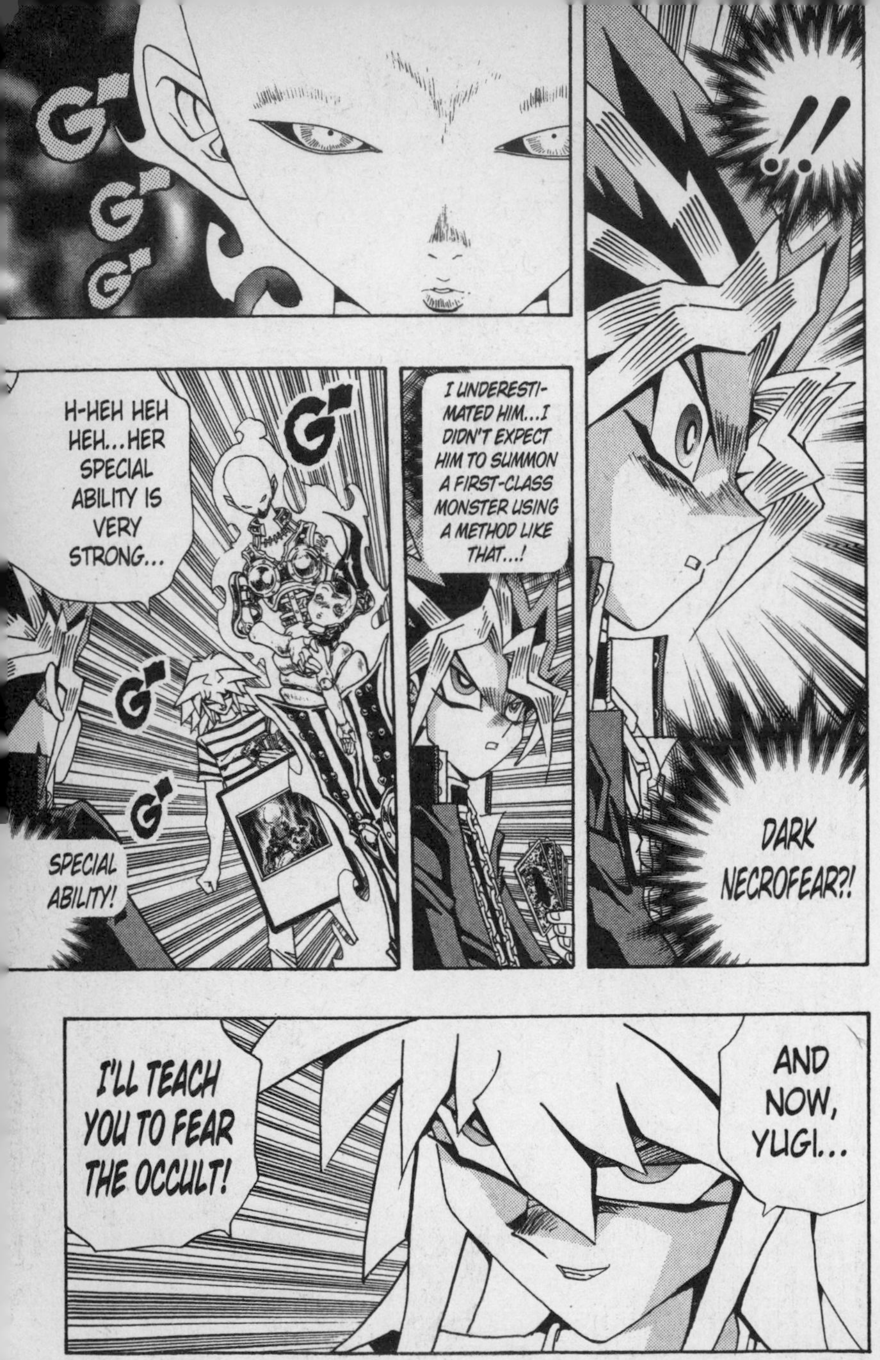
!!
DARK NECROFEAR?!
G G G
I UNDERESTIMATED HIM...I DIDN'T EXPECT HIM TO SUMMON A FIRST-CLASS MONSTER USING A METHOD LIKE THAT...!
H-HEH HEH HEH...HER SPECIAL ABILITY IS VERY STRONG...
G
G
G
SPECIAL ABILITY!
AND NOW, YUGI...
I'LL TEACH YOU TO FEAR THE OCCULT!

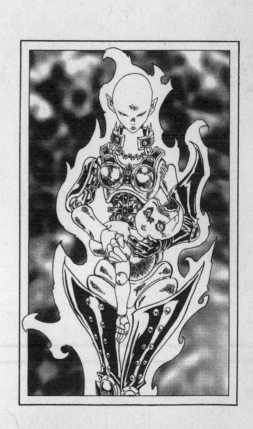

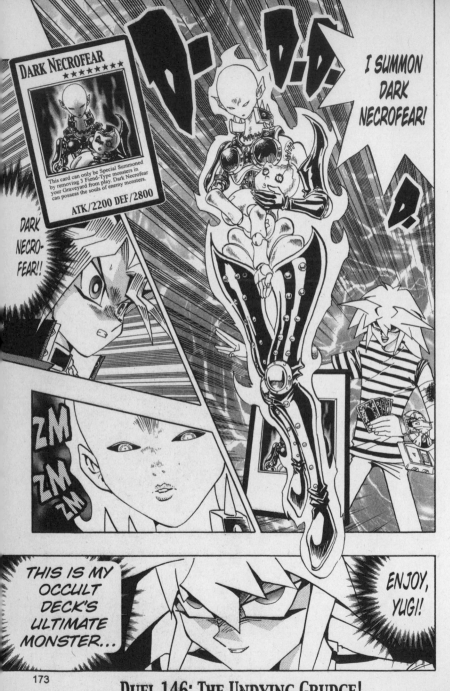

DUEL 146: THE UNDYING GRUDGE!

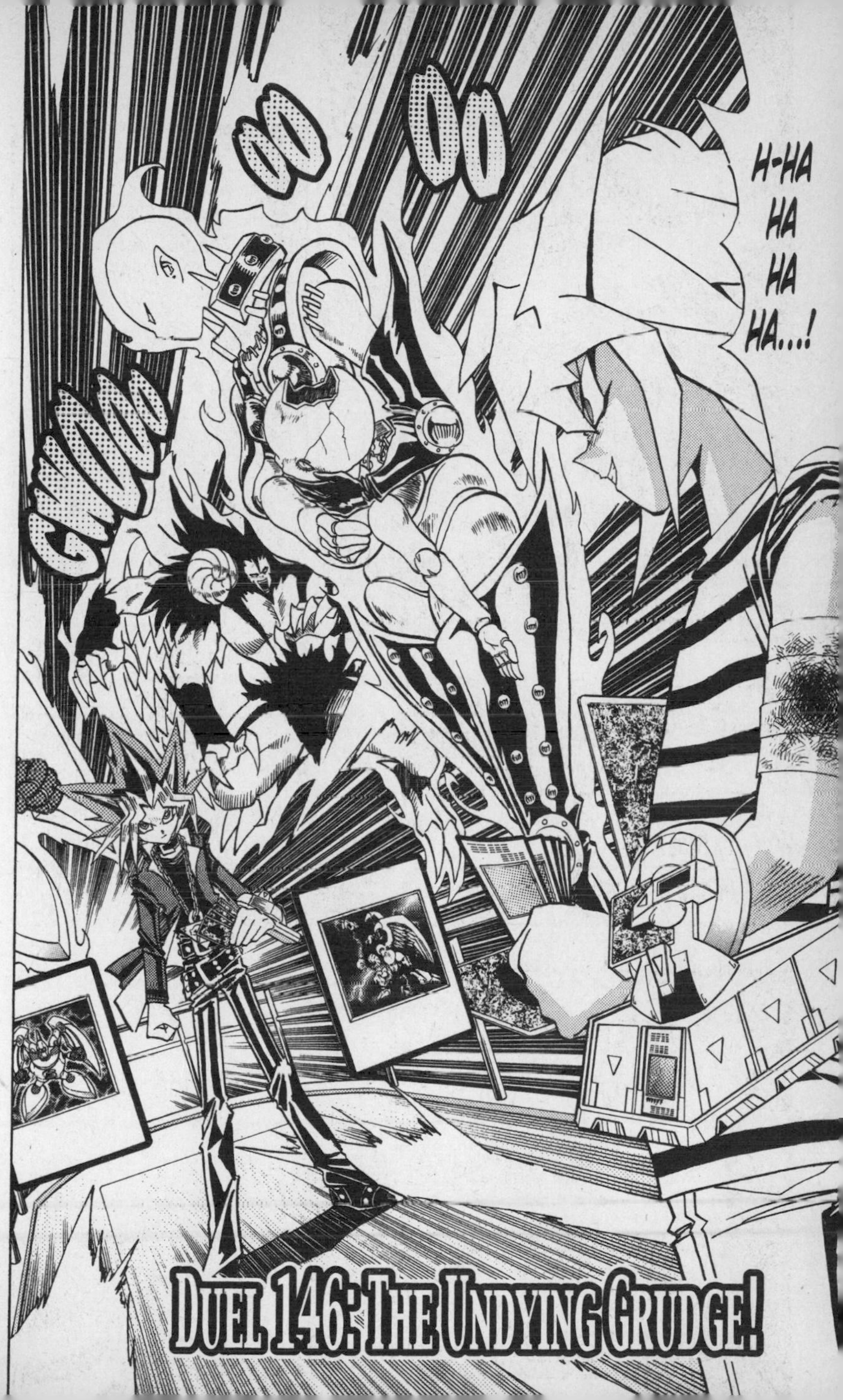
H-HA
HA
HA
HA...!
OO
OO
GWOOO
DUEL 146: THE UNDYING GRUDGE!

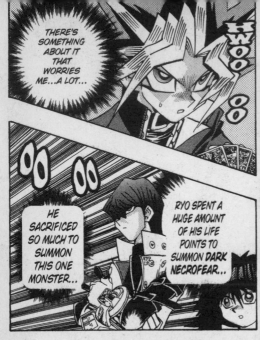

THERE'S SOMETHING ABOUT IT THAT WORRIES ME...A LOT...

HWOOO

A MONSTER SUMMONED BY SACRIFICING THE SOULS OF THREE DEAD MONSTERS!

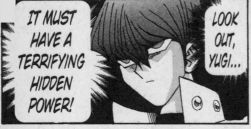

HE SACRIFICED SO MUCH TO SUMMON THIS ONE MONSTER...

RYO SPENT A HUGE AMOUNT OF HIS LIFE POINTS TO SUMMON *DARK NECROFEAR*...

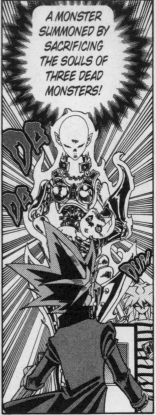

IT MUST HAVE A TERRIFYING HIDDEN POWER!

LOOK OUT, YUGI...

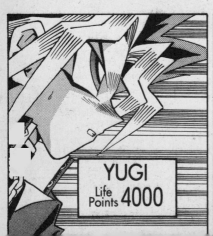

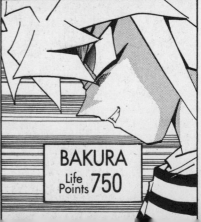

YUGI	BAKURA
Life Points 4000	Life Points 750

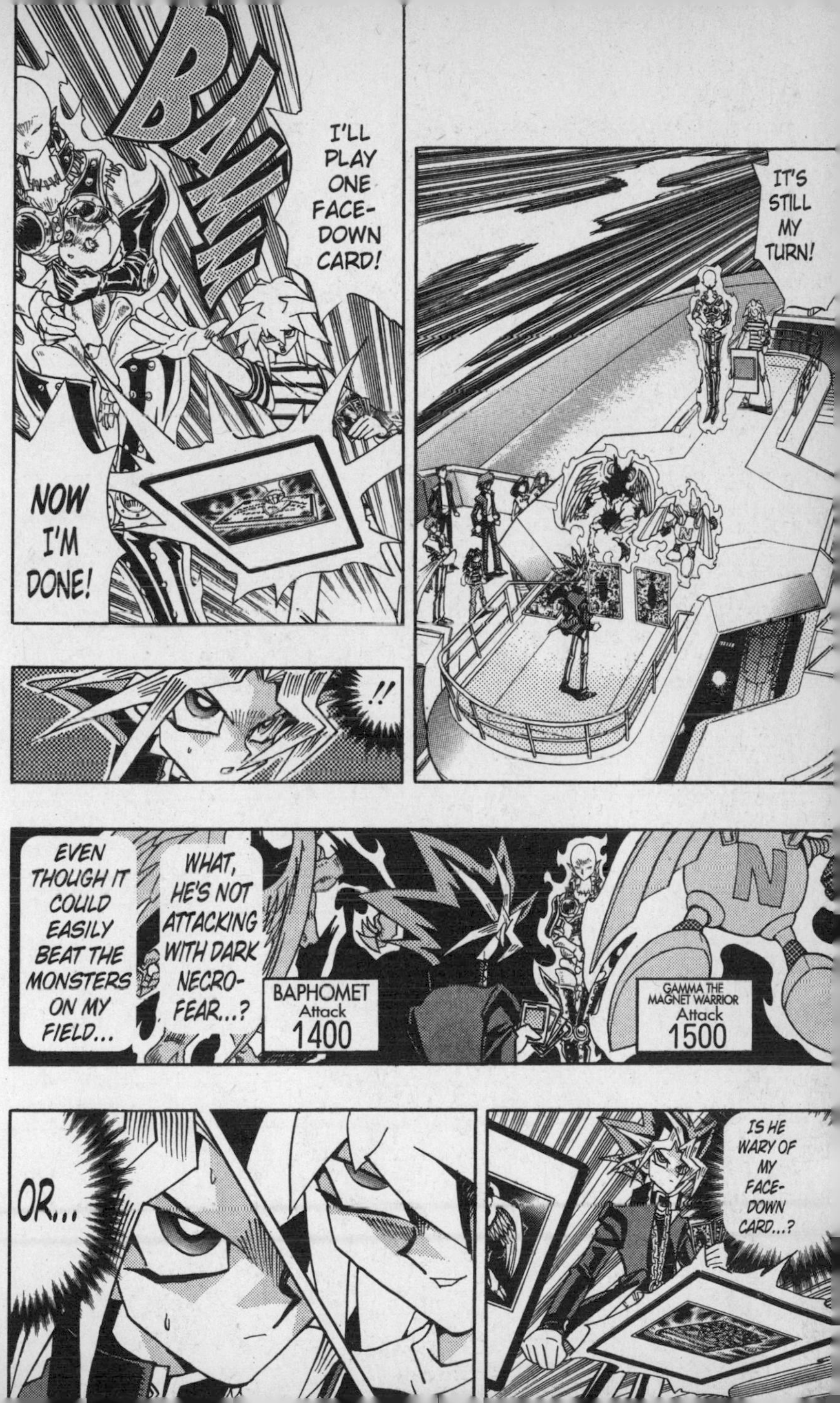
IT'S STILL MY TURN!
I'LL PLAY ONE FACE-DOWN CARD!
BAM
NOW I'M DONE!
!!
GAMMA THE MAGNET WARRIOR Attack 1500
BAPHOMET Attack 1400
WHAT, HE'S NOT ATTACKING WITH DARK NECRO-FEAR...?
EVEN THOUGH IT COULD EASILY BEAT THE MONSTERS ON MY FIELD...
IS HE WARY OF MY FACE-DOWN CARD...?
OR...

READ THIS WAY

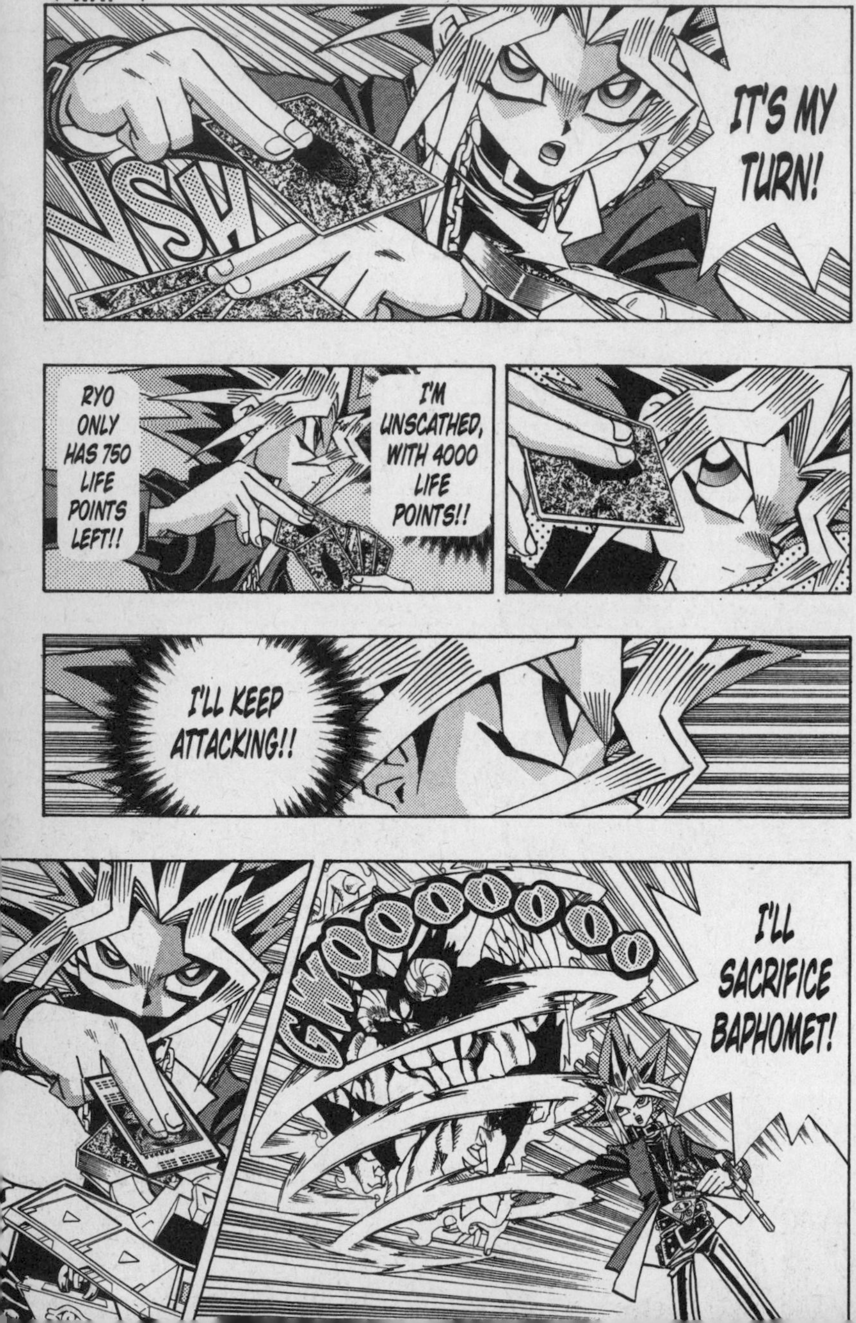
IT'S MY TURN!
I'M UNSCATHED, WITH 4000 LIFE POINTS!!
RYO ONLY HAS 750 LIFE POINTS LEFT!!
I'LL KEEP ATTACKING!!
I'LL SACRIFICE BAPHOMET!
GWOOOOOOOOO

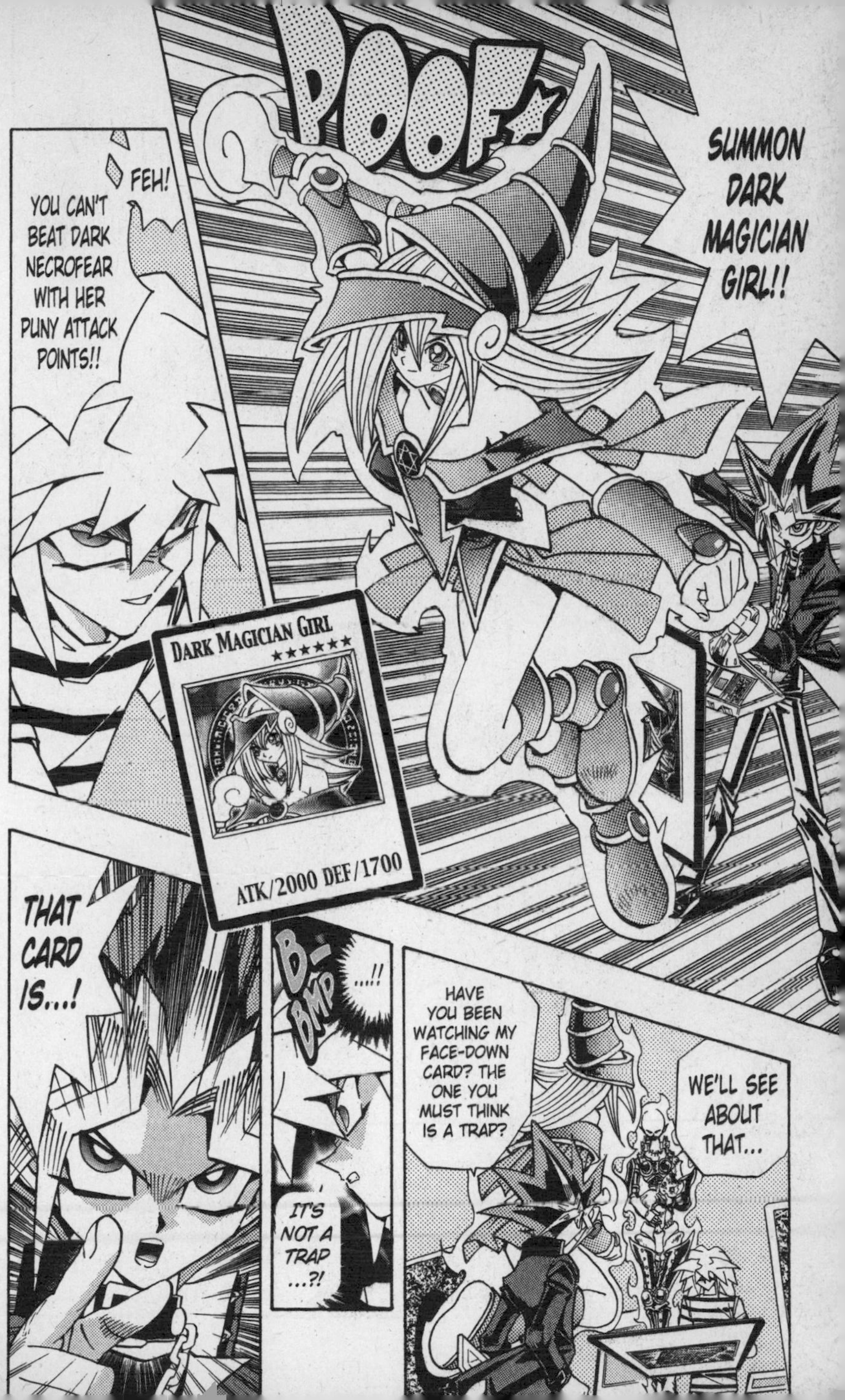
SUMMON DARK MAGICIAN GIRL!!
POOF!
DARK MAGICIAN GIRL
ATK/2000 DEF/1700
FEH!
YOU CAN'T BEAT DARK NECROFEAR WITH HER PUNY ATTACK POINTS!!
HAVE YOU BEEN WATCHING MY FACE-DOWN CARD? THE ONE YOU MUST THINK IS A TRAP?
WE'LL SEE ABOUT THAT...
B-BMP
...!!
IT'S NOT A TRAP ...?!
THAT CARD IS...!

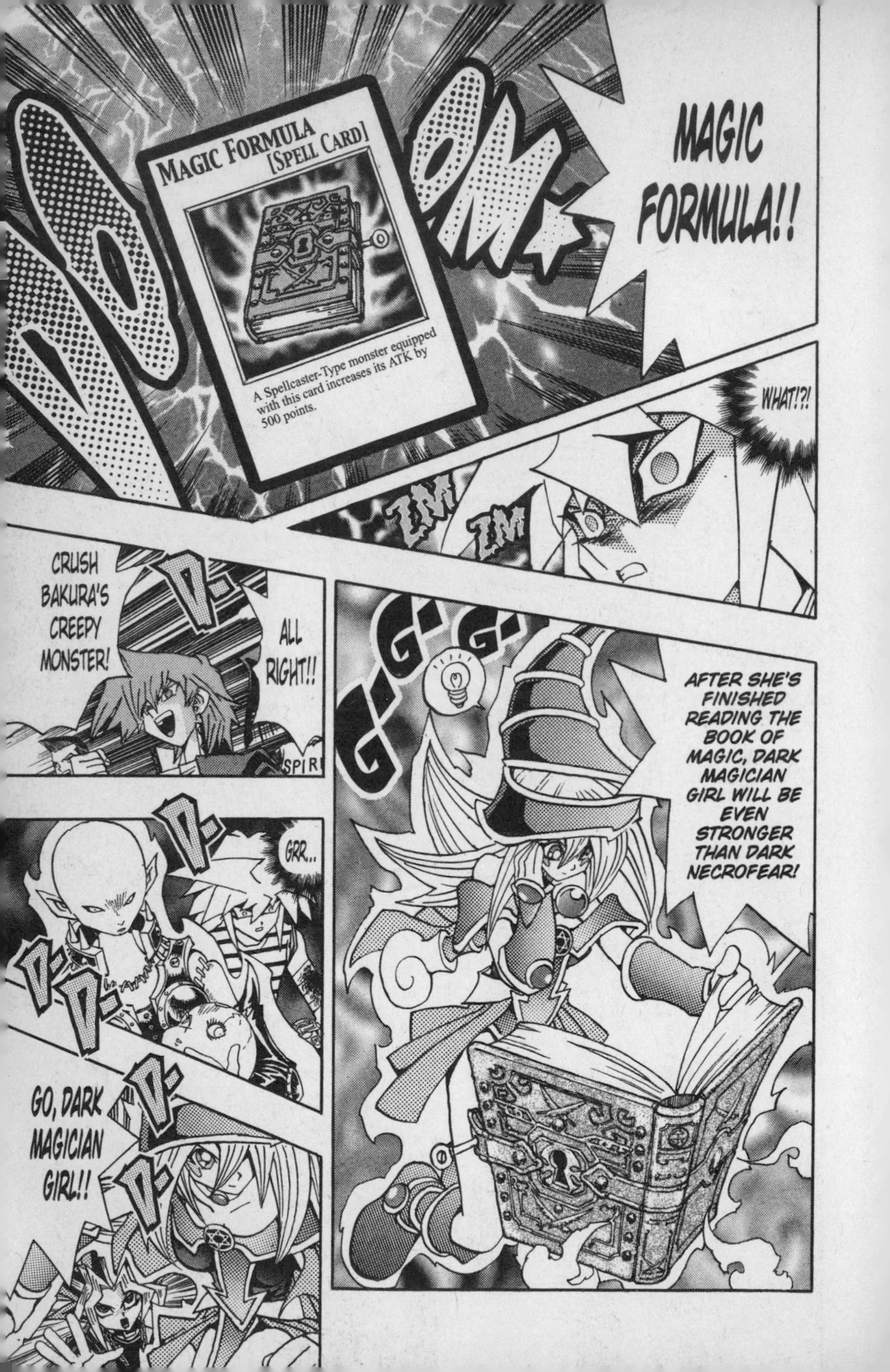
MAGIC FORMULA
[SPELL CARD]
A Spellcaster-Type monster equipped with this card increases its ATK by 500 points.
MAGIC FORMULA!!
WHAT!?!
AFTER SHE'S FINISHED READING THE BOOK OF MAGIC, DARK MAGICIAN GIRL WILL BE EVEN STRONGER THAN DARK NECROFEAR!
ALL RIGHT!!
CRUSH BAKURA'S CREEPY MONSTER!
GRR...
GO, DARK MAGICIAN GIRL!!

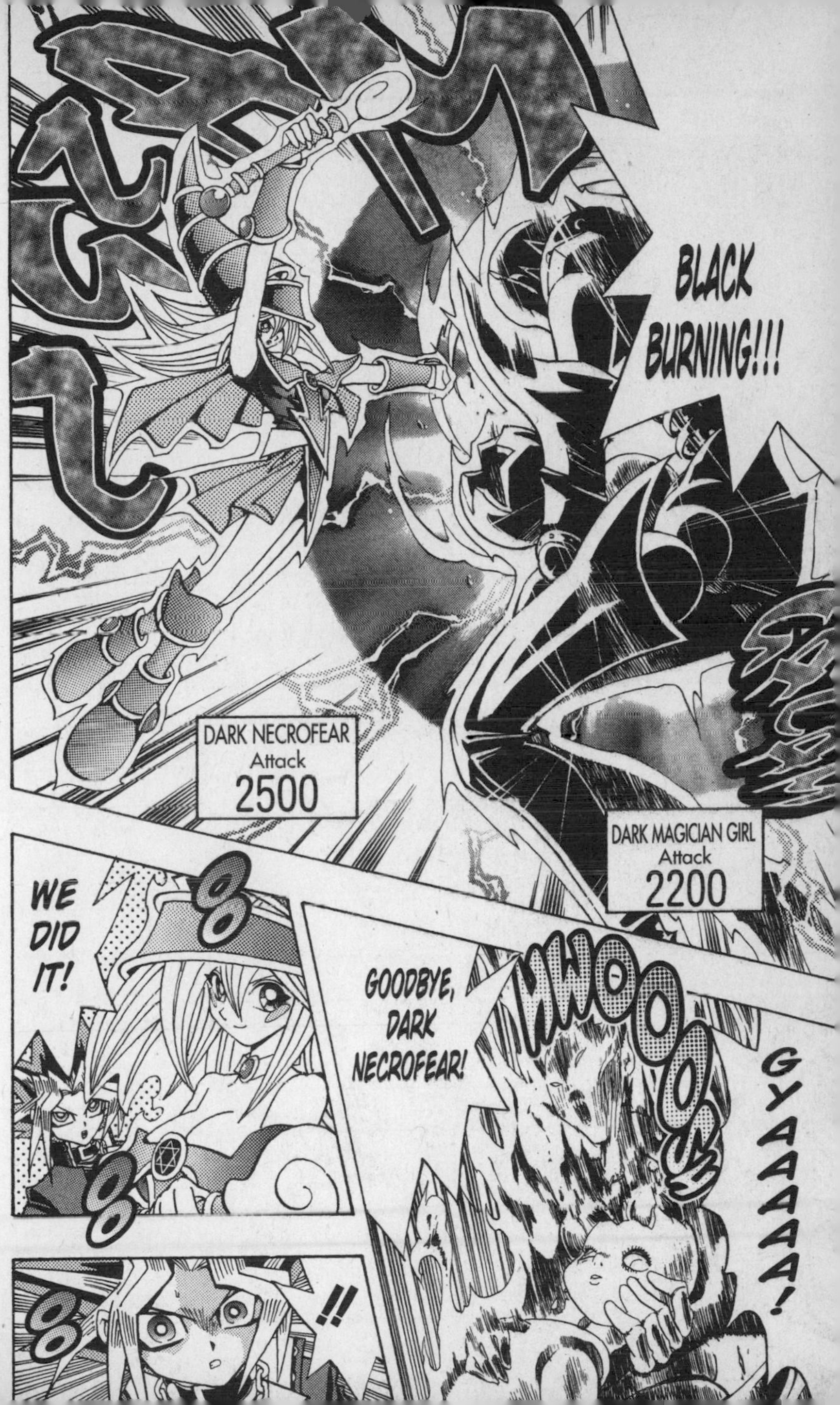
BLACK BURNING!!!
DARK MAGICIAN GIRL Attack 2200
DARK NECROFEAR Attack 2500
GOODBYE, DARK NECROFEAR!
GYAAAAAA!
WE DID IT!
!!

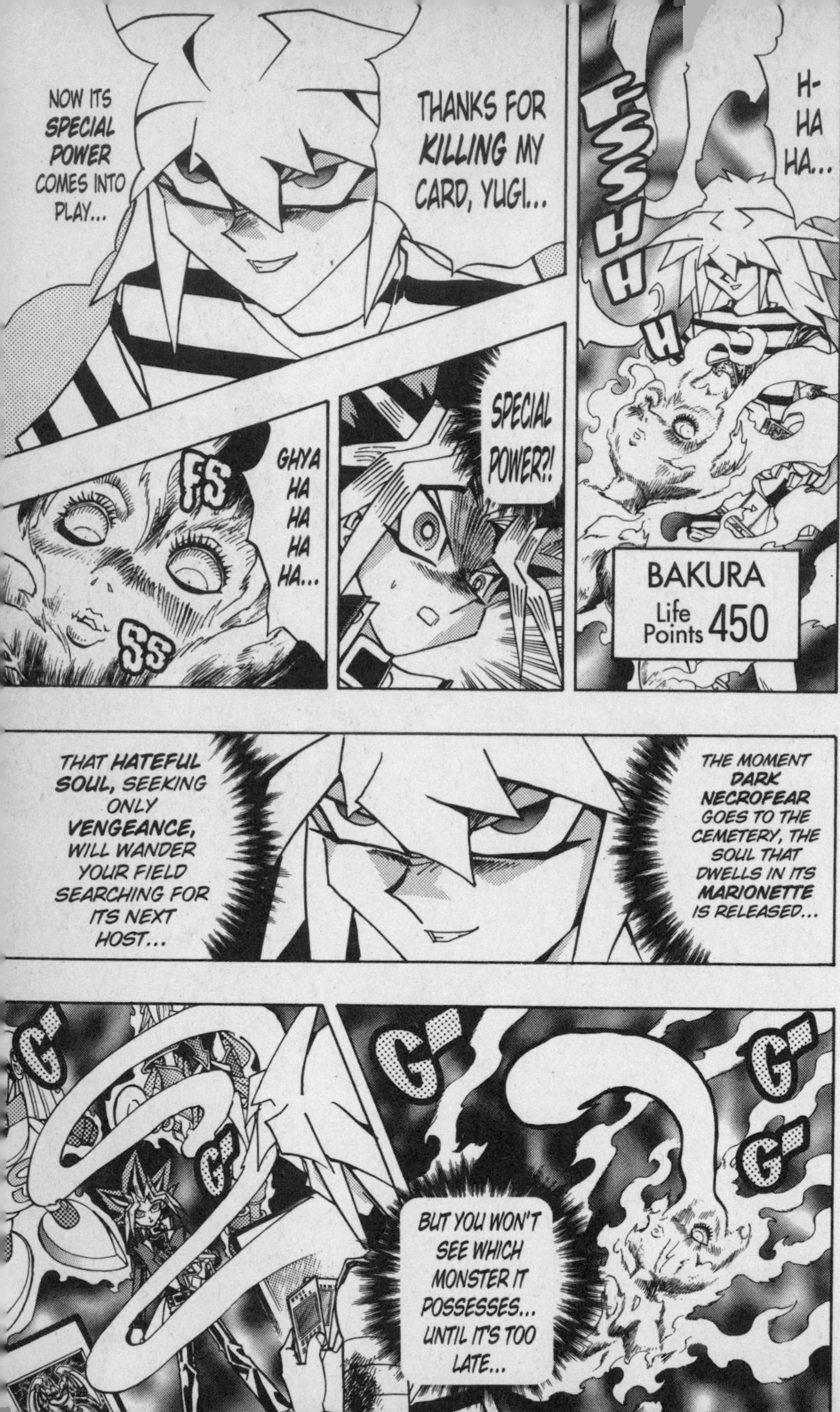
H-
HA
HA...
FSSHHH
BAKURA
Life Points 450
THANKS FOR KILLING MY CARD, YUGI...
NOW ITS SPECIAL POWER COMES INTO PLAY...
SPECIAL POWER?!
GHYA HA HA HA HA...
FS
SS
THE MOMENT DARK NECROFEAR GOES TO THE CEMETERY, THE SOUL THAT DWELLS IN ITS MARIONETTE IS RELEASED...
THAT HATEFUL SOUL, SEEKING ONLY VENGEANCE, WILL WANDER YOUR FIELD SEARCHING FOR ITS NEXT HOST...
G
G
BUT YOU WON'T SEE WHICH MONSTER IT POSSESSES... UNTIL IT'S TOO LATE...
G
G
G

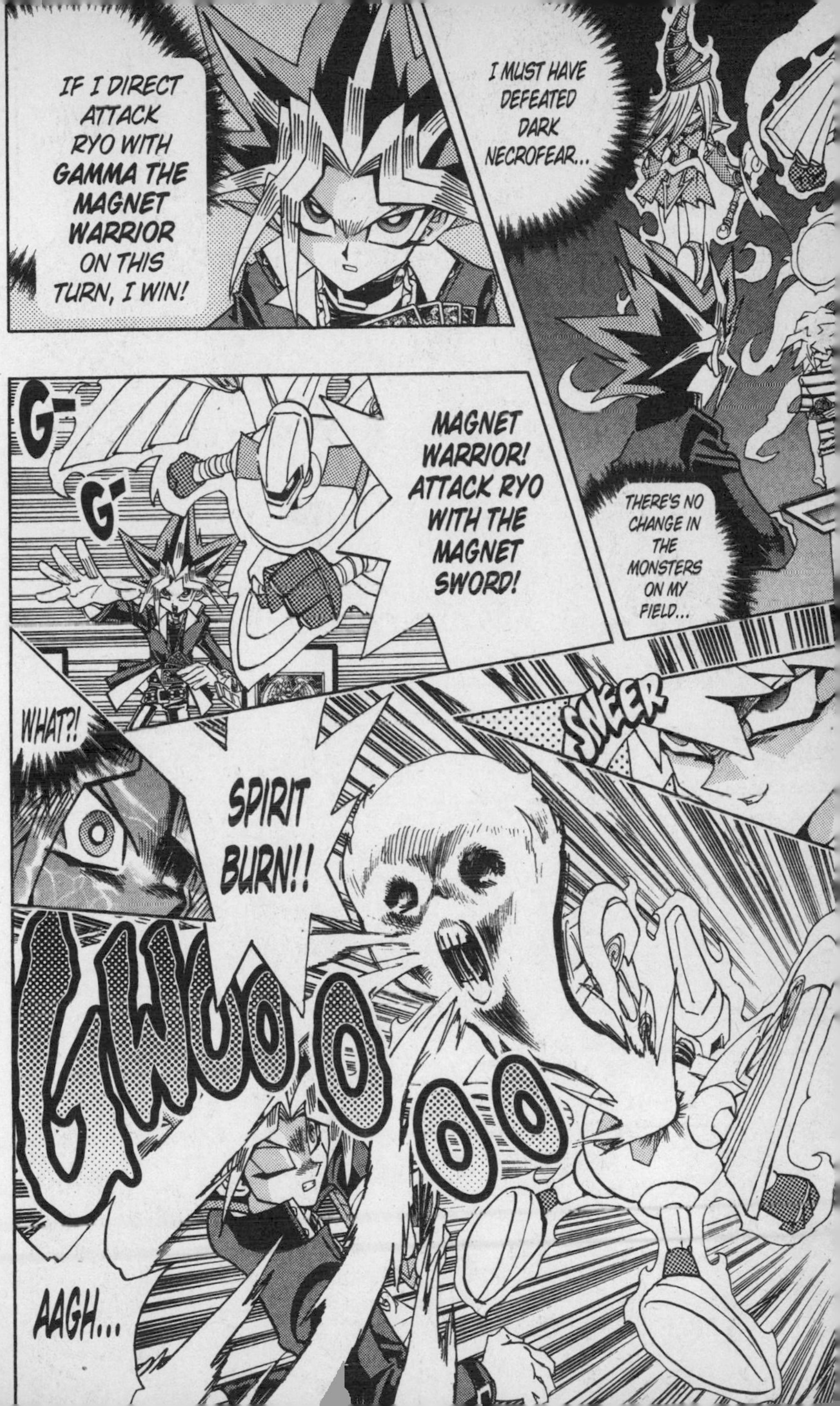
I MUST HAVE DEFEATED DARK NECROFEAR...
THERE'S NO CHANGE IN THE MONSTERS ON MY FIELD...
IF I DIRECT ATTACK RYO WITH GAMMA THE MAGNET WARRIOR ON THIS TURN, I WIN!
G-
G-
MAGNET WARRIOR! ATTACK RYO WITH THE MAGNET SWORD!
SNEER
WHAT?!
SPIRIT BURN!!
GWOOOOOO
AAGH...

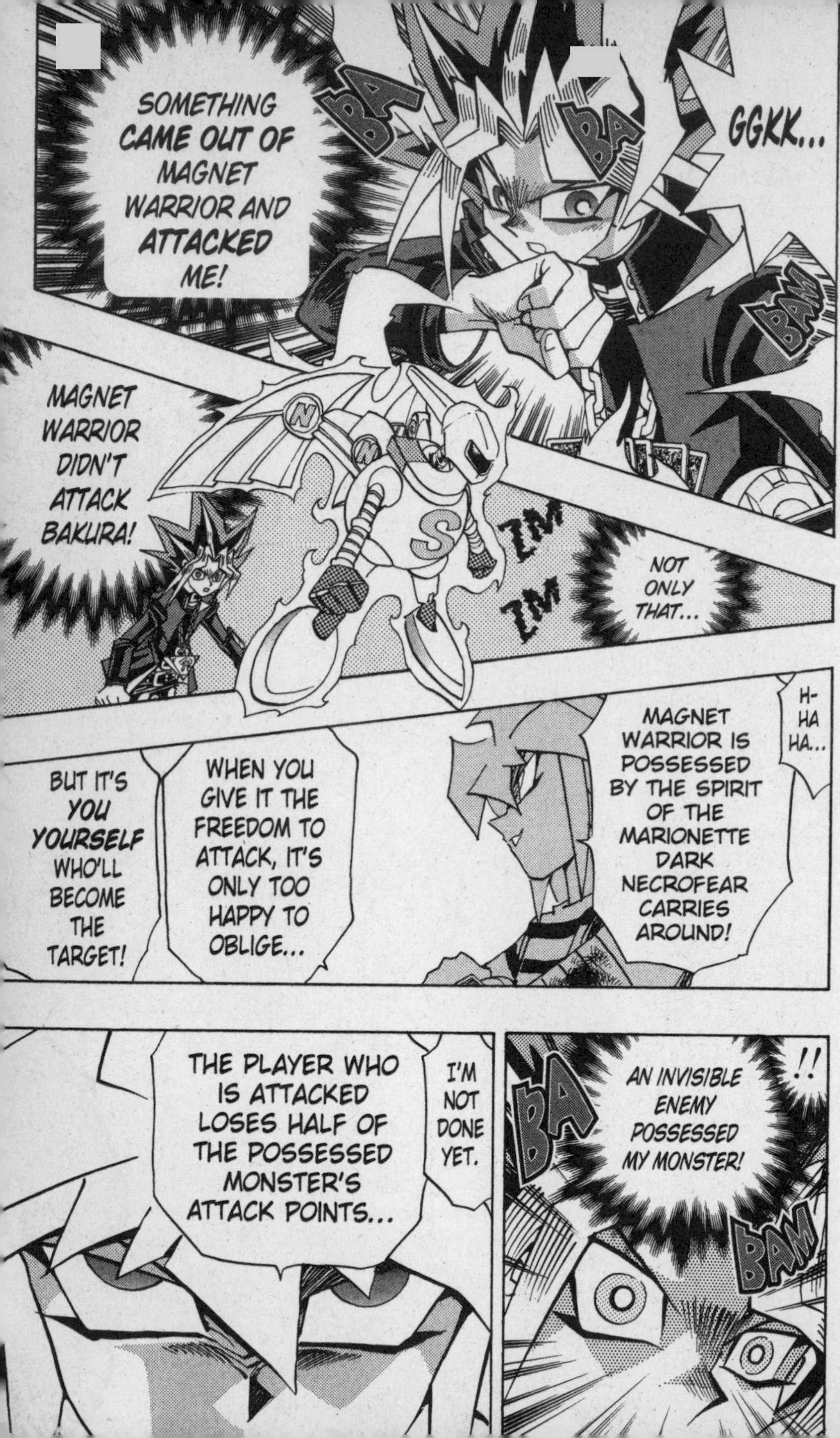
BA
BA
GGKK...
SOMETHING CAME OUT OF MAGNET WARRIOR AND ATTACKED ME!
BAM
NOT ONLY THAT...
ZM
ZM
MAGNET WARRIOR DIDN'T ATTACK BAKURA!
H-HA HA...
MAGNET WARRIOR IS POSSESSED BY THE SPIRIT OF THE MARIONETTE DARK NECROFEAR CARRIES AROUND!
WHEN YOU GIVE IT THE FREEDOM TO ATTACK, IT'S ONLY TOO HAPPY TO OBLIGE...
BUT IT'S YOU YOURSELF WHO'LL BECOME THE TARGET!
!!
AN INVISIBLE ENEMY POSSESSED MY MONSTER!
BA
BAM
I'M NOT DONE YET.
THE PLAYER WHO IS ATTACKED LOSES HALF OF THE POSSESSED MONSTER'S ATTACK POINTS...

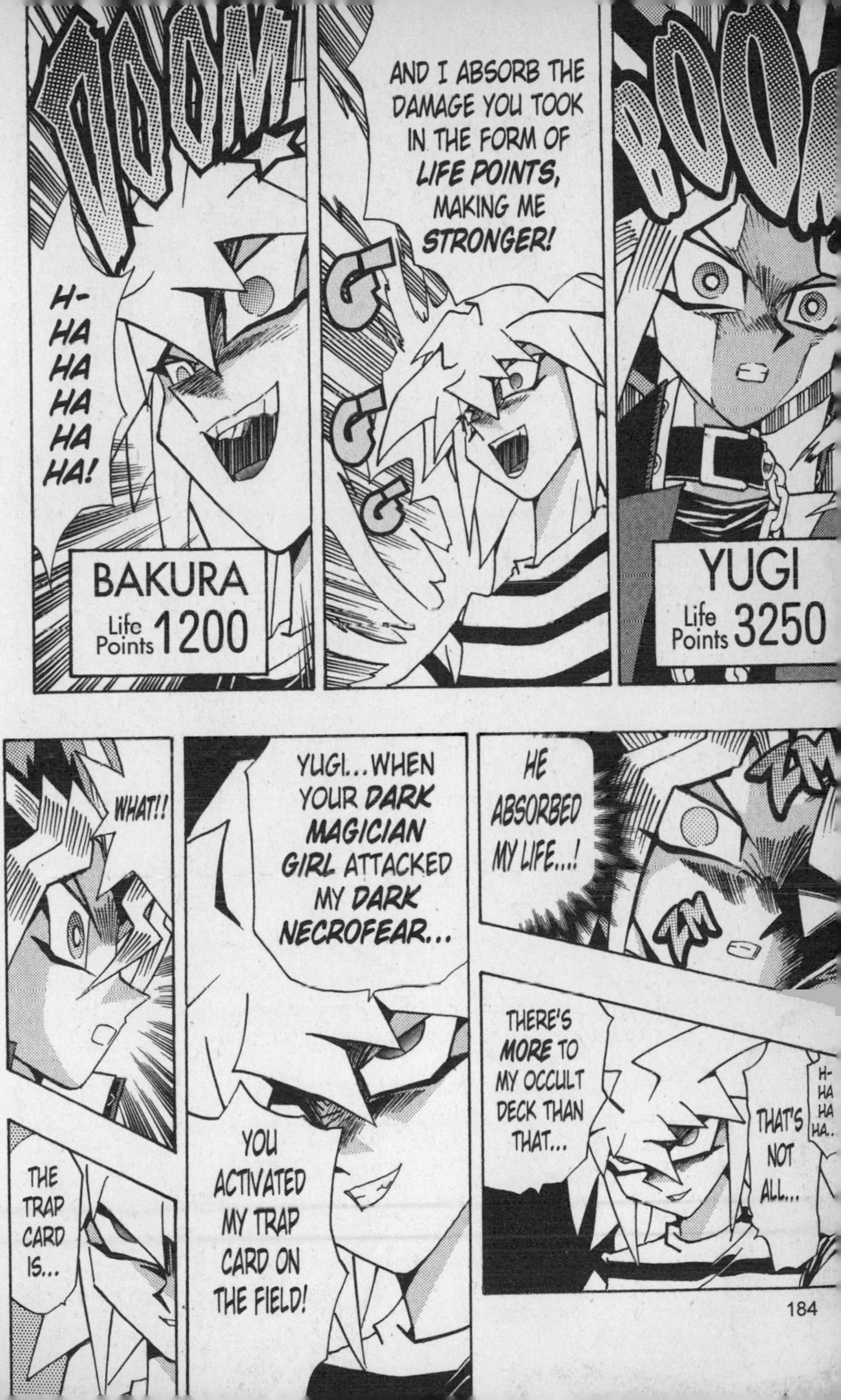
BOO
YUGI
Life Points 3250
AND I ABSORB THE DAMAGE YOU TOOK IN THE FORM OF LIFE POINTS, MAKING ME STRONGER!
G G G
H-HA HA HA HA HA!
BAKURA
Life Points 1200
HE ABSORBED MY LIFE...!
ZM ZM
H-HA HA HA...
THAT'S NOT ALL...
THERE'S MORE TO MY OCCULT DECK THAN THAT...
YUGI...WHEN YOUR DARK MAGICIAN GIRL ATTACKED MY DARK NECROFEAR...
YOU ACTIVATED MY TRAP CARD ON THE FIELD!
WHAT!!
THE TRAP CARD IS...

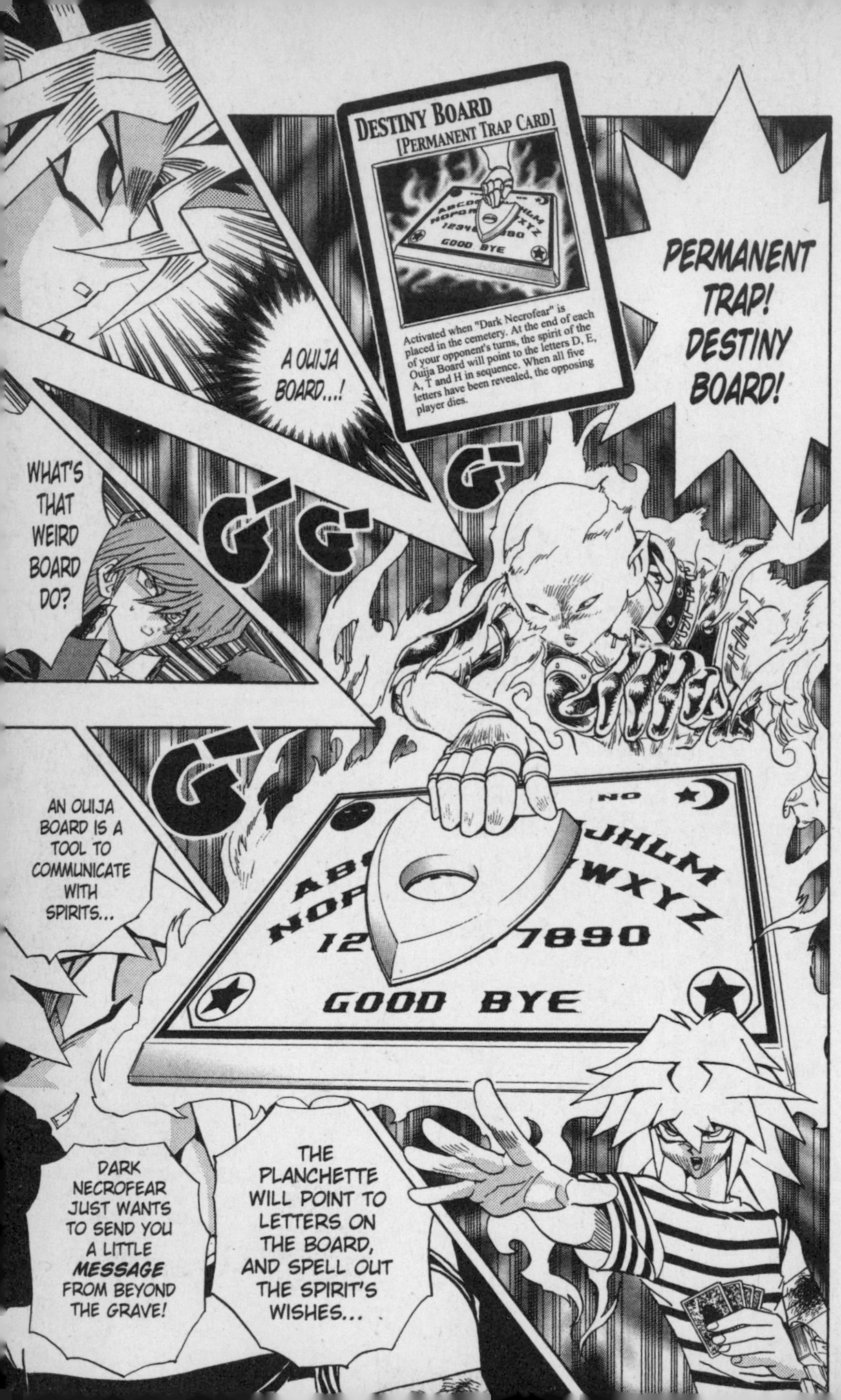
PERMANENT TRAP! DESTINY BOARD!
DESTINY BOARD
[PERMANENT TRAP CARD]
Activated when "Dark Necrofear" is placed in the cemetery. At the end of each of your opponent's turns, the spirit of the Ouija Board will point to the letters D, E, A, T and H in sequence. When all five letters have been revealed, the opposing player dies.
A OUIJA BOARD...!
G
G G
WHAT'S THAT WEIRD BOARD DO?
G
AN OUIJA BOARD IS A TOOL TO COMMUNICATE WITH SPIRITS...
GOOD BYE
THE PLANCHETTE WILL POINT TO LETTERS ON THE BOARD, AND SPELL OUT THE SPIRIT'S WISHES...
DARK NECROFEAR JUST WANTS TO SEND YOU A LITTLE *MESSAGE* FROM BEYOND THE GRAVE!

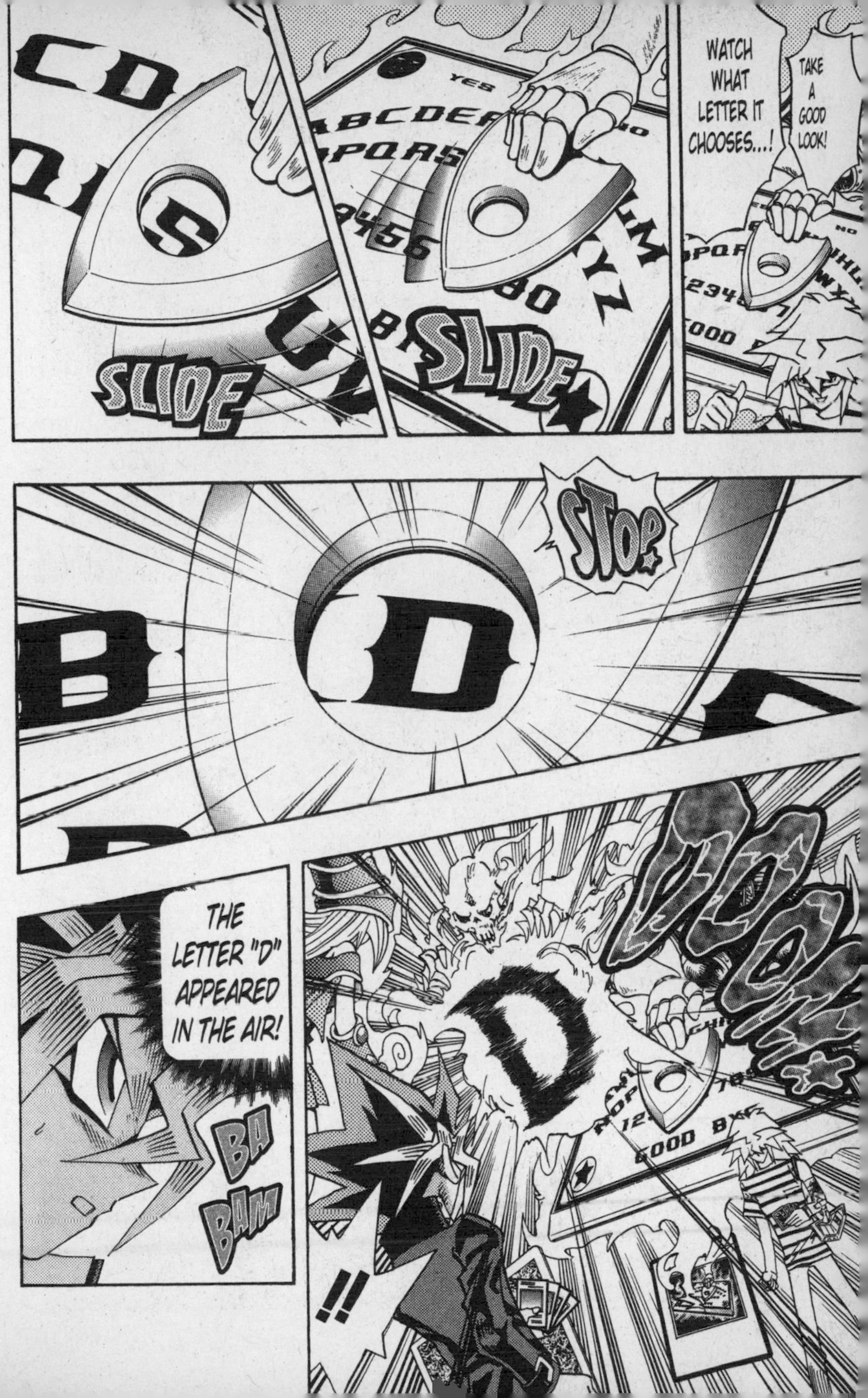
TAKE A GOOD LOOK!
WATCH WHAT LETTER IT CHOOSES...!
SLIDE
SLIDE
STOP
DOOM
!!
THE LETTER "D" APPEARED IN THE AIR!
BA BAM

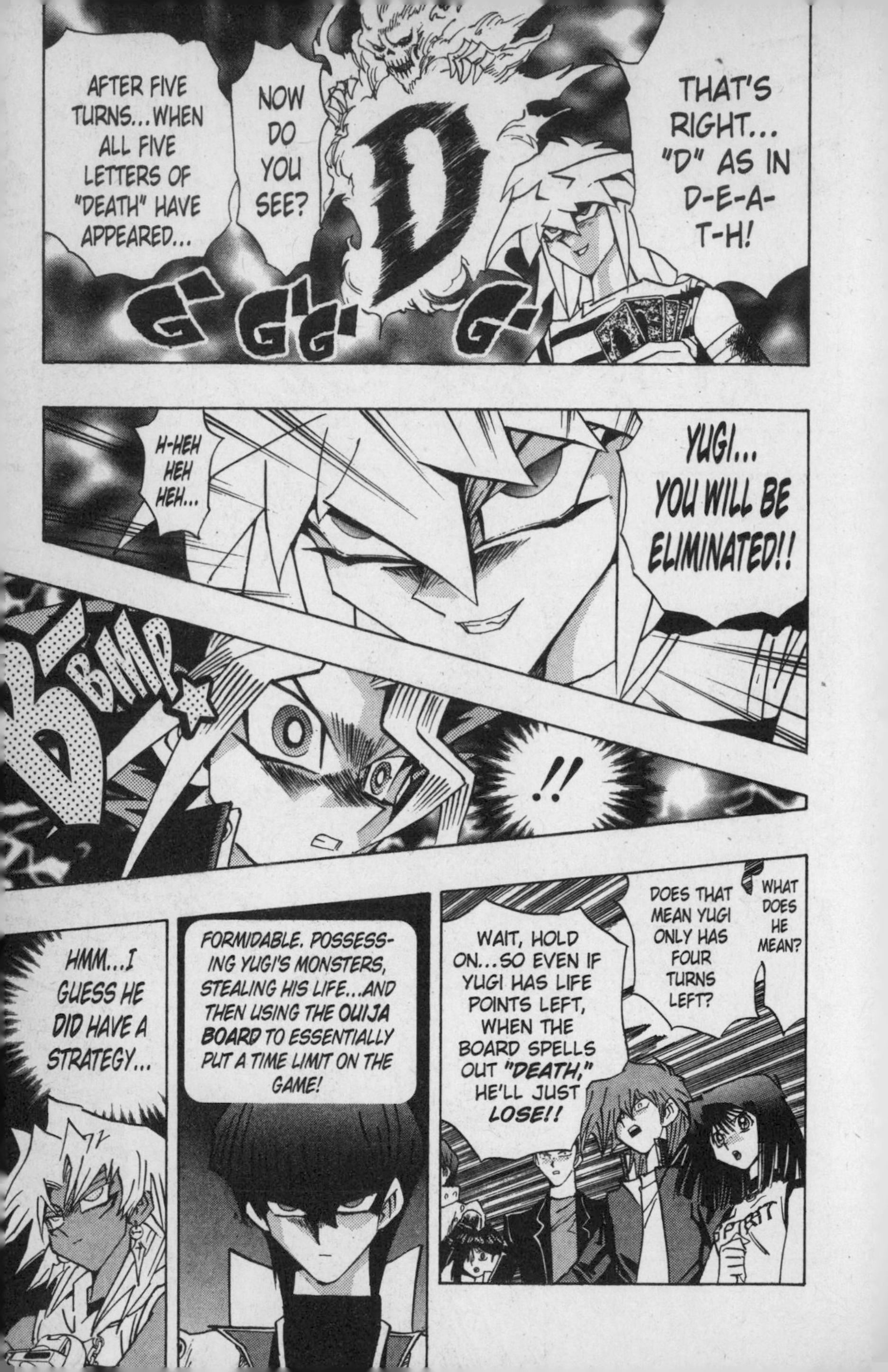
THAT'S RIGHT... "D" AS IN D-E-A-T-H!
NOW DO YOU SEE?
AFTER FIVE TURNS...WHEN ALL FIVE LETTERS OF "DEATH" HAVE APPEARED...
G G G G
YUGI... YOU WILL BE ELIMINATED!!
H-HEH HEH HEH...
!!
BBMP
WHAT DOES HE MEAN?
DOES THAT MEAN YUGI ONLY HAS FOUR TURNS LEFT?
WAIT, HOLD ON...SO EVEN IF YUGI HAS LIFE POINTS LEFT, WHEN THE BOARD SPELLS OUT "DEATH," HE'LL JUST LOSE!!
FORMIDABLE. POSSESSING YUGI'S MONSTERS, STEALING HIS LIFE...AND THEN USING THE OUIJA BOARD TO ESSENTIALLY PUT A TIME LIMIT ON THE GAME!
HMM...I GUESS HE DID HAVE A STRATEGY...

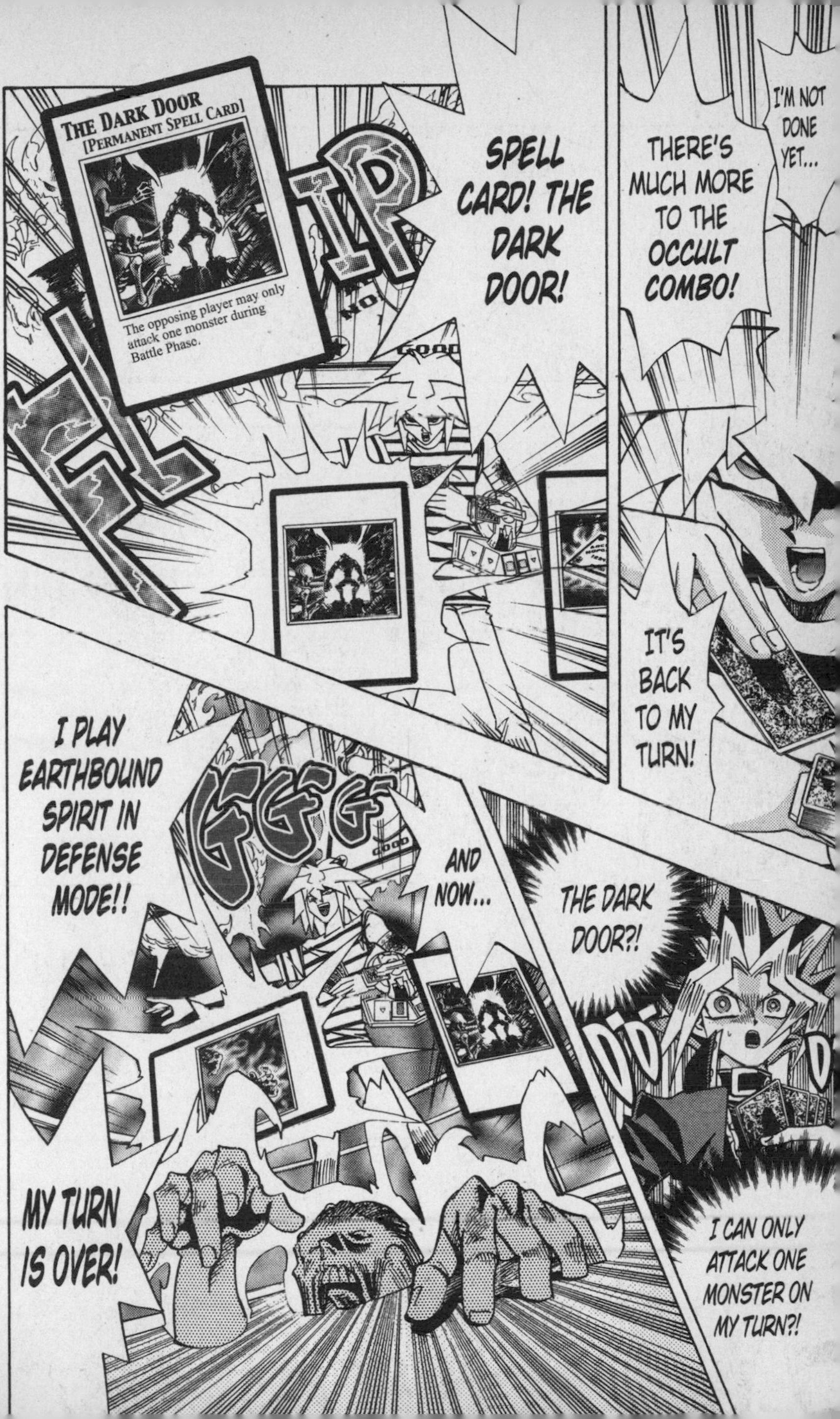
I'M NOT DONE YET...
THERE'S MUCH MORE TO THE OCCULT COMBO!
IT'S BACK TO MY TURN!
SPELL CARD! THE DARK DOOR!
THE DARK DOOR
[PERMANENT SPELL CARD]
The opposing player may only attack one monster during Battle Phase.
THE DARK DOOR?!
I CAN ONLY ATTACK ONE MONSTER ON MY TURN?!
AND NOW...
I PLAY EARTHBOUND SPIRIT IN DEFENSE MODE!!
MY TURN IS OVER!

READ THIS WAY

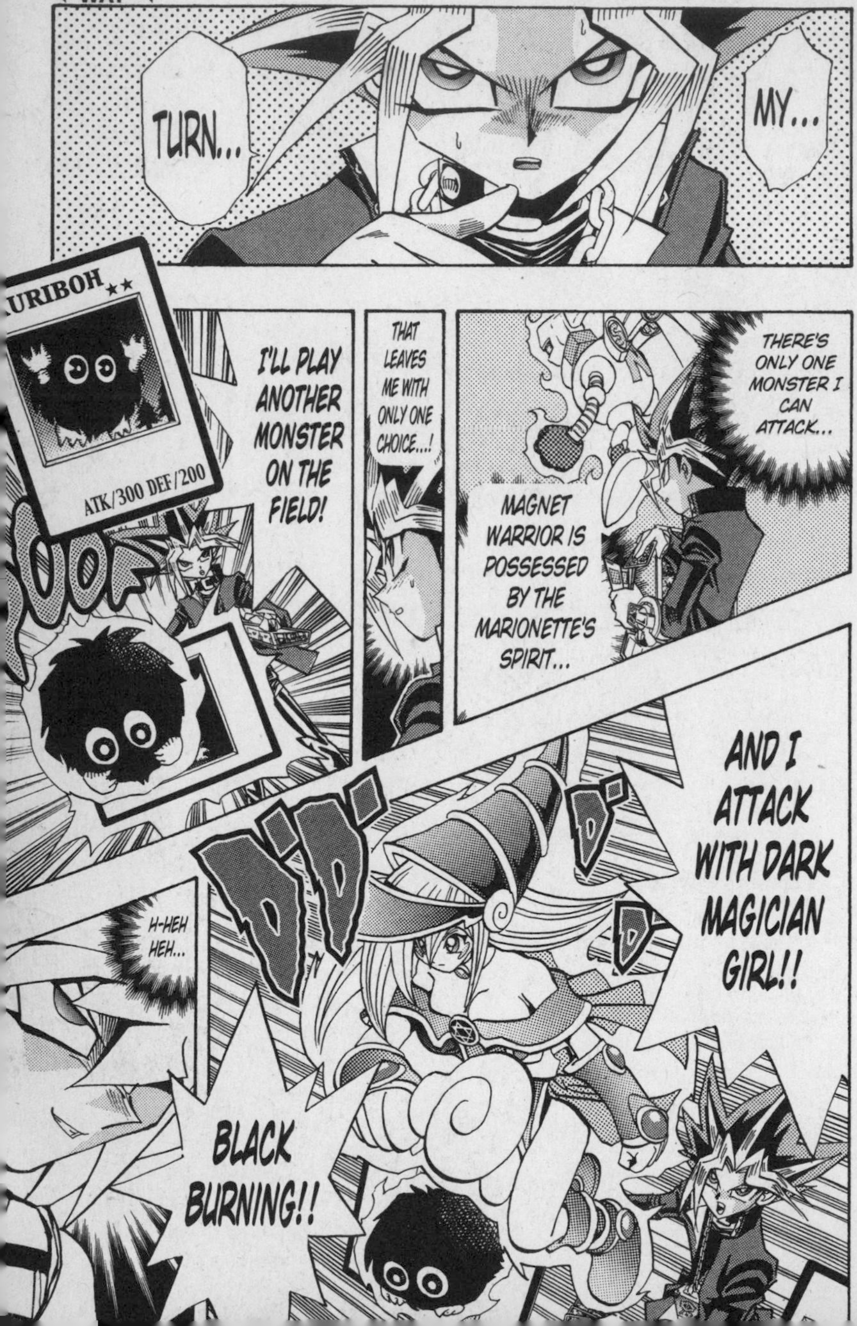

MY...
TURN...
THERE'S ONLY ONE MONSTER I CAN ATTACK...
MAGNET WARRIOR IS POSSESSED BY THE MARIONETTE'S SPIRIT...
THAT LEAVES ME WITH ONLY ONE CHOICE...!
I'LL PLAY ANOTHER MONSTER ON THE FIELD!
URIBOH ★★
ATK/300 DEF/200
AND I ATTACK WITH DARK MAGICIAN GIRL!!
H-HEH HEH...
BLACK BURNING!!

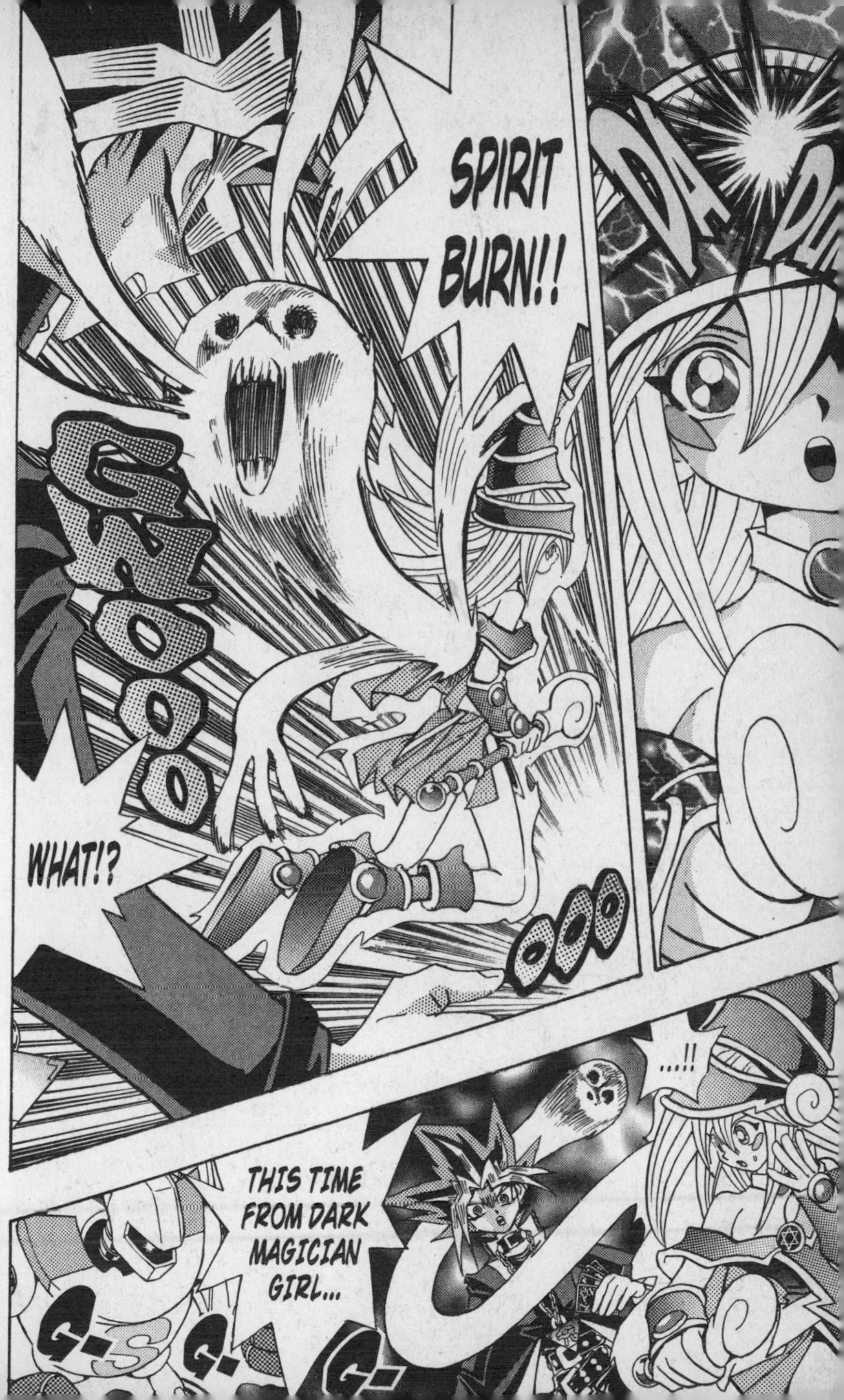
SPIRIT BURN!!
WHAT!?
...!!
THIS TIME FROM DARK MAGICIAN GIRL...
G- G- G-

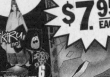
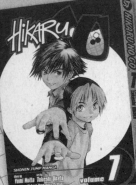
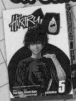

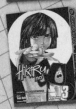

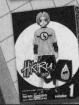
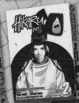

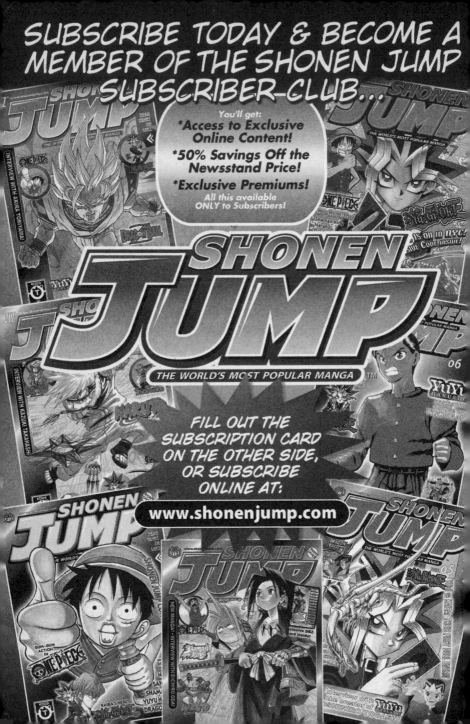

SHONEN JUMP

THE WORLD'S MOST POPULAR MANGA

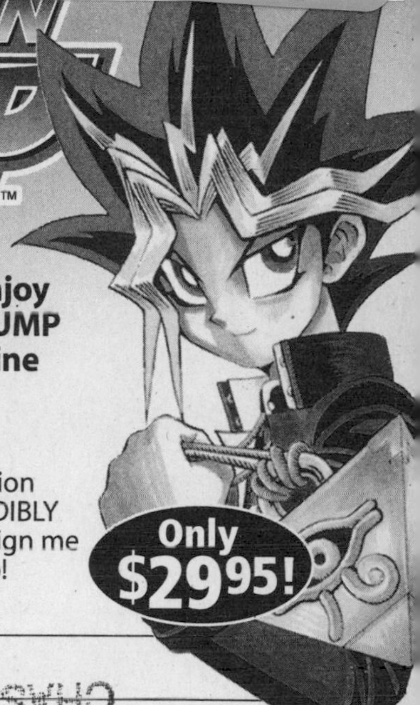

SUBSCRIBE TODAY and SAVE 50% OFF the cover price PLUS enjoy all the benefits of the SHONEN JUMP SUBSCRIBER CLUB, exclusive online content & special gifts ONLY AVAILABLE to SUBSCRIBERS!

☑ **YES!** Please enter my 1 year subscription (12 issues) to *SHONEN JUMP* at the INCREDIBLY LOW SUBSCRIPTION RATE of $29.95 and sign me up for the SHONEN JUMP Subscriber Club!

Only $29⁹⁵!

NAME

ADDRESS

CITY   STATE   ZIP

E-MAIL ADDRESS

☐ **MY CHECK IS ENCLOSED**   ☐ **BILL ME LATER**

CREDIT CARD: ☐ **VISA**   ☐ **MASTERCARD**

ACCOUNT #   EXP. DATE

SIGNATURE

CLIP AND MAIL TO ➤
SHONEN JUMP
Subscriptions Service Dept.
P.O. Box 515
Mount Morris, IL 61054-0515

Make checks payable to: **SHONEN JUMP.**
Canada add US $12. No foreign orders. Allow 6-8 weeks fo...

P6SJGN   YU-GI-OH! © 1996 by Kazuki Takahashi / SHUEISHA Inc.